READING FOR MEANING

An Integrated Approach to Language Learning

JANET SWAFFAR
University of Texas at Austin

KATHERINE ARENS
University of Texas at Austin

HEIDI BYRNES
Georgetown University

PRENTICE HALL
Englewood Cliffs, New Jersey 07632

Library of Congress Cataloging-in-Publication Data

Swaffar, Janet K.
  Reading for meaning : an integrated approach to language learning
/ Janet K. Swaffar, Katherine M. Arens, Heidi Byrnes.
      p.   cm.
  Includes bibliographical references and index.
  ISBN 0-13-753765-4. — ISBN 0-13-761826-3 (pbk.)
  1. Language and languages—Study and teaching.   2. Second language
acquisition.   3. Reading.   I. Arens, Katherine, 1953–
II. Byrnes, Heidi.   III. Title.
P53.75.S9   1991
418′.007—dc20   90-14211
                                                          CIP

To Sylvia Kagan,
Elisheva Iushewitz Schwartz,
and
Betty Nance Weber

Editorial/production supervision
  and interior design: Virginia Rubens
Cover design: Marianne Frasco
Prepress buyer: Herb Klein
Manufacturing buyer: David Dickey

© 1991 by Prentice-Hall, Inc.
A Division of Simon & Schuster
Englewood Cliffs, New Jersey 07632

Printed in the United States of America
10   9   8   7   6   5   4   3   2   1

ISBN 0-13-761826-3   P

ISBN 0-13-753765-4   C

PRENTICE-HALL INTERNATIONAL (UK) LIMITED, *London*
PRENTICE-HALL OF AUSTRALIA PTY. LIMITED, *Sydney*
PRENTICE-HALL CANADA INC., *Toronto*
PRENTICE-HALL HISPANOAMERICANA, S.A., *Mexico*
PRENTICE-HALL OF INDIA PRIVATE LIMITED, *New Delhi*
PRENTICE-HALL OF JAPAN, INC., *Tokyo*
SIMON & SCHUSTER ASIA PTE. LTD., *Singapore*
EDITORA PRENTICE-HALL DO BRASIL LTDA., *Rio de Janeiro*

Contents

Preface

One of the current fashions in literary criticism is to question the status of the author. In his essay "What is an Author?" Foucault points out that the proper name of an author "is functional in that it serves as a means of classification. A name can group together a number of texts and thus differentiate them from others. A name also establishes different forms of relationships among texts" (123). In the literal sense of authorship—the writing of this book—I am the author. In the actual sense of authorship—the creation and explication of the ideas presented in this book—Katherine Arens, Heidi Byrnes, and I have written this book together. Article versions of some chapters have appeared elsewhere under various combinations of our names. And, of course, in the larger meaning of Foucault, in the sense of discourse rather than the usual scholarly sense, there are many authors. The shared authorship with names cited in the bibliography and the chapters on testing and a metalanguage for grammar goes without saying. This preface attempts to acknowledge key people whose more personal discourse has also shaped the thinking in this volume and to explain how the book came to be.

My classroom research began with Freda Holley, with whom I investigated reading, vocabulary acquisition, and error correction in the early seventies. In 1974, encouraged by my colleague Betty Weber, I worked as senior author (King with Weber & Holley) on a chapter dealing with reading for the *ACTFL Annual Review*. On the basis of the model developed in that chapter, Betty Weber and I began working with early introduction of unedited texts. Together we developed a program with a listening and reading emphasis for beginning classes in a foreign language. We were aided by a team of excellent graduate and newly graduated students from our institution: Maria Beck, G. Truett Cates, Phyllis Manning, Martha Morgan, Donald Stephens, and Margaret Woodruff.

In 1977 a department proposal for development of a comprehension-based curriculum in high school and college was funded by NEH (Stephens & Swaffar). Results after the pilot year of our study gave us some clear indications about needed revisions (Morgan). First, students were unenthusiastic about many of the texts used in the experimental program. They proved to be too didactic and narrowly Germanic for our audience. Emerging research in schemata suggested that we needed to rethink our selection criteria in light of our students' backgrounds and interests. Second, although the cognitive advantages of comprehension-based learning reduced the need for study time to achieve credible results (Swaffar & Woodruff), that advantage apparently led to lax study habits: students in the experimental group acknowledged spending one fifth the time in outside study that was reported by the four-skills control group. We saw that our program had to ensure a greater amount of time on task, or learning benefits such as automatic processing and maintenance of language abilities in the long term would be vitiated. Third, we discovered that the experimental students' advantages in language creativity and fluency were offset by their deficiencies in mastery of formal features. Students in the four-skills group were more hesitant than the experimental group about expressing themselves, but the experimental group used formal features less accurately. Issues such as monitoring and repair, indeed the entire framing of our enterprise, needed to be reevaluated in view of what we had learned. Initial efforts in that evaluation were made in a monograph by Cates and Swaffar.

When Betty Weber died in an automobile accident in January of 1979, there was a period during which it was extremely difficult to proceed with this effort. Those who knew Betty Weber will appreciate that her death was a devastating personal as well as professional loss.

In the fall of 1980 Katherine Arens joined our faculty. As a graduate student she had worked with Kurt Mueller-Vollmer, Walter F. W. Lohnes, and Orrin Robinson III in Stanford University's German Studies Department. She had also been an instructor in the Humanities Special Programs. With her background in linguistics and philosophy, Katherine brought new perspectives to the dilemmas posed by the study of the University of Texas group. Together, she and I decided to review the data collected during the NEH grant and attempt to address the problems we saw there. Our objective was to revise the reading model so that it would specify a reader focus on textual meaning, text-based approaches to linguistic rules, and a cognitive sequence that linked L2 reading and language acquisition. It was Katherine who realigned our efforts, and, in so doing, created many of the features of this book: the concept of systematic organization for textual topics and comments, the insistence on a cognitive hierarchy in learning, the details of a metalanguage for thinking about ordering ideas prior to expressing them.

Heidi Byrnes' authorship began in her role as a reader of initial drafts of this manuscript in the summer of 1988 during her work with the Summer Language Institute jointly sponsored by the University of Texas and the Texas Education Agency. The ensuing discussions with her co-authors led to revisions in the emphasis and content of the original. A Secretary of the Navy Fellowship enabled me to work in close proximity with Heidi Byrnes in the early months of 1990 so that essential revisions in the volume's content, diction, and style could result from ongoing discussion and teamwork. Heidi Byrnes brought to the book her background in a broad spectrum of linguistic theory, her work in assessing language performance (e.g., proficiency orientation, national test development), and her active involvement in numerous professional organizations (e.g., MLA, AATG, JNCL, Northeast Conference).

All three of us share a heavy involvement in and strong commitment to classroom teaching at all levels—teaching that respects the intelligence of learners and challenges them to involve themselves in their language learning. This teaching is informed by the conviction that pedagogy should reflect theory and research, not only for the sake of appropriate pedagogy but for the sake of valid theory and research as well. This book was written out of the conviction that second-language teaching must be brought out of its traditional isolation and must be connected to general educational issues, including those articulated at the national level.

In the past decade we have been fortunate in finding support both within and outside the University of Texas. As noted above, my Secretary of the Navy Fellowship provided an essential opportunity for talking things out with Heidi Byrnes. At the University of Texas, the authors owe a great debt to Vice-President William Livingston, The University Research Institute, and Dean Robert D. King for their support and patience throughout the long genesis of this book. At an essential juncture in my work with its core ideas Renate Schulz and David Benseler gave vital encouragement. Robert Swaffar contributed his knowledge of computer applications and his gift for identifying essential components. Richard Kern brought his research perspectives in French and reading theory. Claire Gaudiani included me in initial conferences for the development of Academic Alliances and thereby provided an invaluable forum for discussion and reaction to the concepts in the book. Over a period of ten years, a series of Goethe House workshops under the direction of Manfred Heid brought the three authors together with like-minded colleagues both here and abroad.

To our outside readers—Nina Garrett, Gilbert Jarvis, Alice Omaggio, Milton Azevedo, Bill Fletcher, and our in-house readers Neil Anderson for an ESL perspective, Dieter Waeltermann for his "Frisian" eye for detail, Andrea Winkler for her vantage point from outside the immediate field—goes our gratitude. In the sense of Foucault, all these people have contributed to the "author-function" of this book (125).

The debt to the National Endowment for the Humanities, particularly Program Grant Officers Janice Litwin, Gene Moss, and Richard Ekman, who worked with Janet Swaffar and Betty Nance Weber in the late seventies, is simply that, without them, this effort would never have been possible.

Janet Swaffar
The University of Texas at Austin

CREDITS

Introduction

After the first year of second-language instruction, curricular expectations about language learning change. While the current impetus to use the target language in the classroom remains high in courses for beginners, that impetus is often lost as students continue their studies into a second year and beyond. Classes with a strong reading component tend to resort to English when discussing meaning or implications of texts, particularly if students are reading literature. A verbal chasm seems to exist between discussion of facts involving content questions such as "How old is the heroine?" and interpretive or analytic questions such as "Why does she decide to leave home?"

One reason for this chasm is that students have little opportunity to practice answering synthetic or analytic questions in the second language. They may use discourse gambits in expressing personal opinions (e.g., Fanselow; Kramsch 1981), but they rarely practice analyzing a text on its own terms. Indeed, even in their native language, students are often unable to analyze the content of a topic. They may give subjective analyses, but articulate and dispassionate assessments are rare. The need for training in such reasoning is only gradually being recognized in the humanities.

It is a rare course that encourages students to think about the content of what they read, and to assess the implications and significance of that content when they write. Most L2 classes do one of two things: they focus on practice with well-formed sentences, or they replicate the factual content of the reading. In beginning courses the emphasis is, naturally enough, linguistic. We teach formal features of language and information. We teach declension of adjectives. We teach people, places, and events. When we teach content, however, it is largely in terms of explicitly stated details in the text, not the connections between details and reader response to messages.

True, functional use of language structures such as comparative forms of adjectives is being linked to students' perceptions in newer texts for beginning L2 instruction, e.g., those that offer contextual practice. Perhaps a comparison is made: "The family is closer knit in France. Children live at home longer than they do in the United States." Rarely, however, is functional use linked to the content of a reading text. Consequently, classroom activities or tests which combine names, descriptors, and action verbs for people, places, and events with ways to think about people, places, and events deal with simulations of the real world rather than the fictive realities of a text.

There is a tacit consensus in L2 teaching that if students practice speaking about concrete objects and events they will eventually be able to convey meaningful thoughts about abstract ideas.

Classes begin with replication practice and then move to creation of language about concrete information, and the ability to make requests and inquiries. It is possible for the student to perform these tasks without ever having been exposed to extended discourse or discussions conducted at a level of abstraction that is removed from the listener / reader. At the advanced levels, however, students are expected to be able to negotiate or articulate alternative realities. We believe that this is, in view of dominant practices at the beginning and intermediate levels of L2 instruction, an unfair expectation. Functioning in alternative realities, in visualizations of scenes removed from the immediate environment or speculations about alternative procedures and behaviors, involves high-level, abstract thought processes.

It seems only fair to presume that, in order to conduct these tasks, a student must first have extensive practice. Yet as most curricula are currently designed, we teachers of language apparently expect students to leap magically from the verbally designated worlds of objects, people and physical behaviors (e.g., "Joel fishes. He likes to fish. His father likes to fish, too.") to the verbally created worlds of comparison, instrumentality and causality (e.g., "Joel is a better fisherman than most nine-year-olds. Probably his father's interest in fishing has prompted this enthusiasm.").

It is the thesis of this book that students must have such exposure from the outset of their instruction in a second language. They must hear and read about verbally created worlds. To become articulate speakers of a foreign language they must practice mental and verbal reconstructions of the logical coherences of a reality other than that of their immediate physical environment.

If we fail to teach the connection between language and the ability to manipulate language to analyze or speculate, a discrepancy exists between what we ask students to learn and what we want them ultimately to be able to do. We presume that control of structure constitutes literacy because we presume that control of structure results in comprehension and observations about that comprehension. In this sense we language teachers have had a dual system of expectations for our students. In our curricula, materials, teaching, and testing, we reward formal competence with another language's structure. Ultimately, however, we want our students to demonstrate a literacy which transcends the constraints of skill learning and response. We want them to use the grammar rules and vocabulary lists of a foreign language to be functionally literate in that language. To put it another way, we want our students to be able to use the other language's structure to mediate the comprehension or expression of meanings outside their immediate experience.

This book argues the proposition that this second, covert definition of literacy— the ability to comprehend and express the meaning of alternative realities—must become the profession's overt goal. Institutions (in curricula, testing, and teaching practices) need to rethink the literacy model they are now using because at worst it excludes and at best it denigrates the ultimate objective of literacy: the use of language to convey new ideas. The issue is not what knowledge to acquire, but rather what knowledge students can create with language. This issue is the subject of widespread concern in our profession. Scholars have observed that the current methodological pluralism in language pedagogy and in literary criticism is an oblique expression of confusion about the role of meaning in language study.

This book presents the procedures for integrating language learning and meaningfulness (see Chapter 5 ff.). The procedures are built on assumptions about the learner rather than on assumptions about the text. A growing body of thought from several disciplines supports learner-based theories. To mention several prominent ones: the genetic epistemologies described by Piaget (psychology), the progression from recognition and recall to synthetic and analytic levels outlined in Bloom's taxonomy (education), research in schema theory and metacognitive strategies, the ideas of literary critics who view protention and retention of text meaning as phenomena realized by the reader.

In other words, learner-centered instruction employs a learner's higher-order cognition, cognition that includes but also goes beyond recall and recognition or concrete operations. To access our students' metacognition, an L2 curriculum must both present opportunities for practice with reasoning processes and reward their successful execution. This book will emphasize and exemplify components of a literacy standard which nurture L2 students' reasoning ability and which integrate that literacy standard with a standard of language learning.

One

The New Paradigm
in Language Learning

THE HISTORICAL DILEMMA

A comparison between research in foreign-language acquisition from the mid-sixties to late seventies and today tells us much about the current state of our art. A "then and now" perspective suggests why we changed our minds about what we are supposed to teach. The biggest problem which faced foreign-language (FL) teachers in the sixties and seventies did not need statistical analysis to be understood—the raw facts spoke for themselves. Enrollments in foreign-language programs were declining and language requirements had virtually disappeared. In a pragmatic society the elite scholar, the traditional foreign-language learner, was a vanishing species. Higher education in America was in transition. It seemed as though half of our audience wanted to be engineers or business executives, and the other half was seeking gurus in the Far East or the Arizona mesas. For both groups, foreign languages—indeed, humanist studies as the heritage of Western thought—were suspect. Liberal arts colleges looked like an endangered species. In the high schools, always sensitive to influences in higher education, language enrollments also declined.

Foreign languages were in particular jeopardy because they were at odds with themselves. After World War II the advent of audiolingual approaches to language learning seemed to change our mission—but only in appearance. No audiolingual program, whether in high schools or colleges, gave rise to an advanced student who represented an acceptable alternative to the elitist scholar. Schools wanted to produce standard-bearers for the "high culture" goal of language learning. Many academicians viewed an emphasis on speaking skills as contrary to our scholarly aspirations. As a result, an uneasy compromise was made to maintain the *status quo*, yet afford the appearance of change.

5

While it was well and good to emphasize the spoken language in first-year study, advanced students still got down to the business of learning to read and to display grammar mastery. Since reading generally meant translation, as it had for much of the history of language study, the students' communicative skills suffered (Chastain & Woerdehoff). At the same time, dissenting and often divisive views about what beginners should be learning were found in many departments in colleges and universities. There, the disparity between initial semesters of "language training" (the remedial work) and later "scholarly training" (the academic mission) was evident. The preparation of language majors and graduate students remained a substantively unaltered, "high culture" enterprise.

During this same period, problems of a very different kind were emerging for teachers of English as a second language (ESL). The changing demographics of American society were changing the status of ESL, which had been a peripheral feature of public and post-secondary schools prior to the seventies. For the past two decades, growing numbers of students who speak Spanish and Eastern languages have been entering public schools across the country. As a result, the numbers of ESL classes have increased dramatically.

Concomitantly, pressure is increasing to consider immersion programs for speakers of English as well as speakers of Spanish. The training of teachers to assume this dual task of instruction in language and content has assumed national importance. Moreover, at the post-secondary level the nation has experienced a similarly large increase in the numbers of foreign or foreign-born students who must pass TOEFL tests and function in the university system. In addition to the challenge of a growing immigrant population, post-secondary institutions must cope with the fact that more and more third-world countries are sending students to the United States to study. As graduate students, these non-native speakers often instruct undergraduate classes.

These developments have merged the concerns of FL and ESL instruction in a practical way. Across the country, in major institutions such as Berkeley, Ohio State, and the University of Texas, undergraduate, MA, and PhD programs in language pedagogy are assuming a vital role in preparing qualified instructors. To build these programs, institutions are integrating the resources of educational psychology, ESL and FL instruction and research. At the college and university level, research in learning theory and teaching practice is gradually assuming the status of traditional scholarship in literature and linguistics. This shift can be partially traced to national concern about the international marketplace. Aggressive marketing practices of other nations have raised Americans' awareness that they must become articulate in languages other than English. To some extent, however, the change in attitude toward language studies can be attributed to a rethinking of the language learner's traditional role.

NORMATIVE VERSUS COMMUNICATIVE STANDARDS FOR SECOND-LANGUAGE LEARNERS

Among applied linguists, the second-language research emphasis of the fifties and early sixties was on comparing the beginning learner's audiolingual skills with skills resulting from other types of training, often in terms of contrastive analysis. Unfortunately, correct answers on the standardized tests—for example, the Modern Language Association's achievement test battery or the examinations produced by the American Association of

Teachers of Spanish, French, and German—depended largely on knowledge of surface language rules: sentence-level grammar or discrete vocabulary items. The comparison was really between acquisition of discrete skills rather than acquisition of functional language use. Consequently, methodological comparisons focused on replication of form alone: e.g., language out of context. The criteria for accuracy were idealized norms for speech in the abstract rather than real-world situations.

Such purely linguistic criteria reflect the beliefs of a speech community about *how* one should talk. Typically associated with social class distinction, they tend to focus on the correctness of form rather than on the delivery of meaning. They often impose on the spoken language norms developed for a reflective, deliberate written variety of the language. Consequently, normed standards assume that correct sentences equal effective communication. Normed language takes itself seriously. It is sanitized—cleansed of aberrations such as double meanings or colloquial irregularities. In this sense, one illustration of norming is "received" English—the elite linguistic world of educated Britons and the BBC, the world Monty Python satirizes so effectively.

When students do rote work they focus on a language norm, formal and dictionary equivalents that purportedly mean the same thing in another language. Language tests that ask for the "right" word on the basis of a part of speech or a translation presume such a norm. If we fill in the blank in the sentence "Jennifer is a _____ (adjective) girl," we perform a purely linguistic act. A correct answer is whatever adjective is formally correct. "Interesting" will be wrong in English, because following "a" the adjective must begin with a consonant. It might be factually correct, but it would be grammatically incorrect.

What happens when two very different methods—say, for example, audiolingual and grammar translation—share the premise that the language to be learned is normed language? To begin with, different instructional treatments end up with a lot in common: they produce similar results. In research comparisons, statistical measures of language learning with audiolingualism, cognitive code, and grammar translation methods revealed minimal performance differences. Moreover, regardless of method, the average performance at the end of two years of high school or college was not high enough to encourage expectations that students would be able to use that second language in some practical way (Scherer & Wertheimer; P. Smith). This result made our enterprise look like an exercise in futility and explains another significant generalization that can be made about such research. A comparison of the student numbers in all these studies reveals that language programs were losing about half of their students between the first high school year or college semester and the end of the second high school or college year.

Another reason that the upper-division programs in colleges and universities failed to attract and keep students was that, until the mid-seventies, programs consisted of literature and formal linguistic courses. At this level the research findings were no more encouraging, however, than for beginning instruction. John Carroll's 1967 study of language majors, whose findings influenced subsequent assessments of the profession's goals, revealed that most foreign-language majors failed to achieve more than intermediate-level competence. Regardless of the size or prestige of their colleges and universities across the United States, only those who spoke the foreign language in the home or had visited the foreign country for an extended period of time were able to perform on an MLA examination at levels that approached *functional ability* of an adult user of that language. It was time for the profession to rethink both the means and the ends of language instruction in the United States. And that is, more or less, exactly what happened.

COGNITIVE RESEARCH ABOUT PRAGMATIC LANGUAGE LEARNING

Developments in the foreign language research of the seventies present a classic instance of paradigm shifts in the sense of Kuhn and Foucault. Carroll's findings about the achievement of language majors revealed the unreasonable expectations at American colleges and universities: mastery of surface language was not feasible even in four years. In the course of the 1970s, the profession began to divest itself of a theoretical framework based on normed language. The teaching of *langue*, the notion that teaching comprehensive linguistic rules would result in comprehensive foreign-language skills within two years of college training, quietly disappeared.[1] The *normative input / language replication* paradigm, with foreign language learning defined as the ability to meet an absolute standard of grammatical correctness, was supplanted by multiple interpretations of a less exclusionary goal. Instead of normative use or *langue*, our job was to teach functional use or *parole*. We redefined second-language learning as the ability to perceive and operate within real-world situations, in order to perform real-world tasks.

A new curricular goal, a paradigm of *authentic input / language creation*, emerged. Rather than measuring student performance against an absolute norm for vocabulary and grammar mastery, the new standard acknowledged the value of achieving specific communicative objectives. The profession began modifying curricula to encourage adults, even in their beginning language courses, to express their own feelings and thoughts. Thinking and intentionality became integral to language use at any level. We incorporated linguistic creativity into our agenda.

The curricula that are evolving in the wake of Carroll's findings stress two innovations: (1) expectations that language performance will result from the learner's total knowledge have replaced narrow expectations that performance results only from language ability, and (2) student use of language data for specific purposes has replaced the demand for replication of the total system of normed language. This shift changed the measure of language comprehension. Vocabulary knowledge no longer is the sole predictor of comprehension. Now the profession acknowledges a role for reader schemata. For example, we recognize that although a student knows that the German word for city is *Stadt*, a misreading of this word can occur in a reading assignment about *Karl-Marx-Stadt* if the student fails to realize that a city in East Germany bears this philosopher's name (Bernhardt 1986a: 111). Similarly, in measuring speech production, the old normative standard for accuracy could be expanded. With the new communicative standard, a student's successful circumlocution could be considered as accurate an answer as knowledge of the "right" word or phrase.[2] Changes in the theory of foreign language instruction parallel differences in the way language, cognition, and affective factors were assessed thirty years ago and how they are assessed today.

The definition of language in the old paradigm ignored learner cognition and affect. If the language in the head of the learner was inaccessible to observation, then speaker intent was hidden as well. What remained was surface language and accuracy defined by a language norm. The language to be learned in the paradigm of the fifties and early sixties had a single reality governed by rules for *langue* or standard speech in the abstract, where learners filled in slots or engaged in pattern drills. The dominant linguistic theory was structuralism. The dominant learning theory was behaviorism.

To the behaviorist, the learner was a *tabula rasa* whose learning resulted from conditioned responses to outside stimuli. In the days before computer technology, observable data were what the student produced in words or writing. Neither models of artificial intelligence nor multivariate statistical measures existed. Because thinking could not be observed, learner comprehension became known as a passive activity. Since learner processes were not evident, there was no way to assess their existence. The learner was a blank slate to be written on by appropriate instruction.

This text does not intend to denigrate the work or research of either behaviorists or structural linguists. Moulton's *The Sounds of English and German*, for example, remains the acme for teaching distinctions in pronunciation. The point is to illustrate what happens when a paradigm shifts and conversely, to demonstrate the things that are virtually impossible before that shift occurs. The case of Bartlett, whose book *Remembering* was published in the 1930s and subsequently forgotten until the 1970s, illustrates what happens to unallowable thought. In Bartlett's volume, the unallowable thought was rationalism—the theory that each human being is born with innate ideas that interact with external stimuli—the converse of the then dominant empirical notion of the human being as a *tabula rasa*. Bartlett's *Remembering* proposed that humans learn by using cognitive strategies to integrate prior knowledge with new information. The subdiscipline he founded, schema theory, was about learning as problem-solving. Fifty years later, thanks to work in computer models for artificial intelligence and extensive neurological research (e.g., R. Anderson), the rationalist model of cognition has become viable.

Rosenblatt's *Literature as Exploration* (1938), the classic case for the reader's right to interact with textual meaning, received a similar reception. Her book, written during the heyday of formalist criticism, went virtually unnoticed until the emergence of phenomenologically-oriented theory some thirty years later.

Today, given a model for language creativity, students' choice of the "right" answer depends as much on their cognition and communicative interaction as it does on language competence. In short, we no longer teach or assess linguistic behaviors in terms of linguistic proficiency alone. That is the new option in our discipline. Thus the *ACTFL Proficiency Guidelines*, for example, encourage teachers to focus on communicatively effective language as a classroom goal. The *Guidelines*, as they are currently described, reward the linguistic creativity of learners rather than rewarding accuracy *per se*.[3] The ways in which scholars are trying to substantiate a functional standard for second-language instruction suggest new directions for that instruction (Byrnes 1988; Magnan 1988).

THE CURRICULAR IMPLICATIONS
OF FOCUS ON THE LEARNER

To the degree that Carroll's findings dispelled myths about teaching input for output, subsequent research supported the feasibility of the *authentic input / language creation* paradigm. Work in discourse analysis and artificial intelligence confirmed that demands for knowledge of particular vocabulary and syntax change radically with subject matter or social demands. Cognitive sciences supplied us with data about how creativity—rethinking and reformulating language—promotes depth of processing (e.g., Craik &

Lockhart). Using second-language students to confirm these first-language findings, early research by Winitz, by Postovsky, and by Asher demonstrated that perception and action prompted by language cues contributed as much as or more to learning a foreign language than did rules and generalizations about grammar—insights suggested in Krashen's popularization of the distinction between acquiring and learning a language.

In short, the new creativity paradigm has redefined our concept of language to include both the language created by the speaker and the language as normed by the speech community. Language, if located in the speaker's head as well as in the outside world, consists not of one, but of multiple levels of measurable speaker experience: experience manifested in deep structures as well as surface structures, in macro- as well as micropropositions, in the parole of an actual speech community as well as *langue* in the abstract. Rather than representing a single level of surface language, all these theories represent language as the result of multiple experiential processes and innate factors.

The new relationship between cognition and language has led to completely new ways of researching language learning. Rather than focusing on language as such, research now examines the language product as a result of cognitive process. User manuals for ERIC and *Language Abstracts* reflect the altered definition of our field. Descriptors such as "Adult Learning," "Age Differences in Language," "Neurolinguistics," "Language and Culture," "Sociolinguistics," and identifiers such as "linguistic intuitions," "learner variable effects," and "metalinguistic awareness" all reflect the new model of research: one that defines language as a creative process which occurs within a social context. If their research design is compared, the two paradigms emerge as a set of contrasting emphases:

Language norm + task	*Language setting + learner*
Methodological comparisons	Analysis of learner errors
Contrastive analyses of languages	Error perception by others
Efficacy of memory tasks	Interlanguage
	Affective studies (attitude / motivation)
	Ethnographic research
	Metalinguistic research
	Schema research
	Formal / informal learning
	Language loss
	Child / adult learning
	L1 / FL language acquisition

Although relatively few in number, the categories on the left side of the chart reflect a substantial body of research. They are reminiscent of the hallmark studies of the era referred to earlier, such as Scherer and Wertheimer or Phillip Smith's Pennsylvania report. Work in contrastive analysis looked exclusively and with invaluable thoroughness at differences in formal realizations of language (e.g., Kufner, Moulton). In the fifties and sixties leading researchers such as Pimsleur, Lado, and Politzer established limits on learner recall of output: vocabulary or dialogues. Seminal insights about language transfer or Lado's concept of "linguistics across cultures" are seen today in terms of a different role for both linguistics and the learner (e.g., Gass & Selinker). Nevertheless, the language replication paradigm of the earlier period precluded research designs that belong in the right-hand categories.[4]

Prior to the sixties, psycholinguistics hardly addressed the question of differences between child and adult learning. The behaviorist viewed the language learning of adults as very similar to the language learning of children. After all, since language learning was assessed as the normed product of conditioned response, there was little reason to assume that the adult's learning differs from that of the child. Ironically, the contrastive analyses of the fifties and sixties highlight the extent to which pronunciation and command of formal accuracy in adults compares unfavorably to those same abilities in children. If we look only at those comparisons, adult language learners are relegated to a second-place status. Language instruction in high school and college is remedial work. The adult confronts learning obstacles that would not have existed if the language had been taught in grade school. From the empiricist perspective, the adult student is no longer a blank page to be written on and can, therefore, never overcome the handicap of permanently established behaviors.

The paradigm shift to learner cognition changes the status of the adult language student. In the seventies, L2 researchers worked with variants of Piaget's theory of *Genetic Epistemology*, the notion that human ability in problem-solving is related to a sequence of stages that characterize cognitive maturation. Colleagues in Canada have been particularly informative in this respect. Studies of their immersion programs reveal that, although adults often fail to acquire phonological capabilities and the mastery of formal features of which children under fourteen are capable, they acquire conceptual and discursive capabilities in the second language at a faster rate than children (Sternfeld 1988). Swain's work (1985) suggests that adults learn discursive and conceptual aspects of language more successfully than children do. Whereas early studies looked only at sentence-level correctness, expansion of the focus from sentential to supersentential discourse necessarily includes the grasp of complex ideas and the use of discourse features to connect those ideas in longer texts. As a result, today we think that cognitive maturity may be an advantage because adults can more easily acquire relatively complex ideas and the language of those ideas. Disadvantages in learning formal features are therefore offset by advantages in conceptualization.

Once the learner becomes the focal point of research, the effects of a host of learner variables reflected in the two lists—different language backgrounds, different maturational levels, or different motivations—become desirable design features. Interlanguage research illustrates the shift away from contrastive analysis of learner performance measured against a correctness norm, to the analysis of performance as stages in learner development (Selinker & Lamendella). Similarly, concern arises about how long language ability lasts once it is acquired (Lambert & Freed). Related to this concern are studies of error perception, which focus on the degree to which different problems in surface grammaticality interfere with message comprehension rather than weighting all errors as equal. With the focus on learner apprehension of language rather than on language *per se*, research emphasis shifts from *what* is learned to *how*: the strategies students use to confront authentic materials and communicative situations. Aside from cognitive benefits to students, Barnett (1988a) suggests that strategy use enhances student confidence about forthcoming advanced work.

Just as the theory and research of twenty years ago failed to acknowledge the cognitive benefits of maturity, it had also been relatively incurious about whether or not affective differences existed between children and adults learning a second language. Since children were the L2 learning model and children were uninhibited, it followed that the research of the period simply neglected the role of inhibitions in adults. The notion of production of errors as part of the learning process was not part of the behaviorist paradigm. For the empiricist, errors were irremediable. Today we are willing to accept errors since we believe that learner capacity for self-correction is a sufficient countermeasure to the otherwise damaging influence of faulty language production.

The impact of research has been to create a new curriculum for the adult learner. Rather than concentrating on the memory tasks assumed for the child, the focus has shifted to problem-solving skills that are commensurate with mature cognition. In conjunction with language, the focus is on context and communicative intent. In elementary language classes the practical implications can be summed up as follows:

LOWER-DIVISION CURRICULAR SHIFT: MATERIALS / TECHNIQUES

Previous Paradigm	*New Paradigm*
Culturally neutral dialogues, edited texts, separate skill practice	Personalized language Authentic texts as basis for oral, written work as well as reading
Sentence drill (fill in blanks) Grammar rules linked to rules in formal accuracy	Integrative use: Grammar linked to meaning in a sentence as well as to meaning in paragraphs and discourse
Grammar rules taught in class (30% or more of class hour)	Grammar rules learned by students mainly as independent activity outside of class
Cued by translation or grammatical terminology	Most of class time devoted to contextual practice cued by situational variables
Vocabulary lists to be memorized for active use—largely cued by translation	Distinction between actively-used and comprehended words—vocabulary understood and cued in L2 context

These distinctions must be viewed warily. Practitioners know that most "new" programs are actually implemented on a sliding scale between previous and new convictions and that it is easy to pay lip service to new terminology. The crux of the matter is how those new terms are realized in practice. References to "traditional methods" abound in our literature, yet we recognize that these methods continue to exist on a mutable scale in syllabi, text selection, lesson plans, and testing. Curricular decisions frequently reveal which paradigm is allowable beneath the rhetoric. Factors such as the use of authentic texts that reflect the interests of adult students, the notion that adult learners should generate original utterances in simulations of their real world, or that tests should differentiate between receptive knowledge and command of grammar and vocabulary all imply a learner-centered definition of language instruction.

Another feature of the new paradigm is that it encourages non-majors to continue upper-division work. Whereas previously a small percentage of language students continued course work as majors in a second language's literature or linguistics, today departments are developing courses and programs for the specialists in other fields. Strong indications that, once basic language abilities are in place, adults perform better with materials geared to their cognitive levels and interests, have been translated into new upper-division programs for non-majors or double majors. Again, these shifts can be seen in a comparison between departmental programs twenty years ago and today:

UPPER-DIVISION SHIFT: CURRICULAR ADDITIONS

Previous Paradigm	*New Paradigm*
Canon of literature as genres, periods	Literature as part of cultural values: • popular culture • multi-media options • intertextuality rather than formal genre • thematic rather than period emphases
Language for sentence-level accuracy (major = elitist scholar)	Pragmatic use of language in: • double majors • culture tracks • language in careers • study abroad

---

In the mid-sixties, close to ninety percent of all American colleges had a language requirement for graduation. By the early eighties that figure was reduced by over forty percent. Since then the numbers have again been on the upswing.[5] Increasingly, upper-division programs in area studies, comparative studies, and international studies assume an audience of students with second-language ability. Pilot projects such as the one in international business and liberal arts at the City University of New York, College of Staten Island (in conjunction with the local Italian-American community) or the five-year program in international engineering at the University of Rhode Island reflect changes in the role of language departments. Indeed, popular interest in second-language learning is being tapped within the community as well. Adult Americans outside the university have responded to subject area or practical language use as seen in flourishing elder hostel sessions, weekend immersion programs, language cruises, and summer programs abroad.[6]

The paradigm shift is by no means restricted to the undergraduate program. In graduate programs, changes reflect new definitions of the relationship between cognition and language. The bases for adult perception—our cultural schemata and complex intentions—are now the subject matter of new language curricula. In the chart that follows, cultural schemata appear in the guise of ethnographic, historical, and gender features within the literary canon (called here the shift from national to thematic literatures). Unlike the structuralist program, whose divisions into phonology, morphology, and syntax reflected a model of surface language, today's linguistic program reflects a parallel processing model for adult speech. As in the elementary program, these courses deal with the language created by the speaker and language as a norm within the speech community.

GRADUATE PROGRAM SHIFT: RADICAL CHANGES

Previous Paradigm	*New Paradigm*
Canon as UG majors + depth	Thematic rather than national, e.g.: • cultural geography • dialect studies • colonial literatures • women's studies* • minority studies
Text-immanent interpretation	Literary theory = *text-external* as well as textual phenomena • reader response* • psycholinguistics* • translation as reception
Diachronic linguistics: *Separate realms* • phonology / morphology / syntax	Diachronic & synchronic: *Formerly isolated factors integrated* • speech acts* • discourse theory* • supersentential grammars* • metacognitive grammars • pragmatic grammars
• stylistics (metrics, register)	• text-linguistics*
• etymologies, frequencies	• sociolinguistics*

On the right side of the chart above, the subdisciplines in graduate work are starred. The stars refer to interdisciplinary research. The motor driving the new undergraduate vehicle for adult language acquisition is integrated research among those fields emerging in current graduate programs: rhetorical organization in discourse; psycholinguists' concern with propositional realization of speaker intent; reader-based conceptualization in schema theory and semiotics. Sociolinguists now assess the cultural-psychological factors that affect both learner perception and language use. These research interdisciplines support a radically new role for second languages in the American curriculum—one which replaces standards for mastery of form with standards for construction and expression of meaning.

Course work now acknowledges adult conceptual ability and background by tapping macro-understanding, command of first-language discourse, and prior knowledge in a particular subject. As a consequence, language research has expanded the dimensions of the language classroom and turned second-language study into an intellectual discipline for real-world use rather than a remedial discipline of dubious practical value, whose data had to be learned by rote.

This is the plus side—the new hopes created by the learner-centered paradigm. On the minus side are the hazards of this new enterprise for teachers of elementary language courses. The paradigm shift has complicated definitions of instructional tasks. Language is no longer a single, relatively mechanical collection of rules and vocabulary for assembly of grammatical sentences with slots for nouns, verbs, and adjectives. Instead, language study today implies multiple subtleties and proliferating nomenclatures. Depending on whom teachers talk to, "language competence" may mean command of the discursive rules of a given social setting, realization of intentions, or understanding the contrasting noun phrase structure underlying the surface congruity of "John is eager to please" and "John is easy to please," to mention just a few of the options. In the old paradigm, teachers asked their students to reproduce language according to a fixed standard of correctness. Today we are encouraged to reward a flexible standard of intelligibility. The distinction can be expressed as follows:

Assessment Criteria	Fixed Standard	Flexible Standard
Linguistic accuracy:	Surface grammaticality	Degree of listener effort at understanding syntax, lexemes
Linguistic function:	Mechanical skill with L2	Appropriateness in terms of speaker task, intent and context of the speech act; clarity of messages to others
Linguistic content:	Culturally neutral situations	Culturally authentic situations

The term "flexible standard" refers to still largely unspecified parameters of language as a communicative act. Despite lip service paid to the new paradigm, classroom reality is still far from the learner-centered definitions of language instruction. At recent symposia and conferences, papers have pointed to a need for readjustment in classroom practice. The strategy analyses of Oxford and Nyikos reveal that adults who begin to learn a second language engage in behaviors "likely to be useful in a traditional, structure-oriented, discrete-point foreign language instructional environment" (9). Consequently, these students are less likely to practice functional use of language. In view of the large sample population, Oxford and Nyikos' conclusion that "expectations imposed by standard academic approaches to teaching and testing limit the motivation of most language learners to try new, creative, communicatively-oriented strategies" (19) is damning. It suggests that current teaching and assessment practices defeat communicative objectives.

In studies that confirm and specify the particulars of defeating practices, Horwitz argues that anxiety arising out of performance expectations in a normed curriculum has a negative effect on linguistic performance. An ethnographic study of an elementary French class at Michigan Technological University explored those norms. The conclusions to be drawn from the fact that beginning French students preferred written rather than spoken activities because writing gives them time to think, have their correlative in Laeufer's analysis. She demonstrates that recent inquiries into the critical period hypothesis, a presumed feature of Chomsky's Language Acquisition Device or LAD, strongly suggest that adults need to change their perceptions about the foreign language before a change in language production can take place. The value of listening and writing discrimination activities is well established in research (Winitz). Apparently such activities remain unincorporated into adult language curricula and testing practice.

The dismaying feature of such research is that, despite the success of well documented handbooks such as River's *Teaching Foreign Language Skills* and Omaggio's *Teaching Language in Context*, the beginning language curriculum has resisted teaching and testing the performance goals of the new paradigm. Rule-centered instruction still predominates at this level. Teachers cling to old practices in the absence of direct, positive evidence about new ones. The anomaly is understandable, however, when the problems posed by the new paradigm are considered. A learner-centered program necessarily introduces a balancing act: the selection and presentation of the second language juxtaposed with reasonable expectations about the learner. Those expectations are no longer the tangibles of language structure and vocabulary lists. Quite the contrary, choice of vocabulary and syntax will vary with the discourse situation and cognitive strategies a student uses.

These realizations about the learner role have also radically changed our needs in evaluation of student performance. If language learning involves situational competencies and cognitive strategies, then we need to teach and assess students in terms of particular discourse frames and our learners' extralinguistic knowledge.

THE EXPANDED DEPARTMENTAL OPTIONS

In addition to complicating decisions about teaching goals and curriculum planning, the *language creation* paradigm has radically modified departmental options. Functional language frees us from the elitist-scholar straitjacket. Liberated from the narrowly "normative" or "high culture" standard for language learning, departments can be practical.

What are some of the consequences of acknowledging that discourse functions, the learner's interests (the affective component), and learner background (schemata) play a major role in language acquisition? One result, depending on faculty background and interests, has been the increase in culture and subject-area courses at the college level.[7] While such courses often result in a new subject emphasis for majors, the so-called culture track, many of these classes appeal to the non-major as well. As departmental offerings expand beyond the limits of formal literary and linguistic analysis, the non-majors are beginning to be regular participants in advanced classes. The growing participation of students who are not majors in our upper-division language courses is another relatively new development. It is a development that runs counter to the traditional schism between lower-division classes stressing language mastery and upper-division classes designed solely for language specialists. Such repercussions from our shifting paradigm also push us to rethink the gap between lower-division and upper-division course work.

THE CURRICULAR CHANGES

Early subject-matter emphasis. Language learning can include learning subject matter through a second language. Both majors and non-majors seem to make the transition from elementary to advanced course work more readily when exposed to substantive information about topics of interest (Sternfeld 1989). As a result of research demonstrating how to use schemata and learning strategies to compensate for deficient language abilities (Wolff), authentic second-language materials have become feasible for use in beginning instruction.[8] Second-language research supports the findings of cognitive psychologists for first-language learners: students in secondary and post-secondary schools acquire greater language proficiency when they study subject matter presented in the second language than they do when they study second language *per se* (Stern). Comparative research on immersion programs in Canada has revealed that, folk wisdom to the contrary, after only two years of study most "late immersion" students (in this case, children in seventh and eighth grade) can match the language proficiencies of children who started immersion programs in first grade (Genesee). In addition, early subject-matter emphasis has popular appeal and eases curricular transitions between classes, thereby further enhancing the learning benefits.

Objectives. Within the span of ten years, then, the *parole* concept has also changed objectives in our language curricula. Both the lower- and upper-division course offerings and performance objectives in American language departments address new student audiences with an expanded vision of our role within our institutions. Earlier fears about becoming "nonacademic" or, the correlative evil, a "service" department without an autonomous identity have now been assuaged by the new importance of interdisciplinary programs. Administrators and funding institutions reward us for writing across the disciplines or integrating language study with programs in other fields. Ethnographic findings encourage us to believe that awareness of cultural differences facilitates successful communication and promotes successful interaction with other cultures. Increasingly, the success of ESL programs is measured by their students' performance in content areas of study rather than by their achievement as students of English. Perhaps FL departments need to decide whether they want to consider such criteria in assessing their program's achievements.

OUR EXPANDED ROLE IN THE ACADEMIC COMMUNITY

Equally important are changes in the liberal arts that reinforce altered concepts of the second-language curriculum. Humanist studies today are moving in an interdisciplinary direction. The recent debates stemming from E. D. Hirsch's book castigating America's "cultural illiteracy" and Allan Bloom's thesis about the "closing of the American mind" have engaged language faculties in discussions about solutions to cultural insularity. The negative image of service that adhered to a department offering courses for students of business or international studies has been supplanted by a more positive interdisciplinary framework.[9]

Can the profession integrate language and content study in coherent, well-defined stages in language acquisition? If language knowledge is to have a role in the real world, we need new programs in both secondary and college curricula. Will the content emphasis, in and of itself, be sufficient? Or will the new paradigm founder on the shoals of debates about proficiency levels and disagreement about classroom objectives and their assessment? While debate is always healthy, it needs to begin with agreement about which issues are being addressed. Whatever the shortcomings of the *ACTFL Proficiency Guidelines*, they represent a national effort to identify systematically the relationship between the adult learner's functional and formal abilities. However, the *Guidelines* are not intended to apply directly to the classroom. Teachers must still decide what to teach and test every day so that their students can become proficient.

In adult language acquisition, the first decision we face is what grammar to teach. We are now implementing a learner-centered model with the old sentential grammar, when we should be working with a dependency grammar or a text-based, superesentential grammar. Many text grammarians and discourse analysts view the two as complementary components, with sentence grammar subordinate to discourse grammar as a whole (van Dijk). Developments in text grammar and discourse analysis touch directly on the business of language learning not only because they are concerned with supersentential grammar, but also because they necessarily emphasize the role texts play in the definition of grammar (Hopper). Hence, language theorists have proposed that grammar rules are appropriately viewed as a repertoire of strategies for creating texts.

To some extent the appearance of such a grammar will depend on whether we discover that grammar learning is unitary, driven by a central cognitive motor, by the same macrocomputer in the brain, or whether the learning components are modular.[10] The current discussion about universal grammar models has particular significance for adult language acquisition curricula, since it implies instructional approaches and learner strategies emphasizing a limited number of contrastive distinctions rather than learning the complete rule ordering of the second language.[11] Practical confirmation of that theory would help identify the essential components of supersentential grammar. If parameter settings are blind spots in adult perception that inhibit grammar accuracy in the second language, we might learn about those blocks in perception and devise ways to teach formal accuracy through use, not usage.

A second, related consideration raised by the new paradigm concerns task hierarchies in foreign language instruction. Rather than implying a fossilized learning ability, recent indications suggest that the adult language learner has modified acquisition ability. But what modifiers? At present we only speculate about the fundamental premise of adult language acquisition: adults can learn a language better when distinctions in meaning are emphasized as the basis for distinctions in form. As yet we have virtually no indications about how to capitalize on this premise. For example, let us assume that changes in verb tense signal vital distinctions in a foreign language text. In reading a passage on bridge construction an engineer wants to know what gets done first. We have some evidence from cognitive psychology that that engineer may learn verb tenses more readily when studying a text about sequential problems in bridge building than when memorizing lists of principal parts and plural forms. If language learning occurs in conjunction with the learner's comprehension of meaning, we need to develop techniques that encourage a learner-centered style of comprehension. Presumably, new techniques would foster development of strategies for text creation as well as comprehension.

The third major point concerns foreign-language testing. Everyday instruction still lacks a testing approach for material studied or taught in class that is based on language creativity. Despite enthusiasm for the new learner-centered paradigm, in actual practice, apparently, few tests of classroom achievement measure and hence encourage this orientation. Understandably, teachers continue to present formal features of language and stress vocabulary in their midterm and final exams unless they have viable alternatives. Consequently, tests are rarely designed to reflect and encourage creative, communicatively-oriented strategies on the part of students. Particularly beyond beginning language instruction and initial oral proficiencies, the issue of what students need to be able to do based on a given level of foreign-language instruction seems to be in doubt. Despite a plethora of methodologies and a growing body of research supporting the claims for the new language learning paradigm, there is no integrative theory that serves as a facilitating link between proliferating grammar theories, learner-centered research, and classroom testing of achievement.

This volume tries to develop such links. The chapters that follow draw on current evidence about optimal links between linguistic behaviors, learner cognition, affect, and subject matter to support their claims. The resulting comprehension-based model attempts a working definition of meaning, one applicable to beginning language learners as well as advanced ones. The premise of the model is that once meaning is unambiguously comprehended by the learner, accuracy in spoken and written language can be based on that comprehension. In this sense the theory tries to account for the sequential stages in comprehensible input *and* in comprehensible output. Chapters 2–4 evaluate current reseach literature in order to explain the relationship between top-down / semantic and bottom-up / linguistic processing in a reader-based creation of meaning. Chapter 5 is a procedural model for applying this relationship to reading and language learning. The applications of this model in Chapters 6–12 suggest ways to change curricular practice and a rethinking of our instructional tasks, for beginning as well as intermediate, advanced, and interdisciplinary courses.

NOTES TO CHAPTER 1

1. The terms *langue* and *parole* are being used here in the sense of de Saussure (1966) as a distinction between the language system accessible to the entire speech community (*langue*) and the language used by a particular group for particular purposes (*parole*). This distinction frequently is, but should not be, confused with Chomsky's differentiation between competence and performance (1965). The latter refers to *the individual speaker's* potential versus actual articulation capability under real-world constraints. De Saussure's distinction concerns language. A complete inventory of all language use by all speakers of a language (its most comprehensive dictionary and grammar) is *langue*, whereas speakers in specific speech communities use *parole* (i.e., academic or business jargon). Chomsky's distinction concerns the speaker. A speaker's actual language under real-world constraints is performance, whereas the inventory of a speaker's language use under all circumstances is that speaker's competence.

2. One of the criteria cited in the *ACTFL Proficiency Guidelines* (1986).

3. For a representative articulation of concerns about the actual validity of these claims, see Savignon (1985) or Kramsch (1987).

4. More recently Robert Politzer has made significant contributions to our knowledge of the relationship between the learning strategies, motivation, and achievement of ESL students.

5. The MLA's 1987–88 survey of foreign language entrance and degree requirements showed that 381 (25.7%) of the responding baccalaureate institutions have a foreign-language requirement for entrance and 862 (58.2%) have a requirement for the Bachelor of Arts degree. In the 1982–83 survey only 14.1% reported entrance requirements and 47% BA-degree requirements. The peak year reported was 1964–65 when 33.6% had entrance requirments and 88.9% had a BA-degree requirement (see "Language Requirements Survey," *MLA Newsletter*).

6. See, for example, the community programs at the State University of New York, College at New Paltz under the direction of Henry Urbanski.

7. The University of Wisconsin Foreign Language Department at Eau Claire developed a questionnaire for its undergraduate majors in French, German, and Spanish and discovered that over 70% wanted courses about current events and cultural concerns.

8. For research validation, particularly with regard to enhanced student confidence about forthcoming advanced work, see Barnett (1988a).

9. For descriptions of pilot projects such as the one in international business and liberal arts at the City University of New York, College of Staten Island or the five-year program in International Engineering at the University of Rhode Island, see "Fund for the Improvement of Postsecondary Education Resources: The Comprehensive Project Descriptions 1987–1988." Descriptions of a wide variety of program types can be found in Hill's collection of essays on innovations in study abroad. In addition, Goodwin and Nacht's (1988) volume on issues and policy decisions involved in planning these programs is recommended reading for departments involved in study abroad.

10. If the learning components are modular, then the affective, metacognitive, and grammatical capabilities could be driven by cognitively-independent processors. The modular theory could account for the relative ease adults have in macroprocessing of concepts and discourse settings on the one hand, and the difficulties of adults in pronunciation and details of grammar on the other. A modular model presumes that in the critical stage, the native-language parameter settings are established. If these settings result in accurate applications of sentence-level rules, it follows that they must be modified in adults before surface rules in a second language can be acquired. Chomsky describes the modular concept with the metaphor of a universal language system as a complex network with a series of switches (parameter settings). "Each permissible array of switch settings determines a particular language. Acquisition of a language is in part a process of setting the switches one way or another on the basis of the presented data, a process of fixing the values of the parameters" (1986: 63). He notes that this discussion limits itself to "core language," thereby excluding vocabulary, idioms and the like. When they explore the concept, semanticists will probably take a more inclusive view.

11. Oller has argued the case for student predisposition or expectancy for grammar learning as a function of a general language proficiency factor (the unitary hypothesis). For a summary presentation of various theoretical models and the current status of research in Universal Grammar, see Birdsong. For a pragmatic investigation of the curricular implications of the competing unitary and modular models, see Beck.

The Legacy of History for Practice: Why New Paradigms Are Hard to Implement

In the past decade, the shift to learner-centered language instruction has been most evident in the profession's rethinking of the reading process. Viewed in the past as either a top-down (gist) or bottom-up (letters and words) procedure, reading comprehension, we now think, results from interactive variables that operate simultaneously rather than sequentially (e.g., Samuels & Kamil). Research into one of these variables, schematizing—the reader's prior knowledge applied to text assertions—suggests that, in second- and foreign-language learning as in L1, what is understood depends on the reader rather than on the linguistic difficulty of the text (Anderson & Pearson; Grabe). In literary criticism, reader-response theorists support this view with the claim that "meaning has no effective existence outside of its realization in the mind of the reader" (Tompkins ix). Increasingly, researchers in many fields find that the text cannot be described apart from the comprehender (Anderson & Pichert).

THE READER'S ROLE: LANGUAGE MEANING AND TEXT INTERPRETATION

What does a text *mean* to a given reader? Why do reading experts reject the notion that a text can "mean" the sum of dictionary definitions (*langue*) that exist independent of reader response? Because semioticians from de Saussure to Eco tell us that once words are in a context (*parole*), they cease being mere abstractions. Words in texts function as signs within a culture-bound system. Consequently, any product of the reader's comprehension will depend on the reader's grasp of the constituent systems, a coherent pattern of textual concepts.

Fluent readers synthesize textual subsystems (e.g., content, context, intent, language) into a larger metasystem of meaning. When readers correlate these multiple reader and text factors, they *encode*. In contrast to an interactive process of encoding, a reader may choose to attend primarily to letters and words, a practice characteristic of young children or illiterate adults learning to read. Such a reader confronts the text as a series of dictionary entries—words out of context. Often theorists refer to this word-based style of reading as *decoding*. Definitions of encoding and decoding vary among researchers, with some preferring a distinction between comprehension (decoding) and articulation of comprehension (encoding). For purposes of discussion in this volume, decoding refers to reader replication of textual language without reference to reader or textual framework of meaning. For example, a decoder might mistake the word "money" for the word "many." Encoding, on the other hand, refers to reader construction of text meaning on the basis of multiple interactive factors which will be discussed in this chapter. Such a reader might register "dimes" rather than "money"—recognizing a semantic similarity. Whether encoding is articulated in spoken or written form or not is less important than the distinction between comprehension of isolated bits of language and comprehension of a discourse system.

Iser describes how readers interact with (encode) systems of signs in a text. He illustrates the process with an example from Thackeray's *Vanity Fair*, pointing out that the first time Becky Sharp manipulates someone, the reader registers this as an isolated fact. By the second or third manipulation, however, the reader will probably see a pattern of "habitual opportunism" (115). For this reader, Becky's actions are no longer isolated events; they belong to a recurring schema. The reader has synthesized textual information (Becky's motives, behaviors, impact on others) and constructed from that synthesis a system of expectations linked to his or her prior knowledge of her actions.

DEFINING COMPREHENSION: THE READER'S ROLE

Comprehension has often been equated with a reader's capacity to replicate a text (e.g., in summaries of facts, translations, or matching exercises). Recently, that view of comprehension has been replaced by a conceptual model influenced by research on the role of creativity in memory and recall. Emerging from that research are two recently verified assumptions: (1) that short-term memory is incapable of storing information read or heard for more than about ten seconds unless it is rehearsed (Murdock), and (2) that rehearsal is conducted in "working memory," a function within short-term memory. Working memory reclassifies incoming information by *assigning it to existing configurations in the mind* (Kintsch 1977a). Consequently de Beaugrande (1982), among many others, concludes that "what is in fact comprehended is not sentences, but conceptual content" (180). In short, *readers comprehend a text when they construct a mental representation for incoming pieces of verbal information.* We contemporary readers might construct the mental representation "Becky Sharp is an opportunist" for Thackeray's words, sentences, and extended discourse from another era.

DEFINING THE TEXT

Rarely, if ever, do mental representations of a group of readers concur. *How* readers comprehend will depend on their individual perspectives and background because "the meaning and structure of a text are not inherent in the print but are invited by the author and imputed to the text by the reader" (Schallert, et al. 272). Are there different kinds of imputations? Hermeneutic models distinguish among three: (1) conceptualizing of *explicitly stated information*, (2) conceptualizing of *intentionality* created by the author's structuring of that information, and (3) conceptualizing of the *significance* that the author's message system has for the reader (Hirsch 1967). The first factor, textual assertion, is verifiable in the text. The second factor, inferences to be drawn from explicit language, links text- and reader-based information. The third factor, significance, is verifiable only as a reader-based component (Swaffar 1986a). Together, these three factors are the basis for a reader's textual imputations.

Why does a text invite different readings? Reader point of view provides one answer. Readings change when conducted from different perspectives. A feminist might see Becky as the victim of a chauvinist society and be more sympathetic than the canon of scholarship which has been produced largely by male critics. In and of themselves, different perspectives and goals alter a reader's perceptual processes and recall (Frederiksen 1982). Objective agreement about textual content and meaning is, therefore, necessarily limited to explicit statements and arguable inferences made about any text.[1] From the standpoint of interactive research, a text consists of *explicit assertions and logical implications about these assertions* as assessed by a community of readers. Therefore readings will differ among different linguistic, ethnographic, and historic communities.

TEXTUAL MEANING IN RELATIONSHIP TO READER PROCESSING

Propositional analysis seems to be a key to unlocking the puzzle of how we can assess the relationship between disparate reader processing and textual meaning. Propositions are idea units of the text (Fillmore). These units can reflect the four tasks that are essential for conceptualizing coherent reader processing: (1) propositions can be aligned with textual main topics or with details of those topics; (2) they can be assigned hierarchical relationships (properties, causes, sequences); (3) they reflect reader inferences about concepts not explicitly stated in the text; (4) they can represent ideational and syntactic complexity. In short, propositions can represent the conceptual core of textual assertions and their implications.

Although they are widely used in language reading research, definitions of the term "proposition" vary. Gagné characterizes propositions as units conveying an idea (the man) and a complete idea (the man fixed the tire); each complete idea has *arguments* (the man) and *relations* (fixed the tire). Others call these same components *topics* and *comments* (Kintsch & van Dijk), implying that the proposition represents the reader's perception rather than the actual text language ("some guy" rather than "the man"). If the propositions are text-based, text linguists use the terms *themes* (man) and *rhemes* (fixed the tire). Both themes and arguments can have different functions within a sentence and are not synonymous with a sentence *subject* (Vipond). Most important, not all propositions are equal. Results of analysis vary, depending on how propositions are defined and weighted in relative importance (as macro- or micropropositions).

If connected coherently by the author, important ideas or macropropositions create a text's *schema*. Propositions relevant to textual schema are usually recalled better (by a factor of two or three) than propositions that are not (Kintsch & Keenan; Meyer & Freedle). However, how a reader schematizes will depend on that individual's goals. When a reader's objectives ("This is what I want to find out") align with the textual presentation, he or she assigns textual propositions to appropriate categories of "gist" and "detail." The reader's sorting of gist and detail is called a macro-operation (Kintsch & van Dijk). When the reader's goals are vague or the text lacks coherence (explicit or implicit), schemata are likely to be random, macro-operations will be unpredictable, and the reading outcomes will be "haphazard" (374). Under such circumstances Becky Sharp might become a poor dear instead of a selfish opportunist. Comparing reader recall of a text with an analysis of its weighted propositions can reveal which readings are haphazard and which are justified by the text.

Research has, then, redefined the text vis-à-vis the reader. Text messages interact with reader perceptions. If we could isolate those interactions they would add up to eight distinct components:

Top-down factors: reader

1. reader background (semantic knowledge);
2. reader perspective (reading strategies).

Top-down factors: text

3. text schema (topic);
4. text structure (organizational pattern of the information);
5. episodic sequence (scripts or story grammars).

Bottom-up factors: text and reader

6. illustrative detail (micropropositions);
7. the surface language features of the text in letters, words, and individual sentences;
8. reader language proficiency.

The components in reading reflect interaction between text and reader on many cognitive levels. This insight helps clarify problems with current reading practice. If the reader's task is to construct meaning, reading in terms of one or two of the components shortchanges the comprehension process. Historically, that is exactly what has happened. We have, more by misadventure than by malice, encouraged students to look only at surface language—word-for-word reading and discrete details—in assignments, classroom practice, and tests.

READER FOCUS OF ATTENTION AND COMPREHENSION

Word-for-word reading, whether as translation or transliteration of synonyms, poses practical, purely functional problems for the foreign-language reader. When the focus of student attention is on surface details rather than communicative substance, translation encourages dictionary dependency and word-for-word reading habits. Such habits discourage both pleasure reading and self-reliance in using foreign-language texts. A learning focus on precise matching of semantic, morphological, and syntactic features undermines reader strategies such as "chunking" or skimming and scanning, the techniques of successful readers in both foreign and native languages (e.g., Hosenfeld). Let us show how the various interactive components facilitate reading in order to demonstrate the key element in this interaction: meaningfulness.

The illustration and the cognates of the passage opposite render it meaningful to most American students, even if they are totally ignorant of the Dutch language. Title and format suggest a short movie review. Most American readers are familiar with the rhetorical organization of such reviews. If, however, readers lack familiarity with the *Star Trek* television series or the subsequent movies, they will find this a more difficult

CULTUUR

FILM

RUIMTEVAART

„Star Trek II, The Wrath of Kahn", Ruimtevaartspektakel voor de liefhebbers van geraffineerd trucagewerk. Alle figuren uit de legendarische tv-serie (ooit gestart in 1966) zijn terug in de tweede, groots opgezette speelfilm gewijd aan de avonturen van het ruimteschip Enterprise. Admiraal James T. Kirk leidt opnieuw de crew (en blijkt ineens een echt verleden te hebben alsmede een flink uit de kluiten gewassen zoon). Een grote rol is deze keer weggelegd voor mr. Spock, die wat sinistere kruising tussen een mens en een bewoner van de planeet Vulcan. Booswicht in deze aflevering is Ricardo Montelban als Kahn, een gemenerik die met behulp van een soort generator van nieuw leven alle bestaande leven wenst weg te vagen. Het einde van deze Star Trek-film is „open" genoeg (is mr. Spock nu wel of niet dood?) dat we met vertrouwen naar nummer III kunnen uitkijken.

text to comprehend since they lack subject matter schema. Certain formal features will be unfamiliar in any event, since the passage is an authentic text taken from a magazine written for Dutch speakers. When confronted with the combination of unfamiliar subject matter and new language features, students often resort to surface reading—matching or decoding every word of the passage—components seven and eight of the list on p. 24. Surface reading can be avoided if students are guided to read interactively for a particular *message*, thereby adding components one through six.

APPLYING TOP-DOWN PROCESSES

Textual messages are about something or someone (the semantic structure) and organized in fairly predictable ways (the metasyntax or rhetorical structure). Generally the global subject matter suggests rhetorical treatment. For example, once students recognize that the Dutch text is a film review, the relative length of the passage suggests a short summary rather than an analysis of the film. Summaries deal primarily in facts—the itinerary or microdetails of the macrosubject, in this instance key figures in the film: who they are and the implications of their roles (words which suggest importance or relative unimportance, villainous or heroic behavior). Pinpointing such information is relatively easy and demands far less command of linguistic features than the surface-translation or transliteration task. Even readers who do not know Dutch can find familiar information, especially if they have watched *Star Trek* on television. Of course, we are speaking here about capitalizing on the fact that most students in foreign-language instruction in the Western Hemisphere and Europe share a knowledge base, an alphabet, and the cognates common to most Western languages. This background is one major aid in the interactive processing of texts.

A second major aid is the awareness of how a text topic guides rhetorical structure. Rhetorical organization sorts the meta-syntax, the relationships between the people, places, and events of the passage. In the movie review, Kirk, Spock, and Khan are presented with a brief list of characteristics (Kirk leads the crew, Khan is evil). Students will look in vain for judgments about the quality of acting or an assessment of character development. Moreover, reader interactions between the top-down levels of metasyntax and bottom-up levels of language details will do more than yield a list of names.

In most cases, for example, knowing about Captain Kirk aids the reader. She is better able to speculate about the general or even the precise meaning of words which follow mention of his name. A reader feels reasonably secure in conjecturing that "leidt opnieuw de crew" means "leads the crew." To be sure, "opnieuw" may mean "again" or "at the head of" or nothing intelligible, but it precedes the recognizable concept "crew." If the reader has registered similarity between movie and TV series in a preceding sentence, no serious misreading is likely to occur ("opnieuw" as having the captain "destroy" or "get rid of" his crew, for example).

If the reader's working memory has made a connection between the TV series and the movie, background schema suggests a strategy for isolating the text's global and detailed topics. In the case of this passage, a strategy of establishing sets and subsets yields a considerable degree of comprehension. Most of the recognizable language ("Ruimtevaartspektakel," "generator," "Admiraal," "speelfilm," "figuren," "tv-serie," "avonturen," "rol," "ruimteschip," "planeet," "nummer") and consequently some of the unknown words can be organized into coherent categories of global and subsidiary topics along the following lines:

Topic	Comment
ruimtevaartspektakel	Admiraal Kirk, planeet
speelfilm	avonturen, tv-serie
Spock	"grote rol," "sinister"
Khan	"booswicht," "generator van nieuw leven"

Although some words may be imprecisely or erroneously understood, a reader who has applied top-down factors minimizes the distraction of vagueness or errors. A reader will not, for example, attribute connotations of "sinister" to Kirk or to the movie as a whole, if "sinister" is related to Spock alone.

Such distinctions are vital. Failure to encode textual detail will lead to global misreading. Global misreading can be averted when details are assigned to a comment or subcategory (Spock = sinister) rather than to the text topic as a whole. Apparently, awareness of the difference between top-down and bottom-up strategies is useful for the reader with a weak language background. Research suggests that an interactive reader unfamiliar with Dutch or any other foreign language relies more on *content schema* and *organizational schema* (both top-down processes) to guide comprehension (Wolff). Prior familiarity with subject matter in an essay enhances ability to schematize its content (e.g., Koh; Levine & Haus): what is already known about the crew of the Starship Enterprise and its mission can then be linked to new linguistic information in the text.[2]

Glance at the second Dutch text below to see that, conversely, when people lack background schema about either the content or the structure of a passage, the language appears much more "foreign." A comparison between the task of "reading" a passage about *Star Trek* and reading a passage about a uniquely Dutch subject matter illustrates the difference between reading familiar subject matter in which the eight components can interact, and reading unfamiliar subject matter, in which only language factors are applicable.

Boze winkeliers: meer politie, meer cellen

Staatssecretaris *Van Zeil* van economische zaken kreeg het vorige week voor zijn kiezen in Amsterdam, waar zeer boze winkeliers tijdens hun bijeenkomst hun beklag deden: „De kleine criminaliteit moet nu eindelijk eens aangepakt worden; het kan echt niet langer zo." Voorbeelden van een wanhoopssituatie: enkele malen achtereen werden bij dezelfde drogist de ruiten ingeslagen; een sigarenwinkelier gaat voor zijn deur posten en laat scholieren slechts twee aan twee naar binnen anders wordt zijn zaak leeggeroofd; een andere winkelier heeft tijdens de schoolpauzes extra personeel in zijn zaak; weer andere winkeliers zijn bang langzamerhand hun klandizie te verliezen omdat de auto's van klanten aan de lopende band worden opengebroken tijdens het winkelen. Oplossing kan volgens de winkeliers (mede) gevonden worden door: meer politie op straat. Waarom zijn agenten wel beschikbaar voor het administratief werk van het uitschrijven van parkeerbonnen, maar moet je uren wachten voordat er iemand komt om een winkeldief te arresteren? Meer cellen, het oude verhaal: de winkeldief is al weer doende terwijl de winkelier nog bezig is met de aangifte. De daders zouden zelf de aangerichte schade (ook uit de mond geslagen tanden bij voorbeeld) moeten betalen. Ten slotte: de media zouden aangepakt moeten worden want wat te denken van een radio-uitzending waarin haarfijn wordt uitgelegd hoe je het best proletarisch kan winkelen? □

THE CONTROVERSY ABOUT BOTTOM-UP PROCESSING

Why do extant assumptions and practices work against interactive reading in a foreign language? After all, extensive word-for-word translation is rarely recommended in textbook exercises or curricular guides, even in beginning language instruction. Yet experience is more persuasive than pedagogical claims. In L2 reading practice, teachers and students turn to extensive translation or word-for-word reading because they lack convincing alternatives. The issue is not an occasional rendering of a word or phrase in the students' native language. As used here the term translation refers to rendering textual language in either first- or second-language equivalencies.

Although laborious, there are pedagogical advantages to a purely bottom-up style of text-based reading. Surface language matching of English or the L2 synonyms with textual sentences is verifiable, whereas the structures for establishing whether students think sensibly about a text vary. With translation or L2 answers to discrete-point questions (true / false, who, what, when, where questions), it *appears* that students comprehend the text. The appeal of word-for-word reading is particularly great when the L2 is a foreign language and students have little or no language input outside the classroom. The conscientious teacher would rather be safe than sorry. But can reading of detail at the sentence level be equated with comprehension? Do surface language renditions prove that students understand what the text says?

Mounting L2 evidence about comprehension says no. Perrig and Kintsch's L1 students who were able to identify close to fifty percent of the textual propositions on one test of a reading passage were unable to draw an accurate map of the town described in the passage. Only the second testing instance revealed the "contrast between, on the one hand, the subjects' ability to recall a text reasonably well . . . and their inability to do anything with this remembered information" (509). Good recall accompanied by poor functional comprehension explains the anomaly that, although the ability to decode vocabulary (context-free recognition) is a key facilitator in both L1 and L2 reading, this ability is no guarantee of understanding.

Cooper characterizes the behaviors of poor ESL readers as showing "excessive veneration for each word" and treating a passage in the classroom as "a quarry for vocabulary" (124). These same conclusions suggest themselves in every investigation of the problem in the past decade. Either students focused too narrowly on lexical meaning (e.g., Hosenfeld), or they failed to activate appropriate schemata due to deficiencies in language skills (M. Clarke 1980; Hudson). The key to successful interactive processing seems to be what Carrell (1988) calls "bidirectional processing"—a blend of text-based and knowledge-based processing. Over-reliance on one or the other style of processing leads to a "unidirectional bias" (103). If the bias is knowledge-based, a reader tends to fill in details not motivated by the text and make unsupported inferences. If the bias is text-based, readers tend to *exclude* inferential thinking. Either bias leads to inaccurate comprehension.

Our concern is that a vocabulary focus in reading is often confused with the concept of text-based reading. Word-for-word reading is only *one* text-based option, exclusively a bottom-up strategy. As the list on p. 24 indicates, text-based readings occur at intersentential and segmental levels of the text as well. Indeed, without these levels no synthesis of textual information can take place and the reader has only unconnected pieces of information. Without connections or a gestalt, information is harder to organize in working memory and consequently harder to link to structures in long-term memory. The issue, then, is to recognize that text-based readings involve various levels of linguistic knowledge, top-down and mid-level processing, and supersentential and sentential as well as lexical processing. It follows that if unidirectional processing is ineffective, a single type of unidirectional processing is even less effective.

We argue that reading word for word—reading with a dominant focus on vocabulary or formal features rather than textual message—is an inadvertent by-product of second- and particularly foreign-language instruction. Since the days of audiolingualism the foreign language profession's tradition has been to emphasize speaking and speech situations as the basis for learning the four skills. Despite widespread discussion in the past decade about comprehensible input, one parameter has been overlooked: If input is limited to what students can be expected to produce in their own speech, the language for listening, reading, and writing is unnecessarily restricted.

Challenging listening, reading, and writing, if presented in terms of student interest and information value, are complementary activities that provide practice in processing unfamiliar linguistic detail. Unlike language practice that focuses exclusively on simulated communicative situations, listening, reading, and writing allow students to use higher-order cognitive skills. They afford a level of learning that is more appropriate for the adult learner than one based narrowly on the linguistic limits of speaking activities, tasks necessarily more confined to production of everyday words and formal features than to recognition of language expressing concepts and information normally associated with higher education.

In high school and college, students listen, read, and write for purposes other than learning a foreign language. Adults read and listen to learn about new information and ideas. Based on their reading and listening, they record information and express a point of view. Yet in the United States *the goal of instruction in foreign languages has been to learn the language rather than to use the language to learn.* Here is the crux of the new efforts in proficiency testing and the emerging interdisciplinary programs. Foreign-language departments must set their sights on using a foreign language to learn. As long as the profession continues to teach the rudiments of language *qua* language, we leave ourselves open to accusations that language teaching is remedial instruction better conducted under auspices other than the university (e.g., Redfield).

Virtually all instructional materials, even those claiming to represent communicative learning methods, encourage surface translation behavior. Students' main reading in initial semesters of language study consists of sentence-level exercises. In beginning textbooks, assignments and class activities deal with tangibles instead of ideas. Often, writing practice involves discourse gambits—sentence series revolving around the students themselves or around simulations of life in the foreign culture—its institutions, home life, or work environments. Notably lacking is a balance between such tasks and cognitively challenging reading and written work. As Byrnes points out, L2 textbooks fail to use to their advantage "the fact that learners possess *different degrees of control* for different tasks" (1987a:32).

Publishers' reluctance to break new ground is understandable. Their success depends on teacher acceptance and use of their books. Teaching for recognition and partial control, despite the lip service paid to these aims in the wake of the *ACTFL Guidelines*, has been contrary to traditional teaching in the United States. Comprehension-based instruction is distinctly a feature of the new rather than the old language learning paradigm. Hence, the authentic materials that enliven many of the more recent books do so more often as realia than as tasks designed to activate bidirectional processing for reading comprehension.

The value of recognition and partial control is often subverted by classroom materials. Rather than offering a mix of comprehension-based instruction and stages of increasing control, textbooks inadvertently promote the idea that mastery of textual vocabulary and structures is requisite for reading (or listening comprehension) in a foreign language. Initial texts are simplified, making it easier to practice bottom-up processing at the word and sentence level to the exclusion of other strategies. Students are therefore rarely motivated to undertake bidirectional processing. In effect, students are "learning" that focusing on vocabulary is the way to read a second language. The usual, integrated uses of reading are largely neglected in first-year language texts for colleges and high school: reading for the information and entertainment value of the text, listening to discussion of the text in the second language, writing about the text to reveal comprehension of the content or analysis of its messages.

Instead, exercises treat vocabulary and grammar as entities in themselves, distinct from functional use. Neither reader- nor text-based processes are related to linguistic processes. Rarely is an attempt made to connect grammar and meaning by asking students to subordinate, for example, one idea or event to another, or use adverbs that connect sentences and reveal author intent. In textbook presentation and treatment of reading materials, learning the formal properties of language still has clear priority over the gamut of interactive processes that result in reading comprehension.

HOW TEXTBOOKS CAN SUBVERT INTERACTIVE PROCESSING

Like reading, writing exercises are directed toward teaching form rather than integrated meaning. Despite improved exercises for speaking, most books still cue items with one word in English or the foreign language. Confronted with instructions to rewrite sentences or parts of sentences, the average student manipulates words rather than connecting concepts. Whether it occurs in an initial learning task or as part of a reading assignment, this tactic reinforces surface translation behavior. Comprehension is directed towards manipulating language, not towards understanding how language manipulation affects a framework of meaning. Consider the cognitive activities of students who are asked the following questions:

1. Fill in the correct form of the verb "estar" in the following sentences. (Juan _____ aquí. [is]   Juan y Carlos _____ enfermos. [are] etc.)

Why or whether Juan should be here or elsewhere, why both boys are sick or how seriously, what impact sickness will have on them or others, is all immaterial to the learning task. The statements have little communicative significance. What matters is form.

To complete these exercises, the student selects the correct form from a paradigm, preferably from memory. Even if another cognitive task is added, the choice of the two verbs *estar* and *ser* for example, the item is still executed as a series of surface translation tasks. The student who selects a form of *ser* for the sentence "Juan _____ un niño" has only the words in the sentence to confirm or disconfirm the choice. The correct answer will depend on the student's translation of *aquí* as an adverb of location, of *enfermos* as an adjective describing a temporary condition or *niño* as a noun. Piaget distinguishes between concrete operations (discrete choices) and formal operations (synthesis of multiple choices). Exercises that look at details without a contextual frame are concrete operations on *langue*, whereas reading is a formal operation on (textual) *parole*.

Alderson and Urquhart criticize textbooks on these same grounds, pointing out, for example, that most of the time "the presence of a passive construction triggers an exercise on the passive, with no apparent aim of improving students' understanding of the text" (25).

Consider the preceding illustrations with regard to learning how to recognize and use connected discourse—verbal cohesion. Since *aquí* lacks cohesion (e.g., without preceding or subsequent elaborating sentences we can't guess what it refers to), only context-free recognition can be used to decode it. With single-sentence exercises one rarely resorts to reasoning about meaning. The reader cannot say to herself "because the previous sentence says Juan is at the travel agency this afternoon, *aquí* probably is an adverb referring to his location." She lacks the data to make inferences about either cohesion (language reference) or coherence (contextual reference) factors.

Similarly, the formats of most beginning language readers do little to encourage interactive reading. Consider the content of most introductions to a reading assignment. Advanced organizers are becoming more common, but they rarely orient the student to either the rhetorical scheme or the context of the selection. Introductions tend to give additional facts extraneous to readings, rather than provide the first step toward understanding what they are about. They rarely point to language features that create particular structural bridges between episodes. Yet we know that sequence words such as *first, next, later*, or contrast markers such as *but, nonetheless, on the other hand*, are often essential for identifying rhetorical structure (Chaudron & Richards), as is an orientation to familiar and unfamiliar content (Floyd & Carrell).

Selections are often excerpted from a longer work, simplified or abridged. Such changes rob the reader of the very continuity and redundancy features which could encourage reading for development of ideas. Even if only a portion of the language describing Juan and Carlos' illness is grasped on initial reading, a long discussion, in and of itself, implies that the illness deserves reader attention. Ironically, attention to meaning is complicated in edited texts because their language is simplified and, inevitably "sanitized." If the cause of Juan and Carlos' illness is traced to contamination of a well in a Guatemalan village, for example, readers will be more likely to infer the absence of drinking water in the homes of that village. If that discussion is deleted on the basis of a large number of difficult words, not only language but cultural information about living conditions is deleted, as well.

Another feature of most anthologies that renders them difficult to read interactively is the absence of sensitivity to both reader interests and background in text selection. We know that texts dealing with subjects that students know about and that they find interesting to read compensate for their language deficiencies (e.g., Levine & Haus). Moreover, without orientation to cultural differences, serious misreadings occur even in

L1. Steffensen, Joag-Dev, and Anderson found that East Indian readers of a letter about an American wedding were preoccupied by references to the bride wearing the grandmother's wedding dress and her decision not to exchange gifts. For East Indians, the implications of these "facts," described in their native language, were recast by their cultural frame. While these are perfectly normal arrangements in the United States, in India the image of a bride without a new dress or a dowry is cause for sadness and dismay.

To compound the problems inherent in text selection and editing, exercises at the end of the passage frequently focus on isolated details. The commonly found "true / false comprehension checks" or "who, what, where, when" questions encourage the extraction of detailed information from the text, but not in a cohesive way. Answers to discrete-point questions about the *Star Trek* film review ("Who leads the crew?" or "Who has a large role?") suggest neither what information is important (e.g., the film is similar to the TV series) or what is implied (if you liked the TV version you'll enjoy this film). True / false questions often prove frustrating because a correct answer hinges on a property of grammar rather than meaningfulness. For example, when the speaker has just said "I'm not very hungry. I think I'll have a salad," the true / false item "the speaker is not hungry" is open to interpretation.

For the other exercises commonly found in reading anthologies for foreign-language students, discussion or short essay questions, students lack the practice in connecting facts and meaning, i.e., awareness of the way thought is developed in a piece of writing (in the Dutch review, as a series of descriptors of major roles) and what the reader can assume as a result.[3]

It is in the foregoing ways that an exclusive language focus in beginning instruction sabotages interactive reading. Training in reading as language practice fails to promote behaviors characteristic of successful interactive readers: skimming for information or redundancies, engaging in hypothesis formation, chunking phrases in multiple sentences into larger meanings. On the contrary, the word-for-word emphasis is an unsuccessful strategy if comprehension is the goal (Barnett 1988b). This emphasis conditions the beginner to think of foreign-language reading as a mechanical activity in which the task is to fit all the parts of the puzzle together rather than, as in native-language reading, using the pieces to create a picture. Small wonder that the reader's good L1 strategies tend to be "short-circuited" in L2.

The problem can be summed up succinctly: the language of everyday communication is not the same as the language of texts. Language for communication involves matching words and grammar to references in the real world. Texts are reflections of the world rather than real-world actualizations. Their meanings, whether fictional or not, exist only in discourse.

THE CASE FOR COMPREHENDING DISCOURSE
WHILE LEARNING LANGUAGE

Current curricula and testing practices in foreign languages are both still under the influence of behaviorism. How so? Primarily because that tradition postpones reading and writing, tasks that are cognitively challenging for adults, until an unspecified level of language mastery is achieved. It is a tradition without pedagogical practices that link a learner's first-language knowledge of topics or rhetorical and linguistic structures to that individual's second-language learning. Even today the profession lacks a systematic pedagogy that connects comprehension with eventual speech production—hence the reluctance among textbook publishers to venture into this uncharted territory.

To be sure, a relationship exists between command of syntactic and semantic detail on the one hand and the ability to read and write successfully on the other (Barnett 1986; Berman). But why use one kind of practice to the exclusion of the others? Why, when we have adult students who want to use a foreign language, expose them initially to only the language of spoken communication? Why be reluctant to have them engage in different degrees of control for different tasks? In an era of learner-centered instruction, the profession remains notably hesitant to activate the learner's capabilities.

After all, we know adults can derive meaning from schematically or structurally familiar texts despite unfamiliarity with some words (e.g., Carrell) and syntactic forms (Lee 1987b). We know adults are capable of generalizing about formal features in discourse because mature speakers of English (or Spanish or French) use subordinate clauses or infinitive phrases whereas children have yet to learn how such things are done *in any language*. Listening, reading, and writing about stimulating texts written for an adult audience informs a broader range of skills and applications of discourse functions than is the case if exposure is limited to edited texts and sentence-level written exercises. The work of Valdés, Lessa, Echeverriarza, and Piño finds that students in first-year college Spanish are capable of listening comprehension based on long segments of uninterrupted speech which are "propositionally and linguistically complex" (421). Even first-year high school students derive meaning from authentic texts they have never seen before (Allen et al.). As for writing, the consistent findings reveal no improvement on the basis of sentence practice. Quite the contrary, improvement seems to follow practice in essay or notebook writing (Lightbown).

In sum, earlier introduction of challenging reading and related listening and writing tasks cries out for consideration in the light of current evidence. Translation of texts or providing correct answers to discrete-point questions is no guarantee of comprehension, nor do accurate answers based on mechanical clues (fill-ins, dehydrated sentences) guarantee coherent self-expression.[4] By the same token, practice devoted solely to sentence level transactions seems to have negligible impact on writing performance. One of the few areas of agreement in research on composition correction regards correction of surface errors. Although students, particularly those studying a second language, often claim to need and use it (Cohen), corrective feedback on mechanics addresses only one aspect of the writing process.

Studies comparing correction styles conclude that "detailed feedback may not be worth the instructors' time and effort" (Robb et al., 91). Zamel's suggestions (1976, 1987) based on ESL composition research, as well as Dvorak's summary of foreign language research on writing, cites similar conclusions. More recently, Connor's research summary concludes that second-language teachers need to develop criteria for textual analysis in order to foster our students' writing processes. Ultimately all of these suggestions add up to one conclusion: The profession needs to develop pedagogical practices that utilize the adult learner's needs and extralinguistic capabilities.

HABIT LEARNING AND STANDARDIZED TESTS
OF COMPREHENSION

Aside from tradition itself, the second motive teachers have to eschew learner-centered practices is the pedagogical reality of language-centered testing. Quantifiable and verifiable data have tremendous appeal. Machine-graded tests can assess large numbers of students with a minimum of time and money spent on evaluation. Normed to national standards, test items, even those for reading, tend to test context-free language rather than comprehension of textual discourse. Only recently have researchers begun a systematic study of the ways context affects language use and assessment (Douglas). In conjunction with consideration of contextual influences, a recent study indicates that a greater share of instructional time should be devoted to helping learners make accurate self-assessments about their language ability, their interests, and how to apply those interests to a particular level of language study (LeBlanc & Painchaud).

By definition, both objective classroom and national standardized tests lack several components with which to assess interactive reading, chiefly: (1) specification of the behavioral domain for a particular language ability such as reading (Henning 1988), and (2) a construct that accounts for a reader's ability to connect meanings, their implications, and their significance.

Even when objective questions about discourse levels and episodic structure are added to the traditional items dealing with word and sentential meanings, these tests remain necessarily unidirectional, text-based assessments of reading comprehension. If comprehension is measured by a student's ability to recall pieces of data, reading and listening are indeed "passive" skills. Whether true / false or multiple choice, answers on listening or reading tests tell us what the student comprehends in terms of a particular question, but offer few clues about how or why a particular answer is chosen, or how that answer informs the reader about the text. Current debates about whether the profession needs to research and test "process" as well as "product" (Long 1984) are, in essence, debates about whether or not we need to encourage and test thinking as well as results.

Although it is seldom used in FL tests of reading comprehension, many advocate a cloze procedure as the objective solution for assessing reading comprehension. Cloze procedures consist of connected discourse with periodic word deletions for which students supply the appropriate insertion. While it is a product-oriented test, cloze nonetheless is more text-based than either true / false or multiple choice answers. The common assumption that *nth* deletion cloze tests assess understanding of text discourse rather than understanding of phrase and sentence level features is debatable, however. There is evidence to support both sides, but opponents marshal persuasive arguments. Alderson (1983) concludes that cloze testing assesses knowledge of formal features rather than comprehension of discourse. The thrust of Alderson's argument is that a random *nth* word procedure should be abandoned in favor of a deletion procedure that is based upon a theory of language processing (213). Kintsch and Yarbrough's comparison showed that a cloze deletion test failed to correspond with a test of rhetorical structure. After analysis of L2 studies, Farhady raises questions about the validity and reliability of cloze as a test of text-based comprehension (256–57).

The impact of product tests such as true / false, multiple choice, and cloze on reading practice can be illustrated with the Dutch text. When students read the review, whether using one or all eight interactive components, the struggle to understand is between them and the review. With true / false and multiple choice questions, on the other hand, that dual struggle becomes a triad. The student must first read the review and then the student must read the test. In effect the testing item asks students to compare *two different* "texts." All of us are familiar enough with standard tests to appreciate the dilemma. If different readers comprehend texts in different ways, the student's real job is to get into the head of the person who wrote the item. When the questions ask for "main" ideas, we may well ask, whose idea of the main idea? The reader's or the test maker's?

When, as is more frequently the case, standardized questions ask for detailed information, the comprehension of isolated parts rather than coherent wholes is emphasized. That amounts to a variant of surface language reading: demanding precision without concern for how precision informs. A multiple choice or true / false question about the meaning of "opnieuw" or who has a "grote rol" asks for facts for their own sake. A multiple choice test rarely reveals students' understanding of how these pieces connect. Alternatively, it may reveal only whether or not the student understands which pieces the test maker connects. Meaning, in our century at least, is not ontological. There is no consensus about truth. Eyewitnesses contradict themselves. Perceptions vary. Or as Frank Smith puts it, "comprehension is relative" (1978, 86–87).

Standardized tests fail to teach students to identify and express their relative perceptions because their question type either asks about unconnected facts or dictates preconceived connections. Neither of these questioning techniques acknowledges native language reading behaviors: educated guessing about word meanings within the context of the passage (Saragi et al.); grasp of text coherences (Bensoussan); independent thinking about the implications of textual vocabulary or coherences (Bernhardt 1986a). Standardized tests, whatever their merits as evaluative measures, fail as bidirectional tests of reading. They fail to indicate how students interpret language based on reader construction of textual meaning. And since we know that clever students study for tests, it seems fair to assert that standardized tests fail to motivate such students to learn active reading. At best, such tests motivate students to learn the language in a reading passage. That's not to say they aren't valid as language tests. It is to say they are not necessarily good tests of reading.

Teachers too have been conditioned by the behaviorist legacy. After decades of a paradigm of input / output and comprehension as a "passive" skill, it is hard to think of ways to teach that acknowledge the way our students think. We are hard-pressed to devise activities that reveal the way words register in the brain, i.e., whether "leidt" is more memorable than "opnieuw" and why. Just how do we distinguish between apprehending words as individual sounds or letters and apprehending words within connected thought? Similarly, how do we acknowledge the role of personal feelings as a feature of comprehension? Whether or not the student reacts to the hero of the TV series, i.e., has nostalgic feelings about a childhood hero or thinks Kirk is inconsistent and rather silly, is hard to assess.

The great advantage of excluding meaning and affect under the old paradigm is that teachers and students operate within clear limits. Dialogues, vocabulary lists, and paradigms are tangible. Communicative goals are not. They lack what the behavioral goals have: cleanly defined parameters within a closed system. The replication pedagogy spells out what language students have to learn (the data), what tasks the teacher uses to implement learning (the method), and how to measure outcome (the goals). These objectives may be formidable, but they are definite and involve primarily rote learning and discrete styles of language practice.

Communicative emphases lack these secure limits. Their premises have shifted instructional goals from skill in language manipulation to skill in language use for a specific situation. Instructional emphasis therefore moves from language *per se* to the language of specific situations. Proficiencies within a communicative frame result from three different but related factors. Each of these factors is not only new to, but also irrelevant to, older behavioral approaches. The first factor is our students' background—what they know about the world and how they think. The second is their pragmatic as well as scholarly needs—what they will do with their language knowledge. The third factor follows from the first two: our selection of subject matter. What we teach at both initial and advanced levels needs to be tailored to student needs and backgrounds.

Together these three factors will determine the language—the *parole*—to be taught, in both initial and advanced curricula. As a result, the *parole* taught will vary between different institutions and different student populations. Formerly, the goal of mastery of *langue*, the purview of elite scholars, gave language instructors a shared standard of measure. Today the profession's very real problem is how to measure the diverse proficiencies inherent in learning diverse *paroles*. In the chapter that follows we will look at the sources of those problems and why the profession is facing difficulties in dealing with them.

NOTES TO CHAPTER 2

1. The critical debate on textual meaning and author intentionality is a paper in and of itself. Briefly, in the fifties New Critics Wimsatt and Beardsley (1954) deplored the then relatively common practice in both positivism and *Geistesgeschichte* of text interpretations emanating from what the author said about or experienced with regard to his or her writing. They argued for text-intrinsic readings, insisting that the text must speak for itself and that the reader's job should be limited to assessments of tone and authorial objectives manifested in the choice and arrangement of text words and narrative structure. This view is one fundamental position in current theoretical discussions. Critical divergence today concerns *how* to assess words and structures (see the range of theory in Tompkins).

2. For research in the first language on the effects of textual organization, suggesting that readers have high recall for the story structure and episodes within a text, see Kintsch (1977b); Mandler & Johnson; Meyer & Freedle. Second-language investigations suggest that these effects are significant for L2 readers as well. See, for example, Carrell (1985); Connor; Lee (1986b).

3. Claire Kramsch's book on *Discourse Analysis and Second Language Teaching* (1981) presents the theory and practice of group work linked to either short texts or situations. These practices are vital in discussion of longer texts as well.

4. Lightbown, in her longitudinal study of morpheme development among sixth-grade speakers of French who received formal ESL instruction, concludes that "one important observation of this study is that there was relatively little improvement over time in the accuracy of learners' use of the six grammatical morphemes in obligatory contexts even though grammatical accuracy was always the focus of their ESL classes" (241).

Three

The Practical Differences Between Language Learning and Reading

In beginning instruction, the choice of what grammar and vocabulary to teach remains reasonably secure. Linguistic limits exist because, for beginners, the classroom fixes context in a concrete world. Hence, even the most "natural" or communicatively-oriented instruction, despite its emphasis on meaningful acquisition, shares many premises of behaviorism. New grammar and vocabulary occur in an incremental progression. Naturally, new forms must be practiced. As a result of communicative emphases today, formal practice is more likely to appear as contextualized speech gambits, rather than as rote drill.

The range of speech gambits in the beginner's classroom reflects the way concrete situations restrict the opportunities for speech innovation. Requests, denials, explanations, and expressions of gratitude, for example, need be no more than one or two simple sentences if the speaker is asking for a hotel room or trying to get out of paying a bill. While variations in intonation and explicatives may be virtually infinite, morphologic and syntactic choices decidedly are not. In beginning instruction most language practice is fixed within concrete settings such as the post office or a restaurant in which students talk about and respond to a restricted (and in this sense predictable) set of familiar meanings.

How does learning language as a beginner affect the way L2 students read? The professional literature has been relatively silent on this subject—and understandably so. Most FL curricula still reflect the implicit assumption that practice in speaking and listening comprehension in real-life situations will always lead to reading comprehension. Yet in actual practice this transition fails to occur. The transition to reading is a shock, not a natural development.

The shock results from erroneous assumptions about the learning sequence. In the pedagogy of language replication, reading and writing were among the last skills to be learned in the L2 sequence. Yet, as was argued in Chapter 2, when supersentential reading and writing are absent in beginning language instruction, students have trouble adjusting to these tasks at a later time. College and university students often report frustration with what appears to them to be a total shift in goals and learner tasks (Jakobovits). They find themselves unable to integrate their acquired skills with the new reading emphasis. Faced with a focus on reading, students frequently lose ground in skills acquired earlier (Chastain). Historically, fewer than five percent of students who begin to study a foreign language continue to enroll in courses beyond those that are required.

This chapter presents the view that development of reading facility *can* complement beginning instruction if the differences between reading and speaking tasks are acknowledged in course development. We will present arguments to support a pedagogy of complementary relationships between language learning and reading for meaning. Among these arguments is evidence of more positive attitudes and willingness for continued study. Such developments are possible, however, only if reading tasks are not equated with the tasks of beginning instruction.

THE DIFFERENCE BETWEEN READING AND BEGINNING INSTRUCTION

Why is reading a very different activity from beginning instruction? Many of the answers to this question have already been presented. The eight factors in the interactive list in Chapter 2 (pp. 24) suggest reasons for our failure to introduce reading of informative texts at the onset of instruction. Interactive reading involves more than the ability to recognize and manipulate words. A student who knows how to say "I can run" in Spanish or French can read a "Dick and Jane" text. But what about the level beyond children's readers? What about texts in the real world that present words in a non-literal way? If, for example, their native language lacks similar metaphorical references, the differences between actually "running a race" in a marathon and "running a [political] race" or "running away from a problem" will fail to register with such students.

Learning to use L2 words to express her own meaning ("I am running") is no guarantee that a student has automatically learned to apprehend someone else's quite different use of those same words in reading ("He's been running for president all his life"). Unambiguous situations reinforce literal meanings. When someone says "Just hand me a pen. I'll sign on the dotted line," the fact of a document in their hands leaves little room for doubt that the speaker is going to sign a specific piece of paper with a specific pen. In a short story or a film, such a statement could be either literal or figurative. If it occurs at the end of a convincing plea for funding, it could mean concretely that the statement is made by someone who will write a check or, figuratively, that that person agrees with the arguments presented.

Beginning classrooms specialize in unambiguous meaning. Talk occurs in a concrete setting (pen, document) with a teacher-designated intent ("You are in a restaurant and wish to pay the bill with a credit card"). The concrete situation is closed, "safe," as it were, since clear contexts and fixed intents preclude serious misunderstandings. By comparison, virtually any written text is open-ended. Most texts synthesize abstract systems with implications that are rarely self-evident in the surface language. The relationship between text schema, organization, information patterns (i.e., weighting, organizing, and omitting data), and language is not fixed. "I'll sign on the dotted line" can mean many things, depending on the writer's intent (e.g., serious or sarcastic) and the textual context (e.g., whether or not a real document is involved). Separately or together, macrofeatures complicate a reader's text construction unless that reader knows how to recognize and encode these features.

In Chapter 2 we asserted that the context of spoken language is the real world whereas a text creates a reflection of the real world. Another way of saying pretty much the same thing is that the beginner's learning environment is tangible or closed, while the literate reader's textual environment is intangible or open. Three features of the beginning language classroom render it a "closed" or fixed learning environment.

1. *The setting.* Whether classroom focus is on speech or comprehension, beginners learn the language of their immediate surroundings. They learn words for room furnishings, classroom paraphernalia, and clothing. Few books, if any, begin with discussions of truth and beauty, quite rightly recognizing that such abstract discussions are unsuitable for the elementary L2 audience. Unless they are introduced to encoding strategies and texts at their intellectual level, L2 learners in the first semester will deal with names of objects they can manipulate or experience in their own world. Beginning language instruction, regardless of its methodological presumptions, necessarily emphasizes the tangible.

2. *The situation.* As a result of the tangible classroom setting, the intent of what is to be said and understood is straightforward. To minimize language difficulties, good beginning classes are designed to have all procedural rules as clear as possible. The cards have to be on the table or the novice speaker cannot play. The teacher's job is to have students practice articulating speech acts, e.g., to share information, possibly persuade others to adopt their point of view (or an assumed point of view), or express opinions. There are relatively few subtexts ("Whatever did she mean by *that!*"). Any inferences will be of sentences rather than expanded discourse. In a way one can say that listeners tend to listen between the lines while readers look for subtexts.

3. *The focus.* Beginning instruction is concerned with language detail. Whether they are acquiring language via comprehensible input or learning to conjugate verbs, decline nouns, and discover generally how the grammar of the L2 language differs from the native tongue, students are expected to be able to use certain types of language in certain situations. They are tested accordingly in class and on examinations. Consequently, successful beginning students learn that primary attention to language is appropriate.

These three features characterize most L2 approaches because beginning instructors must teach language structure and vocabulary. The goal of most structural *and* communicative approaches in the United States is to have students who function in real-life situations with reasonable accuracy. As teachers, we must ask beginning students to learn language detail, we must present clear rules for accurate language use, and we must use concrete language at the elementary level. The point in this chapter is only that teachers must activate a somewhat different set of learning strategies to promote successful reading. Regardless of L2 methodology, student expectations developed in beginning instruction, even at the post-secondary level, are predominantly language-based. And language-based expectations impact on the later learning behaviors of those same students (as well as their teachers) when they start to read.

How can language-based expectations present an obstacle to successful reading? Consider the demands in the three learner situations cited above and contrast them with the demands on the reader. First, beginning instruction emphasizes immediate, real-life situations. Texts present abstract meanings, removed from the reader's world. Second, beginning instruction provides a clear, univalent speaker and listener intent. Texts have message systems that often contain covertly as well as explicitly stated purposes, unstated as well as articulated objectives. Third, textual message systems utilize lengths and structures uncharacteristic of the discourse in first-year classes. Fourth, beginning instruction emphasizes student attention to detail whereas the reading process appears to operate most effectively when student focus is on main meaning line or "chunking" smaller pieces of information at a rate too rapid to afford verbatim recall in all but short-term memory.

A COMPARISON BETWEEN LANGUAGE-BASED
AND INTERACTIVE READING

Compare L2 student Paul, an in-class reader, with L2 speaker Irene, whose English is no better than Paul's but who reads by choice, not because reading was assigned in class. Paul will probably be asked in class to identify or recreate equivalencies, to match a fact in one sentence with a verbal statement or question. He may be tested later with items that match an array of multiple choice options: to fill in blanks in individual sentences. He is not asked to predict or second-guess. His job is to apprehend the text, not to demonstrate what he thinks about the text.

How does Paul's approach differ from Irene's self-motivated reading? For Irene, reading is not an assignment, but an activity she chooses. She reads a newspaper article about the Russian nuclear plant in Chernobyl in order to discover what she *thinks* about what is written. While Paul will read the same text for detail, for Irene facts are read in a cognitive scheme rather than as a collection: whether or not sufficient data has been supplied about the Chernobyl disaster (her question), who's supplying the information (the text's answer), and how reliable such sources have been (her analysis). Unlike Paul, she can be critical. Irene is free to decide whether the reporting style is prejudicial, naive, contradictory or inadequate (her synthesis of textual and her own language competence).

To confirm that she has synthesized appropriately, Irene may discuss the article with acquaintances, some of whom will agree and others question the validity of her interpretations. She may modify her views as a result, but she won't necessarily conclude that what she understood was "wrong." After all, she has comprehended in terms of her point of view. Her reading intent was never to recreate either the whole or portions of the text verbatim. She could arrange textual information on *her* terms.

Consider the impact of Paul's and Irene's reading objectives when they read the following from a 1987 *New York Times* article about Chernobyl.

"It may be months or years before the world learns exactly what happened at the Soviet Union's Chernobyl nuclear power station and why radiation was spewed over much of Europe. But one thing that emerged with striking clarity in the days after the incident was first reported was the profound difference between the surfeit of speculation, questioning and information that flooded the West and the few facts divulged in the East" (Schmemann Section 4: 1).

Where does each reader begin and how will each proceed? Paul's class-preparation assignments probably encourage him to begin at the microlevel, with words. As a result, his reading will tend to be linear, and therefore his apprehension is more likely to be restricted to the sentence level. With his attention on processing words, his working memory will probably not have time to focus on text structures beyond the sentence level. Consequently, he makes few second guesses about word meanings or their registers in terms of episodic features (e.g., the shift from a recounting of events to an analysis of their implications) or text topic (how a free press alters public perception). What happens to his processing as a result? He may examine words or chunk phrases according to their lexical functions (verb phrases, adverbs), but he will correlate their meaning in terms of dictionary definitions rather than probable textual semantics. Thus, relatively infrequent vocabulary such as "spewed," "profound," "surfeit," and "divulged" are classed as adjectives, nouns, and verbs, but without a "negative implications" tag impugning the integrity and behavior of the Russians, a tag that would not only guide guesswork, but also narrow the range in selecting dictionary synonyms.

Confronted with a definition for *spewed* as "ejected from the stomach; vomited; poured forth," Paul may be mystified. He lacks a strategy for connecting language details to textual macropropositions (e.g., action verb + radiation + negative tone in the press release) with likely microspecifications. Hence, Paul is unprepared for metaphorical associations or their likely register, and is confused by comparisons of radiation with vomit (because the dictionary associates "spew" with stomach problems), smokestacks belching smoke (because the dictionary associates "belching" with indigestion), or radioactivity "raining" death.

By way of contrast, Irene begins by predicting and encoding. She employs macrolevel background schema about the text's real-world probabilities, focusing her attention initially on a presumed input. "Aha," says Irene. "In the current political climate (Chernobyl occurred prior to the Gorbachov / Reagan rapprochement), look for indications of disparagement." She expects a few loaded words and phrases spaced at a discrete distance from one another. Consequently, she can encode "was spewed" as "passive verb + radiation over Europe = negative term for 'spread, disseminated, sent.'"

The difference between these two readers is that Irene's reading relates her views and those of the text: what she comprehends lies in the tension between her perceptions about the passage and her perceptions about the world. Her synthetic stance necessitates a predictive focus, even if it's no more than "Is this worth reading?" or "I've got to see if there's anything to this!" Such questions are inappropriate for Paul if his views are not rewarded in-class or integrated into reading assignments.

Is Irene's approach superior to Paul's under all circumstances? Any such claims are pure speculation. Until we have more research in reading styles and the impact of purposeful reading, answers will depend on variables such as the match between text and reader background, time factors, opportunities for rereading, or specific reader goals.

Let us assume that Irene and Paul both possess an L2 vocabulary of only 1000 to 1500 words. In that case any number of Irene's guesses will probably be very general, perhaps even incorrect, and she may miss factual details. By contrast, Paul will be able to decode some specific facts by accessing his knowledge of words or consulting the dictionary for unfamiliar vocabulary, but the overall message of the text may well elude him.

The polemics in the Irene / Paul comparison serve only to illustrate the need for an instructional component that encourages a combination of factors, reader- as well as language-based objectives. Input and ouput must be corrected.

Krashen's monitor, if seen as an input processor as well as a production governor, "may be described as the directing of attention to specific input (or output) items" (Nagle & Sanders 17). The Paul illustration is intended only to suggest how training in interpreting texts can help L2 readers cope with overload. Like word recognition, practice in recognizing rhetorical organization can become automatic. Without such practice Paul must make a considerable cognitive effort, if he chooses to attend to linking concepts represented in text language. As a result of his unidirectional rather than interactive reading he will tend to exhibit:

1. less integrative cognitive processing (speed, depth of processing);
2. less tendency toward organization of information (focus, attention);
3. less tendency toward generalization capacity (and consequent ability to generate utterances) than interactive reader Irene.

As a language-based reader, Paul works at recognition and recall of textual words, phrases, or even individual sentences. And frequently, this is precisely what his teachers expect him to do, often for lack of better alternatives.

Alternatives do exist. Excellent reading guides such as those of Grellet and Nuttall provide the instructor with suggestions about how to teach specific aspects of reading for specific purposes. Games developed to augment a communicative approach can help bridge the transition between language and reading practice (Littlewood; Omaggio 1986; Wright et al.). For example, Di Pietro's scenarios, in which the reading text is transformed into imaginary dialogues and scenes by the students, are both excellent previews (to clarify environment and what character types should be expected in reading) and final exercises after reading (to work creatively at generating implications going beyond the intent of the immediate text message). Similarly, the previewing exercises described by Kast or Krusche help students to identify their own preconceptions and expectations about a text situation before they proceed to those of the text, thereby forestalling misreadings.

But the question remains: How to teach interactive reading? What cognitive sequence is linked to what reader processes? What reader attention focus should the teacher and the materials emphasize at various points in the reading process?

These questions must be addressed for several practical reasons. Evaluation that is only language-based will fail to assess both text-based and reader-based factors. On the other hand, both teachers and students feel uneasy without the structure of word lists and paradigms (Horwitz 1986). Student tasks that fail to state what vocabulary and grammar is to be learned and how it is to be learned appear to lack rigor. Even extensive familiarity with subject matter is no guarantee of comprehension. And what about the need to read for a degree of detail? If top-down factors are essential, so is a certain amount of language facility. The question is, how much? Studies attempting to answer this question are often called "threshold" research.

PROFICIENCY THRESHOLDS
AND INTERACTIVE PROCESSES

The mind has limited processing capacity. When there are too many problems in recognizing the printed words on the page, memory overload results. For the L2 reader, proficiency problems activate controlled processing, conscious attention to words and letters. The preferable alternative is automatic processing. When vocabulary meaning is instantaneously recognized (i.e., processed automatically without the conscious effort of the reader), comprehension is faster. The less time spent on an effort to remember individual words, the more memory is available to attend to other meaning factors (Schiffrin & Schneider). Hence, a lack of proficiency in language mechanics inhibits text comprehension. Without some automatic processing the reader is unable to allocate attention to context factors (schema) and the "chunking" or nucleation presumed necessary for recall (Pike).

Schema research measures the effect of particular reader strategies on language processing. Ten years ago the profession was arguing about top-down versus bottom-up styles of reading. With interactive research, interest has centered on the degree to which inhibiting effects of low command of language can be offset by reader strategies (Alderson 1984). A convincing number of studies demonstrate that schematic strategies help increase the comprehension of intermediate-level L2 students (e.g., Carrell 1985). Schema research is concerned with how the reader conceptualizes textual language. What is it about language that is not understood? How does it affect comprehension? How much language proficiency is necessary before a student's background and cognitive strategies can be used to increase comprehension?

Such explorations involve a reassessment of the interaction between reading and overall language learning. The traditional skills point of view separated reading from speaking, writing, and listening. These notions are being replaced with approaches combining acquisition and learning theories (e.g., Higgs). Studies look at unitary proficiency (Oller 1983) and examine the effects of various proficiencies on one another. Indeed, the words "modes" and "domains" rather than "skills" identify research concern with interactive rather than isolated learning behaviors. A domain is an area of competency rather than the competency itself. The studies that look at the domain of vocabulary or syntactic function acknowledge that variables such as metacognition, subject matter, and motivation can affect performance along with threshold factors such as textual readability. Traditionally, readability has been measured by factors such as introduction of unfamiliar vocabulary and sentence length. In assessments of readability based on schema theory, linguistic and cultural background may play as important a role as the formal properties of the text. Other schematic influences such as learning level and the age of students may be important features as well.

Threshold research, then, is aimed at clarifying classroom priorities. How much time should we devote to what kinds of activities?

VOCABULARY LEVELS AND DOMAINS

Vocabulary remains one of the greatest stumbling blocks to fluent reading. Often, unfamiliar vocabulary appears only once or twice in a text. For example, Carroll et al.'s word frequency study (1971) noted that 81,000 of 86,000 words occur only ten percent of the time in the passages he assessed. Subsequent L1 and L2 studies agree that about 5000 words in any language constitute ninety percent of the words needed to read a text for comprehension. Coady's inference from such research is that the evidence argues for teaching high-frequency vocabulary to a point of automaticity.

Opinions differ regarding the amount of vocabulary necessary to read, how much of that vocabulary can be "passive" (for recognition only), and how to go about learning it (Cowie; Meara). The structuralist legacy, emphasizing linguistic structure, deemphasized vocabulary until the late sixties (Bolinger). For L2 teachers, the assumptions of that legacy are still with us today. Saragi, Nation, and Meister suggest that 3600 forms with a "far higher number of meanings" are necessary to read unsimplified material in English, and that even then the reader confronts a dozen or more unknown words per page (72). Similarly, Ostyn and Godin cite claims that a 1500-to-2000-word vocabulary (the goal of most elementary two-year L2 sequences) is inadequate for reading authentic texts. Like Carroll, Coady suggests that a minimum of 5000 words is essential. Such thinking is supported by Tarnóczi, whose research disputes the theory that a 2000-word vocabulary will enable understanding of seventy-five percent of most texts.

Even higher estimates for command of vocabulary are conceivable if register, i.e., discourse-specific vocabulary, is taken into account. Register studies show that vocabulary varies widely from one text to another. Different texts fail to share a high percentage of words. Even works by the same author may vary widely. Simmons found that fewer than one third of the words in three Schiller plays were repeated. Salling's analysis of different English text types yielded somewhat narrower variations (densities from $1:2.6$ to $1:9.8$) with the caveat that unknown words tended to be low frequency and are therefore harder to guess and to remember. At issue is the juncture at which an insufficient vocabulary makes both decoding based on context and any top-down processing impossible.

Sciarone, for example, claims that when fewer than ninety percent of the words are recognized, one's overall understanding is based on guesswork at the expense of precise understanding. This claim seems reasonable; however, he had subjects do a cloze deletion to establish its validity. Multiple choice insertions rather than deletion of difficult vocabulary might have improved scores (Crow).

The three methods used in cloze testing define vocabulary knowledge in very different ways. A cloze deletion asks for a grasp of vocabulary and text that enables a reader to replicate exact language. A flexible cloze deletion asks only that the student create suitable language, or recognize a general meaning within a broad semantic or syntactic category (e.g., any preposition indicating location rather than the particular preposition that is correct in usage). A deletion by clause rather than *nth* word may direct student attention to discourse meaning beyond the sentence level, particularly if conjunctions and adverbial markers are chosen.

Regardless of test validity, the questions still remain: How much vocabulary should be learned to the level of automaticity and what is the best way to learn L2 vocabulary? Two styles of learning seem to be the subject of debate: learning lists of lexical items (dictionary definitions) and indirect learning of vocabulary through a reading context.

DIRECT LEARNING OF LEXICAL ITEMS

Can list or word pair learning (L2 word with L1 translation) aid reading comprehension? Nation summarizes studies that demonstrate an average of learning as high as 166 words per hour (16–17). Teaching word pairs also circumvents guessing, a negative learning factor in the college-level study of Lado, Baldwin, and Lobo, who found that guessing after initial word pair presentation resulted in better recall. Numerous studies have been undertaken to assess optimal word pair learning.[1]

THE RELATIONSHIP BETWEEN BEGINNING LANGUAGE INSTRUCTION AND DIRECT VOCABULARY LEARNING

In the discussion of initial language learning, we pointed out that lexical items generally have concrete references. The requisite 2000 to 5000 words can often be confirmed in the movement or manipulation of objects. In beginning learning, objects or actions appear to correspond with particular verbal signs (vocabulary). Word recognition results from a mental equation system that may be influenced by but is not discourse determined. At the onset of reading, however, this equation relationship (word = specific correlation) changes. Words are no longer defined by word pairs but rather by textual reference and by the discourse contexts in which they occur.

The notion that the word is a sign having a signifier (phonological and orthographic representation) and a signified (the definition and implications within a culture-bound system) goes back to de Saussure. Wittgenstein distinguishes between an ostensive definition (an apparent, but actually erroneous assumption of correspondence between a word and a referent in the real world) and a verbal one. Modern-day semantics (e.g., Katz, Lyons) is concerned with the contextual variables that alter lexical meaning within a given discourse (the "Cinderella" of Grimm's fairy tales versus the "Cinderella" of presidential candidates). Possibly the difference between learning a dictionary definition and a contextual definition is comparable to a contrast between usage and use. The question remains: Can learning lexical items in translated pairs facilitate reading comprehension in a foreign language?[2]

INDIRECT VOCABULARY LEARNING

Recent experiments have examined the impact of reading and text discourse factors on vocabulary acquisition. Nation cautions that because of the lack of experimental controls in context studies (e.g., variation in length of time, covert translation, context difficulty as a background rather than vocabulary problem, etc.), conclusions should be considered "statements of belief" (24). Certainly this caveat remains valid for the research about to be discussed.

Interactive processes are concerned with a completely different approach to word learning: the recognition of semantic features and how new combinations result in new meanings. Just as the meanings of *awesome* change in a teenage conversation versus a church sermon, so will the meanings of other words associated with awesome, such as being impressed or intimidated. When polyseme recognition, the ability to recognize multiple definitions for a single word depending on the context, is essential for comprehension, then word pairs are not of much use. To assess polyseme recognition (*Wüste* as *desert* rather than *wasteland*), contextual practice is essential. And since the language of texts is often metaphorical (the dark continent as opposed to the dark night), meanings are obscured unless readers learn to recognize semantic extensions or polysemes of words.

Native language research shows unequivocally that ease of recognition of a word is influenced by its frequency of occurrence (Rubenstein et al.) and by the context in which it appears (Tulving & Gold). Does extensive reading increase vocabulary for the non-native reader? One problem facing such research is ascertaining what words advanced L2 readers already know. Various controls have been used. After reading the novel, L2 readers recognized many of the 241 *nadsat* words that Anthony Burgess invented for *A Clockwork Orange* (Saragi et al.). The average *nadsat* word is repeated fifteen times in the book, but ranges vary widely. The volume has approximately 60,000 words. Subjects were not told in advance that they would be tested on vocabulary. Ninety *nadsat* words which reflected the range of occurrence frequency were put in a multiple choice test with four English word choices. The median results were seventy-seven percent correct, indicating that repeated words can be learned incidentally through extensive reading.

Unfortunately, the study fails to mention the number of students involved and gives no information regarding their relative proficiency (e.g., learning and respective proficiency level, prior familiarity with and interest in subject matter). Useful as *nadsat* words are for discrimination purposes, the effects of their unfamiliarity (as non-normative English) may have heightened reader attention and, consequently, artificially enhanced recall. Moreover, as special vocabulary, students may have processed them differently. These variables help explain why results in this contextual study are superior to other L2 work on this topic (e.g., Grabe & Zukowski-Faust).

More L2 studies of vocabulary gains after reading longer texts are needed. Research on short texts necessarily relocates encoding concerns from apperception of macro- to microstructures, since short passages lack redundancy of vocabulary occurrence and elaboration of context factors. Kintsch and van Dijk find that studies examining immediate recall of short paragraphs look at readers' subprocesses (392). Such experiments yield more detailed recall (microprocessing) in which macroprocesses play only a minor role. In this sense, short text study examines the reinforcement of lower level context effects and comprehension of micropropositions.

In a short text study without recall protocols, Bensoussan and Laufer gave sixty students from parallel English classes a list of seventy words to translate into their native tongue, Hebrew. A week later, students received a clean copy of the same list and a 574-word text containing these words. In order to confirm whether or not prior exposure to the word list contaminated later encoding, an additional control group of thirty-five students received only the word list and context passage. Comprehension questions at the end of the passage verified general understanding. No significant differences between the two groups were found. We are not told if any of the seventy words were already known to the control group. If all of them were unknown, this would mean over twelve percent of the words in the short passage were new, yet comprehension and encoding occurred.

The authors found indirect contextual clues (e.g., contrasts, collocations) for only twenty-nine of the seventy words in the passage. Of the remaining forty-one words, clear clues (e.g., explicit definitions, illustrations) were found for only thirteen. Of the total forty-one possible, then, students exploited contextual clues for only seventeen or twenty-four percent of the total seventy words. The authors concluded that, although results were statistically significant, context showed limited practical value for vocabulary acquisition (22).

Since Bensoussan and Laufer asked students to match vocabulary and definitions rather than encode from the passage, the study was language-based. Theoretically, the use of a word list would discourage the very contextual guessing the authors sought to assess. This design feature of the Bensoussan and Laufer study might also explain other studies that have more encouraging findings for adherents of contextual approaches. For example, in both an early study by Seibert and more recent work by Laufer and Sim, context training increased student effectiveness in interpreting the meanings of words found in texts.

In an analysis suggesting priorities for training in contextual guessing, Bensoussan looked at data from several context studies in light of discourse factors. She diagnosed semantic misreadings at both macro- (text structure and reader schemata) and micro-structural levels. At one text's macrolevel, the examples cited show how failure to utilize schema results in a mistranslation of a polyseme: *cried* (out) becomes *wept* instead of *yelled*. In cultural misreadings of illocutionary intent, good-natured requests became commands or disagreements (402). She found that students' failure to identify correctly the sex of the speakers (macrosemantics) caused low-level misreadings as well. Such effects of faulty gist and detail perception correspond to Sim's findings that L2 readers' failure to recognize sentence connectors (*since, while, nevertheless*) inhibited their understanding of the larger context.

SEMANTIC FIELDS VERSUS LEXICAL PRECISION

Researchers in L1 propose that we resolve the context / list learning debate by grouping words according to their semantic relationships (Johnson & Pearson). When they are taught semantic fields, students learn to recognize a generic meaning for an unfamiliar word in context. A reader who associates "coach" with "mode of transportation" as well as with organized team sports can continue reading the gist of a Cinderella story even though nuances of style and the image of a horse-drawn carriage are lost.

Advocates of a word field approach reward students who recognize that "ugly" and "uncomely" convey a similar thought. It doesn't matter whether those students select the conventional or the unconventional word for the stepsisters' appearance. In a study of advanced ESL students, Crow and Quigley found the group being taught semantic field recognition developed receptive control of twice as many words as those using list- and synonym-learning techniques. Crow concludes that teaching and testing practices should emphasize learning words as segments of a larger schema rather than as synonyms or dictionary definitions.

Other types of investigations also indicate that lexical definitions are no guarantee of comprehension. Bensoussan, Sim and Weiss conducted three studies on the effects of use and non-use of dictionaries on students' performance in L2 reading tests. Less proficient students referred to bilingual dictionaries and used them more frequently than did proficient readers. As we might expect from strategy studies, the better readers either did not use dictionaries or used monolingual ones. Most important, dictionary access did not alter performance on test scores. There were no statistically significant differences in the performance of dictionary and non-dictionary groups. In a comprehension test where readers connect textual meanings, those connections, not dictionary definitions, determine the success of the reading. Indeed, dictionary definitions may interfere with comprehension. This is Johnson's tentative explanation for data comparing two groups that had studied definitions of target words before reading. One group referred to glosses; the other did not. The group *without* glosses displayed superior comprehension and recall.

Johnson conjectures that glossing may have encouraged a word-for-word reading that had a negative impact on conceptualizing (514). On the other hand, a recent FL study which compared reading performance with glossed and non-glossed texts indicated that glosses had a positive impact on comprehension (Davis 1989).

EYE MOVEMENT

Along with vocabulary studies, eye movement research reveals how the reader processes words and structures in a text.[3] It can tell us what the eye fixates on and for how long (relative significance) or at what point regressive reading occurs (processing difficulty). We know, for example, that readers of English seem to spend over twice as long looking at content words as they do looking at function words (Carpenter & Just), that reading difficulty is reflected in reading rate, and that different reader objectives (e.g., learning versus pleasure reading) predict different rates (Anderson & Armbruster). Whether the same distinctions hold true for foreign-language readers is unclear, because L2 research in eye movement is only beginning.

Bernhardt (1987) assessed eye movements of native and non-native speakers who read easy, difficult, and natural (e.g., unedited) texts. She used three groups of students: inexperienced L2 readers, experienced L2 readers, and L1 readers. Her quantitative conclusions support L1 models: Inexperienced L2 readers need more processing time overall. Moreover, their fixation durations suggest that inexperienced readers need significantly longer to sample information from the text. Unlike the experienced readers in L1 and L2, the inexperienced readers failed to adjust their processing time (and presumably their processing strategy) in the three passages. One explanation of long sampling time is that the working memory is overloaded with analysis of individual words and structures, functions that have become automatic for the more experienced reader. Presumably, slow reading correlates with lower comprehension because attention to letters and words inhibits reader attention to conceptual and schematic information.

Apparently, decoding problems affect the L2 reader at least as much as they affect the poor L1 reader (e.g., Perfetti). An increasing number of studies suggest that inadequate command of language increases reliance on graphic information and inhibits use of effective L1 strategies (Alderson 1984). The fact that Bernhardt's inexperienced group maintained the same inefficient eye tracking strategy in all three texts parallels findings in other L2 research (M. Clarke 1980). However, these studies do not look at the possible effects of reader background and strategy training on the behavior of students with low L2 proficiencies. Kern's work suggests that strategy training is a significant aid for this specific student group. And while we have studies on the impact of student schemata on the readability of L2 texts, we have no studies that tell us whether schematically familiar texts promote more automaticity in word processing. Since familiar schemata foster readability, the logical inference should be that recognition and recall of vocabulary are also enhanced.

EFFECTS OF STRATEGY TRAINING
ON VOCABULARY LEARNING

Laufer and Sim (1985) compared performance among ESL classes at Haifa University to find out if strategy training would improve reading performance of students with an extremely limited command of English vocabulary or grammar. Their rankings resulted from a matching of class grades with student performance on a section from the Cambridge First Certificate in English. The authors concluded that first-year students who scored below sixty-five percent on their EFL class grade could not "handle an academic text" (408). Their results also led them to conclude that, at lower limits, reader strategies fail to compensate for language problems. If reader strategies break down at low language proficiency levels, the instructional strategy of presenting texts that deal with subjects familiar to and of interest to the L2 reader seems all the more important (e.g., Lee 1987b; Levine & Haus; Wolff 1985).

Another compensatory strategy would be to activate reader attention by varying the comprehension goal. How can attention styles affect comprehension? Again we return to the role of a single interactive factor: language proficiency, viewed by psycholinguists as a level of "automatic processing."

McLaughlin, Rossmann, and McLeod assume that successful language processing is based on automatic processes that free the learner to attend to performing, to speaking or writing in L2. Unfortunately, when readers fail to recognize L2 vocabulary or syntax, they need to resort to *controlled* processing to read. They must concentrate on words to the exclusion of other processing factors such as background or text structure. The effort to connect language and meaning may cancel out if the "controls" put all the attention on language. If automatic decoding is essential for good reading in any language, the issue is how teachers can foster this capability.

One solution to the overload problem is to practice language. Unquestionably, the more automatic the word recognition, the freer the L2 reader will be to engage in controlled processing of unfamiliar language. Viewed in this light, "language mastery" and "automatic processing" can be equated, and the "language learning equals reading" theory would seem to have strong support. With psycholinguistic models, experts speculate about how mental processing works. Several features of processing frequently referred to in the literature are: an affective filter (Burt & Dulay), a monitor (Krashen 1982), and an executive component (Selinker & Lamendella). Each model weights the role of a particular factor differently or suggests that the role may vary under different circumstances.

The "executive," for example, makes decisions about attention based on affect or learner goal. Krashen's monitor has been criticized for lacking specifications about the basis for decisions and their subsequent impact on processing. Fundamental to all models is the presumed and empirically supported distinction between long-term and short-term memory (Atkinson & Shiffrin; Miller 1956).

Since long-term memory stores learning, researchers have tried to establish whether exposure to rules about structure and vocabulary lists will result in rapid and accurate decoding in reading. As research on language drill suggests, automaticity itself is no guarantee of comprehension. Learning occurs according to the learner's style of apprehension. Neurological research suggests that learning *combines* controlled and automatic processes. Shiffrin and Schneider define controlled processes as those that utilize "a temporary sequence of nodes activated under control of, and through attention by, the subject" (156). Automatic processes are those consisting of an established sequence of nodes "activated without the necessity of active control or attention by the subject" (155). In other words, to become automatic, apprehension processes need to be trained on the basis of a high degree of learner attention. Drill alone will not suffice. Only a "focal attention" builds configurations that can become automatic. McLaughlin, Ross-man, and McLeod use these insights to illustrate styles of information processing in second language learning:

TYPES OF INFORMATION PROCESSING IN L2 LEARNING

	Information Processing	
Focus of Attention	**Controlled**	**Automatic**
Focal	(Cell A) "Intentional" performance of a new skill	(Cell B) "Intentional" performance of a well-trained skill
Peripheral	(Cell C) "Incidental" performance of a new skill	(Cell D) "Incidental" performance of a well-trained skill

From Barry McLaughlin, Tami Rossmann, and Beverly McLeod, "Second Language Learning: An Information Processing Perspective," *Language Learning* 33 (1983): 125–58.

As the table illustrates, learners need to intend to match new data to preexisting knowledge, whether the processing is controlled or automatic. Controlled processes involve more learner attention because new input and processing occur simultaneously. Consequently, "intentional" performance of a new skill puts high demands on various memory functions. Short-term memory in reading has, by the most generous estimates, an outside limit of four or five seconds. If, in that time, the amount of incoming information proves too unfamiliar or too extensive to be linked to existing memory patterns, learning fails to occur. Similarly, if the learner must transfer too much unfamiliar phonologic, orthographic, lexical, morphologic, or syntactic information from short-term memory to long-term memory, incoming data will interrupt concentration. Interruption, in turn, interferes with storage processes (Rivers & Temperley).

As a consequence of these insights, more and more researchers are arguing for automaticity in processing of high-frequency vocabulary—the 5000 words that constitute ninety percent of most texts (e.g., Coady). Just how many words readers have to be able to process automatically before they can read is by no means clear. Neither is it by any means clear *which* words will be on the list.

Whether the most effective mode for acquiring vocabulary is to read in context or to learn words is equally unclear. Nagy and Anderson begin an L1 study of vocabulary acquisition with the observation that direct vocabulary instruction fails to account for a "significant proportion of all the words children actually learn" (304). Yet another study of Nagy et al. (1985) suggests that, while incremental learning of vocabulary occurs in the course of contextual reading, the rate of that occurrence is fairly low. Their estimates of probability range between .05 to .15 and vary considerably between experiments. Grabe and Zukowski-Faust found even more discouraging results when they replicated the Nagy et al. study with non-native speakers. Apparently, at least under the particular constraints of these studies, non-native speakers failed to experience the incremental learning of vocabulary in context which was achieved by native speakers.

The problem in reviewing the apparently low impact of contextual reading on vocabulary acquisition is that these studies cannot duplicate the quantitative reading many theorists presume is a precondition for acquisition of a large reading vocabulary. It is, we think, the reading outside of class—the daily reading of newspapers and magazines, comics, sensational literature, or trivial texts—that fosters automaticity. Unfortunately, such conditions are difficult to reproduce and control in a research study.

In Chapter 4 we will examine some of the evidence that suggests top-down factors may aid bottom-up processing. We will look, for example, at Kern's study, in which FL students received a range of strategy instruction including work in text-based vocabulary recognition. Students in this case showed significant improvement in reading comprehension, particularly those at low- and mid-levels of reading ability. Similarly, the FL research of Allen et al., Lee and Musumeci, and Levine and Haus suggests that various factors other than language level affect readability. Allen et al. point out that when recall protocols rather than multiple choice or cloze tests are used, even beginning students of L2 can derive meaning from authentic passages. In short, we will explore how students' familiarity with a text's subject matter, the testing instrument used to collect data, and the extent of students' diagnostic practice with strategies all affect reading performance.

THE ROLE OF VOCABULARY INSTRUCTION IN READING

The selective evidence presented in this chapter is supported by a larger literature in the field which suggests that L2 learners need a command of vocabulary to read. An undetermined level of automaticity for high-frequency vocabulary seems to be essential for L2 readers. Techniques for learning vocabulary need to be part of any instruction in reading (e.g., V. Allen; Barnett 1990; Nation). The positive long-term effects of vocabulary instruction in L1 (e.g., Perfetti) speak eloquently for such efforts in L2. The style of this vocabulary instruction can, however, no longer be reduced to a case of either word lists or contextual learning. If L2 readers are to establish automaticity in vocabulary recognition, teachers must find a middle ground between the word lists and reliance on reading in context.

The strategies and the reading approaches presented in later chapters of this book suggest instruction that encourages a large cognitive role for the L2 student's vocabulary work. We have L1 evidence that readers link lexical items to meaning in their memory storage (Abramovici; Hayes-Roth & Hayes-Roth). It seems fair to assume that a similar linkage is made in L2 reading. Due to the fact that apparently all readers, including L2 students, connect language and meaning on the basis of their focal attention, instruction should follow suit. Students need guidance on when to guess—and when not to (Haynes). They need to spend class and test time on diagnostic work that links the meaning / lexeme connection in monitored practice.

Consider the two hypothetical readers we discussed earlier. Assuming they both have an equivalent word recognition vocabulary, which of the two is more likely to develop automaticity at the word level—the language-based (purely lexical) or the interactive reader? At first blush, Paul's job is easier. His focus is on words. To "learn" what the text says involves recognition and recall. Irene, on the other hand, reads to see if anything is said about workers at the plant, possible solutions, long-term effects of the disaster. Her cognitive focus is driven by synthetic and analytic reasoning. Aside from the affective advantages of background interest, Irene has cognitive advantages as a language learner because she engages in more depth of processing. She organizes language information within a limited system of discourse. Paul's task is far more demanding. He must recall linguistic information within the virtually limitless system of language. The language base is essential to both readers. But there are other essentials as well.

COMPREHENSION AND INPUT PROCESSING

Language-based and interactive styles each reflect a particular kind of processing. How cognitive processes operate to promote comprehension and learning is still a matter of conjecture. Even the relationship between comprehension and learning is itself unclear. The two are generally considered complementary, "interdependent, but distinctive cognitive phenomena" (Nagle & Sanders 20). Learning theory and comprehension theory, while not interchangeable, share many features. A major feature they share is a concern with cognitive processing. The difference between the concerns is that learning models look at what the mind does *to learn input*. Comprehension models look at what the mind does *to modify input*. In other words, comprehension research attempts to look at how the mind treats input and how that treatment modifies what is learned. Potentially, interactive reading can involve both learning and comprehension.

Nagle and Sanders propose a comprehension model in which processing of input shifts with the attention mode of the apprehender. They note that "attention may stimulate rehearsal and retention in STS (short-term storage), narrowing of focus or monitoring and initiation of controlled processing" (19). Factors such as task demands or context may arouse attention. Compare the shifts in Paul's and Irene's attention in reading the Chernobyl text. A graph of Paul's language-based attention would show that, as that attention moves from word to word, rehearsal and storage of words is interrupted. Breakdown occurs when language overload occurs. Unfamiliar words disrupt his attention to connected words in the text.

A graph of Irene's reading, on the other hand, is less likely to reveal these blips in her attention. Due to her high motivation ("I want to read this") and background (she has been to nuclear plants, may know of previous, less well-publicized failures), her attention is focused less on the unknown language than on familiar concepts. Since she starts reading within a secure frame of meaning, she can either ignore or make inferences about unfamiliar words. Hence, the trace decay (fading sensory output) and interference (from unfamiliar words) that plague Paul's word-based efforts are less likely to short-circuit Irene's attention to concepts. She can escape Paul's overload sequence of language-based reading, which might be visualized as the following:

Stage 1—attention alters processing modes
Stage 2—processing modes alter retention
Stage 3—storage breakdown occurs
Stage 4—attention dissipates

Unfamiliar subject matter and unfamiliar language pose formidable obstacles to Paul's comprehension. Even if he can maintain his attention, Paul's language focus in reading is on the unfamiliar, the unknown words. Consequently he has little opportunity to join ideas.

The hierarchy of Bloom's taxonomy illustrates the difference between registering information and connecting ideas to generate thought. First in Bloom's taxonomy are recognition and recall, so-called lower-order cognitive tasks. Recognition and recall involve little "thinking about" and draw heavily on retentive capability. When a person recognizes or remembers a phone number by thinking about it, by trying to visualize or recreate similar configurations, she is edging over into the next category of "higher order thought." Unlike recall and recognition, the so-called "higher order processes" of synthesis and analysis create systems of meaning. They permit applications of knowledge.

CONCLUSION

What has the analysis in this chapter tried to show about the teaching of reading? First, since reading is a creative process, what we know about how the mind works argues for interactive rather than language-based reading. Second, familiarity with textual subject matter seems to compensate for low language proficiency. Differences in reading "proficiency" frequently depend on what it is students are reading about (Bernhardt 1986b; Lee & Musumeci) rather than on their language level. The argument for reading familiar material in beginning classes is that logical reasoning seems to enhance learning. The more ways we can get our students to think about something, the more likely they are to remember it. The language proficiency / reading proficiency debate seems to boil down to three concerns for our teaching objectives.

1. If students are to read to learn text language, they need to be trained to pay attention to that language. If we want students to read to learn information and comprehend texts, they must use multiple styles of attention: attention to message coherence, to cohesive markers, to redundant features, to morphologic clues, to syntactic clues, and so on.

2. Since the practical distinction between language proficiency and reading proficiency is fluid, each requires complementary instructional and testing approaches: approaches that acknowledge both language processing and interactive processing. For language processing, recognition and recall of language will be emphasized; for interactive processing, synthetic and analytic reasoning.

3. Students need to realize that language knowledge and reading in a second language are complementary but distinctly different abilities. The unpredictability of students' interests and needs argues for practice with authentic texts in beginning as well as advanced instruction. Otherwise the implied assumption that these are one and the same tasks will make the transition to interactive reading more difficult.

The evidence we have presented suggests that neither a language-based nor an interactive reading focus is "right" or "wrong." The two styles do, however, access different learning strategies. Those strategy differences need to be acknowledged by teachers and evaluators. Students need to practice both styles of reading. To capitalize on top-down factors that facilitate language learning in the reading process, initial reading must combine in-class reading with the assignment of outside reading of less demanding texts. We must overcome academic prejudices about the canon of literature or subject matter and encourage students to read magazines dealing with sports, movies, and notoriety. They must read trivial works of their own choosing such as thrillers or romances; in short, texts that are fun and have few intellectually redeeming features. The point is that, to develop automaticity in word recognition, students need L2 texts that are of interest to them, texts which they can read quickly and easily. Acquisition of vocabulary in context seems to occur when students read texts that have familiar contexts, familiar rhetorical organization, and familiar subject matter.

When intermediate proficiency levels have been achieved, indications from ESL studies discussed above suggest that L2 students in their second year of high school or second semester of college should be able to read successfully in schematically familiar content areas. As students advance beyond threshold language, instructional emphasis can introduce increasing quantities of intellectually challenging texts in conjunction with easier readings.

In sum, the "language proficiency versus strategies" debate seems to be an issue of approaches to reading rather than an issue of delaying interactive reading or authentic texts until a language threshold is achieved. The language level no longer dictates when students can begin to read for meaning, but rather when students can graduate from reading familiar subject matter, even texts of negligible intellectual quality, to reading about unfamiliar subject matter which challenges their analytical capacities. Language level becomes a type of readability index. It helps predict the extent to which students will have to rely on prior knowledge and command of encoding strategies (top-down processing) to comprehend the gist and the degree to which they will probably encounter problems with textual detail (bottom-up processing).

Prior to the threshold point, when unfamiliar ideas create a cognitive overload for students with skill deficiencies, teachers can profitably emphasize interactive reading for a comprehensible input of gist. The interactive goal at beginning levels is to enhance automaticity in decoding language that is only recognized or partially controlled. Although language-based goals (decoding skills) are also served, texts that contain information and reflect students' prior experience allow learners to practice an interactive approach to reading. Familiar subject matter helps to develop the language facility necessary for the classroom emphasis to shift from *reading practice* to *reading for content*. The chapter that follows presents reading activities that can help students develop past a language threshold—ways to practice cognitive strategies students need in order to comprehend texts that present new information and new ideas.

NOTES TO CHAPTER 3

1. For an annotated bibiliography of recent L2 vocabulary research, see Meara. Cowie's review of Meara's work offers a succinct interpretation of the implications of this research. Of the various mnemonic devices suggested for list learning, the keyword method has received perhaps the greatest L2 research attention (e.g., Pressley).

2. All we know at present about learning vocabulary in lists are the competency parameters: pronounceability enhances recall (Rodgers); self-generated associations, whether visual or acoustic, are good mnemonic aids (Cohen & Aphek); imposed images are useful for children but the reverse is true for adults (Pressley) or they must be used with caution (Omaggio 1979b); cognate study aids readers (Lobo, Seibert); even long lists (several hundred words) can be acquired and large numbers of lexical meanings recalled (Lado et al.); when words to be learned are nouns or adjectives, retention is higher than for other parts of speech (Rodgers); yet Guarino and Perkins' contextual research with ESL students suggests that multiple interactive factors (from reader world knowledge to discourse-grammar knowledge) may be equally or even more significant (82). Hence, the nagging performance question remains: To what extent does vocabulary learned in lists enhance reading comprehension?

3. Research in reading rate or eye movements (eye tracking) has been used extensively for L1 models of bottom-up processing, since such movements appear to confirm the theory of a linear sequence of what readers look at and for how long. Eye movements can be measured in voltage changes in light reflected into the eye of someone reading from a screen. Voltage signals indicate the direction and extent of eye movement, where the eye fixates spatially (rightward and down, leftward and up, back and forth). Monitors sampling voltage values 500 times per second can measure the length of time the eye stops, the fixation duration, and the total reading speed. Computer programs convert voltage signals into numbers and calculate fixation positions, duration, number of regressions, and reading rate. The resultant calculations are concrete evidence of strategy shifts (Carpenter & Just 1983).

$$\mathcal{F}our$$

Strategies, Text Topics, and Language Levels: Reading to Learn

THE CASE FOR READABILITY AS TOPIC, DISCOURSE, AND ORGANIZATIONAL FEATURES

In Chapter 3 we looked at research about low thresholds of language ability and how such thresholds inhibit L2 reading comprehension. We argued that when instructional strategies make use of their students' extralinguistic knowledge, readers can offset their linguistic deficiencies. In effect we challenged the assumption that before reading comprehension can occur, a threshold of language learning is essential. The threshold position implies that adult L2 learners at novice-to-low-intermediate stages in language proficiency are very much like child learners of a native language. They are word-based until they learn sentences. Thereafter they construct meaning interactively. But are adults, with their cognitive maturity, like children who cannot reason above the level of their ability to express ideas? Surely the very opposite is true: adult students reason considerably in excess of their L2 linguistic capabilities.

We have argued that linguistic difficulties provide all the more reason for activating metacognitive strategies for efficient decoding and encoding. Metacognition, defined as "an individual's awareness of strategies and mental activities while carrying out various cognitive processes such as memory, comprehension, learning, and attention" (van Kleeck vi) is learnable. Learning metacognitive strategies involves multifaceted training in levels of awareness about reading. Activation of content schemata, for example, may not occur to students unless they are trained to apply prior knowledge. We can "know" the schemata of Grimm's fairy tales, yet be unaware of their altered presence in Hans Christian Andersen's stories.

An argument can be made that current instructional parameters in L2 inhibit meta-cognitive processes. Let us consider in turn the variables of (1) text length, (2) reader background, (3) text topic, (4) authenticity of texts, and (5) rhetorical structure of texts in conjunction with their discourse markers. Most elementary reading is of short edited texts or short assignments in longer edited texts. Students who read short texts tend to do more word-for-word reading since the demands on memory in a 200- to 600-word text allow for greater attention to detail than would be the case with a text of several pages. Consequently, students who read short texts use word-level strategies more than text-level ones (Kintsch & van Dijk). Allen, Bernhardt, Berry, and Demel suggest that "lengthier texts may well be more cohesive and, hence, more interesting, for learners" (170). As yet, information about the relationship between the metacognition of L2 students, linguistic ability, and variety in their reading materials is scanty.

The second variable concerns reader background. If, as indeed seems to be the case, reader background is a key to comprehension of texts, we need to know more about how readability criteria and years of study or levels of language competence interact. Current studies, to be discussed in depth later in this chapter, suggest that we are seriously underestimating the adult student's capacity to read for meaning.

Third, and closely related to the background variable, L2 readers must have an opportunity to reveal comparative comprehension on different text *topics.* The available evidence from comparisons of text topic and reader performance (Koh; Levine & Haus) sheds light on automatic versus controlled processing, because it reveals that familiarity with text topic enhances reading performance.

The applications of the fourth variable, authenticity, have resulted from work in discourse analysis. Such research reveals that we may have been doing our students a disservice by presenting them primarily with "simple" texts. Simplification often alters textual patterns of redundancy and rhetorical organization, thereby rendering the edited passage *less* readable than the original. Moreover, edited texts tend to be culturally sanitized, culled of the very idiomatic and metaphorical expressions that L1 studies suggest can make reading more memorable and, in this sense, "easier" (Reynolds & Schwartz). The formatting, topic headings, and illustrative material of authentic texts also provide additional clues to encoding both macro- and micro-details of the passage.

The fifth variable, rhetorical organization and discourse patterns, is the least documented in L2 research. In an analysis of the impact of discourse features on readability, Baten, using Thorndike's L1 research, compared eight presumably similar texts. Organizational features (e.g., structural ties between propositions, numbers of restatements, etc.) rather than structural features such as sentence length were assessed. Logical reorderings (negative effect) and thematic consistency (positive effect) distinguished between the easy and the difficult text groups (144–46). On the basis of traditional readability standards, the difficulty ratings assigned to the texts did not correspond with Baten's analysis. Diagnostic analyses of how L2 students use coherence and cohesion suggest that success or failure in constructing textual propositions correlates with multiple discourse features, from numbers of new propositions to features such as narrational voice or pronoun references (Bensoussan; Bernhardt & Berkemeyer).

L1 work supports the notion that rhetorical features, such as an expressly stated gist ("the big problem today . . ."), organizational development ("a major aspect of this problem is . . ."), and overt links between ideas ("as was stated at the outset . . ."), help readers use effective strategies. Standard rhetorical forms that structure texts (their macrostructures) act as a schema for the reader. Their absence leads to poorer reading performance (Meyer, Brandt, & Bluth). Kintsch and Yarbrough found that when students read two versions of the same text—one well organized and one whose paragraphs were reordered—reading performance differed. Students were asked to perform two tasks: (1) tell what the two versions were about, and (2) note two main points in the article. The researchers found that "answers were correct 53% of the time when subjects were given the texts in the good rhetorical form, but only 29% were correct when the rhetorical structure was destroyed" (831). Similar findings have been documented for L1 by Frederiksen (1982) and for L2 by Carrell (1984).

GENERIC TEXT TYPES AND READABILITY

Questions of discourse are, in our view, the hidden agenda expressed in concern about any presumption of text typology. Language level is the related piece of this puzzle. As yet we have little idea about how grasp of macrofactors relates to understanding words in sentences. In Kintsch and Yarbrough's study, for example, rhetorical form strongly affected the students' ability to answer topic and main idea questions, yet analysis of student performance on a cloze test using the identical texts revealed negligible differences (832). Word- or microlevel processing in sentences was *not* affected by rhetorical organization, at least as measured in a cloze test. Only when macroprocesses (main idea, gist) were elicited did differences emerge.

Kintsch and Yarbrough's findings underscore a major problem in all research about how people think. The problem is that different thinking processes yield different information (R. Anderson et al.). In the absence of direct evidence about the way people think, we must rely on a variety of tasks that we hope reveal thinking processes. Inevitably, different tasks yield different results, as was the case in the Kintsch and Yarbrough study. Yet in the absence of direct evidence there is always "potential uncertainty in assessing whether differences in test performance are due to the quality of the memory for information encoded or the inappropriateness of the test for assessing the information that was learned" (B. Stein et al., 707). Did the test reveal the learning we were looking for or something quite different? What is the relationship of various reading factors to student performance?

Since L2 research with interactive reading tasks is just beginning, we have a very incomplete picture of the relationship between such factors as discourse features, reader perspective, text types, skill hierarchies, and language levels. We do know from Carrell's ESL (1984) and Lee's FL work (1986a) that, as with L1 texts, some rhetorical structures are more memorable than others. However, no one has yet compared the performance of L2 students on texts with good and poor rhetorical organization or uninformative discourse markers. All we have are indications that notions of L2 readability need rethinking, particularly with respect to text types.

In their study of the relationship between text type and time spent in language study, Lee and Musumeci tested 210 students, drawn from eleven classes of college Italian in the first through fourth semester. The researchers selected passages to correspond with their interpretation of descriptors in the *ACTFL Guidelines*. In subsequent discussion, several scholars cited by Lee and Musumeci disassociated their work and the *Guidelines* from these interpretations (see "MLJ Forum"). Regardless of the validity of their interpretation of the *Guidelines*, the substance of Lee and Musumeci's findings, together with those of Allen and his colleagues, sheds light on two important questions:

(1) Do text types influence readability? and (2) Do conventional test items register variance in reading performance as sensitively as recall protocols?

Lee and Musumeci found that their subjects at each language level could answer forty-four items about different text types with almost equal facility.[1] Moreover, analysis of student performance in the four semesters did not indicate that either genre or years of study were significant variables in student comprehension. For example, in terms of correct answers given by students, travel or registration forms, though compact and abbreviated, proved to be as difficult as reading about current events or literary texts. Presumably, for adult readers, the burden of processing additional vocabulary and syntax in the newspaper and literary passages was offset by the advantage of a connected narrative that develops ideas.

The study of Allen and his colleagues cited earlier examined the reading performance of an even larger sample of high school students. The 420 students were enrolled in French, German, and Spanish from years one through five. These subjects read four authentic texts, each of which reflected a particular "text type" mentioned in the *ACTFL Proficiency Guidelines*, a high incidence of cognates, and topic content of international interest that was presumably familiar to high school students (166). These factors effectively replaced the "grammatically sequenced and graded perspective" of traditional L1 and L2 readability formulas (164; see also Bernhardt 1986b).

With regard to the first major issue, the relationship between the amount of time spent in language study and reading performance, the findings of Allen and his colleagues differ from those of Lee and Musumeci. A "significant main effect by level" *was* found (169). Rather than five levels, however, the five years of high school work seemed to translate into three different levels of advancement with, for example, second-year students performing at about the level of first-year students. However, the three distinct levels did not translate into the same progression of advancement for each language, a result that leads the authors to "caution against viewing separate languages in a generic sense which maintains that general principles can be applied to all languages across all levels for all learners" (170).

Why would college semesters or high school years of study fail to emerge as a significant factor in either comparative study? Possibly a critical factor, only one study (Allen et al.) used recall protocols as measures of performance. Another important unknown is the time spent on this task. Neither study checked linguistic ability on the basis of other measures. Viewed together, these studies raise the question of whether the difference in "language level" (Lee and Musumeci's term) corresponds to time spent in language study (Allen and colleagues speak of "exposure time"). In the absence of such data, possibly *five years* of study in high school yields more discrete differences than *two years* (four semesters of study) in college. Possibly too, maturational differences revealed in L1 studies (e.g., Meyer & Freedle) play a role in differentiating text types in different languages. Regardless of these questions, the finding shared in both studies is that a particular content or "text type" failed to provoke a main effect *per se*.

Related to questions about whether the type of text predicts readability is the issue of linguistic complexity. Authentic texts, for example, often present unfamiliar idioms and formal features. The traditional readability standard held that texts be lexically and grammatically simplified. Otherwise, it was believed, these features would interfere with the comprehension of L2 students. Even when studies fail to discuss the word count/sentence length standard for readability, research with more challenging texts questions the validity of that claim.

For example, Lee (1987b) designed a study to assess whether "the comprehension of a particular linguistic structure [the subjunctive in Spanish] is necessarily a function of prior instruction in its form and uses or if comprehension can be achieved without the benefit of such instruction" (51). The author compared 180 students from twelve different classes. Half the students, the pre-instructional group, were in first-semester Spanish. The post-instructional group had been taught the subjunctive and was drawn from second-semester classes. Lee's analysis revealed an absence of significant differences in performance between the pre- and post-instruction groups (54). He concluded that *"perhaps foreign language teachers have been underestimating learners' comprehension because of the way they have been assessing it"* (55, italics added).

For curriculum planning, the insights of Lee (1987b), Lee and Musumeci, and the article by Allen, Bernhardt, Berry, and Demel, in conjunction with studies on the positive effects of schema cited earlier (see Chapter 2, pp. 22-24), support the assertion that the L2 profession has tended to underestimate students' potential for reading comprehension of authentic texts. These studies indicate that L2 students with relatively little language training can comprehend authentic texts as long as selections reflect the cognitive and content background of adult learners. Music students can read about music with greater ease and comprehension than if confronted with text topics chosen at random on the basis of either language factors or typology.

Let us turn briefly to prior thinking about text content and specific reading functions, views challenged by the foregoing research. In her book *Language Teaching in Context*, Alice Omaggio includes a planning guide for reading developed at the Defense Language Institute. The description differentiates types of content, function, and accuracy goals "a teacher might work on at each level of proficiency" (152). Omaggio stresses that while "some activity types are more appropriate to one level of proficiency; many of them . . . can be used at various levels" (153). A comparison between the qualitative and quantitative factors in the DLI chart (153–56) reveals how multiple variables make prediction of readability difficult. As we read them, the qualitative distinctions Omaggio presents imply a sequence in which three factors correspond:

1. Reader perception (listed under *function* and *accuracy*). Beginning readers will grasp mainly gist at the novice and intermediate levels. While novices will be assumed to have minimal comprehension except when reading memorized material (gist, key words), intermediate-level readers should experience misunderstanding only of finer points. The advancement in intermediate levels and above will be characterized by an increasing grasp of supporting detail.

2. Text topic (listed under *content*). Beginners are limited to general topics (weather, seasons, self-identification, forms). Intermediates can read narrative on familiar topics and everyday survival topics, while advanced readers may read nontechnical prose and a wider range of topics. However, professional topics in special fields of competence or particular areas of interest characterize only the superior level.

3. Text type (also under *content*). Concrete or tangible information (menus, biographical information, meeting arrangements) characterizes lower levels. Only at the advanced level are newspaper accounts, instructions and directions, academic texts and routine reports listed.

In addition, the taxonomy's suggested readings reflect quantitative characteristics: early emphasis on short texts. Intermediate readers have ads or simple letters or realia such as menus, headlines, maps or program schedules, while intermediate readers have text types such as short narrative / descriptions, nontechnical prose, newspaper accounts. The superior level begins its suggested text types with a reference to "lengthy narratives and descriptions of all types," "most practical, social, abstract, and professional topics," listing also special fields of competence and particular areas of interest (Omaggio 156).

ACCESSING THE READER'S COMPREHENSION ABILITY THROUGH INSTRUCTIONAL OPTIONS

The problem facing the DLI descriptors and many recommendations for L2 reading of authentic texts is the unpredictability of the interactive reader. Both the DLI and the *ACTFL Guidelines* very appropriately stress that topic familiarity eases reading difficulty. But what constitutes a "familiar topic"? When professional topics occur only at the superior reading level, students with extensive knowledge in a particular field may be denied the opportunity to apply that background at early levels of language learning. Yet we know, for example, that scientists read scientific texts with greater success than business students with comparable L2 capability (e.g., Bramki & Williams; Koh). Similarly, the registration form included at the novice level ignores the fact that a person familiar with such forms will outperform someone who is not. As someone who spent her research time in the Federal Republic, Janet Swaffar would be reduced to guesswork given a bill of fare from an Austrian café. Katherine Arens, who wrote her dissertation in Vienna, would not only recognize every item on the menu, but could provide enthusiasts with recipes upon request.

What about the identification of main ideas and their supporting detail as a standard for intermediate readers? In Chapter 3 and again in Chapter 7, we discuss the evidence that these abilities can be modified by classroom practice with strategies and particular reading perspectives. If successful, such practice could enable beginners to comprehend both gist and detail of texts about familiar topics. Possibly, extensive reading in a lengthier text would enable a person with relatively low language abilities to improve linguistic abilities. In short, beyond the first few weeks of language instruction, whether restricted topics or text types are more or less readable may well depend on their readers, not on their inherent features.

Because the profession needs common standards of measurement, questions about criteria for readability affect all of us. But how do we establish standards for grading reading materials and assessing comprehension of those materials? In order to be reliable, a reading test must be normed to a population of students with heterogeneous backgrounds, all of whom use very different kinds of knowledge and experience to understand a text. The solution we propose is to reframe the problem. Although intuitively appealing, research evidence speaks for caution in presuming that some text types may be more readable than others by virtue of genre or brevity. Correlations between the text types and the discourse markers or rhetorical features of a text type seem to depend on the author, not the genre. Genre itself is nonpredictive. L1 research suggests that if reader background factors are equal, an author's use of discrete discourse factors and rhetorical structures predicts a degree of readability. The same generalization may hold for L2 texts as well. As yet we lack confirmation of that assumption.

In addition to underestimating the adult student's potential to read for meaning in the second language, we may also have been underestimating the positive effects of authentic texts on language acquisition. Vigil (1987) conducted research into integrative learning through early use of authentic texts. She established that not only was comprehension of such texts by beginning students very high, but also that her students' *language* capabilities increased with the contact as well. Vigil compared a spectrum of instructional effects on two groups: users of unedited and edited texts in two beginning Spanish courses. She found significant differences favoring the unedited-text group at the end of an eleven-week course.

Moreover, these differences were apparent not only in reading comprehension, but also in students' compositions and oral performance. "The results suggest that learners exposed to language structures in the context of authentic text develop the skill to produce language coherently rather than as isolated components of the language" (100–101). At the same time, as would be expected with texts emphasizing command of surface language, the group using edited texts made fewer errors in spelling and concordance. This correspondence between type of reading material and learner processing suggests that both reader strategies and text factors *do* have an impact on overall language learning.

The L2 evidence about text types, discourse, and language levels argues for three revisions of current practices in teaching and evaluating performance in L2 reading: (1) that we teach and test without particular regard to text type as such, i.e., not assuming particular text types for novice, intermediate, or advanced readers; (2) that we assess text difficulty on the basis of text-internal discourse factors—both linguistic and conceptual; (3) that adult students be evaluated on the basis of a hierarchy of procedures or *tasks* (a reader process orientation) rather than a hierarchy of *skills* (a text-based product emphasis). An assessment of relative task difficulty would first have to be evaluated empirically to establish reliable measures. To be sure, task complexity is a traditional measure of cognitive development. We argue for it here on the premise that *L2 reading comprehension is a function of cognitive development, the ability to think within the framework of the second language*.

The scoring of such a test would depend on the student's ability to execute a comprehensive range of reading tasks rather than to display a particular skill capability. The items in such a test would consistently address the word level or local detail of a given text as well as its global features. The criteria for such items would be that they reflect or elicit discourse: coherent language with clear communicative intent. A picture is emerging of the types of procedures that are relevant—the global tasks and their relationship to the subtasks of comprehension. We will present the research basis for these suggestions here and their practical applications in the chapters that follow (see particularly Chapter 9 on testing).

STRATEGY TRAINING AS AN INSTRUCTIONAL ACTIVITY: EVALUATIVE STUDIES AT THE INTERMEDIATE LEVEL

Both L1 (Baker & Brown; Carroll 1967; Palinscar & Brown) and L2 studies (Barnett 1988a; Carrell 1985) about adult metacognitive processing suggest that strategy training can improve reading comprehension. Of the studies that have examined training effects (e.g., Barnett 1988a; Floyd & Carrell; Hamp-Lyons; Kern 1985), only Laufer and Sim suggested no value for strategy training beneath a given language theshold.

Several of these strategy studies have used authentic texts as the basis for training and evaluation, because such texts are felt to be richer in the discourse features that aid comprehension than are edited texts. As we have seen, particular discourse features seem to promote effective reading (e.g., Baten). What do these evaluations say to practitioners?

With twenty-four ESL students, Hamp-Lyons conducted two semester-long classroom treatments of reading (two hours weekly). She matched three groups on the basis of pre-test scores to compare the effects of a "traditional" and a "text-strategic" classroom approach. Hamp-Lyons compared two classes having traditional formats with one text-strategic group. In the former, she encouraged students to replicate discrete information from the text as well as formal grammar features at the sentence level; in the latter, she encouraged reading for a range of responses, emphasizing text schema and discourse features. Scores on cloze tests suggested that the most significant gains were made by the text-strategic group. With the lowest pre-test mean, the experimental section outperformed the control groups in the post-test.

Carrell (1985) conducted a study comparing training and non-training in recognition and use of text structure—an evaluation of one version of a particular instructional activity. The sole difference between classroom treatments was that the control group received no training on top-level rhetorical organization and the strategy for using that information for reading and recall. Conversely, the experimental group spent that much less time on grammar practice. Each group received a pre- and post-test that were scored for high-, mid-, and low-level idea units recalled. Whereas pre-test scores were equivalent, post-test results for the experimental group yielded significantly higher scores for all levels of idea units recalled. Since the recall of low-level ideas is often assumed to be based on knowledge of linguistic detail, one would anticipate a superior gain in low-level ideas for the control group. They, after all, received more training in linguistic detail. A post-test conducted three weeks after the reading showed that training effects persisted for the experimental group. In other words, the immediate gains in recall after the conscious use of strategies seem to last over a three-week interval.

Carrell's data (1984, 1985) lend support to the notion of "text-strategic" emphases on discourse features and main meaning. However, she and Hamp-Lyons were both using students with high intermediate proficiency. Two variables relating to proficiency need to be considered: (1) Would students at lower levels of proficiency respond as well to top-down strategy training (the threshold or language-level problem)?; and (2) What is the effect of the language in which strategy instruction was conducted and the language used in student recalls? At present, non-training comparisons indicate that, when the native language is used, greater recall is elicited than when the non-native language is used (Lee 1985). This approach is not practical in ESL studies whose subjects have multilingual backgrounds, but may be useful in L2 studies of students who share a native language.

Barnett (1988b) conducted such a study. Four sections of fourth-semester French were encouraged to predict as they read, analyze their reading style, skim, scan, and guess at word meanings from context. She compared their performance with students in fifteen non-treatment sections at the same level. Barnett found, as she expected, that "students who read through context better are more likely to perceive that they use effective strategies, and they also comprehend better" (157). Contrary to expectation, however, direct training in strategy use was not a significant variable. In this study, Barnett's null findings on strategy use contrast with results from a year-long experiment in which early special training in the second and third semesters did help students comprehend better than their peers who lacked such training (Barnett 1988a). She speculates that the effects of strategy training may require more than one semester to register in comprehension gains.

Barnett's findings also support the assumption expressed in Chapter 2, that *early* training may be a key to helping L2 students read with better comprehension. By the fourth semester, student strategies for L2 reading may be entrenched. Consequently, the time when strategy training will make a significant difference is in conjunction with beginning L2 instruction for the reasons outlined in Chapter 3. The fact that ESL studies of students at intermediate levels reveal significant gains after strategy training, whereas Barnett's L2 study did not, is possibly a result of the acquisition-rich environment available to ESL students. Logically, ESL students, unlike their FL counterparts, have more opportunities to focus on contextual as well as language factors during beginning instruction. Hence, strategy training at intermediate levels of ESL students may be more likely to promote processes whereby the reader considers and remembers context.

Why does strategy practice help L2 readers? Because construction of another person's textual logic is *linguistically* undemanding, even though it represents a complex *cognitive* task. Such construction asks only that students select and categorize textual language in a meaningful pattern (e.g., in a sequence or cause and effect relationship). For such a task, linguistically complex articulations (e.g., sentence series that students must generate) are unnecessary.

One reason why good L1 readers probably engage in metacognitive strategies on an automatic level is because they employ reader strategies in text selection itself. This is not true for L2 readers. Texts are selected for them. Reading, particularly if viewed as "an assignment" only, tends to be text-based. Hence the L2 reader is less likely to introduce her own perspectives or focus goals (i.e., reading to find out the answers to a particular problem or find out how to save money). At least in speaking and listening practice, the first-person focus in most classrooms often shifts attention to strategies for discourse (requesting, thanking, etc.), rather than analysis of discourse.

We presume that, for this reason, L2 readers need to learn and practice mental shorthand to activate metacognitive strategies in working memory. L2 readers must consciously access the equivalent of, for example, the statement "Even though there are a lot of new words here, I have to remember this is a review of *Star Trek* and these are descriptions of the crew, all of whom are familiar to me." Otherwise they are in danger of focusing an undue amount of controlled attention on syntactic detail or unfamiliar vocabulary.

High language level will certainly promote advanced and superior levels of comprehension. When students focus exclusively on "main ideas" or "gisting," the likelihood exists that they will misread, fail to perceive cultural nuances, or remain oblivious to subtextual implications. A grasp of language detail is essential for full interactive comprehension. In order to read for meaning, global text features must be accurately linked to their detailed exposition, and detail focus involves a whole series of vital subtasks. From an instructional standpoint, therefore, the first stages of L2 reading must clarify global propositions and the manner in which the text presents them. Only after the text topics have been established is it fruitful to turn to the way the text elaborates those topics.

STRATEGIES AND SUBTASKS

What are the language subtasks of reading comprehension? Which helps comprehension more, content or function words? Are semantics more meaningful than syntax? Does recall follow from recognition? Again, research evidence suggests that we should revise our thinking.

Content or function words. One prevalent notion about reading is that content words are more important than function words. Ulijn (1984), testing Dutch readers learning English, found that conceptual knowledge in conjunction with word knowledge was the critical factor in comprehension. Concepts resulting from content words (nouns, verbs, adjectives, and adverbs) proved more significant than function words (prepositions, pronouns, conjunctions, and auxiliary verbs). These findings seem to contradict research in discourse markers which suggests that function words are essential to identifying cohesion in texts. The critical difference in comparing contradictory findings may be in how the data is gathered.

Sim and Bensoussan, for example, analyzed 103 multiple choice questions designed to test whether students scored higher on questions about function words (e.g., the discursive function of "as a matter of fact" as contradiction, elaboration, agreement) than on questions about content words (e.g., the meaning of "climate"). They used a non-cloze test because they wanted to examine lexical skill, recognition, and decoding rather than the encoding they assumed for cloze tests. Function words proved as difficult for students to identify as content words. Bernhardt's eye-tracking experiments (1984, 1989) support Sim and Bensoussan's findings. Her eye-movement research indicates that both native and non-native readers fixate regularly on function words, particularly in more difficult texts. Moreover, native German readers (as opposed to experienced non-natives) tended to devote more attention to function words in a phrase than to the content words in the same phrase. The group of inexperienced readers, on the other hand, attended primarily to content words.

Semantics versus syntax. Since function words mark cohesion in written texts, these studies bear directly on the controversy over the relative importance of semantics (content words) over syntax in comprehending. Reconsider Ulijn's findings in terms of the conceptual impact Meyer and Freedle document for the reader who identifies text structure. The technical texts used by his students have an organization that favors contextual guessing of structure (Bramki & Williams). With such texts the reader can expect a given rhetorical organization for data discussed. The necessity for encoding connective features is therefore reduced. The emphasis of Ulijn's subjects on semantics may therefore be a result of their familiarity with the macrosyntax of their sample text. Yet students in Ulijn's study may also have had inadequate background familiarity for them to predict semantic meanings. The background in formal schema could have compensated for deficient language competency in decoding syntax, but it would not compensate for deficient semantic capability.

Cooper examined the performance of practiced and unpracticed non-native readers of English, i.e., those who had pursued their previous education through the medium of English and those whose prior education had been in the native tongue. The testing instrument looked at a variety of semantic (e.g., non-contextual affix identification, contextual identification of hyponymy, synonymy, or antonymy) and syntactic variables (e.g., cleft construction, complementation, cohesion markers, and awareness of logical relationships between sentences). All item types discriminated between practiced and unpracticed readers. The sharpest discrimination was between performances on the intersentence section. The author concluded that unpracticed readers were particularly uncertain about the meanings of sentence connectors. To glean additional information, Cooper asked unpracticed readers to list unfamiliar words in a text and discovered that a high proportion of these words were common across subject areas. What is striking about the list he provides is that many are discursive connects such as *despite*, *nevertheless*, *consequently* or markers of macropropositional logic such as *contrast with*, *similarly*, *function as*, *characterize* (133). For this reason Cooper concludes that classroom training should help unpracticed readers understand and "create" large, coherent text relationships (135).

This is a key issue in teaching practice. The pedagogical literature dealing in classroom approaches emphasizes semantics in both textual and extra-textual activities. Leading theorists as well as practitioners have stressed the primacy of semantics over syntax. However, variables in research design (e.g., whether the test is of recognition or recall), may account for different results. Generalizations about "syntax" and "semantics" are like generalizations about "truth." One wants to know whose syntax, what semantics?

To answer these questions, researchers are turning to statistical tools designed to assess interactive variables. Examination of interactions between syntax and semantics or reader background and language level can yield quite different data than if those same factors are looked at in isolation. To assess the interaction between syntax, lexicon, and recall of short French texts (600 to 650 words), Barnett (1986) examined syntax and vocabulary as independent factors in a rational deletion cloze test, i.e., filling equivalent numbers of deletions by selecting one of three answers for each.[2] Recall scores obtained from English protocols were then factored as a dependent variable. Her subjects were 124 fourth-semester college students.

Her results support Berman's conclusion about the importance of syntax in comprehension of L2 textual details as well as L1 studies investigating similar variables. Barnett found that recall increased according to both vocabulary *and* syntactic proficiency. In other words, the results showed parallel effects. Students with either (a) low vocabulary scores or (b) low syntax scores were unable to increase their abilities in the opposite area. In both instances recall scores were consistently low. She therefore concluded that for these French students "knowledge of syntax and vocabulary interact to allow a reader to understand a text" (347), a finding supported by Twyford's work with beginning students of Italian (1980).

PRACTICAL IMPLICATIONS FOR THE CLASSROOM

At this point, amid a wealth of data about variables in reading comprehension, we return to the question posed at the outset of this chapter: How do the insights about interactive processing apply to the L2 reader, particularly at higher levels in the curriculum? What follows is our analysis of the significance of current research and the issues it raises for us as classroom teachers.

Issue #1: How do we teach vocabulary for reading? Threshold studies suggest that vocabulary building is an essential facet of proficient reading. At the same time, evidence suggests that lexical lists fail to solve the reading / vocabulary problem. The alternative has the reader build his or her own vocabulary. There are several pragmatic reasons to encourage students to do this. When the learner decides what to commit to memory, the salience and consequent retention is presumably higher. Moreover, not all students need to learn the same words. Saragi, Nation, and Meister refer to a vocabulary test based on the 1000 most frequent English words. Analysis indicated that, although the class average was eighty-nine percent on the exam, only forty percent of the words tested were known by every learner (72). If word lists are made, then, it is probably students, not teachers, who need to identify the words they need to know.

Crow stresses the value of contextual understanding, Bensoussan the value of uninterrupted reading for meaning. To link textual meaning and vocabulary, classroom presentations must look at discursive and thematic relationships rather than dictionary definitions (e.g., Grellet 128; Nuttall 64 f.). Assessments of dictionary use (e.g., Bensoussan, Sim & Weiss) and glosses (Johnson) indicate that, rather than by extensive emphasis on such formats, our students may be better served by more pre- and post-reading vocabulary discussion that connects text and reader schemata.

In-class vocabulary practice should ask students to find additional words that relate to the same semantic category (semantic fields or synonymy), identify how the same words are redefined by different contexts (polysemy), provide opportunities to increase awareness of pronounceability, and identify affixes, suffixes, or parts of speech. Good vocabulary exercises represent strategies for vocabulary monitoring and repairing misreadings. To facilitate recall, we must link vocabulary to macromeaning factors: familiar schemata, a topic of student interest (reader-based macrofactors), text structure, and gist (text-based macrofactors).

Issue #2: What is the role of syntax?   Research expands our current focus on syntax within sentences to include intersentence and inter-episodic text levels. In independent studies, Cooper, Bensoussan, and Sim have demonstrated the significance of student recognition of logical connectors. While Bernhardt's eye-movement studies (1986c) of German, French, and Spanish native-language readers suggest that the relative concentration on function words may differ from one language to another, additional time devoted to ends of clauses and sentences were significant in all cases. Because modifiers and logical connectors are among the vocabulary items hardest to guess in context yet essential for accurate text reconstruction (Bensoussan & Laufer), they must be taught, particularly in prereading exercises. And since intersentence connectors identify relationships between macro- and micropropositions, they are most logically discussed as links between high-, mid- and low-level text structure ("find words that tell you what follows is a result of what has gone before"). In building mental representations of text structure, L2 readers need syntactic cohesion factors to connect semantics.

Issue #3: How do we trace reader conceptualization?   As recall protocols and oral interviews illustrate, we frequently fail to appreciate that students arrive at aberrant textual reconstructions in perfectly reasonable ways (e.g., a child may match "fly" and "elephant" after seeing *Dumbo*). Differences in background knowledge may lead to logical inferences that teachers judge incorrect because they lack that background data.

Readers of a second language inevitably experience misreading. Indeed, some misapprehension of textual meaning is a common phenomenon in any reading. To prevent discouragement, teachers must help students repair flawed comprehension in a nonjudgmental way. Readers need to have opportunities to explain decisions about meaning. As with successful reading perspectives (Block; Connor 1984), topic-oriented verbalization styles promote learning (e.g., Michaels' L1 study). Strategy work in small groups can help students verbalize links between the text topic and what they understand of it (Kramsch 1981), i.e., which events in the story lead readers to draw inferences and conclusions. Instead of judging those conclusions, readers and teachers need to focus on the process of understanding and the concepts resulting from that process.

Unless classroom diagnosis is encouraged in class, teachers can too easily assume that language deficiency is the culprit in misreading, when in reality student schemata are overriding their command of language. To cite an instance from our own experience, a fourth-semester German class read an authentic text about the latest dieting fad. Armed with a German language preview about American dieting fads, the class established the schemata of the passage. As a result, students had no difficulty in engaging in contextual guessing about the following idea units: three needles in the ear would do something (unknown word) to hunger. "Something positive or something negative?," we asked in German. Something positive, of course. Thus encouraged, the class speculated that the needles would inhibit, stop, or prevent hunger. The needles would also eliminate something—another unfamiliar word. While less certain about what would be eliminated, the students picked concepts like cholesterol, waste products, and toxins from a longer list that included vitamins, minerals, and red blood cells.

At this juncture the class read a sentence in which they understood every word: "The dieter can drink as much as he or she wants—soup, mineral water, tea, or coffee." Yet it was at this point that the class misread. They were convinced that the dieter could *not* drink all she wanted. When asked to explain in English why they interpreted the sentence this way, their answer made perfect sense: how could wastes or toxins be eliminated from the body if one drank coffee or tea? Caffeine is, after all, unhealthy. As unidirectional readers, the students in this class rewrote—indeed, they improved on the text—in order to fit their preconceptions. The occurrence was a reminder of the importance of bidirectional reading. Beyond that, the incident also illustrates the diagnostic value of conducting some reading work in the students' native language.

In addition to clarifying the basis for misreadings, use of native language may yield more accurate assessments of L2 readers' comprehension and recall (Lee 1986b; Tan & Ling). Reconsideration of native language use in reading and testing of reading is a fairly radical suggestion in today's communicatively-oriented classroom. For the past forty years, from the days of audiolingual precepts to Krashen's "input hypothesis" (1982), the notion that maximal exposure to the second language fosters comprehension has dominated at least the theory if not always the practice in our discipline. Contextually-oriented approaches such as those described by Omaggio (1986) and the reading formats illustrated in the comprehensive exemplifications of Nuttall and Grellet stress text-based models designed to elicit L2 use. Some teachers may feel that the price paid in reading comprehension is compensated for in language learning. On the other hand, successful readers also increase their overall language learning (Oller 1983). Occasional use of L1 in outside reading, small group work, and testing may teach more L2 in the long run.

In a communicative program, L1 use would be an incidental check of student conceptualizing and strategy practice, not translation. Because translating involves surface mapping between languages, it generally fails to activate reader conceptual processes. On the other hand, some research has suggested that native language recalls enhance comprehension and help identify conceptual problems, e.g., the misreading when *cried* is translated as *wept* and not *called out*. In order to find out whether language interferes with how our students comprehend a text, we need to test and compare formats that use both L1 and L2.

Issue #4: How does reading interact with other competencies?   The answer seems to depend on the type of test used to determine such interactions. Standardized tests have been criticized for failing to integrate different modes of learning. Oller's *Language Tests in Schools* (1979) concludes that testing which separates skills results in a lower performance than testing which integrates them. Students who not only recognize a Dutch synonym for "sinister," but know how to write the word and use it in conversation as well, do best. Just because our brains apparently compartmentalize comprehension (Wernicke area) and production activities (Broca area), doesn't argue against using several compartments at the same time. It does, we think, argue for careful looks at a learning task sequence. The legacy of habit learning is the teaching of four skills and discrete "behaviors." We suggest that the profession needs to think of reading in terms of instructional sequences in integrative language use, rather than thinking of reading as a single skill.

Issue #5: Does interactive reading affect current definitions of readability? Computer programs that account for the interaction of top-down and bottom-up factors point to current thinking about assessing readability. Up until now most readability scales have emphasized language features such as sentence length and vocabulary difficulty. Now we know that background, discursive, and motivational factors must also be weighted. Features we often fail to register consciously, such as factual inconsistency, can nonetheless inhibit recall (Zabrucky). How do classroom teachers judge text selection in light of research theories that are still evolving (Schallert et al.; N. Stein.)?

Coherence counts. Schema research began with the study of ambiguous passages in which writers or storytellers failed to specify whether, for example, a fight was verbal or physical, or which event was being celebrated and why. These are the text types to avoid. Similarly, texts that leap from personal stories to factual analyses or from one situation to the next are hard to understand, particularly if students lack background knowledge to fill in the gaps. What we as teachers need to do with our reading assignments and with our test construction is to monitor texts for stylistic factors that make reading hard. We must also teach students to identify nonlinguistic as well as linguistic text features that inhibit comprehension.

Issue #6: How can we evaluate interactive reading? The research presented here calls many of our current testing practices into question. Our tests generally fail to account for interactive variables such as: (1) reader background, (2) different language skills (see Canale on including comprehension and production items), (3) the text's macropropositions (topics, text logic) and micropropositions (their detailed elaboration), (4) different types of texts tested in different ways (for learning, for locating gist on the one hand, or particular information on the other). In their format, reading tests rarely vary in question type. They provide true/false or multiple choice answers but rarely incorporate open-ended questions or recalls. Only this item variety lets us diagnose problems and give students a chance to show us why they understood a text in a particular way.

Issue #7: How can we teach components of interactive reading? Interactive models suggest that not only the reader's but also the teacher's role is of greater significance than has been thought up to now. L2 teachers who want their classes to interact with texts have to be facilitators of the reading process rather than monitors of performance. They have a fourfold task: (1) to activate reader schemata, (2) to guide students to an awareness of text structure, (3) to assist in strategy development, and (4) to promote relaxed interaction between students and text. Beyond these four functions, the teacher's challenge is to choose tasks for different students' backgrounds and language competencies. Drawing on the research discussed here, we suggest the following.

First, in view of the evidence that a reader's L1 strategies are often not applied in L2 reading, we suggest that students read authentic texts from the start of language instruction for the sole purpose of training in gist comprehension or top-down processing. Practice with unedited texts could offset the dominance of word-for-word decoding tendencies that can result from initial language-learning practices. Such reading would also make students aware that, even as elementary learners, they are able to deal factually with popular, familiar topics (travel, films, music, television, reports of current events). Finally, this activity teaches students that not all L2 texts are equal, and that their own interests foster a higher degree of comprehension for some types of reading than for others.

Second, we need information about students' backgrounds and interests to select texts for L2 reading. At the very least it would be useful to know what our students would like to read. From a commercial perspective, anthology editors might do well to consider market research findings. What are the interests and text preferences of the teachers and the students who will be the prospective audience?

Third, experiments with as little as one classroom week of intensive strategy practice and accompanying metalanguage has yielded significantly improved reading. It seems self-evident that we should introduce this activity in our classes. We may also wish to consider tutorial work with our weaker readers based on oral interview techniques. If we lack the time, student tutoring often proves effective (Feeny).

Fourth, previewing work to establish the content and logical organization of the text is essential. Since recognition of schema enhances both comprehension and recall, the case for prereading cannot be overstated. Bernhardt's (1985) examples of the enduring effects of initial misreadings (discussed in Chapter 3) show how important it is to help students avoid faulty constructions.

Fifth, students need practice in reading longer texts. To do so, they must be able to identify middle-level or episodic structure, e.g., changes in scene or time, sequence developments, or shifts in perspective. Being aware that such changes will occur, either through a prereading exercise or assignment questions, can aid processing significantly. If such interference problems in middle-level coherence and cohesion are recognized in advance, the reader can concentrate on other processing.

Sixth, L1 research in directing reader attention (Frederiksen 1982; Schallert) can be applied to rereading tasks and can thereby reinforce both the language and ideas of the text. Once students have completed an initial reading, they can be asked to reread from another point of view (e.g., as burglars, policemen, or home owners) or another structural logic (problems and solutions instead of comparisons). Such activities treat comprehension as a fluid process rather than as a particular result. They also provide a language review within a novel conceptual frame.

Seventh, since affect and text-extrinsic perspectives can distort comprehension (Block), students should be encouraged to synthesize textual facts and assertions as neutrally as possible. However, this practice applies only to their initial reading. After constructing textual meaning, students learn by taking issue with textual ideas. Differences of opinion provide opportunities for bridging the gap between comprehension and production, particularly in small group practice.

CONCLUSION

If L2 readers are to participate actively in identifying cultural and author codes they must use texts for the total language learning process: (1) for *text-based comprehension* of new information, of logical systems, of differences in meaning found in different language use, and of author perspective, and (2) for *reader-based articulation* of individual understanding of schemata and details, as well as for a variety of perspectives that may or may not correspond to those of the author. In short, interactive reading is an integral part of communicative language learning. Consider the processes that must be practiced and assessed. Prereading links the students' existing knowledge with their language capabilities. When a teacher asks students to decide what they know about the subject matter of a text (their reader schemata), the teacher has students practice L2 language in the class's L1 context. Beginners may only be able to label choices "right" and "wrong," but any output beyond that represents an attempt to express ideas. As was stressed in Chapter 2, the articulation of first person *knowledge* (in contrast to *opinions*) is not linguistically demanding. Subsequent to the reading assignment, students will probably think about the text in their native language. If given the option of connecting that thinking to textual language, however, they can practice integrative learning. Reading can become a reasoning task connected to a language task.

For curriculum planning, the use of authentic texts to teach subject matter of interest to students is a feasible instructional undertaking. Like L1 adults, mature L2 students need reading for many reasons: to learn specific facts, to be entertained, to comprehend text gist, to interpret author intent, and to locate cultural messages. The skills involved in reading for this range of goals are metacognitive as well as linguistic. Research evidence supports the notion that both FL and ESL students with a grasp of metacognitive strategies can read authentic texts, and are even able to undertake extensive reading in a longer text or in a particular field of study at earlier stages than we have previously thought.

For students of European languages that share a common alphabet, comprehension does not appear to be absolutely inhibited by language level. If materials are chosen with familiar schema and interest level in mind, relatively early reading in a content area offers L2 students the advantages of using their knowledge of a foreign language to learn. Equally important, electives taught in the second language let students choose topics of interest to them.

In the chapter that follows we will present an instructional model for skills-integrated reading. The model's procedures move from comprehension to production in L2 reading. The pedagogical standard used for these tasks is that their execution reveals how readers interact with the language and concepts of the text.

NOTES TO CHAPTER 4

1. Increase in accuracy from one semester to the next amounted to about one percent (Lee & Musumeci 177).

2. Although her sample distinguishes between lexical and semantic items, Barnett groups them together as "vocabulary." Originally a three-factor analysis of variance between vocabulary, syntax, and story features was conducted. However, the story variable yielded no significant differences and was discarded (1986: 345).

Five

A Procedural Model
for Integrative Reading

SIMILARITIES AND DIFFERENCES BETWEEN
THEORETICAL MODELS AND A PROCEDURAL MODEL

Theoretical models of interactive reading in L1 are frequently characterized as either reader- or text-based, yet they differ in other ways as well (Samuels & Kamil). Grabe points out that all models have gaps and are, in that sense, only partial accounts of interactions (63). The model presented in this chapter makes no claims to completeness or originality. It is indebted to the theoretical models in L1 and the practical applications of those theories in L2 (see Chapter 3 for discussion).[1] It shares the hypothesis common to all interactive models, that reading involves an array of processes—bottom-up as well as top-down. By isolating key stages in L2 reader processing, our procedures attempt to account for incremental sequences suggested by theoretical models. Unlike theoretical models that are frequently labeled text-based *or* reader-based, this is a pragmatic sequence. It identifies both text features and features of reader processing.

　　One of the knotty problems of reading comprehension in any language is not only to avert misreading, but also to avert a reader's truncation of text on the basis of that reader's incommensurate knowledge or preconceptions. Often, L2 students don't see the discrepancies between *their* background and convictions and the quite different framework of an L2 text. Without sensitivity to these discrepancies, distortions of the text or lacunae in reader comprehension occur. Without sensitivity to the text's cultural preconditions, even advanced language students tend to register facts, but fail to register the textual inferences that are embedded in cultural assumptions. Hence the first requirement of a procedural model for L2 reading is that it account for a monitor that links reader- and text-based processing stages.

Theoretical models agree that the reader uncovers the meaning of a text's language by establishing a pattern of textual repetitions and modifications of its global messages. Psycholinguists refer to the reader's identification of global features—macropropositions, episodic features, or story structure. Many ESL researchers consider global features to be exclusively reader-based and microfeatures to be exclusively text-based. We disagree. An extensive body of literary and linguistic theory argues for the phenomenological status of text at the macrolevel. Texts have global features that multiple readers can verify and reproduce. Multiple readers agree about the junctures at which a story line changes or new characters appear. Whole schools of criticism have been erected on the notion that diverse readers will recognize the same macrofeatures in a text because those features exist independently of individual readings (Ingarden). Indeed, the phenomenological status of macrofeatures is a keystone in any theory of reader response, hermeneutics, or post-structuralism. Literary critics refer to the reader's "protention" and "retention" of main events, processes that are essential to establishing the data base for interpretation (Iser).

If our model's first departure from usual practice—the synthesis of text- and reader-based features—posits parallel sets of information to be processed, this second departure posits commensurate levels at which text messages exist and at which their reader apprehends them. The procedural model assumes two sets of top-down and bottom-up processes: one set that is attributable to the reader, one set that is attributable to the text (see list, Chapter 2, p. 24). The practical distinction between these two sets is that the reader brings speculative meanings to bear on any given subject, while the text focuses and informs those speculations. Comprehension—the synthesis of text and reader views—occurs when these divergences are resolved. The successful reader discards speculations that are irrelevant to the intent, context, information structure, and language used in the text.

A third important feature of a procedural model involves the status of language and comprehension: they are relative rather than absolute. Textual language is defined as only *one of many features that convey textual meaning.* This definition alters the status of reader processing in our model from one of autonomy to one of increasing dependence upon the text. Why, then, insist on the independent status of reader and text? The best analogy that comes to mind is that of a driver and a car. The reader drives; the text transports. The reader decides where to go, but needs a vehicle, some gas in the tank and air in the tires to get anywhere. How fast and effectively they travel together depends on features of both reader and text, how the two interact. During the journey, text factors will dominate, indeed dictate, successful reader behavior—the parallel here between, for example, clear transitions and a well-oiled engine. At the end of the trip, however, the reader is again dominant. How to start and what to do after completing the reading trip is up to the reader. Like the driver of a car, the initiator and concluder of interaction with the text is always the reader.

When comparing styles of reader interaction with the text (e.g., an analytical mode versus personal identification with textual events), the literature talks about reader *perspective.* For L2 readers and their teachers, perspective has particular significance because, as the research discussed in Chapter 3 indicates, different perspectives seem to yield very different quantities and qualities of recall. We have seen that reader reaction to a text (e.g., affective factors or reading focus such as Block's integrator and nonintegrator styles) can influence comprehension. In this same vein, different reader purposes (e.g., pleasure, study, survival) influence how reading is done and what is apprehended.

We know from L1 work in metacognition that reader perspective can link or inhibit linking of comprehension to textual factors at both top-down and bottom-up levels (Baker & Brown). Intent, context, information structure, and language competency have both top-down and bottom-up functions. All four factors inform accurate comprehension of *parole*, closed within the frame of a given discourse. Whether in conscious or unconscious application, an L2 reader must use metacognitive strategies and schemata to encode the text's context and intent within that context, its content and the semantics that express that content, its information, and its formal language properties. Without relevant strategies and background, even the best bottom-up processing often results in misreadings or inferior comprehension when compared to top-down or meaning-based processing (Devine).

On the other hand, deficiencies in bottom-up processes also disrupt comprehension. One difference between first- and second-language reading seems to be that the L2 reader, even at advanced levels, focuses longer on vocabulary than the L1 reader does. Increased time in decoding reduces comprehension. The language barrier remains the L2 reader's most apparent obstacle. To recall the review of this problem in Chapter 4: Native language readers have automaticity in their processing of vocabulary and greater ease in synthesizing meaning levels in texts. The non-native reader tends to have a longer eye fixation on individual words; slow processing results, inhibiting comprehension. Given the paucity of evidence regarding vocabulary learning outside of context, one may well posit that texts that maximize positive effects of secure top-down processing may offer the best language practice for L2 students who want to develop automaticity in decoding.

To conclude, all interactive models share some preconditions. They all assume that comprehension results from parallel processing of multiple types and levels of information. The model presented in this chapter is procedural—not theoretical. Theoretical models *predict* reading processing. Procedural stages *guide* reader behaviors. Although the presumption of parallel processing exists, a classroom model must isolate those processes in incremental stages. These stages reflect the organization of features of several theoretical models that were developed to explain how reading comprehension occurs. Our model is pragmatic and differs from most theoretical approaches in addition to many suggestions in ESL theory in three other ways: it views text and reader as independent interactors, it assumes complete parallelism of features of that interaction (both display top-down and bottom-up characteristics), and it treats language as one of four features that aid reader comprehension.

In all other respects our model shares the fundamental premises of its theoretical cousins. These shared assumptions of interactive models can be summarized in four statements:

1. As long as it is reasonably well written from a rhetorical standpoint, the text is the basis for ascertaining integrated information, not isolated pieces of information.

2. The language of the text communicates specific messages in a specific context (*parole*), not abstract language potentials (*langue*).

3. The reader must assemble and consider all factors of the text—its cultural context, its author's intent, its arrangement of information, and its degree of linguistic

complexity (i.e., how the lexicon, semantics, and syntax of the text suit its topic and message).

4. Reading leads to an *active reconstruction of both the sense and language of the text.* Anything short of reconstruction, even a summary act of memory, will bypass significant aspects of the text's meaning.

As a model, the interplay of text- and reader-based procedures can be visualized as follows:

INTERACTIVE FOCI AND TASKS FOR THE L2 READER / LEARNER

Text Focus	Meaning Focus	Student Task	Linguistic Focus
1(a). Macrosemantics: content & context	Preview of topic (global factors)	To frame factors HYPOTHESIZE	Words recognized that suggest topic
1(b). Macrosyntax: rhetorical pattern of text frame	Identification of structure, episodes	To construct information pattern as topic / comment CONFIRM INPUT HYPOTHESIS	Words, phrases that suggest macrorelationships
2. Microrealization of macrofeatures	Text implications	To reconstruct, i.e., link implicit & explicit text language	Statements that refer to text data and constitute inferences from data SENTENTIAL OUTPUT
3. Weight and organization of textual propositions	Text significance	To express opinion (linking reader language to text propositions) CREATE DISCOURSE	Connected sentences, writing that develops an argument; reader demonstrates verbal command SUPERSENTENTIAL OUTPUT

⟶ TEXT INTERPRETATION (subsequent to foregoing processing)

SEQUENCING TASKS

Practically speaking, how might teachers present texts so that students can meet the conditions represented above? How can students learn to proceed from interactive rather than solely top-down or bottom-up, text-based or reader-based premises about language? What instructional approaches put *the determination of discourse meaning in first place*?

Intake would follow in sequences of reader attention that move from stages in textual comprehension, through use of textual language, and ultimately, through applications of textual concepts to the L2 reader's world. Meaning must guide comprehension from the outset, or else textual input will not lead to learner intake, i.e., the comprehensible input the learner actually registers (Long 1985). Beyond intake or comprehension *per se*, the L2 reader needs to practice using intake as output. Practice must help readers connect their *a priori* logic and background schema with a specific text utterance. At the same time, the reader must confront textual features without being overwhelmed by any of them. The following sequence of reader and text interactions explores those requirements:

Stage 1: Students preview work to establish the content and logical orientation of the text.

Class activity: Class reacts for 5–8 minutes to a teacher-suggested topic followed by a subsequent cursory reading (skimming or scanning) of a text dealing with that topic.

Reader-based phase: Prior to looking at the text, the class has reacted to and speculated about the scope or focus of the text topic.

Text-based phase: After scanning the text, students delimit the topic of the article exclusively by means of words and phrases in initial paragraphs.

Stage 2: Students identify middle-level or episodic structure.

Class activity: Class spends 3–5 minutes finding shifts in topic, character, events, and setting of the story or text.

Reader-based phase: Students scan text format, semantics, and discourse markers that divide the text into subsets of the global topic.

Text-based phase: Practice in recognition of discourse markers—their function and impact on language usage in the text (e.g., changes in word order).

NOTE: Stage 2 is generally superfluous with shorter texts (those with fewer than 500 words). Both types of recognition exercises focus student attention on language that connects messages in a passage.

Stage 3: Students read for detail—beyond gist or global comprehension.

Class activity: Recognition of micropropositions related to global or episode propositions.

Reader-based phase: Students scan sentences for the ways they relate to the main concepts (stage 1) or episodes (stage 2) of the text, initially a class activity, e.g., 20 minutes to skim a 500—1000 word text.

Text-based phase: Students read silently to a predetermined point in the selection to locate 2 to 3 examples of text language representative of that logic and create a matrix from that information in matrices.

Stage 4: Comparison of word- and phrase-level reconstruction of textual information in matrices.

Class activity subsequent to reading outside of class: Students assess their matrices—preferably in the form of written précis—through class discussion, small group work, and teacher evaluation.

Reader-based phase: Students organize text phrases that convey details (micropropositions) in a way that is consistent with the textual pattern of main ideas (macropropositions) they perceive.

Text-based phase: Only lexicon from the text may be used at this stage. Students' matrices reveal only minor adjustments in text language, e.g., some changes in singular or plural forms, deletion of words they judge superfluous.

Stage 5: Sentence-level reconstruction of textual information.

Class activity based on writing done largely outside of class: Students generate sentences based on their matrices.

Reader-based phase: Students create the language of factual details in the text that relates to perceived macromessages of that text.

Text-based phase: Students expand the text phrases in their matrices into simple sentences. They modify formal properties of textual language according to the teacher's assessment of their chief deficiencies in comprehensible output (e.g., transformations such as tense changes, negation, etc.).

Stage 6: Supersentential construction of the reader's opinion about textual information.

Class activity based on writing done in small groups or outside of class: Students generate at least four or five connected sentences based on their sentential statements. Relevant discourse markers and their impact on formal features, such as case or word order, must be emphasized by the teacher.

Reader-based phase: Students extrapolate from the language of factual details in the text to create their own macromessages about the implications and significance of those details.

Text-based phase: Students use the text as a reference to confirm their assertions and the formal properties of relevant language.

RATIONALE FOR THE PROCEDURES

There are several advantages of a sequenced approach to reading. First, the procedures let both teacher and students monitor comprehension in discrete steps. Second, both accuracy in language production and automatic processing are reinforced when readers use text language as the basis for sentences that they generate. Third, since the model progresses from lexical to sentential to supersentential language, students must attend to the details of vocabulary and grammar as they relate to the larger textual message. Each level of activity also focuses student attention on the relationship between text meaning (propositions) and language function (the formal properties that convey propositions). Fourth, the model integrates a text-based with a reader-based perspective. Fifth, it enables readers to confirm their inferences and express their ideas about the implications and significance of their reading. Sixth, because they elicit text- *and* reader-based perspectives, the procedures encourage students to use a fuller range of metacognitive strategies than they might employ with a purely text-based approach.

Considered in terms of discrete procedures, the model can be seen as consisting of a series of dialogues between texts as well as sets of sequential tasks. While these tasks are presented in a learner sequence, the ultimate goal is to enable the reader to access all stages as interactive processes.

Briefly stated, the foregoing description of the model suggests a progression in which reading leads to use of listening, speaking, and writing capabilities. The relative emphasis on reading and writing reflects the FL learner's situation in the United States and, indeed, the ethnographically isolated L2 learner as well. FL students lack communicative input outside the classroom. Hopefully the expansion of computerized materials and use of video will augment the FL learner's current options for listening comprehension and speaking practice.

At present, however, for the FL student who is an adult, the best hope for linking all four skills in input / output practice outside the classroom is by doing more reading and writing. Why? Because reading for meaning and writing to express ideas have been seriously neglected in the language curriculum. Consequently, students lack practice in integrating functional language use and subject matter with their own thinking. Reading and writing are ideal skills from which to build such integration, because FL and L2 learners can tailor both tasks to their individual capabilities (e.g., reading and writing style, review, self-correction). If the procedures outlined on p. 76 are used incrementally, reading and writing can capitalize on adult background and cognitive capabilities. When texts speak to the interests and needs of students, reading and writing will be interesting to them. The sequence minimizes student anxiety about all skills—speaking, listening, reading, and writing—because goals are clearly defined at each stage. Moreover, embarrassment or a sense of failure is less likely since the classroom focus is on problem solving, not right or wrong answers. Because language learning occurs as a function of recognizing or expressing meaning, that learning should be more memorable and should encourage students to pursue reading beyond the formal classroom. Independent student use of the FL or L2 outside the classroom should be the profession's ultimate measure of success.

IMPLEMENTATION OF INDIVIDUAL STAGES

The foregoing discussion presents a major premise of this book: Tasks that integrate speaking, listening, reading, and writing are preferable to tasks that address practice by separating subject matter and skill. The following stages in implementation demonstrate how such integration can take place.

Stage 1: Students preview work to establish the content and logical orientation of the text.

Reader-based phase: Focus on a personalized aspect of the text topic. For example, with a passage about what makes a good marriage work, it would be appropriate to ask students to make observations about characteristics of long-lasting marital relationships. In so doing the instructor can ascertain what and how much the students already know about a topic. As students convey their concepts, whether they do so in the L2 or English, the instructor writes comments on the board in the language to be learned. Cognitive, linguistic, and affective goals are all served in this process because emphasis is on student knowledge rather than the text data, e.g., true / false or discrete-point questions.

Since the language demand is optional, those students who are uneasy about using the L2 tend to feel more relaxed about expressing themselves. Cognitive goals are served when students reflect on the multiple potentials in a passage and the probable limitations of its topic. The instructor's record-keeping serves the initial linguistic goal of vocabulary recognition: All verbalized comments appear in writing in the second language. Visual input is then followed by a review of the comments. The oral review in the foreign language affords additional practice that can lead to partial control of vocabulary and structures on the blackboard.

Text-based phase: *Focus on the topic of the text, based on its language.* The instructor gives students several minutes to skim a passage. If it is longer than about four hundred words, instructions should specify whether students are to read only initial paragraphs—generally the first two paragraphs will suffice to orient the reader to the text as a whole. Since L2 readers often ignore pictures, subtitles, and even titles of passages in that language, step two involves calling attention to these features in conjunction with the text—asking for textual statements that elaborate its title, for example. At this juncture a second list of words (the textual complement to the first list generated by student schemata) is put on the blackboard as students search out the relevant language of a passage's main ideas. If the notion of looking for names or descriptors of people, places, or objects is clear, students will select appropriate nouns and adjectives from the text. From a text on marital success, typical responses in L2 might be (having) *similar backgrounds, family support, reasonable expectations*, (wanting) *lasting relationships.*

Since students respond optionally and are selecting information from the text in front of them, the problem of accuracy does not arise. In essence they read aloud from the first two or three paragraphs of the passage. If students provide an answer that does not seem to fit, it is entirely appropriate to ask why they made that selection. Just as it activates schemata, prereading practice should also uncover possible sources of misapprehension and address them. Occasional mispronunciations can be dealt with as inhibitors of communication and opportunities to match pronunciation and orthography ("Did you say 'cat' or 'caught'?").

There are several pedagogical advantages of these two stages. First, students isolate key vocabulary functions, a linguistic goal. Second, they juxtapose textual statements with their own schemata to confirm or disconfirm their understanding, a meaning goal. Third, and perhaps most important, are the cognitive and affective benefits. Students participate in terms of what they know or can reasonably be expected to recognize. Too often, language classes emphasize students' ignorance, and they experience anxiety as a result (e.g., Young & Horwitz). In this sense, the procedures foster affect that seems to promote cognitive and linguistic success.

In phase one, the reader focus, the instructor finds out what students know. Pooling that knowledge reinforces a strategy of activating reader schemata rather than resorting to a word-for-word decoding process. Moreover, the classroom activity has set up a framework for narrowing the range of schemata in a text. In phase two, the text focus, misunderstanding of textual schemata (failure to identify main ideas accurately) can be forestalled. The teacher's record-keeping ensures that the language of the text (student selections in phase two) is overtly compared to the language of student expectations (phase one).

Stages 2 and 3. Students identify middle-level or episodic structure.

Reader-based phase: Many L2 texts which students read initially have no real episodic structure. A 500-word text may not do more than introduce a problem and present its characteristics. Like the *Star Trek* text in Chapter 2, short readings often have only one topic and focus. In such cases the teacher will call attention not to episodes, but rather to the words that lend cohesion to the single message system. If the presentation is chronological, words such as *next, whenever, afterwards* will provide rhetorical direction. Similarly, a presentation of a contrast, such as the photo-copier ad discussed in Chapter 6, uses words like *on the other hand, however, in comparison*, keying, in this instance, positive and negative characteristics.

Text-based phase: Recognition of discourse markers—their function and impact on language usage in the text (e.g., changes in word order). In a shorter text such recognition will be mainly of individual words—adverbs and conjunctions that signal connections between text ideas. In longer texts the reader's attention may need to focus on macromarkers in the sense of Chaudron and Richards—phrases or clauses that connect global features of the text (e.g., *as was stated at the outset, a major feature of the problem*). In the case of fiction or a longer article, shifts in topic, setting, or characters may signal a major subset of the textual message.

To encourage flexibility in recognizing such shifts, the teacher should, at least with novice readers or readers with low proficiencies in language, identify the type of features to be recognized: individual words, phrases, or clauses that overtly refer to previous text or signal a new direction in that text, or introduce new people, places, and locations. Assignments and activities must indicate how to identify macrodevelopments in texts, their message grammar. In a short text such as the hypothetical passage about happy marriages, three or four adverbs may be sufficient to point to the relationship between topics (e.g., happy couples) and comments (e.g., are *often, frequently, rarely, seldom* best friends). In a longer text on the same subject, a teacher might ask the class to find the points in the text where description of enduring marriages changes to discussion of societal changes that impact on marital stability. In a story echoing this topic, students might scan to pinpoint where "new characters are introduced" or at what point "the husband's thinking shifts from reflections on his marriage to speculations about single life."

Whether such assignments should be integrated into the students' outside reading or conducted in class or as a small-group activity will depend on language level and students' prior experience with successful encoding. As with stage one (the preview for content and rhetorical organization), stages two and three commence with the learner and subsequently direct the class to the text—to recognize and recall specific types of textual language. When conducted as an in-class activity, opportunities for feedback and clarification increase. By listening to hypotheses and comments that students make, teachers gain insight into their students' strategy use and understanding of discourse relationships.

In-class work with these procedures helps students reinforce actual use of metacognitive approaches to texts, strategies to which they may pay lip service but which they do not actually employ (Phifer & Glover). Apparently students must recognize that a strategy is useful before they will use it routinely or give up unproductive strategies (Baker & Brown). For example, L2 users of dictionaries in test situations have no advantage over non-users (Bensoussan, Sim & Weiss). If students see in daily practice that they can comprehend an L2 text without recourse to a dictionary, they will be more likely to attempt reading for gist rather than spend time on excessive dictionary use. In a classroom where reading emphasis is on reasonable inferences and rhetorical patterns rather than decoding a particular word, those metacognitive strategies are more likely to become routine.

The cautionary note here is that blanket assumptions about the value of particular strategies appear unfounded (Carrell 1989). Apparently, teachers do better to encourage strategic behaviors than to insist on specific strategies (Harri-Augstein & Thomas). As an illustration of how to engage a class in practice with open-ended strategies, Kern suggests Stauffer's Directed Reading, Directed Thinking Activity (hereinafter DRTA), an L1 reading technique. Because readers commence with speculation about a text topic, at first blush DRTA appears similar to previewing. It more closely resembles a second- or third-stage activity, however, since it focuses student attention on connecting macro- and micropropositions in the text. Usual procedure in DRTA allows students access to one text segment at a time as opposed to those previewing procedures in which students may look at the text as a whole if they choose.

Instead of asking students to find subsections of the text themselves, the DRTA approach asks the teacher to break the text down into segments. Each student has a copy of the text, and a blank sheet of paper. The teacher tells the class to cover some portions. As in the preview, the teacher asks open-ended questions about the title or paragraphs exposed (e.g., "What do you think this text will be about? Do you think this will be a story? an essay? a play?"). As in stage one, all inferences count. Jocular suggestions are welcome. Often the revisions made subsequent to reading are more memorable (the salience factor) when linked to humor or speculations that proved to be irrelevant. In the case of a passage entitled "Enduring Relationships," for example, typical answers might be: "What makes marriages work," "How to be happy in marriage," or "How to give up freedom gladly." As in stage one, regardless of the language used by students, the teacher records suggestions in L2.

Once several ideas have been offered, students read to test the different predictions just proposed. Like all strategy-based activities, DRTA works exclusively with open-ended questions. The goal is student processing of the text, not specific information. Consequently, when the class has finished reading the first segment, the teacher asks about student experience with the text, not questions about the text: "What do you think now?", "Why did you change your mind?" These questions encourage students to trust their own thinking rather than to rely on instructional guidance. Given such freedom, the class often uncovers additional details or questions the validity of original speculation (e.g., "This is a sociological study about marital happiness, not a personal story.").

Follow-up, like initiation of DRTA, involves more experiential questions: "What made you change your mind?" or "Why do you think that's an important idea?" Often when students explain the logic behind their statements and support their hypotheses by citing relevant portions of the text, seemingly unfounded or erroneous conclusions are clarified and make sense. Stipulating that students justify their positions with textual evidence not only discourages haphazard guessing, it also allows the teacher to better understand students' comprehension processes.

A wealth of reading activities is to be found in L1 literature. The only caveat here is that in FL classes, at least initially, neither absolute language restrictions (students may use either English or L2) nor mandatory participation characterize the interactive reading recommended in these procedures. As discussed in Chapter 4, students may benefit from conceptualizing a text in their native language. While they should be encouraged to use the L2, a higher priority for students lacking immersion practice is a relaxed class environment. This atmosphere alone promotes openness to a whole range of reading strategies. Research evidence increasingly suggests that students' strategy use is a very individual matter.

Students learn that there is no single way to read for meaning, that texts mean different things to different people, and that by pooling their L2 knowledge and various backgrounds they can teach one another. Students find in-class activities that explore their thinking (as opposed to their language ability) relatively enjoyable. Studies that measure the learning that occurs in small groups support claims that students profit from interaction with peers (e.g., Long & Porter; Pica & Doughty).

Stage 4. Comparison of word- and phrase-level reconstruction of textual information in matrices.

Reader-based phase: Students have already hypothesized about the global topic and comment of the text in stage one and substantiated the validity of that prediction in stages two and three. Although the text is the source to be confirmed, all of these tasks are reader-based to the extent that appropriate choices are the reader's responsibility. As long as they are text-based, those choices can be inaccurate in only two ways: (1) They can fail to correspond to the global features because they are trivial or extraneous to important information; (2) They are redundant or inconsistent.

These problems can be best illustrated by comparing two matrices, one adequate and the other flawed by trivial or inconsistent entries. Let us refer again to the hypothetical article on successful marriages. The class has established that information in this passage is organized around marital circumstances (features of the topic) and impact of those circumstances (comments on characteristics of the topic). Students create matrices, selecting two sets of textual information, one for the topic and one for the comment. The matrices look something like the examples below except for the fact that both would be written in the L2 of the text.

STUDENT #1:	*Types of Marriages*	*Characteristic Decisions*
	both husband and wife with careers	no children
	wife at home	two children, not enough money
	wife works temporarily	can buy a home, delay family

STUDENT #2:	*Types of Marriages*	*Characteristic Decisions*
	both husband and wife have careers	no children
	not enough money	two children
	wife a lawyer	husband a lawyer

Assuming that she has created an adequate reflection of the text, only student #1 conveys an informative pattern. Student #1's marriage and decision categories contrast and are consistent. In the left-hand column all entries present features of people. The right-hand column lists the impact of circumstances in column one with respect to the couple's priorities (children, home, money). The reader of this matrix will have a sense of what the article said. Student #2 does not fare so well. She disregards both the standard of contrast and consistency. Thus, when her matrix is read horizontally, the last entry of both the left- and right-hand columns is uninformative. The fact that both people are lawyers may be important information in another context, but not by the macrorelationships suggested by this matrix. The fact that one partner is a lawyer neither influences, contrasts with, nor creates problems for the other lawyer-partner in this matrix. The information is redundant, adding nothing to a reader's grasp of the text.

As an example of the second problem, inconsistency is revealed when the information matrix is read vertically. Student #2 mixes people and money in the left-hand column. Not enough money is a comment, not a topic of this matrix. Money shortages may arise in the course of a marriage, but only people and their activities are responsible. Subsuming career choices and money shortages to the topic *types of marriages* reveals a logical problem.

This comparison illustrates the metacognitive skills needed to produce an informative matrix. Students must be able to group sets and subsets of information. Random or summary entries fail to convey comprehension of textual relationships. The entry *not enough money* might be the result of poor career choices or spendthrift ways. If the entry *not enough money* was opposed by the entry *unable to go to school*, the relationship would be clear. It becomes even clearer when the global topic of the text is identified as *problems of the unemployed* and the macrocomment as *origins of those problems*.

Text-based phase: Since the student task is to identify information, the teacher must assess whether that identification is adequate to the text. That is not always an easy task. The problems are less a matter of inherent difficulty than of suspicion of the task. Teachers have been trained to interpret texts, not to first engage in neutral assessments of their content. Particularly FL teachers, many of whom are trained in applying theories of critical analysis, have relatively little training in monitoring the distinction between registering information and interpreting it. Awareness of the difference between acknowledging what the text says and interpreting what the text says is a metacognitive distinction that students need, or their conclusions about text meaning will fail to distinguish between text and reader.

Registering what the text says as a meaningful "other" is an essential step that precedes interpretation. It is in such registering and sorting of textual propositions that practice in linking meaning and language occurs. Of unquestioned value as well is the bridge between input of global meaning and intake of the details, the groundwork for later interpretation.

What happens when that groundwork is not laid? Think back to classes in which students confirm registration of meaning in discrete questions and then suddenly have to answer interpretive questions. Silence ensues. Students often resort to answers in their native language. Despite this relatively common experience, textbooks persist in presenting one set of questions to confirm the students' ability to answer questions about isolated facts (e.g., "How many of the married women who work have children under five years of age?"), followed by a second set that asks students to interpret textual messages (e.g., "Discuss whether married women with young children ought to work."). Such questions are frustrating and unproductive if they are asked before the issues in the text and the language expressive of those issues have been clarified in the students' minds.

The plea here is for a registration of textual messages on the text's terms. Student matrices need not be extensive. What good matrices do is to exhibit a student's awareness of the way information is weighted and organized in the text. If, for example, the text about happy couples dealt with how couples married for a long time felt about each other for ninety-five percent of the text and made only a few parenthetical comments about two family breadwinners, the very logical statements made by student #1 above would be incorrect. The matrix could consist of beautiful statements, logically presented, but those statements would be an inadequate representation of the text, a failure to replicate textual emphases on fundamental messages.

Stage 5. Sentence-level reconstruction of textual information.

Reader-based phase: Readers engage in small-group work or written assignments based on in-class practice in which the instructor introduces the particular sentential features relevant to the text read (e.g., adverbs of time, subordinating conjunctions, relative clauses, tense or mood changes, negation). Students expand the text phrases in their matrices into simple sentences. They modify formal properties of textual language according to the teachers' perception of their chief deficiencies in comprehensible output.

In so doing, students create the language of factual details in the text that relates to perceived macromessages of that text. The complexity of the sentence-level work will depend on the learning level of the class, for it is at this point in the sequence that mastery of formal features becomes a major learning goal. To some extent the text itself dictates the linguistic features to be dealt with (e.g., a descriptive text with many relative clauses). Often, however, suitable exercises can be devised by the instructor. For a text about enduring marriages, the creation of simple sentences on the basis of text language might be challenging enough for beginning levels. Based on her matrix of information, student #1 might expand her table into descriptive sentences as follows:

Features	Implications
Both husband and wife work.	The family has no children, owns home.
The wife stays home.	The family has two children. Money is short, family rents home.
The wife works for some years.	The family buys a home. The family has children later.

To render these sentences more readable and introduce notions of current trends in family life, students might be asked to insert adverbial expressions such as *frequently*, *occasionally*, *sometimes*, *increasingly*, *less and less*, and *more and more*. As a further illustration, if the instructor feels students need practice in using *neither*, *no*, or *not*, these words could be introduced by asking students to negate their matrix by introducing a reverse logic. Student #1 might create sentences such as *The family has no children*, *The wife does not stay home*. Not all sentences will be negative, however. If the first sentence in the left-hand column is negated (*The wife does not work*), then the right-hand sentence might change (*The family has children*).

Although a limited amount of language is being manipulated, creativity plays a role as long as assignments are keyed by changes in context rather than by formal grammar terms. Contextual drills allow students to think about the sense relationships of their sentences. As a further example of how to link formal practice to expression of thought, students could be asked to decide which behaviors in the matrix were more typical of the white middle class of America in the 1920s as opposed to the 1980s. *In the 1920s women stayed home. In the 1980s more women work.* Here the exercise links changes in verb tense to student perceptions rather than responses to cues about tense. Introduction of modal verbs might occur through a teacher's recontextualization, such as "Introduce degrees of restriction into the statements about women working. Use words such as *can, must, should, will,* or *may*" (e.g., *Women can work. They may have children, too*).

When work with complex clauses is introduced, the matrix lends itself well to practice in joining sentences. As will be discussed in further detail in Chapter 7, adding modals or joining sentences can change the thrust of discourse by introducing restrictions, description, causality, contrast, or expressions of personal conviction (e.g., *I think, suggest, believe*). Joining sentences is a step that leads to supersentential discourse. As with the purely sentential exercises, the assignment is designed to illustrate how various types of complex sentences help communicate a particular kind of thought.

Students need to be aware that different combinations of discourse markers alter communicative impact. Rather than treating formal features such as relative clauses as mechanical changes in usage, recontextualized exercises reveal the communicative function of these changes. They also should result in better intake and more comprehensible output in written and spoken practice.

For example, the passage on women working lends itself well to a discourse on causality—already implied in the matrix as a question of cause (*Both husband and wife work*) and implied effect (*The family is without children*). If students are told that their communicative goal is to clarify cause and effect through words such as *therefore, as a result, consequently,* or *because,* they can manipulate their matrix information by fronting various pieces. They are asked to consider whether the sentence *Both husband and wife work; therefore, the family decides not to have children* has the same implications as the assertion *The family decides not to have children, so both husband and wife work.* In this instance the communicative force of the second sentence subtly alters the impact of work on family life. Whether or not both partners work results from the decision not to have children rather than the other way around.

Shifting factual relationships through introduction of cause and effect is one way in which many presumably factual texts manipulate their readers. When an output exercise keys communicative function to a modified context, it can offer two types of learning at the same time: (1) automaticity practice in developing language skills, (2) cognitive practice for developing awareness of the ways in which discourse techniques can modify textual messages. If these exercise goals are met, comprehensible output based on reading reinforces a student's grasp of the way language modifies comprehensible intake.

Text-based phase: Written manipulation of vocabulary and structures in the text follows initial practice in recognition of vocabulary and structures. Stage four, a selective copying task, represents the student's transition from general recognition of language associated with the text's macropropositions to partial control of that language in expression of micropropositions found in the text. Written practice introduced in stage five is the fulcrum in a hierarchy of comprehension and production tasks. It links recognition and use in terms of textual meaning, because the objective of written exercises at this stage is to actualize reader knowledge in terms of textual structures. Adults prefer to write before they talk about answers because in the written mode they have adequate processing time to reflect (Loughrin-Sacco et al.). Moreover, the design of this sequence combines rereading and analysis of textual language with the writing task, a combination recommended by increasing numbers of studies (e.g., Connor; Dvorak).

The sequence also establishes and distinguishes between reader-based and text-based comprehension before encouraging students to merge these positions in statements about their textual inferences. As the following section illustrates, each stage has a built-in checkpoint between student conceptions of what the text says and actual assertions made in the text. Stage one, previewing, involves both a speculation and a confirmation task. Stages two through five, optionally conducted as group work or assignments outside of class, all ask students to establish textual facts in terms of explicit (text-based) and implicit (reader-based) information. The final stage represents a synthesis of text and reader. In these procedures, interpretation is the point at which the reader's discourse reconstructs the discourse of the text.

Stage 6. Supersentential construction of the reader's opinion about textual information.

Reader-based phase: Students generate at least four or five connected sentences on the topic of their sentential statements created in stage five. As in the preceding level, relevant discourse markers and their impact on formal features, such as case or word order, must be introduced by the teacher. Students use the language of factual details gleaned from the matrix and sentence practice to express a personal point of view, present alternative solutions to textual problems, or critique the messages of the text. In that sense the only text base for this activity is as a reference about language use and confirmation of student assertions. Stage six is predominantly a reader-based exercise designed to promote comprehensible output of extended discourse.

Even when a class has studied the syntactic rules governing discourse connectors in the L2, class time needs to be devoted to illustration of how different types of connections between sentences convey particular meanings or directions in a discourse. This practice helps students keep in mind that the formal features in supersentential exercises enable expression of a particular speaker or writer intent.

Since class discussion of discourse markers emphasizes language use (communicative functions) rather than usage (correctness rules), foreign-language teachers find it relatively easy for the class to stay in the second language throughout the exercise. The language of formal grammar explanations designed to cover all contingencies (usage) frustrates ESL teachers and tempts FL teachers into abstract explanations in English. Limiting the context to a text matrix frees teachers from having to explain the *langue* of speech act potentials and the range of contexts in which those speech acts may occur. Instead, the class works with a finite number of sentences that communicate ideas about a text.

Here are several examples of how a classroom activity with blackboard or transparency review might take place. For an introduction to stage six, supersentential expression of personal opinion, the teacher might commence with an open-ended solicitation of sample sentences from stage five (e.g., "What are typical statements made in this text?"). Sentences that are volunteered are listed at the far left of the blackboard, accessible to but separate from the main focus of the exercise. In the middle of the blackboard is a list of the discourse markers reflecting a particular logic, preferably one established with the help of students responding to the following open-ended prompting:

"I can say 'I believe' it's going to rain today if I want to express my opinion. What other L2 words (verbs) can you use to express your convictions in Spanish (French, German, or English)?" With the resultant list, students can generate sentences that develop ideas.

If, for example, students are asked to express personal convictions after the sentence *Often women stay home to raise a family*, they can choose a second sentence from the left-hand list on the blackboard, but precede it with *I believe that*, or *I think, I am convinced, I suggest*, etc. (*such families have less money, decide children are important*). Naturally the sentences available on the left-hand side of the blackboard reflect the particular sentential practice in stage five. Some discourse gambits are more compatible with particular grammar functions than others. For expression of personal convictions, for example, sentences that use modals or negation are particularly well suited. Reader sentences might yield options such as *I believe a woman can work and still have a family* or *I think that a man should stay home and raise the family* or *I think the wife should not work*.

Alternatively, if students have already reviewed conjunctions in their sentential practice, the discourse logic of contrasts might be appropriate. They would be asked to contrast the advantages and disadvantages of a family in which both parents work. The class would create a list of representative conjunctions that contrast ideas (for specifications of such a list, see the table at the end of this chapter and possibly L2 vocabulary for *advantage* and *disadvantage*). To illustrate the shift in discourse, it is useful to work with a single blackboard sentence. After a sentence such as *Often women stay home to raise a family*, two or three subsequent sentences could each tag a different discourse. The range of options might yield the following:

CONTRAST LOGIC: *But* (. . . women can still earn money, have a job, be happy, etc.)

CAUSE / EFFECT: *As a result* (. . . women delay a career, have no career, spend a lot of time with children, family cannot buy a home, etc.)

As in the preceding example, the discourse direction would depend to some degree on the personal convictions of students. In a cause / effect logic, however, more language is available to follow connectives such as *therefore, as a result, because* than the contrastive markers such as *on the other hand, nonetheless*, or *however*. The text bias is thus revealed to students in terms of the language they have available to express personal convictions. Of course, as students become more proficient, they will need to rely less heavily on the text as a language model. Initially, an inherent advantage of integrating text-based reading with writing and speaking is that it circumvents the temptation to translate. Students whose assignment is to use text language to express their propositions have a disincentive to engage in translation. Whether grammatically correct or not, translation is extraneous to the goals of these procedures.

Subsequent to a five- or ten-minute review of how discourse markers serve as tags for communication, students might want to work in small groups to create essays. Alternatively, the teacher may want them to write out individual assignments outside of class. In this case, the following class session could devote a short time to discussion of essays.

Since the six stages have built student command of language in expanding increments, the final participation task is feasible. Students can reasonably be expected to volunteer to read their statements aloud or to express some of the ideas contained in a written draft. That rare event, class discussion in the foreign language, can now take place with reasonable assurance of representative participation. Often a provoking statement by the teacher ("Who agrees with me that a woman's place is in the home?") suffices to get things started. On the other hand, a teacher must really be interested in divergent views and respect student willingness to participate. Exclusive concern for formal accuracy inhibits spontaneous observations and teaches that fellow students have little to say that is worth listening to. In such classrooms students attend only to the teacher, thereby losing opportunities for listening comprehension.

The tradition of authoritarian classrooms discourages attentive listening to fellow students, since questions and spontaneous observations stem mainly from the teacher. Yet peer input seems to demonstrate pedagogical value equivalent to, if different from, that of the teacher (e.g., Pica & Doughty). If students fail to pay attention to each other the instructor might want to motivate careful listening by constructing a memory game (e.g., "What does student #1 say that student #2 does not?") or by asking the class to take brief notes on each other's statements in order to summarize the gist of those remarks.

After all six stages have been worked through, a first-year language student will have partial control of conjunctions and modals. In effect, stages five and six are both contextual drills which allow freedom to express a personal opinion, but within the limitations set by a specific text. Based on the hypothetical article about modern marriages, the resultant essay might read as follows:

SAMPLE SHORT ESSAY

I agree that it is hard to work and raise a family. A mother at home may be OK. But I believe it can mean less money for the home and children. Working women are able to earn money. A family with children will use lots of money. Therefore I think that both husband and wife should work.

Initial work in speaking and writing connected sentences such as the sample above will be neither elegant nor altogether cohesive. Transitions will be missing. The substitution of pronouns for nouns or fronting of adverbial connectors may not occur unless emphasized as goals of the exercise. But such essays will let students express thoughts and develop ideas in the second language. For beginning language students, the focus is necessarily on a limited number of features representative of a particular discourse logic. Teacher evaluation should set standards for performance within the restrictions of the procedural stages: (1) use of the vocabulary and structures of a text is the basis for simple descriptive statements, (2) reliance on a personal opinion guides decisions about how to restructure those statements, and (3) use of discourse markers is consistent with a particular speech act (e.g., expression of opinions, analysis of ideas).

CONCLUSIONS

The six procedural stages detailed above represent realizations of tasks that attempt to cope with the common hazards of reading for meaning in the foreign language with familiar schemata. Later in the book we will address problems inherent in L2 readers of texts with unfamiliar schemata. Up to now the objective has been to present a model for beginners in language learning that seems operable for more advanced students as well. The procedures are designed to promote three types of cognitive processes in the reader: (1) processes that identify global features of the text as a message system, (2) processes that link global features to their illustrative detail, and (3) processes that enable the reader to establish implicitly- as well as explicitly-stated messages of the text.

While the three processes probably occur simultaneously in an L1 reader, our L2 model stresses a text-based perspective initially. It does so to forestall the misreading or inferior comprehension that results when students read reactively rather than interactively. In the chapter that follows, we discuss the metacognitive strategies activated in these stages and illustrate their application in classroom reading of a short work of fiction.

NOTES TO CHAPTER 5

1. Notable among the L1 models of interactive reading: LaBerge & Samuels; McClelland & Rumelhart; Perfetti; Stanovich. In addition, our construct owes a heavy debt to Meyer and to Kintsch & van Dijk (1978). For L2, the authors have drawn features from models that have dealt with learning theories, notably Bialystok; Krashen; McLaughlin; as well as models of interactive reading in isolation, e.g., Bernhardt, or reading and listening as comprehension equivalent processes, e.g., Nagle & Sanders.

APPENDIX TO CHAPTER 5

The following table summarizes common markers of discourse logic. These words need to be recognized as signals for particular relationships between previous sentences and paragraphs and the text that follows.

TYPES OF INTERSENTENTIAL RELATIONSHIPS

Type of Relationship	Meaning	Connectives
1. *Enumerative*		
1.1 Listing	What follows outlines the order in which things are to be said.	first, second, etc., one, to begin with, next, then, finally, last(ly), etc.
1.2 Time sequence	What follows outlines the time sequence in which things happen.	first(ly), in the beginning, next, then, subsequently, eventually, finally, in the end, etc.
2. *Additive*		
2.1 Reinforcing	What follows suggests a reinforcement of what has been said.	and, again*, also*, moreover, furthermore, in addition, etc.
2.2 Similarity	What follows is similar to what has been said before.	equally*, likewise, similarly*, etc.
3. *Logical Sequence*		
3.1 Summative	What follows summarizes what has been said before.	so, altogether*, overall*, then, thus, therefore, in short, etc.
3.2 Resultative	What follows is a result of what has been said before.	so, as a result, consequently

TYPES OF INTERSENTENTIAL RELATIONSHIPS (*continued*)

Type of Relationship	*Meaning*	*Connectives*
3.3 Deductive	What follows is an observation which may be deduced logically from the generalization that has preceded it.	so, therefore, hence*, thus, consequently
3.4 Inductive	What follows is a generalization based on observations that have gone before.	therefore, hence*, thus so, this shows / indicates that, etc.
4. *Explicative*		
	What follows explains or glosses what has been said before.	namely, thus, in other words, that is (to say)*, by (this) we mean*
5. *Illustrative*		
	What follows is an illustration of an example of what has been said before.	for example, for instance
6. *Contrastive*		
6.1 Substitutive	What follows is a preferred rewording of what has been said before.	better*, rather*, in other words, etc.
6.2 Replacive	What follows is a replacement of what has been said before.	alternatively, instead, (but) then, rather, etc.
6.3 Antithetic	What follows is in complete opposition to what has been said before.	conversely, on the other hand, oppositely, etc.
6.4 Concessive	What has been said before is conceded as true or correct, but what follows is, in contrast, also true or correct.	but, however, nevertheless, still*, nonetheless, notwithstanding, etc.

Note: those with an asterisk occur in initial position only.

From Ronald Mackay and Alan Mountford, "Reading for Information," from *Reading in a Second Language,* eds. Ronald Mackay et al., 1979.

Six

Meaning, Metacognition, and Propositions

Readers' metacognitive orientations are sometimes referred to as their internalized models of reading. Although reading is an interactive process, combining both top-down (gist, story episodes) and bottom-up factors (letter, word, and sentence meanings), metacognitive processes—*the way the reader organizes and acts on textual information*—can affect that reader's success or failure in understanding a text. That organization will involve both top-down and bottom-up strategies. What researchers look for is an effective synthesis between the two. If reading is an interactive process, reliance on a single style of processing generally will lead to problems in text comprehension.

Our procedural model proposed in Chapter 5 synthesizes top-down and bottom-up processes through a focus on textual message systems. Although the procedures refer to different levels of messages and a range of tasks for identifying them, the dominant focus for all stages is the development of textual meaning. Thus, Chapter 6 will look at how reader comprehension processes interact with components of language to create text meaning.

For purposes of discussion, the *meaning* a reader gets from the text is abstract, an unexpressed idea. In other words, text meaning is a nonobservable, mental response to language. When L2 readers identify individual textual lexemes to express their mental response to a text, they are halfway towards language production. In order to express meaning—the basic ideas behind the lexemes—ideas must be structured; that is, they must be organized syntactically. In that fashion they are placed into conceptual relationships that a reader perceives or intends. Therefore, when we talk about language *structure* in this chapter, we mean the speaker's or writer's concrete manifestation of thought in observable language. Before we explore how to structure readers' ideas, however, we must consider how readers determine meaning—what strategies or *metacognition* foster their mental interaction with textual ideas.

MEANING AS METACOGNITIVE PERSPECTIVE

Relatively few ESL and FL studies have explored the correspondence between readers' perceptions of their metacognitive strategies and their reading performance. Research comparing self-awareness about use of top-down (e.g., "I pay most attention to what the reading passage means") or bottom-up strategies (e.g., "I pay most attention to what individual words mean") tends to show three things. First, readers with low proficiency are more likely to use bottom-up strategies (Carrell 1989). Second, conscious application of global reading strategies correlates positively with reading performance at intermediate or advanced proficiency levels (Benedetto; Hosenfeld). Third, explicit instruction in the strategies outlined in our procedural model has a positive impact on reading performance (Barnett 1988a; Kern). Although relatively few such studies exist, these findings are supported by more extensive research in related areas.

Research in L1 supports the notion that metacognitive strategies are pivotal factors in reading comprehension (e.g., Geva; Geva & Ryan; Singer & Donlan). Studies in L2, although limited, seem to suggest that some stages in metacognitive processing may be particularly critical. Apparently, a reader's application of her grasp of text organization and her reaction to content play a seminal role. Both metacognitive research and studies in related fields of schemata and error analysis suggest that the most successful reader and text interaction involves keeping meaning in mind. When a reader's primary focus is on meaning—sometimes called textual propositions or idea units—reading performance is superior to a reader focus on individual words or the pronunciation of words. If, for example, students read "dimes" for "money," they probably encode—they read for meaning. Students who read "many" are not attending to meaning—their decoding is word- or sound-based.

In her ESL work, Devine identifies meaning-centered readers as those "who in their interviews indicated that they considered understanding what the author wanted to say as the measure of successful reading" (Devine 129). Devine's analysis of twenty low-intermediate students of English (ESL) revealed that recall and comprehension of the text was significantly higher for meaning-centered students than for readers who equated good reading with accurate pronunciation or word identification. Devine also conducted an in-depth study of three students who exemplified these reading styles. The meaning-centered student, who had the same language proficiency level as the other two readers, was *"far more successful in her efforts to read in English"* (126, italics ours).

The notion of meaning-centered readers raises the intriguing question: What is "understanding what the author wanted to say"? How much meaning originates with the author? How much originates with the reader? As Block's research documented, not all students' concepts of reading for meaning are equal (Chapter 4). Block's work does, however, shed light on Devine's findings. Devine's successful readers probably had what Block called an *integrated perspective*, the perspective of someone who registered text messages objectively rather than reacting to those messages. In view of the corroborating studies on misreading as being attributable to faulty applications of schemata rather than language deficiencies, Block's research touches on a central issue in the negotiation of meaning between text and reader: establishing the metacognitive components of objectivity.

Block has examined perspective as an overriding strategy—the governor of metacognitive processing. Her integrators "applied information or experience from their own lives to the information in the text" (486). They checked textual information against their personal knowledge and experience and then returned to textual statements to check the match between their background and textual assertions. Such a student might begin reading and observe: "Metal fatigue and air safety. I've read about accidents where planes lost engines or pieces of the outer hull. Here the text reviews the causes of such accidents. . . ." Non-integrators, on the other hand, reacted affectively to textual information, e.g., "Metal fatigue. I'll bet this is about airplane crashes. I'm terrified about flying. . . ." Instead of addressing textual messages, non-integrators talked primarily about their feelings. After these initial reactions, non-integrators rarely returned to the text to reconsider the author's ideas or to distinguish those ideas from their own subjective responses. Most observations were in the first rather than the third person.

INITIAL OBJECTIVITY TO ESTABLISH TEXTUAL MEANING

The dictionary defines objectivity as "exhibiting or characterized by emphasis upon or the tendency to view events, phenomena, ideas, etc., as external and apart from self-consciousness." To effect comprehension, an objective strategist can only be detached up to a point, because to be meaningful, information must be comprehended as a logical system. That is why our model presented in Chapter 5 defines text meaning in terms of *four external factors that must be systematized by the reader*: the two macrofactors of global topic and rhetorical organization of that topic, and the two microfactors of detailed information and the language expressing those details. Whether addressing macro- or microfeatures, all of the procedures organize textual information in the same pattern: as topics (subjects or agents of action) and their comments (what is said about them).

The language is that of the text, but the conceptual organization of that language is the reader's. Literate adults have the ability to synthesize information on the basis of abstract principles. Language manifests that synthesis of text words and the reader's capacity to organize those words conceptually. The organization of language is syntagmatic, a linear pattern of relationships between topics and comments about those topics. The reader must be able to comprehend these units and synthesize them to be able to comprehend a text's meaning as semantics. Because a text exists within the larger systems of human society, the reader must be able to organize its intent, structure, and goals in terms of a message which communicates in its context—its pragmatic implications.

Here we have stated in a very simple way an application of current thinking about functional syntax and pragmatic grammars. Formal grammars, the grammars that represent language on the basis of mapping rules between syntax, semantics, and phonology, can tell us how language works according to an accuracy norm. But they view language itself as a system of internal rules, unaffected by social or personal needs. While formal grammars can tell us what sentences can occur, functional grammars will predict when certain sentences are likely to occur. In other words, such grammars examine how speaker intent influences the way that speaker structures a sentence.

Functional grammars explain why Aunt Catherine is more likely to say "Gracious, it's hot today" than "Heavenly days, it's hot today." In a story about Aunt Catherine such grammars point out how the functions of explicit or implicit references about her age, upbringing, and convictions form a pattern that leads her to say "gracious" and not "heavenly days." Functional grammars treat text language and text message as polysemes—congruent systems.

Whether at the word, phrase, sentence, or discourse level, textual messages are realized as topics and comments. The topic is always an agent or an experiencer (stated or assumed). If an *agent*, the comment expresses an observable *action, physical state*, or a *change of state or condition*. That comment may include a receiver of the agent's actions—what it or they do (e.g., "hit the ball"); or how it or they behave (a physical state such as "had good outfielders") as well as when they do it ("Saturday afternoon") and where ("Wrigley Field"). If an *experiencer*, the comment is about an unobservable *mental state or condition* (Chafe; Fillmore). Typically a mental process or disposition is described, e.g., "[batting records] were considered" or "[she] heard the crowd roar."[1]

Thus macrofeatures of both topics and comments can be identified in semantic terms just as they are set up in stage one of the procedural model: *who* (nouns or pronouns), *what* (verbs), *when* (adverbial expressions of time), and *where* (nouns, prepositional phrases, adverbial expressions of location). The pattern of propositional cues that relies totally on semantic cues and simple verbs will be descriptive or locutionary. Those cues and possible statements could look like this:

> *who* (agent) + *what* (past action) = She saw the girl. [or] They had lunch.
> *who* (agent) + *when* (future action) = = I'll arive at 3 p.m. [or] I'll return later this evening.

CREATING SIMPLE STATEMENTS WITH PROPOSITIONAL CUES

Let us imagine a picture that illustrates propositional cues: for instance, a single-panel cartoon of a little child playing ball in the yard under the full sun. The cue could be "who / what + what." The "who or what" is the topic of the sentence, the main subject matter of the scene. Some viewers conceptualize the drawing as primarily about a "who." For them the grammatical subject of the sentence is "a child." Possible sentences produced from this view might be "The child (topic) is playing (comment)" or "The child (topic) saw the ball (comment)."

For viewers whose attention is drawn to an activity, for example, the scene conveys a "what," e.g., "playing ball" or "throwing a ball." When students focus on the activity rather than the person engaged in the activity, they create sentences such as "Playing ball (topic) is fun" (if the child is smiling) or "Throwing a ball (topic) is boring" (if the child's expression is vacant). When cues asked for "who *or* what," all four sentences are equally valid statements about the picture.

For more specific information, the cue can be limited to "who + what" (The child throws the ball") or "what + what" ("Playing ball is fun"). To be even more specific, the cues can be linked to a definite context, e.g., "who (children in the story) + what" or, if the instructor wants the second answer, the cue might read "what (activities children undertake) + what." These elaborations encourage students to refer to the text both for information and to establish how similar concepts are expressed. Explicit links to a reading passage mean the propositional cues focus on a passage's content—the student's grasp of "who did what" in a particular context. *When linked to a text, cues ask not only for accurate assessment of language usage in the text, but also for accurate assessment of textual facts.*

Both of the preceding sentences are described propositionally as "who + what," a grammatical subject plus a verb plus what that verb requires to finish its sense—in other words, its complement. In writing propositional cues for the comment (the "what"), a teacher may want to include additional information to elicit conceptual details or grammatical forms. As in the preceding example, more cues (e.g., about tense or number) mean the finished sentence will be more predictable in its structural form.

As an illlustration, a " + where" added to the simple cue "who + what" expands a simple description. With the addition of further complements the expansion continues. At the same time, this is no discrete-point activity that limits expressive options. The story might imply multiple responses: "throws the ball in the backyard," "into the air," "at home" (an idiom, not a straight prepositional phrase, in many languages), or even "there / here." A "who + what" cue in no way precludes the addition of adverbial expressions of location; "who + what + where" simply reminds the student that adverbials are appropriate; only "who + what + where (prepositional phrase)" restricts the utterance to a specific category of adverbial expressions. Regardless of the type of cue, students must use either familiar vocabulary or structures, or reread a text to find the appropriate grammatical and vocabulary items.

One advantage of using the text as grammar model has to do with the fact that details of case and morphology are the most challenging for adult learners of a second language. Studies of late immersion programs indicate that these features are a realm where adults, in most respects more rapid acquirers of L2, lag behind children (Swain 1985). If, for example, ESL students read about someone "partaking of" smoked duck as a synonym for "eating," they may be unaware of the difference in structure. With a text model to refer to, however, students can confirm the necessity of the preposition "of." Word lists in textbooks typically obscure these usage distinctions, since they tend to list "to partake," give a definition, and then mention " + of." The frequency and applications of this usage remain abstract. In contrast, if students look at a text's use, they see characters in a story "partaking of [something]." Meaning and language structure are synthesized.

FACTORS IN READER BACKGROUND AND EXPECTATIONS THAT INHIBIT PERCEPTION OF TEXTUAL INTENT

To move beyond description and become illocutionary, the propositional cues above must add some language features: complex verbs such as modals, adverbial expressions, complex sentences with conjunctions. A pragmatic approach does account for extra-linguistic variables: body language, intonation, or situational variables that change meaning. Students in a classroom, however, need to deal with linguistic cues because they lack the information necessary to refocus linguistically-ambiguous statements. For example, if William says "It's really hot" to Katie, who is sitting next to the air conditioner, he could be describing the weather (a descriptive or locutionary statement), or he might be suggesting she turn on that air conditioner (an oblique request or illocutionary statement).

Language students, particularly those studying foreign languages, lack exposure outside of class to the social implications and cultural applications of the language they are learning. Students of English who live in the United States, Canada, or England learn from their immersion experience that context alone can turn a purely descriptive statement about one thing into a description of another. The comment "It's really hot" has no meteorological implications in the context of discussion about a best-selling record.

When they read, L2 students are generally exposed to new contexts for familiar expressions. Part of the difficulty L2 readers have if they do not start reading for meaning early in their language learning is that they do not understand how a word or phrase can assume new implications in a new context.

Intonational patterns or inflections can also alter meaning. The whispered comment "The files go in the *corner* cabinet" could be an implied criticism (i.e., "That idiot can't learn to put things where they belong."). Without intonational emphasis the statement would be a neutral descriptive comment. Here too, classroom learners are at a disadvantage because they lack the linguistic sensitivity to changes in intonation that signal changed intent. Texts, on the other hand, generally provide a clear context and a series of descriptions or events that begin to clarify language which, in isolation, could well be enigmatic.

MEANINGS SUGGESTED BY VERB GROUPS

Unambiguous texts, like unambiguous illocutions, generally use explicit cues about how they should be interpreted. These cues are often syntactic features—complex verbs such as modals to suggest opinion, adverbial expressions that identify time or location, or complex sentences with conjunctions that cue cause and effect or comparison. Taken together, such features express dynamic relationships between topics and their comments. Cumulatively they develop a pragmatic force in the sense of making their message compelling to the reader. Their structural manifestation in language reveals an intent to do something: i.e., persuade, argue, negotiate, satirize.

The force of textual illocution stems from multiple factors—context (e.g., timeliness), content (e.g., intelligibility), and clear rhetorical structure. Clarity in rhetorical structure is a function of links between idea units. The simpler the idea unit, the easier it is to grasp its meaning. At a fundamental level of simplicity, idea units with single-verb groups cue simple sentences that can be visualized as single picture frames of an activity or physical state. Regardless of whether speakers describe an individual who "sings," "is singing," or "has sung," they convey only one image, one camera focus on the activity.

At a more complex level, a synthesis of two pictures or two ideas introduces a speaker's viewpoint or two picture frames. Cues for such sentences have two verb groups (auxiliary or modal verb + main verb, or two clauses, each with its own verb). By using the term "verb group" we distinguish between the ordinary concept of compound verbs as markers of tense, mood, and aspect, and two or more verbs which introduce a dual content in a proposition. "Can go" constitutes two verb groups because it conveys two ideas: "ability + go." In contrast, "are going" constitutes a single group with two pieces: "go" modified by only time and aspectual implications, "go + tense + aspect."

As an illustration, consider a picture of someone with her mouth open and an orchestra in the background. With these visual cues, a viewer might express the following inference: "The woman's mouth is open. There is an orchestra in the background. The woman *must be singing*." In saying "two verb groups," we are referring here to the two verbs *must* + *sing*. The verb *must* modifies the simple proposition of singing. It further suggests a viewer's inference rather than verified fact. This duality between fact and inference, picture and viewer, occurs with all statements of conditions, restrictions, or limits, e.g., "I think she is singing," "I hear her sing," or "She might be singing."

Excluded from this category are auxiliary verbs which emerge only as tense, aspect, or mood markers (go—*have* gone; go—*is* going; go—*would have* gone). Whether we say "She might be singing," or "She might have been singing," the shift in tense does not change the inferential quality of the statement.

Verbs that mark tense, aspect, or mood only expand a single thought: past tense, or "things we *have done*"; progressive, or "things they *are doing*"; conditional past tense, or "things they *would have* done." Such markers never subdivide concepts into two parts because this type of auxiliary verb is inseparable from its main verb. Changes are changes in modality, not in propositional content. Maintaining tense or the conditional is only a consistency factor in a particular discourse.

Conversely, a two-verb group with two types of propositional content can be envisioned separately. A statement beginning with "what I saw" or "what I heard" is one picture, e.g., a cartoon with a person who has a "think bubble" depicting a different scene ("Clark Kent was a mild-mannered reporter"). The distinction can also be visualized as a two-panel cartoon with a before (mild-mannered reporter) and after (Superman) scenario. In either event, the result is a juxtaposition of two images.

At the level of meaning (semantically), these two-image propositions correspond to judging, qualifying, modifying, limiting, or adding conditions ("If," "Thereafter," "I think," "When [I am Clark Kent, Superman. . . .]"). At the level of grammatical form (syntactically), these two-verb-group sentences can have either one or two clauses, or they can be two independent sentences with parallel structures connected through the use of adverbial expressions. For example:

ONE CLAUSE: *who + what* (qualifying) = He is too mild-mannered to be Superman.

TWO CLAUSE: *who + what* (limiting) // who + what = I believe that he is too mild-mannered to be Superman. (// represent clause boundaries)

PARALLEL CLAUSES: *who + what* + adverbial connector = First of all, he is a newspaper reporter. Second, he is mild-mannered.

With modal verbs, for example, a speaker links two ideas by using verb forms. "Superman flies" is one picture; "Superman likes to fly" adds a "close-up" of his smiling face; "he may fly" cuts from the upturned faces of the crowd below to the caped figure on the building above. Since the cues lack referential qualities (i.e., without a reference any "who" will do), a text or a real-life situation must provide the actual focus.

As an example, imagine the situation "things Superman likes to do on holidays." The students' cue is "who + what (auxiliary verb)"—yielding not only "Superman likes to dance" but perhaps also "He prefers to foxtrot." Tenses may be added or formal features specified, e.g., "modal verb, past tense." Regardless of formal specifications, the situation cue must refer to a context in a reading passage. In all situations, the resulting sentences imply simple restrictions on or qualifications of the central propositional notion "Superman dances" expressed in our hypothetical passage.

At this juncture we leave Superman and turn to sleuths. Superman lends himself to exemplification of descriptive options, concrete visualizations familiar to us in cartoons. Murder mysteries have more elaborate structures—rhetorical scenarios of verbally-defined relationships. Consequently they lend themselves more readily to a discussion of adverbial connectors and two-clause sentences with conjunctions—the discourse markers that are keys to understanding discursive intent.

MEANINGS ESTABLISHED
THROUGH DISCOURSE MARKERS

We have illustrated how descriptive propositions become restricted illocutions—a dual or complex perspective necessitating two verbs instead of one. More complicated qualifications take us into the realm of extended discourse or chained propositions. Chained propositions require either two largely parallel sentences with a proper adverbial connector, or a two-clause sentence with a conjunction. As was true of restricted propositions, however, only the general rhetorical outlines of these sentences are prescribed, not the exact grammatical form.

Chained propositions can, for example, elaborate on what the speaker sees, hears, believes, or hopes in a restricted proposition. Assuming a murder mystery scenario, a situation cue of this type could be: "what the speaker believes about [the main topic / comment]"; the propositional cue is "speaker restriction // who / what + what" or simply "who + what // who + what." In their simplest form, two short sentences serve as propositions that reveal discursive relationships: "John heard the gun. The butler did it." The sentences are coherent—they imply a relationship. Rhetorically, cohesive sentences suggest more than they state. A two-clause sentence makes the restriction clearer: "John believes that the butler did it." Other compound verbal expressions are possible in English: "John heard him do it," which also has two distinct verb groups.

When both credibility and logic are to be explicitly rendered, the adverbial connectors or conjunctions become crucial. The sentences must be less circumspect than in the example above where only weak inferences can be drawn. With comparisons / contrasts, an adverbial expression such as "however" or a conjunction such as "but" introduces explicit associations, for example: "John heard the gun. However, Mary saw the butler shoot." Implication: Mary's evidence is more damning than John's. In the average mystery novel, the reader is more likely to encounter a situation in which the positions of various suspects are compared: "The butler disappeared, but Mary called the police," or the more dramatic "The butler disappeared. Mary, however, called the police" (two parallel clues, in the situation "where suspects were," with the propositional cues: "who + what // [comparison] who + what").

Superficially, these last two options—the contrastive conjunction and the adverbial marker—yield equivalent observations. Syntactically, they each contain two similarly structured clauses. The differences in the structure of these clauses may, however, originate with pragmatic factors. In many European languages, pragmatic considerations trigger word order or mood changes. Speakers can, for example, switch discourse topics by using some conjunctions, but not others.[2] The question of whether information is new or old seems to govern the choice of coordinating versus subordinating conjunctions in English and German. Dunbar concludes his analysis of these phenomena by observing that "nonsyntactic, extrasentential factors of speaker assertion such as topic switching, use of presuppositional or assertional material, and the speaker's emotional support for reported material" influence structure in both English and German clauses (160). French prescribes a change of mood on the basis of similar considerations.

Such pragmatic factors apply to a reader's interpretation of topic emphases in the sentences about Mary and the butler. The presence or absence of adverbial connectors and conjunctions affects weighting of speaker assertions. The stentorian "however" in the sentence group "The butler disappeared. Mary, however, called the police" would be appropriate in the mouth of a detective trying to distinguish the likely guilt or innocence of suspects, or said slowly while a conclusion was being drawn. In the sentence "The butler disappeared, but Mary called the police," the conjunction "but" calls attention to a "conclusion-in-process," almost a "read-along" of the evidence with very little affective weight.

The same sorts of two-sentence / two-clause options exist for causal logic or various sequences or hierarchies which students may build in referring to other variants of the murder scenario. Note that the examples just above *compared* suspects on a one-to-one basis. If the situation were "the sequence of events," the suspects would come up in sentences cued differently: "who + what // [sequence] who + what." As two obvious answers: "John heard the gun. The butler left before that." or, "The butler left before John heard the gun." These must be two-clause utterances because they connect two images: John listening, and a butler walking out. Conceptually the rhetorical setting requires that these pictures be sequenced. Syntax accommodates this need by the use of adverbial expressions of time ("before that"), or by a conjunction ("before" + who + what).

If the scenario is altered slightly to a focus on "why Ms. X is guilty," then causality markers suffice as propositional cues: "who + what [guilty] // [causal marker] who + what." And of course, the communicative goals of the situation can also be met without causal markers: "The butler killed him accidentally. Jeeves forgot to unload the gun."

Nonetheless, explicit markers clarify the intent of the utterances: Each of the two options mentioned above, adverbial markers and conjunctions, serve this purpose—each in slightly different ways:

1. THE ADVERBIAL MARKER: "Jeeves left the loaded gun in the gun rack. *Therefore*, Jeeves killed his master accidentally. Count Kinsky picked up the fatal weapon."
2. THE CAUSAL CONJUNCTION: "Jeeves killed him accidentally, *because* his master picked up the fatal weapon."

Each of these alternatives may, of course, be further restricted by adding to the propositional cues: If, for example, " + where" is added, this cue prescribes the location of the shooting, e.g., "Count Kinsky died in the den." A " + when" reminds students to add a time indicator, e.g., "Count Kinsky died sometime between ten and twelve p.m." Even with these cues, students still have a range of rhetorical options, e.g., anything from "inside" or "in the house" or "late at night" or "before midnight."

The inventory of propositional options governing intersentential discourse and their realizations in actual language can be summed up as follows:

1. Single, short sentences may be chained circumstantially. Without adverbial markers, the statements may be clear because they reflect textual information. However, since they demand reader inference, they are the weakest rhetorical option. Consequently, students should be encouraged to mark statements explicitly by adding adverbial expressions drawn from the text.

2. Adverbial markers expressing particular logics can be added and then highlighted through word-order changes (or intonation).

3. Most complexly, conjunctions can form two-clause sentences. Potentially, this has the greatest rhetorical flexibility, but also demands the greatest syntactical monitoring.

The following examples indicate several logical, and in that sense, illocutionary options realized by these syntactic intrusions into the descriptive sentence "Mary saw the butler."

> *who* + *what* // conjunction + *who* + *what* (past) = I know that Mary saw the butler. (judging condition)
>
> *who* + *what* + (modal) = She can see the butler. (potential)
>
> *who* + *what* + (modal) // negation + *what* (contrast) = She will see the butler and not his shadow. (contrast)
>
> *who* + *what* (past) // *who* + *what*
>
> (+ adverbial marker) Mary turned on the light. Then she saw the butler. (sequence)
>
> (+ subordinating conjunction) Because she turned on the light, Mary saw the butler. (causality)

Cueing language structure in this fashion enables the reader to discern a pattern among propositions in a text. The cues highlight redundant syntactic features of individual sentences at both the macro- and microlevel of information. Cumulatively, these features begin to suggest a particular logic. Sentences with temporal references are likely to indicate a contrast between before and after, while adverbial location may convey a distinction between one place and another. The modals qualify statements, as do sentences that begin with "we think," "they believe."

Conjunctions are perhaps the most obvious clues to a particular logic. Students discern fairly readily that sentences beginning with "therefore" will continue with a statement expressing some causal connection with the preceding sentence, whereas "but" or "however" will trigger a contrast or a qualification of the preceding assertion. A complete inventory of such markers and their illocutionary direction is available at the end of the preceding chapter.

Beyond their usefulness as tags for comprehension of meaning, propositional cues apply to language production in writing and testing as well. These applications will be elaborated in Chapters 7 and 9. It suffices here to point out that the advantages of this system for reading comprehension are the same as those for output and evaluation of classroom performance:

1. The cues link conceptual meaning to output;
2. The cues are applicable and intelligible to students with minimal knowledge of the nomenclature of formal grammars;
3. With cues students can produce individual meanings or concepts of text meaning, yet do so within uniform constraints on structure;
4. The structure of student language is based on contextualized language in a particular reading passage;
5. Accuracy questions can be addressed by rules of various kinds (e.g., structural rules, pragmatic rules, sociolinguistic rules).

We have made the claim that propositional cues distinguish between degrees of meaningfulness in the sense of *explicit* illocutionary force, i.e., doing things with words. Out of a discourse context, the statement "It's hot today" is purely descriptive. Even out of context, however, the statement "It's hot today, so let's go swimming" is overtly illocutionary—it conveys a suggestion. If the comments are made to a group of people wondering what to do with their afternoon off, those words can lead to action—and the statement becomes *perlocutionary* (Searle).

THE CHANGED POSITION OF INTENT
IN COMPREHENSION AND PRODUCTION PROCESSES

When intent is introduced, metacognitive processes must be overtly linked with grammar. One function of linguistic rules that reflect intent is to help L2 speakers produce language in context that is intelligible. Until now we have presented suggestions for cueing propositions as a preliminary stage to aid an L2 speaker in identifying and conveying communicative intent. We will now look at what happens when discourse itself is analyzed in terms of propositional options.

Any pragmatic approach to language rules must be flexible enough to accommodate speaker objectives in situations bounded by cultural constraints. When a car tire blows out, people generally respond with one or two words rather than several sentences. Time and apprehension reduce the speaker's options to "What happened?" or "Good grief!" In emergency situations, language use is quite different from that of a high-level peace conference or a church social.

What kind of grammar describes how a speaker's intent can turn into language in any given situation? It will look quite different from grammars that describe the linguistic conditions for accurate use of a language's formal features. Those grammars cover all conceivable situations, all possible speaker intents, and any information at the sentence level. Descriptive grammars aim to be applicable in multiple realities. As a result, their rules place exhaustive demands on learner competency and reader attention.[3] We will now present ways to narrow the scope of these grammar demands to specific textual situations and speaker intents—a conceptual grammar. A conceptual grammar is pre-linguistic. It begins with what a speaker *wants* to say and then proceeds to guide acceptable options in language generation. The text provides the language—vocabulary and formal features—for the L2 speaker to manipulate. The reason that language in authentic texts is usually beyond the linguistic level of our students is, we believe, because those students lack strategies for practicing expression of intent. Our goal is to demonstrate how to connect L2 speaker intent and textual language. When students see this connection, comprehension of a text can be the basis for the learners' speech acts.

If they are reading texts as *langue*, foreign-language speakers have to process a great deal of extraneous information. Extraneous processing (and its demands on attention) can be reduced if texts are read as *parole*, as restricted data about clearly defined topics. In Chapter 5 the procedural model demonstrated how a teacher can eliminate extraneous processing by designating the classes' intent and speech situation. Through reference to texts, L2 students can determine intent and situation in text schemata and narrative structures. When L2 speakers are aware of their cognitive goals (describing, restricting ideas, developing a logic), they have a basis for selecting textual information about language and subject matter. In the pages that follow we will try to demonstrate that when speakers know what they want to do with words, they can use a text to structure their language production.

THE CASE FOR A SITUATIONAL GRAMMAR

There are two theories about communicative processes: The first presupposes a speaker's need to know all conceivable rules for speech production under all conceivable circumstances; the second presupposes that a speaker needs only those rules for speech production relevant to a particular situation. The case in favor of a conceptual grammar is strictly practical. Precisely because they have limited linguistic ability, L2 students must be allowed to concentrate on what they want to do with words in specific situations. Apprehension of intent is the "payoff" stage for native as well as non-native listeners and readers. In other words, we generally have to understand "what," "who," "where," and "when" before "how" and "why" can be inferred.

Texts are particularly slippery in this regard. At what point in the "Friends, Romans, countrymen" speech, for example, do we decide that Antony came to praise Caesar as well as to bury him? In Swift's day, "A Modest Proposal," which suggested in the early eighteenth century that eating babies would solve Ireland's population problem, was considered biting satire rather than a serious suggestion. Could the contemporary reader encode the satiric intent without the context of Ireland's famine and strife with England? If readers employ the strategies outlined in the foregoing chapters in a systematic way, we believe the answer is "yes."

Pragmatic comprehension strategies help students identify the situational grammar of oral and written texts. For the L2 student, unless the illocutionary rules of texts are familiar, their intent is missed or misunderstood. We are not talking here about culturally shared genres such as a television newscast or a soap opera, ads, or instructions. These are the beginners' genres (see discussion, Chapter 3), the ones that provide the listener or reader with straightforward intents whose familiar and predictable situation aids the student in encoding language.

Texts which present unfamiliar situations necessarily pose massive problems in encoding intent. As a tool for identifying intent, propositional cueing provides a framework for thinking about meaning. Aside from its usefulness in eliciting simple sentences, propositional cueing can function as a thinking adult's grammar beyond the second or third semester, to encode texts with *unfamiliar* contexts and intents. To read to learn, these students must be able to encode with open-ended situations and avoid the resultant bewilderment about grammar in discourse where, as Cole Porter would have it, "anything goes." With these caveats in mind, the following sequence in comprehension of textual or oral input is proposed for such a grammar:

COMPREHENSION

APPREHENDED INPUT ⟶ COMPETENCY ⟶ CONTEXT ⟶ CONTENT ⟶ INTENT

In this model, recognition of intent is the payoff for the reader, the comprehender. The situation of the speakers or writers of the second language is the reverse of the comprehender. While listeners or readers have to understand the context of the text before they can encode intent, intent is the starting gate for speakers or writers.

The first rule of comprehensible speech for the producer of language is that a comprehension sequence begins with intent. Let's put it this way: people who speak without a notion of what they intend to say generally have trouble communicating (the *non sequitur* problem). The notion of communication is based on the premise that both sender and receiver acknowledge that the sender intends to do something with words. For the receiver, the apprehension task is to figure out why things are being said this way in this situation. The sender's job is to put that intent into language appropriate within a given context. When clear communication is the goal, the production model inverts the comprehension sequence:

PRODUCTION

INTENT $\longrightarrow$ CONTENT $\longrightarrow$ CONTEXT $\longrightarrow$ COMPETENCY $\longrightarrow$ *APPREHENSIBLE OUTPUTS*

The sequence of meaning factors for listeners and speakers has some explanatory power with regard to language acquisition. Children, the profession has long acknowledged, seem to acquire the formal properties of languages more readily than do adults (Swain 1985). Why? If production output occurs initially at the level of speaker intent, one reason for adult difficulties in language acquisition is that the adult is capable of numerous intents, while young children are capable of relatively few. The cognitive operations of small children develop with age. Four-year-olds generally fail to see that a gallon jug contains more water than a narrow glass which just happens to be taller than the jug. As a result, they have the advantage of living in a fairly simple world. They may want to say "The glass is taller than the jug" but they do not want to say "The jug holds more water because even though it is not as tall, it is wider." As Piaget's work illustrates, a child is incapable of such complex thoughts and their commensurately complex language.

Adults, on the other hand, have to weigh all kinds of prior knowledge and attempt to filter it through subtleties of context and language of which the child is blissfully unaware. "Do you want a cookie?" the adult asks three-year-old language learners, and they will respond "Cookie" or "Yes" or "Tank you" [sic]. Under most circumstances, such answers are dictated by no other concern than getting a cookie. Sixteen-year-olds are quite another story. They may wish to make a good impression ("Oh, thank you, I'm on a diet") or be worried about whether they can slip away to play basketball with their friends ("I really don't think I should right now. Maybe later?"). The intent to negotiate or manage the cookie exchange by means of language places enormous linguistic demands on mature speakers. As a result, the adult L2 learner is attending to more meanings than the child, who need attend to only one or two. And, as we know, diffused attention interferes with memory functions.

The problem of diffused attention is worsened by the fact that, until they become proficient in a language or are given models for thinking in a second language, adults conceptualize in their native language. Teaching approaches have provided few alternatives to thinking in the native language.

We have stressed teaching students how to produce L2 sentences, yet at the same time have paid little or no attention to teaching them about how to use the foreign language to register the underlying thought of those sentences. That distinction harks back to the discussion of old and new paradigms at the beginning of this book, the difference between command of the formal properties of a language and recognition of the function of those formal properties in communication. Both meaning and structure guide a speaker's production. Propositional cues, metalinguistic cues for the propositions of natural languages, forge a tangible link between the meaning of speaker utterances (recognition of speaker or writer intent) and appropriate expression of that intent in L2 structure.

THINKING IN PROPOSITIONS

Propositions as defined here are the pre-linguistic components of meaning apprehension and production: the speakers' gestalt for spoken intent and for the context in which that intent is expressed. According to psycholinguists, we engage in pre-linguistic or propositional thought all the time. Our brains may not work like computers, but apparently Kant was right: the human mind operates more effectively when using categories for perception than when disregarding such categories. Both L1 and L2 research findings on rhetorical organization and memory support this premise.

Yet while the categorical processes may be shared, their articulation certainly is not. Notational systems ("if not P then Q") exist for the truth value of propositions in formal logic. Computer programs and formal logic systems can represent much of the syntax and some of the semantics of languages. Complete processing of natural languages, however, has eluded our capabilities. While the current models help us understand constructs of syntax and semantics, they are unable to tell us how speakers link meaning and language structure. Natural languages often have structural features that are redundant and imprecise. They use words that can mean different things in different contexts. Speakers can express an idea in twenty different ways, each of which may have a slightly different shade of meaning. Therefore what L2 students need is a grammar construct in which all those ways of expressing an idea are acceptable in a given situation, a metalanguage for that situation's propositions.

A metalanguage for such propositions would have goals very different from formalist or computer notational systems, both of which are mathematical rather than language-based constructs. To avoid adding to the processing overload of the L2 student, the system must reflect only fundamental speaker options, otherwise the system will confuse more than it clarifies. At the same time, this metalanguage must be intelligible to both L2 teachers and students. In other words, we are looking for those natural language features that correspond to fundamental distinctions between discrete mental operations.

Let us review the options in discrete mental operations that correspond to operations in natural languages. Presented in the foregoing discussion as propositional cues, how do these speaker options function? Three combinations seem to be available in all languages:

1. Descriptive propositions. When the speaker only wants to describe a concrete context, simple propositions result (single-verb groups). Somebody or something expresses a condition, an action, or a process. Such propositions produce one-verb simple sentences (tense-marking verbs aside).[4]

ACTION: "She runs to the store."
CONDITION: "He is home."
PROCESS: #1 (habit) "We sleep late Sundays."
             #2 (immediate activity) "We are sleeping late."

2. Entailed propositions. When speakers want to introduce an intent into a simple proposition they qualify the simple thought with three types of entailed restrictions (often two-verb groups). Entailments are logical propositions that follow automatically from one another. The usage stems from English law, where it refers to restrictions on inheritance or transfer of property. Entailed property may have, for example, prohibitions against selling the inherited land or relinquishing its mineral rights. No entailed property is completely free and clear. Neither are entailed propositions—they can be restricted by sensory perception (sense verbs), contingencies (modals), or speaker credibility (verbs such as *think, believe, infer,* etc.). Any speaker or listener perspective expresses entailment.

Entailments impose a presumed result on an assertion. For example, any modal verb will introduce a "modality entailment" because the action expressed is modified and cannot be reduced to simple fact. The offer "I can go to the store" is not the assertion "I go to the store." The actual going to the store will be contingent on the implications of "can" in any given set of circumstances outside the statement: the additional information "I put gas in the car" or "I have time." Each restriction reflects a distinct real-world experience of the speaker. Because they restrict the descriptive proposition, the resulting sentences use two-verb groups, the verb of the proposition plus the verb of speaker perspective (verbs of sense perception, modals, and verbs expressing feelings or thought).

PHYSICAL ENTAILMENTS:	*"I saw* him run to the store." (speaker's sense perception of the simple proposition)
CONTINGENCY ENTAILMENTS:	"She *might* be home." (speaker's awareness of possible external conditions that can alter the simple proposition)
CREDIBILITY ENTAILMENTS:	"I *think* that she might be home." (speaker's judgment regarding the simple proposition)

3. Synthetic propositions. When speakers want to develop discourse—a pattern of connected ideas—they generally begin by thinking in terms of no more than four logical patterns: cause and effect, sequence, contrasts, or relationships between things talked about. The resultant sentences are necessarily complex since they combine two simple or restricted propositions. Described in terms of formal features, analytical propositions have two or more clauses or two related sentences marked by characteristic adverbs, relative pronouns, or conjunctions.

CAUSAL ANALYSIS:	"Because the light is on, I know he is home."
CONTRAST:	"Although the light is on, he is not at home."
CHRONOLOGY:	"After he arrived home, he turned on the light."
RELATIVITY:	"The light which he turned on is very bright."

DISTINGUISHING BETWEEN METALANGUAGE CUES FOR DISCOURSE FUNCTIONS AND THE FORMAL FEATURES OF SENTENCE-LEVEL ACCURACY

We believe that the foregoing propositions are the primary mental operations available to the human mind. This is by no means to assert that they are the sole mental operations expressible in language. A host of additional functions that trigger choices in word order, negation, mood, modality, and tense also enter into a speech act. In terms of a metalanguage of meaning, however, these operations represent secondary features of the production process, i.e., they do not signal the intent of discourse, only its consistency. Questions of word order or mood are rhetorical decisions about which formal properties to select. The initial propositional decision, however, is conceptual: the link between the learner's thinking and sound rhetorical decisions about the language features that express that thought. *A metalanguage for propositions sorts out available conceptual differences.* Without a system that distinguishes these propositions, the learner must necessarily rely heavily on knowledge of form rather than commencing with functional considerations.

Moreover, in order to communicate, the conceptual differences between propositions must allow only one notational option. One idea cannot mean two things at once. When there are two or more possible forms for propositions, those forms become a feature of language-rule learning rather than concept learning. Questions of appropriateness are stylistic issues, not dictates of communicative clarity. For example, in the sentence pair, "Derek read the joke" and "The joke was read by Derek" the propositional meaning ("who + what") is the same regardless of the shift in topic (from Derek to joke) and voice (from active to passive). In the sentence pair "Montgomery is easy to please" and "Montgomery is eager to please" there is parallel structure without parallel meaning (The first sentence expresses actuality; the second is wishful thinking.).

Both types of cues, those for concepts and those for formal features, need to be included in any production model, but they represent different stages in processing language. Moreover, often rules such as tense choice or forms of negation are language-specific. Often accuracy involves knowledge of pragmatics—cultural sophistication about when to use given structures, as, for example, the choice of the honorific in Japanese. It might be desirable, in such instances, for the notational system of a metalanguage to ask students to use a particular tense or sentence form. For example, a cue for descriptive language ("who" + condition) might ask students to manipulate the proposition through negation or questions rather than declarative sentences ("No, she is not" or "Isn't she?").

Do such insertions impinge on the speaker's freedom to choose intent? We suggest that this is not the case, that a speaker's use of a particular construction involves a language rule, not a logical decision. To differentiate between thought and form in this way helps the student to recognize when choices can be made (what topics and what comments) and what follows obligatorily from these choices (structural constraints). Consequently, propositional cues can signal grammatical realizations of concepts found in a text without dictating conceptual designs about text content.

When the metalanguage distinguishes between individual choice of messages and linguistic rules, it prevents a linguistic free-for-all. The model "thought + form" links conceptual language to grammar rules already learned. Currently, most L2 grammar instruction is structural. In that case, the propositional notions of places, objects, and ideas are the "what," and animals, people, or Martians the "who." How the "what" and "who" is cued in grammar will depend on the rules the L2 student is accustomed to. After structuralist training, "what" and "who" can be viewed as grammatical subjects or objects, depending on their location in the cue sequence. For students who use case grammars, the agent ("the Martian ran") and the experiencer ("the Martian was thirsty") distinction can be introduced. The relevant point is that cues can vary with the teaching approach as long as they help students think about speech acts on the basis of a limited inventory of terms that represent prelinguistic components.

Since verbs express "process, action, or a state of being," their propositional distinction corresponds to one of these concepts. Therefore, if the speaker wants to describe conditions (the so-called statal verbs such as "feel" or "be"), then a simple propositional formula would be "who (what) + condition." If the speaker wants to describe an action, "who / what + what (action)"; if a process, than "who / what + what (process)."

Aside from encouraging students to avoid translation, the great advantage of this shorthand is that it lets teachers cue statements about texts without restricting students to one or two possible answers. Let us assume that students must produce propositions about the following short ad for Canon copiers.

THE CANON ONE TOUCH MORE.

IT'S ONE UP ON XEROX.

It enlarges as well as reduces. And costs less, too.

The comparison is anything but a draw. The Canon NP-125 simply outdoes the Xerox 2350.

For one thing, the Canon not only has two reduction modes, it even enlarges. The Xerox only reduces.

The Canon has a touch more speed too. It makes 12 copies in just a minute. And requires absolutely no warm-up time.

In fact, the Canon NP-125 doesn't even have a power switch. Copying begins the instant you touch the copy key.

So nothing could be simpler to use. No wasted time, energy, space, or cost.

It's that simple. And that easy. The Canon NP-125 One Touch More.

The Xerox doesn't even come close to touching our price.

To elicit language for descriptive propositions about this text the teacher could ask for the following:

what + *what* (process / condition)
POSSIBILITIES: It costs less. Canon outdoes Xerox. It [the copier] requires no warm-up time.

what + *what* (description)
POSSIBILITIES: Canon is simple. Canon has speed. It is one up.

what + *what* (action / description)
POSSIBILITIES: Canon enlarges. Xerox only reduces. It makes copies.

The criterion of using the text as the basis for meaning provides a standard for propositional accuracy. Sentences constructed on the basis of such minimal "thought" cues reveal what the student comprehends. A student who writes "Xerox enlarges" has misread a piece of the information pattern ("all the things Canon does that Xerox does not"). Similarly, someone who writes "Canon requires warm-up time" has not grasped the importance of negation within this same pattern. Warm-up time is a negative feature and hence belongs with Xerox rather than Canon. The sentence is grammatically correct but wrong in terms of textual argument.

Unlike assignments or tests based solely on grammatical accuracy, metalanguage cues for propositional concepts ask students to account for meaningful as well as grammatical statements. In a propositional approach, weighted grading rewards accurate thoughts as well as accurate sentences. And textual meaning receives student attention when half the points they receive are for accuracy of facts and inferences and half are for accurate language use.

It might be argued that such a weighting neglects grammaticality. We counter that just the reverse is true. If thought precedes language, then awareness of the subject (Canon or Xerox) or negation pattern (no warm-up time = "good" versus no enlarging = "bad") is linked to awareness of form. The way to enhance grammaticality is to enhance the awareness of how distinctions in form are linked to distinctions in meaning.

To elicit language structures for entailed propositions, speakers qualify the description on the basis of (1) their mental perception (credibility entailment), (2) their sense perception (physical entailment), or (3) their perception of a social or external constraint (contingency entailment). These are all two-clause sentences; each progression is separated by a double slash ("//") and has its own grammar form.

> *who + what* (credibility) // what + what (action / description)
> POSSIBILITIES: I think that Canon costs less. We claim that Canon outdoes Xerox. Sam hopes it [Canon] requires no warm-up time.
>
> *who + what* (physical entailment) // what + what (description)
> POSSIBILITIES: We heard Canon is simple. I see that Canon has speed. He shows that it is one up.
>
> *what + what* (contingency: modal or adverb)
> POSSIBILITIES: Canon can enlarge. (or) Generally Canon enlarges. Xerox only lets you reduce. (or) Apparently Xerox only reduces. It will make copies. (or) It definitely makes copies.

With entailed clauses, speakers have to express two simultaneous perspectives. Hence the foregoing sentences ask for two verbs—either two-verb groups for a single clause or two separate verbs in separate clauses. Speakers think, hear, or speculate something about Canon or Xerox on the one hand, while they describe the machines on the other. These sentences account for at least two situational focuses: what speakers perceive and how they qualify what they perceive.[5] This dual focus is reflected in most languages in increased formal complexity, and it is this relationship between speaker intent and language form that speakers frequently fail to notice. For example, speakers are often unaware of the changes in sentence intent wrought by modal verbs that qualify or judge.

What are the advantages to the speaker, hearer, or reader who notices the difference between pure description and a qualified description? Psycholinguistic research suggests several: (1) attention seems to be enhanced when personal concerns are expressed, and (2) linguistic creativity occurs because qualified descriptions, largely expressions of personal opinions and judgments, necessitate use of formal features not modeled in the text. Yet as a rule such creativity is restricted to only a few such features, such as insertion of modals, subordinate clauses, and optional changes in tense or number, none of which reveal context explicitly.

Synthetic sentences are the third group of propositional types. They are realized as sequence sentences, relative sentences, contrast sentences, or causal sentences. Unlike the entailed sentences that have a dual focus within a single proposition, synthetic utterances are combinations of two propositions. They have two complete grammatical clauses containing two topic and comment groups. By connecting topics and comments, they change the relationships of idea units in subtle ways that affect comprehender perception.

Recall the *New York Times* article about Chernobyl presented in Chapter 3. The proposition that "It may be months or years before the world learns exactly what happened at the Soviet Union's Chernobyl nuclear power station and why radiation was spewed over much of Europe" is juxtaposed with "But one thing that emerged with striking clarity in the days after the incident was first reported was the profound difference in the surfeit of speculation, questioning and information that unfolded in the West and the few facts divulged in the East." In this contrast sequence what "the world" (everybody) knows about Chernobyl (topic: the world; comment: has few facts about why the plant exploded) is juxtaposed with a quite different proposition: freedom of information in the West and suppression of information in the East. Hence in sentence two we have the topic "profound difference," the comment "surfeit of speculation, questioning and information in the West and the few facts divulged in the East."

Logically, the two sentences contradict each other. How can we in the West have to wait for months and maybe years to find out "exactly what happened" in the first proposition, yet experience a "surfeit of information" in the second?

The answer, of course, is that the text intends to talk not about Chernobyl, but about the benefits of living in the West. We in the West may not know much, but that is still a lot more than the Russians are allowed to find out in the pre-Glasnost era. Although ostensibly a news story, the Chernobyl piece editorializes with its propositional logic. Implicitly, the juxtaposition of these two descriptive propositions, a contrast between information about Chernobyl on the one hand and treatment of information in the East and in the West on the other, introduces an implication at the subtextual level: "The nuclear disaster illustrates not only inferior technology, but repressive government as well." To read implications, students need to be able to encode the relationships in analytic propositions.

Consider how propositional intent changes with the logic shifts in the following:

1. *what* (location) + *what* // (sequence) *what* + *where*
   After Chernobyl had a nuclear disaster, a surfeit of speculation arose in the West.

2. *what* (location) + *what* // (relative clause) *what* + *where*
   Chernobyl had a nuclear disaster, which led to a surfeit of speculation in the West.

3. *what* (location) + *what* // (contrast) *what* + *where*
   Chernobyl had a nuclear disaster, but few facts were divulged in the East.

4. *what* + *where* (cause) // *what* + *where* (effect)
   Because there was a nuclear disaster in Chernobyl, a surfeit of speculation arose in the West.

The most neutral statement above is the sequential statement. One event follows the other but the events have a linear rather than a weighted relationship. The relative clause introduces an explicit subordinate relationship. The disaster is the main event, the speculation in the West a spin-off or subset of the Chernobyl event. The contrast pair, on the other hand, raises the two propositions to the status of separate, but equal events: "We had P but not much Q." The contrast is between event and information, and although the statement is rife with implications, no expressed connection is made. Finally, it is the cause and effect sentence that subordinates the Chernobyl event to events that follow as a presumed consequence.

The point of these examples is that discursive logic weights propositions in consistent ways, and that encoding of that weighting reveals propositional intent. Here discourse markers, comprehended as the way in which a writer assigns values to topics and comments, represent the tools with which an L2 reader can uncover the logic of Western texts. That logic often flies under false colors. Often the gamut of writing from a scholarly treatise to a news report reveals a variety of subtextual polemics, e.g., the freedom fighters in one revolutionary scenario are the insurgents or terrorists of another. Ultimately, text logic is anchored in cultural context.

Compared to descriptions and assertions, analytical utterances are invitations to verbal interaction that specify a cultural context. When a person says, "The weather looks horrible today," other people's intents remain unspecified—the speaker is not assuming a predictable listener or reader reaction. Descriptive and entailed statements tend to be self-contained. One observation may or may not lead to another. This is not true of synthetic propositions. When we say "The weather looks horrible today, so let's call off the trip to the country," all those in favor of an excursion have been explicitly challenged. Language has forged links between a context (horrible weather) and a resulting intent (canceling a trip to the country).

Inevitably, this context/intent structure of the utterance increases the likelihood of more dialogue with others. Perhaps a child interjects, "But Mama, you promised," or alternative suggestions are made, e.g., "Well, in that case, let's go to the movies." In this way, synthetic statements lead to related responses and arguments. They are the stuff of discourse. In texts, writers use synthetic propositions to create full-blown conceptual realities at the subtextual as well as the textual level. Readers, whether in L1 or L2, must uncover both levels of intent to interact with conceptual realities of textual worlds. Without such capabilities they cannot use language to learn about that language's political, cultural, and social messages. They remain hostages to prejudgment, comprehenders within fossilized conceptual boundaries.

NOTES TO CHAPTER 6

1. For purposes of the discussion that follows, the distinction between agent and experiencer is not stressed since we wanted to avoid limiting applications of propositional cues to a particular grammar model. The distinction is important to a learner-based model of text comprehension, however. Kemper analyzes event chains in texts "according to the actions, physical states, and mental states actually stated in a text" (392). Applying a knowledge-based approach to text comprehension, she has researched readability under the assumption that readers comprehend texts by registering causal connections between actions, physical, and mental states expressed in individual clauses. Her research supports the notion that unless readers can link the elements of a text together as they are reading, comprehension problems occur (see also Kintsch & van Dijk; Schank et al.). The larger the number of causal links which a reader must infer (i.e., that are not stated in the text), the more comprehension difficulties the reader seems to encounter. For applications of this work to readability, see the discussion in Chapter 11.

2. Using the following sentences, Dunbar argues that topic switch in German can occur with *denn*, but not with *weil*:

/5a/ Anna kann schon gut kochen, denn der Karl, der sieht ganz schön gesund aus.

/5b/ ?Anna kann schon gut kochen, weil der Karl, der sieht ganz schön gesund aus.

He points out that 5b, the clause with the subordinating conjunction *weil*, is unacceptable because it makes no sense to the German speaker. The authors are indebted to Mark Louden for his insights on this subject and for calling this reference to our attention.

3. Since Chomsky, the study of grammar has been extended far beyond structuralists' focus on sentence-level surface-structure syntax and morphology. Chomsky's original concept of deep structure added a crucial layer of propositional meaning, and this opened the door to attempts by generative semantics to formalize semantic meaning as rigorously as syntax. Other major efforts to build in a range of other kinds of meaning include Montague grammar (which is concerned with the abstract logic underlying sentence structure), pragmatics, discourse grammars and narratology, speech act theory, and sociolinguistics.

However, these theoretically significant efforts are clearly not suitable either for inclusion in, or as models for, pedagogical grammars, though we may want to make students aware in general terms of the nature of such work, as a kind of consciousness-raising about ways to think about language. But such metalinguistic explorations are not only far too complex and detailed for our students to make use of, they do not in fact address the needs of foreign-language learners. All these extensions of linguistic theory have as their aim a more and more inclusive and detailed description of language as abstract system, of the nature of language knowledge. They do not directly concern themselves with the way speakers and writers link particular meaning with particular choices of words and structure in the construction of texts, nor with the way hearers and readers comprehend texts. Our aim here is to shed light on the constraints and options which influence language learners in *that* attempt.

4. We avoid using the term "compound verb" in descriptions of propositional types because that designation refers to compounds of tense as well as modals. Tense changes do not have the same meaning as verb combinations such as "can sleep" or "think we saw." To avoid confusion, we refer to "one-verb" or "two-verb" as synonymous with "one verb-group meaning" regardless of how many verb forms it contains. For example: English "to be able to" and German "können" are equivalent one-verb groups.

5. The shift in focus which verb groupings reflect also explains why it is difficult to teach students to differentiate authorial stances with edited materials. Such text materials tend to be more descriptive, with little author intent evident and only a self-evident (and hence uninteresting and undifferentiated) context.

Seven

Cueing Pragmatic Use
with a Sample Text

ILLOCUTIONARY FORCE AS A READABILITY FACTOR

Readers find purely descriptive, locutionary texts bland. Locutionary texts have no particular designs on a reader—they lack intent. When purely descriptive texts are contrasted with texts presenting information in terms of causality, contrast, or problem and solution, the descriptive passages are less memorable (e.g., Carrell 1984). We suggest that part of the reason for this lack of salience is that texts with a problem-solving intent stimulate the reader to thought or to action. Only when a text influences readers to think about its meaning does it exhibit illocutionary force. Purely descriptive texts, under ordinary circumstances, rarely do. Hence they fail to focus reader attention.

Recalls of topically similar passages illustrate what Frederiksen (1982) calls "links" (macropropositional logic) to different patterns of recall. Examples of such links are "three geographical areas of the Midwest have been described" (introducing a comparative logic) and "The three areas described are near urban centers and hence would have high rates of visitation" (causal logic suggesting a relationship between circumstances and subsequent events). Presence of some type of linking or macrologic results in different reader recall of otherwise similar information. In one such study, analysis of results confirmed Frederiksen's hypothesis that the way semantic information is organized affects both comprehension and the reader's reconstruction of a text (69).

Student perception of textual organization appears to be an important factor in readability and recall for second-language students as well (Carrell 1984). Students have greater success with texts that convince, inform, and persuade—texts with rhetorical illocution—than they do with readings that are purely descriptive. But, as has been pointed out, cues for rhetorical illocution at the global level are rarely explicit, and when

115

they are explicit, they are often inconsistent. The topic "this book" and the comment "solves all your weight problems" may deal with specific weight problems and how to solve them, but more probably it describes diet and exercise programs (solutions) and how to use them (instructions). The reader must recognize text structure in the pattern of information. The text's rhetorical claims about that structure may be (and often are) misleading (e.g., Anderson & Armbruster).

Reader expectation and background will also influence the quest for textual meaning. Reader purposes or special background influence reader structuring of messages. One reader's exciting message can be another's boring description. Imagine, for the sake of illustration, a young person named Daniel who reads computer manuals avidly. For Daniel, computer manuals are illocutionary—they tell him how to install and operate computers, and they teach him the use of new technology. Part of Daniel's job is to consult with Liberal Arts professors at the University of Texas about how to use their new programs. Most of the professors Daniel works with feel that computer manuals describe obscurity upon obscurity. For these professors, computer manuals fail to do anything with words. They read to find out what the programs claim to do, and then they call Daniel to find out how to use the programs, i.e., to turn the manuals into illocutors.

Texts that intend to do something, in this case to instruct, become purely descriptive when those intents cannot be grasped by the reader. Sometimes that failure is linguistic—the threshold factor for professors who read computer manuals may have something in common with L2 thresholds; sometimes it can result from absent schemata or lack of reader interest.

The point of the foregoing discussion is to highlight the cornerstone assertion of this chapter: *If readers are to comprehend text structure, to understand how its macrotopics and macrocomments fit together in an overt, consistent way, they need to assume responsibility for recreating text structure.* In our view, that is what meaning-based readers know how to do. If meaningfulness matters, then generating message organization on the basis of text language is the keystone strategy in metacognition. Ultimately other strategies to determine meaning—use of prediction, context, redundancy, schemata, etc.—serve this more comprehensive strategy of message organization.

Rarely do texts spell out their rhetorical logic with explicit statements such as "looking at the problems and their solutions . . ." or "we are about to compare . . ." Often when the claim "here is how information is organized" is made, closer analysis reveals it to be specious. One of the insights from reading research is the fact that artificially constructed tests of the effects of rhetorical organization use texts that are more clearly constructed than those the student is likely to confront in the real world (Schallert et al.). Two facts stand out: (1) Rhetorical organization is rarely a consistent event in texts, and (2) Students have better recall when textual information *is* organized (Carrell 1985; Lee 1986a). Therefore, *to reap the cognitive benefits of structured information, in most cases the reader will have to participate in that structuring.*

THE CASE FOR METACOGNITIVE TRAINING

Although recreations of text structure will be individual, practice in meaning-based reading seems to be a viable class activity. Because L2 research on strategy training is still in its infancy, the safest generalization at this point is the one drawn from Kern's research

(1989), namely that "students can benefit from direct instruction in specific strategies designed to assist them in (1) word recognition; (2) inferring the meaning of unknown words; and (3) synthesizing meaning in larger segments of the text" (145). A student's reading comprehension seems to be modified by training in use of background and cognitive strategies (e.g., Barnett 1988a; Carrell 1985; Nemoianu).

THE CLASSROOM AS A FORUM TO ENCOURAGE METACOGNITIVE ATTITUDES

Reading has traditionally been treated as an individual responsibility—a task conducted outside of class. We wish to stress the necessity for classroom practice if students are to become interactive and maximally effective readers of L2 texts. The goal of such practice is metacognitive awareness of reading as a dialogue between text and reader. Rather than promoting any particular techniques, we stress the importance of encouraging problem-solving attitudes such as persistence (keep on reading!), linking global concepts to textual detail, and identifying the structure of messages implied by linguistic patterns.

The procedures outlined in Chapter 5 allow a number of strategic approaches to texts at each stage. For example, previewing suggests emphasis on word recognition, but can also involve inference about word meanings based on background knowledge or redundancy. The matrix exercise promotes both global and local strategies as well as rhetorical structuring. Larger segments of the text must be synthesized, but at the same time students must recognize and use specific words and grammar functions to complete the matrix. When such connections are made, students can apply the matrix format not only to shorter passages but also to quantitative reading (see illustrations, Chapter 12).

Given tasks such as those suggested for each stage, when students report to one another about their comprehension, they pool background information about their range of knowledge, command of vocabulary, and strategy insights. With repeated practice, the internalized models of individual students are expanded by the peer group experience. The immediate advantage of an entire passage read in class is that students' insights about the text will illustrate an interplay of strategic approaches.

The example that follows illustrates the use of a range of techniques in classroom reading. Why choose a literary text? First, most language courses still stress literature in their offerings. Second, articles in science or from periodicals are quickly dated. Third, literature often illustrates differences in attitudes, values, and behaviors in the L2 culture, yet unfolds stories whose ordering (see discussion of story grammars in this chapter) is familiar to adults.

We chose a German text to illustrate some of the cross-cultural factors that can bemuse the L2 reader. American readers may find themselves confronted with alternative views of their culture. Indeed, they may decide that a story about America, written by an Austrian writer, says more about Austria than it does about the United States.

SAMPLE TEXT

SAMPLE SHORT FICTION: "The Story of a Railroad-Crossing Tender" by H. C. Artmann[1]

1. The responsibility of a railroad-crossing tender of the Union Pacific Co. is a big one; not only does it involve concern for humans and animals, but damage to freight must also be avoided insofar as possible.

2. The railroad-crossing tender owns a book, which he reads over and over;

he has owned this book for ten years, but every time he reads it, he stops after page 77, and he starts again from the beginning; he would never read beyond that page; he has premonitions. Ridiculous, he murmurs. Nonetheless, he always goes back to page 1.

3. Most of the time, however, he smokes his favorite pipe; he does not have a wife; he watches the first star glimmer in the evening sky; he steps out into the intimate green of the nettles behind the house; he is usually an early riser and drinks a beer after meals.

4. The last train generally comes through at 9:35 p.m.; he watches the last car disappear in the distance; the brakeman has waved to him; he has been the brakeman's friend for years, although he has never spoken with him.

5. The railroad-crossing tender's book is an old penny dreadful with the title *The Man from the Union Pacific Express*. Today he decides to read the novel to the end, but he is uneasy about doing so.

6. Once a strange brakeman stood on the back platform of the last car; was he an assistant?

7. Towards 11 p.m., the railroad-crossing tender becomes aware of an unusual glow of light; he goes in front of the house and sees a train approach which is not in any schedule; it rolls past him without a sound; on the platform of the last car stands the stranger from that other time, playing a harmonica.

8. The railroad-crossing tender rubs his eyes; that all seems very peculiar to him; he is, after all, completely alone; he goes back into the house; he drinks a second beer and glues pages 78 to 126 together. That, he thinks, would be best.

CLASSROOM EXPLORATION OF MEANINGFUL PROPOSITIONS: ESTABLISHING THE SEMANTICS OF MACROLEVEL FEATURES

Remember that previewing begins with student schemata about the text topic—what do students know about railroads and people who work with trains? The instructor's open-ended questions should elicit most of the words important for comprehension of this text: *train, railway cars, brakeman, crossing.* Key expressions are recorded in the second language. Text-extraneous vocabulary deserves equal footing with terms which appear in the text, as long as the words volunteered belong to the semantic field of railroads. The point of this phase is to prepare students to compare the possible schemata with the actual realizations in the text. As for concerns about the quality of language volunteered, even if students express concepts in English or incorrectly in L2, these words should prove more salient for the class as a whole than teacher-selected vocabulary, because students identify the lexicon meaningful to them. Along with solicitation of facts, questions relating to affect should also enhance memory for vocabulary: What feelings do students have about trains? What do they like / dislike?

USING TEXTUAL LANGUAGE

Students are now ready to look at the text to see if their schema corresponds to Artmann's. They will probably decide it does not. But opinions are not the meat of reading for meaning, particularly at the outset. To forestall the substitution of opinion for textual messages, *readers must always substantiate their answers through reference to specific language in the text.*

Reference to textual language not only structures turn-taking, it also reduces the teacher's guidance and managerial role. When students cite specific paragraphs and sentences, the text, rather than the teacher, substantiates students' comprehension. As a result, fewer opportunities exist for speculation, misunderstandings, and digression—a feature recurrent in classroom interaction studies (Allwright).

Several students may observe that the story has unusual visual features. Paragraphs in this text are numbered, so that the location of specific language can be readily corroborated. In the original German, text nouns are written with small initial letters instead of capitals. In addition to these visual peculiarities, the style is so terse that readers must rely on inferences to fill in informational gaps. Does the crossing tender drink two beers a day (i.e., does "after meals" mean after lunch and dinner)? Does the man smoke anything besides a pipe? When does he read the novel? Does he ever have visitors or go anywhere to get groceries or visit friends?

In a well-crafted work of fiction such gaps will emerge from rhetorical patterns as well. In Artmann's story the overall pattern is playfulness. He activates reader response by teasing—stopping just short of implausible assertions. By avoiding overt causality, Artmann forces the reader to fill in the connections—to draw conclusions suggested, but not confirmed, by the text.

ESTABLISHING MACROSEMANTIC CATEGORIES OF INFORMATION

We have defined macrosemantics as the significant nouns, adjectives, and adverbs, the *who, what, where,* and *when* around which any text, whether fiction or nonfiction, revolves. Most teachers intuitively look for words they think students must know before they can understand a passage. Normally this is the "important" vocabulary that carries the thread of the story. These are typically words that are repeated or varied at least two or three times, even in a shorter text. If the class cannot recognize a lexical item from sentence or supersentential context, the instructor should link the unknown word to the list of macrolevel terms produced by the class.

In the Artmann text, the best example of a key term unlikely to be encoded by students is *railroad-crossing tender.* The concept is antiquated, since railroad-crossing gates are now closed by automatic mechanisms and not by hand. When characterizing the primary people or places in a text, special terms point to important features of the text which students can deduce once they understand the concept. In this case, once *railroad-crossing tender* is defined, students can speculate about how this term helps establish when and where the story takes place.

A number of other unfamiliar nouns not germane to the list of schematic vocabulary for railroads will pose encoding difficulties—*nettles, harmonica, penny dreadful.* But because they play a secondary role in the story, failure to recognize them will not result in misreading or breakdown of reading. In the context of stepping into the backyard, whether the crossing tender steps onto grass or a particular type of weed is interesting but not essential for comprehension of the macropropositions of this text. While the context of the story fails to define these words with precision, it does suggest whether the nouns refer to animate or inanimate, man-made or natural, human or nonhuman entities.

ENCODING THE VOCABULARY OF MACROSEMANTICS

We mention nouns in particular, because studies of vocabulary unfamiliar to the L2 reader of European languages suggest that nouns constitute ninety percent of the unknown words in a text. Aside from being unknown, nouns pose the greatest interference for readers because context often proves inadequate for encoding. Therefore, procedures that distinguish between nouns seminal to text messages at the text or episodic level, and those which are peripheral to that meaning, enable students to function with authentic texts despite vocabulary deficiencies. In classroom practice, verbs and adjectives pose fewer problems for students. For example, most students can guess an appropriate verb to link to a description of the stars, or a reasonable if not precisely accurate concept for an adjective that describes a man's pipe.

Even if lexical guesses about equivalencies are inaccurate, when a word's part of speech is recognized, reading is more successful (Phillips). Despite their ignorance of the precise meaning of those words, students seem to encode sentence meaning more readily if they can recognize unknown words as verbs or adjectives. As part of practice in reading authentic texts, we ask students to see whether they can recognize the grammar function of unfamiliar words. If the unknown items are verbs, they are asked on the basis of context to decide whether those *verbs represent a state of being or suggest an activity*. Such distinctions are often signaled by familiar syntactic features, e.g., She [stands, rests, lies] *next to* the pool. She [jumps, runs, leaps] *into* the pool.

Once students are aware of how to use their knowledge of language as *langue* to uncover meaning of textual language, a particular *parole*, other insights follow. Students rapidly learn that while sentence context is insufficient to define a word precisely, it is often adequate to assign verbs to one meaning category as a state of being or an activity (Crow). Similarly, students can generally deduce from the main story line whether *adjectives describe something in a positive or negative way*, e.g., cocaine derivatives are often referred to as [harmful, destructive, dangerous] whereas an amusement park is generally considered [exciting, fun, colorful].

The story line of the Artmann text concerns everyday activities in the Old West, a scenario familiar to American students: a man working for the Union Pacific Railroad, what he does all day, what he decides not to do. The fact that his decisions are a bit out of the ordinary is offset by the repetitive language describing both ordinary and extraordinary events. Based on student assessment of text-semantics, known to them as the *who, what, where,* and *when* of a text, the results might be:

1. PEOPLE   (a man living alone)
2. OBJECTS   (trains, a book)
3. PLACE   (an isolated spot in the USA)
4. TIME   (before electricity)

ENCODING THE VOCABULARY OF MACROSYNTAX

Once the global situation or macrosemantics are identified by the readers, they can proceed to the *macrosyntax* (i.e., rhetorical organization or intent) of the text. As previously defined, the macrosyntax of a text is the reader's reconstruction of its rhetorical organization, its pattern in depicting dominant relationships between people, institutions, events, or ideas: as a *development* (cause / effect, problem / solution) or a *description* (features / characteristics, comparison). Where do students find textual clues that establish whether the text describes its subject matter or elaborates a development involving that subject? Initial indicators are discourse markers—conjunctions and adverbial phrases that connect sentences and paragraphs. If the Artmann story had intersentential connectors such as "because," "therefore," "for that reason," these might suggest implications of activities described—a type of cause and effect relationship. The story has no such words. Instead, the reader finds three instances of "but," one "nonetheless," and several adverbial markers such as "today," "once," "every night," and "afterward." The occurrences of "but" and "nonetheless" suggest a contrast in the propositions that follow these discourse cues; the adverbial markers indicate a "before and after" contrast.

In order to confirm impressions of a macrosyntax based on discourse markers, assumptions about rhetorical clues must be verified by the episodic structure of the text. Do events, people, or objects in the story contrast with one another between sentences, paragraphs or whole segments of a longer text? In the Artmann story, the second sentence describes an unusual activity (stopping midway through a book and starting over again). Do other unusual events occur? Are they related? With shorter texts, details often confirm or disconfirm initial impressions of the macrosyntax. Consequently, the instructor may want to let students decide about the macrosyntax of short texts such as the Artmann story on their own and come to class the next day prepared to show how the text supports a particular organization of information.

TEXT-BASED TECHNIQUES FOR ORGANIZING TEXTUAL INFORMATION: PRE- AND POST-READING

Establishing text structure has been the concern of both L1 and L2 specialists. Grellet and Nuttall have written excellent handbooks for L2 students that illustrate a range of structuring techniques whose value as learning aids has been established in L1 research and practice: semantic mapping (Johnson & Pearson), graphic organizers (Moore & Readence), idea mapping (Armbruster & Anderson), text structure strategy (Taylor & Beach), story grammars (N. Stein), and story maps (Beck & McKeown 1981).[2] These tasks all try to use reader metacognition to recreate text organization.

Unlike multiple-choice, true / false, or discrete-point questions, text structuring tasks focus on coherence—how the text pieces work together. They rely on a reader's background knowledge or schemata to help in the organizational process. They ask students to isolate the topics and subtopics of a text and to create a visual representation of those relationships. Often the exercises are used as prereading activities or for vocabulary building. Several have, however, proven even more effective as study aids or post-reading activities (e.g., graphic organizers).

Semantic mapping is primarily a vocabulary-building tool. If done as a prereading activity, it is conducted in the same way as the first stage of the procedures outlined in Chapter 5. Students brainstorm about words that relate to a concept stated by the teacher. The technique improves on merely listing suggestions on the board because it divides words and phrases into related categories. The results might look like this:

RAILROADS—TYPES OF TRAINS: freight trains, passenger trains, bullet trains
WHAT TRAINS RUN ON: diesel fuel, steam, electricity
THINGS TRAINS DO: transport people and goods, make noise, run on tracks

Graphic organizers. Similar to semantic mapping, graphic organizers arrange vocabulary in a hierarchy of major to minor concepts. They are particularly appropriate for technical or scientific texts because they reinforce the sets and subsets of terms students must learn. Graphic organizers are generally text-based and are therefore appropriate at stages of reading when the focus is on explicit text meaning rather than textual implications or reader interpretation. As a small-group activity, organizers can be written on index cards and duplicates can be distributed among the various groups. Each group decides how to arrange the concepts. For the Artmann story the result might look at the following categories:

Union Pacific Railroad
Crossing tender

Job	*Recreation*	*Events*
gate opening / closing	pipe	last train at 9:35 p.m.
	beer	unscheduled train later
[pastes book shut]	book	[pastes book shut]

Graphic organizers are less appropriate for works of fiction than for technical or scientific texts. Categories for individual nouns fail to reveal much about the story because the text is not hierarchical—in which case it would, for example, list preferable jobs or a coherent series of job-related events. Although works of fiction correspond to the real world, they rarely do so in any consistent way that can be mapped. As a previewing task for learning new vocabulary in textbooks or technical materials, the organizer introduces a passage's semantic concepts.

One of the reported advantages of this approach is that teachers find themselves better prepared after constructing a graphic organizer. Another advantage is that, in post-reading, the organizer can stimulate discussion if, for example, the teacher asks students to fill in blank spaces in the grid. Such activities also promote the transition from teacher- to student-generated diagrams. As a follow-up for a longer passage, organizers can also serve as points of reference for inclusion of additional insights (e.g., details about train schedules or the mechanics of railroad-crossing gates).

Story grammars and story maps. As their names imply, these techniques recreate the metastructure of stories in Propp's classic work *Morphology of the Folktale*. Stein and Glenn suggest a six-part morphology for a story grammar: (1) *setting*, which introduces characters and location of the story, (2) *initiating event*, which marks the first change in story development, (3) *internal response* of characters, often in conjunction with a goal, (4) *attempt*, the effort to achieve a goal, (5) *consequence*, success or failure to achieve the goal, and (6) *reaction*, a character's response to the outcomes of these efforts. Apparently, even when stories lack one or more categories, L1 readers, especially older ones, tend to fill them in (Whaley). When categories are manipulated by researchers—taken out of story order or intertwined—recall of readers suffers (Stein & Glenn).

A diagram of the story grammar in the Artmann text might look as follows:

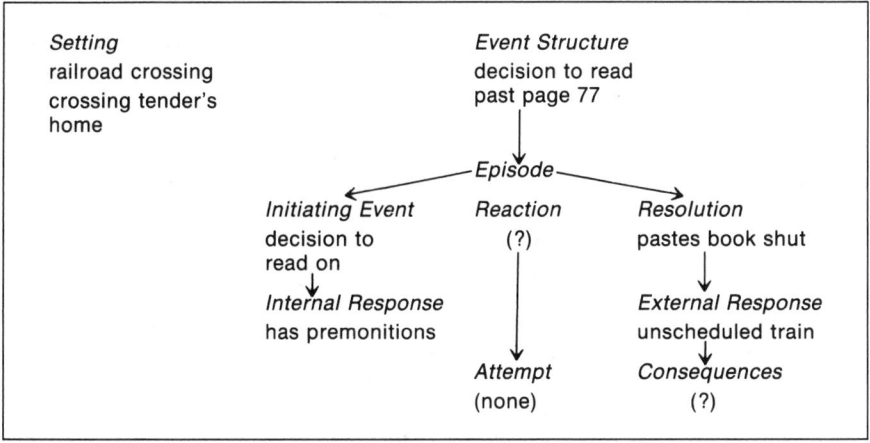

A story map uses many of these same features but arranges them in a vertical flow chart rather than a diagram.

The Setting

Character(s): crossing tender
Place: crossing tender's home at place of work—railroad crossing

The Problem

Crossing tender stops reading his book at page 77.

The Goal

Reading past page 77
     EVENT 1 Crossing tender decides to continue reading.
     EVENT 2 An unscheduled train rolls by, makes no sound.

Resolution

Crossing tender pastes the book shut.

These techniques encourage students to identify critical information in a systematic way. Do they lead to a better understanding and recall of texts? Research results in L1 with elementary school children are mixed (e.g., Beck & McKeown 1981). The problem with such techniques may be that students must organize information in terms of a structure that is imposed on them versus a structure that they generate themselves.

Idea mapping. Mapping has been used in L1 work with high-school and college-level students. Developed so that students could represent the structure of an expository text, the pattern is supposed to provide a spatial representation across the whole text. Practically speaking, like all of the techniques discussed here, idea mapping is completely text-based. As mentioned above, with story maps and story grammars, students select text language to fit a prescribed organizational structure. Possibly because they tend to be more detailed and complex prescriptions, idea maps are generated by the teacher most of the time. They try to be comprehensive, and therefore the necessary amount of detail can result in a formidable intellectual puzzle merely to be filled in by the student (Tierney et al. 139).

Idea maps, like the other text-based techniques discussed in this segment, focus on relationships within the text, but not on connections between text messages and the real world. Consequently, they do little to foster students' perception of textual implications. Their failure to demonstrate bidirectional reading may explain why training in mapping fails to yield long-term gains in comprehension (Armbruster & Anderson).

To sum up reservations about these techniques as a whole, we have tried to illustrate the limitations of text-based activities. In essence, these are the limitations of unidirectional reading (Carrell 1989). Text-based activities most certainly are useful at various stages in the procedures outlined in Chapters 5 and 6: as introduction to texts or textual vocabulary (semantic mapping, graphic organizers), for review of textual information (story or idea mapping), and for testing (as a fill-in exercise). Which activity students choose will depend on the text itself, since several of these activities lend themselves to either expository or narrative readings, or emphasis on content or vocabulary.

What we have tried to illustrate in the examples above is that these activities, because they are text-based, fail to synthesize reader and text propositions. A reduced version of a text may well act as a memory aid or confirmation for students. But it serves to facilitate comprehension of the text, not to replicate it in terms of its message systems and their implications.

LINKING GLOBAL FACTORS TO ILLUSTRATIVE DETAIL— THE MATRIX AS AN INTERACTIVE TECHNIQUE

A text-based pattern may fail to integrate a reader perspective, but at least it is verifiable and reproducible. An integrated or bidirectional reading is, by definition, less predictable. The question is, can readers structure textual information in a manner which reflects individual perception, yet reveals fidelity to the text? How can structuring be text-based, yet allow reader conceptualization of that structure? Will an invalid reading result?

Our answer is that if the textual semantics and weighting are preserved, varied organizations of the text can be equally informative. Illustrations from the resultant information matrices exemplify this point. In the Artmann text it would be possible for the class to agree that the macrosyntax was something like this: *After deciding to read past page 77, the railroad-crossing tender experiences strange events.*

To illustrate this claim, we now turn to multiple structuring approaches to the Artmann text. As a first example, let us presume a student whose reading perspective has been one of cause and effect. To substantiate a cause / effect logic in a matrix structure, that student might organize textual events as follows:

Tender's Action	(implied) *Effect*
reads every day to p. 77	last train goes by every day at 9:35 p.m.
decides to read further	unannounced, silent train at 11:00 p.m., harmonica player in back

If a second student were to focus on the decision (to read on or not to read on), a contrastive logic of "before and after" and the textual information might yield this matrix:

Before Decision	After Decision
reads until p. 77	has a premonition
train at 9:35 p.m. every day	unannounced train
one beer after meals	second beer after seeing unannounced train
book can be read beyond p. 77	book is pasted shut beyond p. 77

What would be significantly different if yet a third student decided to reconstruct an actual chronology?

Chronology of Events	Special Features
Ordinarily: reads book	reads only until p. 77, rereads, owns book for ten years
goes out to watch trains	
has a beer after meals	title: *The Man from the Union Pacific Express*
last train at 9:35 p.m.	
Today:	*Today:*
decides to read past p. 77	has uneasy feeling
11 p.m.—silent train	rubs eyes, pastes book shut after p. 77

All three matrices reassemble important information from the story. However, they use different approaches. One could argue that the third matrix was the least defensible because it is unduly complex—the student had to set up four tables instead of two. The first set in matrix #3, the daily routine, is somewhat artificial since the story lacks a precise chronology. Without more information about ordinary days, the list keyed with "today" does not really contrast with prior routines. Yet that student clearly has a grasp of textual developments. In that sense the answer is quite satisfactory.

Note that with sample matrices one and two, the pattern of information is virtually identical, although the logical frame differs. It has been our experience that *as long as the underlying logic of the reader parallels the meaningful information of the text, the reader may systematize textual facts under a different logic or give that logic different titles and still emerge with fundamentally the same insights.* Categories such as "ordinary events" and "extraordinary events" will, for example, yield the same data as the matrices above.

Although it describes isolated "before / after" situations, the sentence-level exercise with conjunctions lays the groundwork for connected discourse in an "Opinion Exercise" (at the level of the significance of the text for the reader). To express opinions, rhetorical connectors (in this case sentences with conjunctions such as "after" and "before") will probably be necessary. Such connectors predispose readers to consider a related thought. Students who write "After he read the book, some strange things happened" will see the logic of continuing with a sentence that tells what those strange things were.

IMPLICATIONS OF THE PROCEDURAL SEQUENCE

The advantages of this exercise sequence become evident when teacher and students attempt to discuss the story in the target language. The fact that the first levels of the exercise sequence (previewing) have focused on the language of the text reduces the temptation to translate. In the sentence-level assignment, reference to the organized information in the matrix reduces the likelihood that students recall details without perceiving their global applications. Perhaps most important for a communicative classroom, students who have prepared themselves with the written exercises more readily participate in discussion.

Procedurally, students know how the discussion will be managed, regardless of the story. Weaker students can respond with single words or parts of sentences. Just as one would expect from research on individual expression of concepts (Osgood), the relevant information that students locate rarely appears in identical form. The Artmann sentence "Today, he decides to read the novel through to the end, but he is uneasy about doing so" is rendered by the students with simpler sentences. Virtually all students are able to participate at this level, because they need only reveal knowledge of the text. They do not combine talking about the text with language generation.

Let us consider the style of typical student contributions. Characteristic answers and errors for this item are: "Today he wants to read the novel through. He thinks about nothing good"; "Today reads he [sic—word order] the novel"; "Today he ends [sic—word choice] the novle [sic—spelling]; "Today he read [sic—morphology] more." Felix suggests that, as long as student attention is on meaning, students who modify textual language confirm comprehension. Their language use is often faulty, but this is to be anticipated at an interim stage of partial control. The important issue is the degree to which faulty grammar interferes with clarity of message.

Teachers who review answers for meaning clarify ambiguous or grammatically-inaccurate statements first and correct formal grammar second. Although the priority is clarification of meaning, students register covert correction. An inquiry such as "Are you pointing out that today the crossing tender plans to read the novel through to the end or that he has already read the novel?" clarifies a factual point at the same time it covertly emends "today he ends the novel."

For factual as well as grammatical errors, consulting the text is a nonjudgmental way of asking students to repair misreadings of both content and language structure, e.g., "When you point out that the crossing tender reads more, what do you mean? How is that said in the text?"

Teaching repair strategies is preferable to explicit correction because highlighting individual errors embarrasses and disrupts the communicative exchange. Moreover, such overt correction appears to have little influence on students' language use, since linguistic accuracy seems to be subject to individual cognitive development, i.e., the correction may not register until the student is ready (e.g., Faerch & Kasper). Comparing message validity and intelligibility, on the other hand, affords practice in making sense, yet offers students a relatively stress-free environment in which to speak or read aloud from what they have prepared.

In assessing oral and written responses, teachers need to keep in mind that mistakes are more than offset by the fact that students have begun to integrate the story with the language they control. Consequently, instructors who evaluate answers for meaning must clarify ambiguous or discursively-inaccurate statements first and correct formal grammar second. The implication of second-place status for formal grammar implies no denigration, only a priority of clear meaning as the drive behind accurate use of formal features.

MACROLEVEL SYNTAX

Is restructuring the organization of a text in an information matrix tantamount to re-creating the text in reduced form, or is it truly a reader response with independent identity? We propose that a clearly-executed matrix engenders neither reduction nor reproduction. In specifying logic, a choice of syntax, and discourse, the student has created a reading of the text.

Any reassembly of textual language in the information matrix demands cognitive analysis coupled with the ability to manipulate text language (Task # 4 above). Students may choose, for example, to use pronouns instead of nouns ("He reads a book called *The Man from the Union Pacific Express*") or delete language ("reads to page 77"). Regardless of how they label their matrices, student comparisons will reflect "before" and "after" information, because that is the logic of the text: an implied causal relationship between the railroad tender's decision to read past page 77 and the disruption in his life—the mysterious (imaginary?) train at 11:00 p.m.

Matrix organization will not prescribe grammar. It does, however, establish a dominant set of communicative options, because choice of formal grammar to be reviewed is limited by the matrix logic. In the case of the Artmann story, the fourth stage— sentence creation—can be set up in two or three ways, depending on the formal features students would profit from manipulating. If the matrices suggest contrasts ("what happened before / what happened after") or cause / effect (crossing tender's action, ensuing event) the discourse markers of each logic will have to be selected. Of course, clauses can be linked in various ways, e.g., by adverbs of sequence, or conjunctions.

CONTRAST MARKERS: but, however, yet

MATRIX ENTRY: normally reads to page 77 // decides to continue reading past page 77

PROPOSITIONAL CUES: 2 sentences: who + what // adv + who + what
2 clause contrast sentence: who + what // but + who + what

SAMPLE SENTENCES: The crossing tender normally reads to page 77. *However*, he decides to continue reading past page 77 tonight.

SAMPLE SENTENCE: The crossing tender normally reads to page 77, *but* decides to continue reading past page 77.

If the text virtually dictated matrices that compared a *before / after* chronology ("first," "after that," "before he . . ."), adverbial expressions of time and prepositional clauses or phrases expressing time would be appropriate.

ADVERBIAL MARKERS OF TIME: first, usually, sometimes

PREPOSITIONAL PHRASE MARKERS OF TIME: after meals, in the evening

MATRIX ENTRY: reads a book // reads to page 77

PROPOSITIONAL CUES: adverb + who + what

SAMPLE SENTENCES: *Sometimes* the crossing tender reads to page 77. *Usually* he reads to page 77.

If student abilities warrant the challenge, more complicated sentences can be elicited. Complex sentences can be cued along with the syntax problems found in some languages, e.g., word order changes in dependent clauses, mandatory use of conditionals. In the Artmann story, the matrix connects the gatekeeper's actions to an event. Consequently, two separate propositions correspond to two separate clauses which may or may not be linked grammatically. To convey text meaning accurately, however, the two clauses must be linked in discourse, e.g., through cohesion or coherence.

CONJUNCTIVE MARKERS OF CAUSALITY: because, since

MATRIX ENTRY: decides to continue reading past page 77 // silent train rolls by

PROPOSITIONAL CUES: because / since + who + what // what + what

SAMPLE SENTENCE IN WHICH A MAIN CLAUSE
IS LINKED TO A PRESUMED CAUSE: *Because* the crossing tender decides to continue reading past page 77, a silent train rolls by.

OR

SAMPLE SENTENCES IN WHICH AN INITIAL ADVERB SUGGESTS A CAUSAL LINK WITH A PRE-CEDING MAIN CLAUSE:

ADVERBIAL MARKERS OF CAUSALITY: as a result, consequently, therefore, thus

PROPOSITIONAL CUES: who + what // adverb + what + what (2 sentences)

SAMPLE SENTENCES: The crossing tender decides to continue reading past page 77. *Consequently* a silent train rolls by.

The escalation from a weakly implied coherence of events with temporal references to a definitive cohesion in the causality clauses expresses a striking difference in discursive function for the otherwise equivalent information. Such differences in themselves bring home to students the power of discourse markers in expressing overt rather than covert messages. They also establish a basis for considering the fact that Artmann eschews all markers of causality and uses the juxtaposition of events to imply rather than state that such a causality exists. Had he done the latter, the story would have gained explicitness at the cost of its fascination as a metaphor about the power of fictional suggestion.

In the examples above, the sentences may lack elegance, but they represent discrete discursive options. If elegance is sought, an expanded version of the same "Sentence Exercise" could, for example, elicit a series of temporal conjunctions to elaborate on the discourse functions. Such an elaboration would give students practice in linking propositions in an expanded discourse pattern. Consequently, propositions cued in this way demand of the students a greater control of syntax or stylistic options.

Individual adverbial markers such as *previously* and *now* elicit a contrast in simple past and simple present tenses. Temporal adverbs and conjunctions necessitate a contrast between past perfect and past in both German and English. The result would be two sentences such as: "For years the railroad-crossing tender *had read* only to page 77. One day he *decided* to read the book to the end" (a contrast of past perfect and past) or "Before he decided to read to the end, he had only read to page 77" (a contrast of past and past perfect). Such changes in cueing are not only appropriate to review formal features, they also organize complex time references more memorably for the hearer / reader.

Like most discourse markers, these adverbs, conjunctions, and tenses have no absolute meaning. They make relative sense only within a discourse. To become memorable, these markers must be learned in a pattern (e.g., most—least, first—last, always—never). Moreover, when they are learned as isolated vocabulary items, L2 students are tempted to use them in unidiomatic ways.

With a writing assignment that stresses development of ideas, the instructor must evaluate discourse coherence and cohesion as well as formal features. Without corrections of rhetorical flow, discourse logic is obscure to students merely because it has never been pointed out before (Zamel 1985). The explicit link of syntax patterns to discourse intent heightens students' sensitivity to problems of discourse management in the L2. It also reinforces many prior oral activities or gambits by implementing them in the written mode.

MICROLEVEL DETAILS

After the information exercise (in this case, the chronology or comparison of events in the story) has been discussed, it is time to reaffirm connections among these events in a "Sentence Exercise." After the matrix, this next step may appear mechanistic, because to create these sentences the student need only connect propositions already noted in the information pattern. In a second language, however, that task involves sophisticated attention to grammar detail. To express matrix relationships in complete sentences the student must use discrete syntactic or morphological features. Although exercise focus here is more on language detail than was the case in the "Information Exercise," sentence variations help to reinforce links between linguistic structures of the L2 and perception of meaning by the students.

Research suggests that linguistic production does not automatically increase with the increase in passive comprehension of language. In practice, advanced students in many American high schools and universities actually demonstrate a clear deterioration of their ability to connect complex sentences and tend to forget even simpler grammar forms. When students are confronted with a shift from, for example, speaking to reading emphases, production skills usually regress.[3] Consequently, systematic practice in which students connect sentences to develop coherent expression needs to be practiced even at advanced levels of L2 study.

According to Chastain's research, without such practice the gap widens between the sophisticated language of intermediate and advanced reading and the linguistic abilities of the students. When grammar and syntax are separated from the message of a particular text, students cannot build linguistic bridges to textual messages. Students are often able to interpret a text in their native language, yet not in the foreign language (Crow). What is missing is a medial step that stresses student command of syntax in relation to text information. A text-based "Sentence Exercise" that guides students from their comprehension of propositional messages uncovered in the "Information Exercise" to logically-connected sentences can attack this discrepancy between comprehension and production. If managed appropriately, the written exercise can facilitate a discussion in the target language. A number of suggestions follow.

MEANINGFUL REPLICATION OF THE TEXT

After the students have written the "Sentence Exercise," they have connected information to accurate language use on a level between their own abilities and the language of the text. Follow-up activities to reinforce this command are essential. Many texts, for example, lend themselves to pantomimes or visualizations. Even the Artmann story can be acted out with props that designate a house, a book, a paste jar, and a pipe. When the teacher or a student reads a text aloud for others to act out, several advantages accrue. Pantomime makes the text and the nuances of its language less abstract. The activity gives extra practice in matching listening comprehension to actual behaviors and interactions with objects or people. As a classroom gambit, the pantomime is both more fun and more interesting than the traditional reading aloud, because it keeps the attention of the group focused on concrete realization of language.

Reading aloud may have a negative effect on the classroom. When Bernhardt compared the reading comprehension of students who read a text silently and those who read the same text aloud, she concluded that "oral reading as an activity in an instructional environment designed to help students bring meaning to text is clearly out of place" (Bernhardt 1983: 113). She suggests that silent reading is preferable. Silent reading can encourage individual strategies such as skimming and backtracking to confirm comprehension. Reading aloud by students can inhibit active use of these strategies and hence inadvertently encourage inattention.

A pantomime, on the other hand, introduces a dynamic to enhance attention. It allows a visual connection to be established between the sense of a spoken verb and a purposeful activity. Even when students read out parts of the text to prompt the actor, the activity is not a mechanical reading aloud because the pantomime forges a link between acoustic, visual, and kinesthetic memory. Depending on the personality of the class and the teacher, text pantomimes offer not only confirmation of comprehension, but also humor, concrete referentiality, and diversity.

Building on that linguistic base but requiring less of a personal stake, seeing the text as a picture offers students another way to verbalize their individual conceptualization of the story. Drawing pictures places higher requirements of precision on students' expression than do pantomimes, which are limited to acting out textual concepts. Composing a picture according to verbal directions requires more reflection about abstract features such as spatial conceptualization of information relations and the implications of syntactical connections.

Let us assume that one group of students is assigned to draw or diagram the normal scene for the crossing tender. A second group tackles the visual scene after he decides to read the book through to the end. In class, each group must first describe its picture verbally, while it is being copied by the teacher or a designated student onto a transparency or on the blackboard. In one picture, a regular train could show the station clock at 9:35 (perhaps with the moon overhead, to indicate night); the familiar brakeman waves from the back of the last car. The second picture could show 11:00 p.m., a strange train, and another brakeman playing a harmonica. To describe or compare these pictures, students are virtually forced to use relative clauses, prepositions, and adjectives ("Show me the clock on the front of the station which says 11:00"; "Draw a train with an odd glow"; "Draw the man who plays harmonica on the train where he belongs"; and so forth).

Comparing each others' pictures will also require students to observe shifts in tense and time adverbs, the addition of modal verbs to indicate options, and the use of subordinate clauses, e.g., "Before, the train *came* at 9:00; now, it *appears* at 11:00"; "Although the train usually makes noise, the train in this picture does not"; and so on. In order to restrict possible sentences to those anticipated by the "Sentence Exercise" and its variations, the teacher need only point to the relevant part of the picture and specify a logic pattern that students are to use. For example, the teacher can point to the train's glow, and suggest topics that have appeared on students' matrices to key a temporal sentence with two clauses such as "After the crossing tender noticed the strange glow, the train came up," or "he walked out of his house," or "he didn't hear anything." By suggesting such topics for students to comment on, the teacher is reminding the class of the probable syntax that fits their communicative goals.

Such verbal activities give students the flexibility necessary to express their opinions in the L2—to convey ideas. Typical answers to the opinion question "Was the story an adventure?" (referring to the title) were: "The story is not an adventure, because nothing happened. When the strange train came, it made no noise. It wasn't in the schedule. The gatekeeper was dreaming." The opposing view was, surprisingly enough in this case, in the majority. Students used arguments such as: "An adventure is something unusual. After he did the same thing for a long time, the crossing tender did something unusual. He decide [sic] to read the book. When he decided, he gets scared [sic]. Until he sees the strange train, everything is o.k. After the strange train came, he sees that the book has a strange reality, and this reality is dangerous." Regardless of argumentation, all essays needed time references in their sentences. Opinions could not be grounded without proper use of adverbs of time. Despite their lack of elegance, these answers *do* represent coherent chains of discourse.

Although there seem to be advantages to initial strategy practice in the students' native language (see Chapter 4, pp. 68–69), the processing discussed here is designed for successful execution in L2. It commences with top-down factors (global semantics and syntax) and, once these are established, connects relevant bottom-up factors (arrangement of informational details) in the text. Students must recognize and use textual language in initial processing stages. The stage from replication of language to language creativity is aligned with the cognitive transition from explicitly- to implicitly-stated concepts in the text, and with progressive integration of students' language and text ideas.

CLASSROOM ACTIVITIES

After several practice runs with the class as a whole, the teacher can introduce group work, in which three or five (uneven numbers yield better group dynamics) act as teams who offer mutual corrections. On the basis of the homework, a group can prepare an exercise for itself or prepare itself for a contest with another team. The goals of such classroom games should vary. One time, the emphasis can be on correctness ("Which group can make the fewest mistakes?"—with bonus points given to the group that can recognize and correct errors). Another time, rewards can be given for the greatest number of comprehensible variations of one idea ("Which group can think of the most ways to say this?"). In addition to the learning advantages cited in earlier chapters, small groups reduce the instructional time spent on classroom management and shift responsibility for communicative interaction to the students (Allwright; Pica & Doughty).

As these examples illustrate, systematic procedures that link textual propositions to students' language creation can result in statements which are relatively free of mistakes. The main goal in message emphasis is that language moves in the direction of correctness motivated by sense-making. Concern for conveying messages can be derailed by a focus on accuracy for its own sake. Teachers too often reward facility with forms, rather than facility with expression of meaning. The result inadvertently encourages "safe," propositionally-vapid sentences ("He saw the glow"). In a system that looks only at accuracy, more sophisticated ideas embedded in an imperfect sentence construction ("After read he [sic] the book, he the glow saw [sic]") are discouraged.

From a motivational perspective, the safe but vapid proposition has a lower priority than a proposition that does things with words. By rewarding form without attention to content, L2 teachers discourage student efforts to express complex propositions. A learner-centered classroom such as the one illustrated in this chapter rewards starts and correct repairs (Byrnes 1988), rather than looking exclusively at formal properties of language.

OUTLINE FOR A NEW CONCEPT OF READING

The reading model offered here presupposes new procedures for both teacher and reader. The teacher will be interested not in information for itself, but in the logic of the information; not in vocabulary in isolation, but organized in concept groups; not in discrete grammar points, a matter of endings and morphological only changes for their own sake, but in a content-derived morphology and syntax—an unmistakable correspondence with the meaning of the text; not in reading as passive recognition of "an other," but rather as an active cognitive and linguistic process. Finally, the interactive process must be manifested as a position taken by the student writer or speaker vis-à-vis the message of the text. The resulting shifts in presentation of grammar will be briefly sketched here, together with a statement about their effects in the classroom.

Shift #1: Grammar must present a message proceeding from the speaker's logic.

In order to convey a meaning adequately, grammar usage must represent propositional information in a way that makes sense. Such a concept presupposes that there is a necessary connection between speaker / writer logic (propositional intent) and the logic of the sentence (marked by formal features). The task of propositional cues is to identify the correspondences between a specific set of information and its possible expression as sentences, and to use the awareness of these correspondences as the basis for production. The forms which this correspondence takes can be briefly illustrated as follows. For example: when the teacher is asking for specific, discrete pieces of information about a reading text, this information is usually solicited through asking the "wh-questions" (who, what, where, when). Again using the Artmann sketch as a source of information, the conventional grammar approach can be transferred into a propositional framework as follows:

SPEAKER LOGIC / INFORMATION MODEL = "what the crossing tender does"

POSSIBLE SENTENCE LOGICS =

who + *what* (verbal)	The crossing tender is reading.
who + *what* (adjectival)	The crossing tender is alone.
who + *what* + *where* + *when*	The crossing tender smokes behind the house every day.
who (agent) + *what* + *who / what* (receiver)	He sees the last car.*

* Note: This direct object need not be a noun. It could also be referred to by a pronoun (e.g., "he sees it")

This exercise elicits grammar (microdetails) on the basis of the sentence's function as an utterance, not as a mechanical application of rules. Such an exercise cannot be used randomly. In a cognitive sequence that moves from comprehension to production, its procedural position is fixed between the matrices and free expression. As a task that joins the logic of information to sentence structure, the exercise is appropriate only after students' comprehension of textual information has been confirmed.

Shift # 2: Grammar usage must reflect both formal and logical correctness.

When constructing and evaluating exercises and tests for a learner-based classroom, the teacher must distinguish between sensible statements and formal execution. Both elements are important, and each must be given its due. This balance does not usually occur. Between 60 and 80 percent of the grade in most elementary examinations is assigned to students on the basis of their successful realization of details, such as writing out parts of speech, or filling in proper forms of verbs, nouns, and articles, either in blanks or based on dehydrated sentences. Yet research indicates that the details of text language are more memorable when students focus their attention on expressing meaning (e.g., Frederiksen; Meyer). In mechanistic grammar exercises, meaning is necessarily incidental, because such exercises consist of unrelated sentences. They lack coherence. They are not embedded in a gestalt. When sentences fail to connect ideas, either explicitly or implicitly, they cannot "mean" anything. Consequently, the thrust of corrections cannot mean anything either—corrections are often misunderstood or reduced to hollow form.

Out of context, for example, the tenses of verbs seldom alter the meaning of a sentence significantly. In the case of a coherent sequence of sentences, however, tense shifts reinforce the notion of time change. The Artmann story makes this point. Consider the sequence "Earlier, the gatekeeper only read to page 77. Today, he wants to go on." If the student writes "The crossing tender read*s*," a correction focuses on comprehension ("Is he doing it now? Previously?") rather than on morphology. For such contrast pairs (yesterday / today; formerly / now; to this point / now), an accompanying grammatical marker, in this case a shift in tense, is necessary. But the correct form of the verb can be produced (and would be by the more advanced student) without aid of a grammar cue (i.e., without a "past tense" instruction).

As a further illustration, consider the particular problem L2 students of German have with word order, and what shifts in word order imply. The problem, we suggest, is not so much syntactic ("verbs precede subjects when the subject does not start the sentence") as conceptual. As in German, the contrast "Today, the brakeman waved" / "The brakeman waved today" changes not only word order but also meaning. The two sentences occur in different discourses. The first variant ("Today, the brakeman waved") suggests that the time element represents a contrast from what had gone before. Emphasizing this contrast would be the pivotal difference between conventional and propositionally-cued approaches to grammar as exemplified below:

Formal Grammar:

Rewrite the following sentence so that it begins with the underlined word; make any other necessary changes.
1. The train was on time today.
(Desired response: Today, the train was on time.)

Propositional Cues:

Find the reference to time in the following sentence, and underline it.
1. The train was on time today.
Now rewrite the sentence to emphasize the time phrase for the hearer or reader.
(Desired response: "Today. . ." or any additional circumlocution, such as "Today, for the first time, . . .")

Although they are asking for the same final result, the cognitive operations needed to achieve these results contrast significantly.[4] A formal grammar approach assumes that the student will automatically recognize the underlined word as an adverb of time or time expression (an act of grammatical classification) and will be able to apply a generalized rule to this specific case—or to mechanically repeat the change until the generalized rule becomes automatic. For American students, who usually receive little training in formal grammar, this is a questionable assumption. A formal approach further assumes that the system behind the change as an utterance will become clear from the mechanics of the situation.

In contrast, the propositional cues explicitly distinguish these two operations: (1) the identification of a word or set of words as "adverbs of time" or "time expressions," and (2) the functional operation of grammar within the sentence (adverb + change in word order = emphasis). The great advantage in dividing these two acts of comprehension is that the teacher can much more easily determine where errors come from: lexical, syntactical, or cognitive sources. Students ignorant of the grammatical category "adverbs" will fail to function with rules expressed in terms of adverbs, such as "adverbs of time precede adverbs of manner." Yet they may still understand the shift of meaning when an adverb is displaced, because the statement may simply sound right in the L2. Precisely because propositional cues differentiate between formal and functional aspects of language use, they afford a diagnostic and repair tool for students with difficulties. A purely formal approach lacks these cognitive dimensions.

Shift # 3: To create speech acts about texts, grammar usage must be framed by the determinate text situation and a systematic information pattern.

In other words, formal features of grammar should always be taught and tested in context. The advantages of this synthesis for reader comprehension and recall have been widely confirmed in L1 and L2 research (see Chapter 4). The practical problem for the L2 learner is to synthesize the details of language and information (the micro-propositional level or the sentence level) with the macrostructures of the text. The relationship between these two levels must remain clear for the speaker or writer, otherwise "contextual learning" is rhetorical rather than real. To structure production exercises that balance context and language features, students need to have the same constraints: a common reference to situation, content information, and the grammar information necessary to articulate a meaningful, accurate statement. Such a test item could structure these variables as follows:

"Adventure of a Crossing Tender"

(each item: X points for adequate content, Y for formal features)

CONTEXT: the night of the adventure

PROPOSITIONAL MODEL: complex chronology

PRODUCTION MODEL: a sentence with a subordinate clause, using a temporal conjunction such as "since" or "after" and past tenses

Note that although the formal language of different student answers will differ ("After the crossing tender read the book, he saw a glow" or "After he saw the silent train, the crossing tender pasted his book shut"), the discourse and grammatical criteria permit a consistent evaluation. The instructions about the type of sentence to be used also circumscribe the grammatical problems which the student must be able to solve. The setting of a precise environment within the story similarly restricts the text information to be mediated between story and evaluator.

In the grading of the grammar, however, a further weighting is observed: between types of mistakes. In the test items described above, a clear distinction is drawn between those errors which inhibit communication (such as faulty syntax, missed correspondences between singulars and plurals) and those which are mainly stylistic (such as case endings after prepositions, or minimal spelling errors).[5] Consider the student answer "After he read further, the rong [sic] train come [sic]". The textual references are clear and accurate, so that the full three plus points would be assigned for information. Of the two grammar points, one and one-half would be deducted (one for the false syntax "come," and one-half for phonetic spelling). In contrast, a sentence such as "After he read on, he smoked his pipe" is grammatically perfect, but violates the underlying logic of the story. After the crossing tender read on, only extraordinary things happened. Pipe smoking, although it occurs in the story, belongs to the category of routine, normal events in the crossing tender's life. An inference of pipe smoking is inappropriate. Hence at least two out of three points for information would be deducted for content.

These evaluative standards also apply to the reader's oral or written "Opinion Exercise," usually a coherent retelling of the story or a speculation about an alternative end to the story. The exact quantification of plus or minus points always remains a question of classroom practice and program objectives. Our concern here is to suggest that the "democracy of errors" in evaluation fails to reflect current insights into the ties between grammar and meaning. Hence the notion that all errors are equal needs to be replaced with a mode of analysis mirroring communicative procedures—a balance must be struck between awards for correct use of formal features and effective illocutionary use of language to express ideas.

In other words, we find our students' problems in transferring their ability to read, speak, and write in an L2 to be a result of current pedagogical practice rather than a cognitive necessity. We suggest that students can expand linguistic ability and express opinions that are supported by the facts of the text if they can work through a hierarchy of learning activities. Otherwise the multiple processing levels of interactive reading pose excessive demands. By separating those demands and meeting them in a sequence of Preview, Information Pattern, Sentence, and Opinion exercises, students can undertake a structured process of analysis of a text without being overwhelmed by purely linguistic difficulties. At the same time, the procedural model develops the student's ability to unite the content of a text with language competence, a vital component for developing proficiency.

NOTES TO CHAPTER 7

1. The translation was done by Janet Swaffar. This and other illustrations throughout this volume are drawn from actual experience in teaching and representative samples of student work with the texts and approaches described.

2. For a detailed overview of text-based comprehension strategies, including research concerning their effectiveness and exemplification of each model with classroom materials, see Tierney, Chapter 4.

3. The classic results which support these conclusions were presented by Kenneth Chastain. An earlier comparison between audiolingual and cognitive teaching practices (with Woerdehoff) showed clear advantages for the cognitive group in the first year of study. In the second year, however, in which both groups received the identical reading emphasis, statistically significant differences in speaking ability vanished.

4. For the definition and applications of this terminology, see Piaget. To this point, most attempts to implement Piaget's theories have been made in first-language classrooms; see for example: Dasch; Halford; Wadsworth.

5. The question of the seriousness of an error is evaluated differently by native and non-native speakers of a language. Our point is that weighting should reward concepts stressed in class. Students need priorities to develop fruitful study habits. For summaries of available research and a bibliography on error perception in different languages, see Eisenstein or Ludwig.

Eight

Concerns of Colleagues Regarding a Procedural Approach

Previous chapters have looked at the case for reading for meaning in terms of research findings and a procedural model for classroom implementation. In so doing, they have illustrated how that model differs from other approaches to L2 reading assignments. This chapter explores questions of L2 faculty regarding these differences. While previous chapters have stressed the rationale behind these procedures, the discussion in this chapter will focus on the concerns of teachers who want to use them. One of the first questions teachers are likely to have is:

What are key considerations in selecting reading materials for L2 students?

Desirable features of L2 texts are:

1. Topics familiar to the students. No matter what the level of the language class, individual students vary widely in their command of the language. Indeed, they may be more likely to share familiarity with the subject matter than with the language of those texts. We can capitalize on this prior knowledge by selecting texts which present that topic from a variety of perspectives and in the form of different genres.

2. Topics of interest to L2 students. Background in no way insures an interest factor. Students may have the background to understand treatments of ecological questions or the difficulties posed by overpopulation, yet find texts on those subjects unenticing. Because interest level affects level of engagement and consequently, level of performance (Young & Horwitz), teacher efforts to determine particular interests of L2 classes vis-à-vis subject matter probably will contribute to success in L2 reading. (For sample questionnaires to elicit feedback on reader background and interests, see Appendix to Chapter 11.)

3. A substantive, readily-discernible plot or message system. If L2 reading is to be worthwhile, the texts read must be competently written and worth reading. Such texts exhibit clear development of their ideas and intend to say something that offers readers an opportunity to think, to learn, and to enjoy themselves in the process.

4. Clear sequential development. Narratives in which the time scope is framed as a series of events as in fairy tales, or history texts which present those events in sequential order, are easier to follow than prose in which a chronology has been reduced or pulled apart. If past, present, and future are juxtaposed, as in some philosophical texts or fictional works such as Margaret Atwood's *The Handmaid's Tale*, the reader must rely on linguistic features to clarify when events occur and what chronological relationship they have to one another.

5. Well-marked episodes. Closely aligned with the problems they face in texts that lack clear sequential development, readers' comprehension is lessened when the language that signals transition between episodes—changes of people, place, topic, or action—is vague or inconclusive. When readers are told only "On that same day that St. Paul had a blizzard, the sun was shining elsewhere" they may have no idea where the "elsewhere" subsequently discussed might be. As a result, they will be less likely to recognize that what follows is a description of a day in Austin, Texas, than if the transition statement had read "On that same day that St. Paul had a blizzard, the sun was shining in Austin, Texas."

6. A recognizable agent or concrete subject. Stories about identifiable people or situations will be more readable than texts that are more abstract in nature. An editorial about American attitudes towards saving will probably pose greater comprehension difficulties for a reader than a text about particular individuals who have gone into debt through their misuse of credit cards. The text about credit cards will offer some quotations and present facts about individual situations. As a result, the number of concepts or idea units per sentence will probably be smaller than in an editorial that addresses the general problems of bankruptcy, deficits, and materialism. Generalizations must be qualified, and qualifications often result in complex modification of sentence structure or sentence connections.

7. A minimum amount of description. Texts in which something happens necessarily contain the rhetorical features mentioned above—predictable chronology and recognizable agents involved in events. Conversely, lengthy description depends on the flavor of language to create atmosphere or foreshadow events. Unless the scene is concretely visual or supported by illustrations, extended description, like texts lacking clear chronology, often places excessive demands on the L2 reader. With their tendency toward highly differentiated and specialized vocabulary, these texts require such a high level of reader investment in schematizing and language detail that they put the L2 reader at both a cognitive and linguistic disadvantage.

8. An unambiguous intent. Texts which treat a topic from a humorous, or parodistic perspective frequently say one thing but mean another. Consequently, such texts easily confuse L2 readers. Only after students have read about a subject presented from several straightforward points of view are they likely to grasp subtextual humor. Assignment of texts that allow students to compare serious with humorous or parodistic texts will provide readers with the accepted message systems before introducing them to objections to those views. The discrepancy in a humorous text between the surface or denotational statements and their connotational messages can only be appreciated after students understand the connotations and denotations of a serious treatment of the same subject.

9. An appropriate length. Appropriate length for texts will depend on institutional, program, and course goals. For several reasons, teachers may want to rethink the traditional notion that short readings are preferable to long ones. If read in conjunction with the procedural exercises discussed in foregoing chapters, longer texts that are carefully structured and fulfill the criteria above need to be no more difficult to read than shorter ones with equivalent features. Indeed, if a short text lacks these features, it may prove more difficult to comprehend than in the original. Similarly, if episodes or key figures have been edited out, or if the passage is excerpted from a longer work, a short version of a text may actually prove more difficult to read than a longer one. But such an assertion is cautionary only and must not be construed as a blanket indictment of edited texts.

Observations about editing and authenticity. As writers are keenly aware, editing is not inherently bad. The issue of concern is the motivation behind the editing. Simplification in and of itself is not an adequate basis for editorial decisions about L2 texts. If the editor seeks only to reduce lexical difficulty and alters the text without regard to other features that reinforce the text's messages, simplification will probably result in obfuscation. On the other hand, competent editing undertaken to clarify a text's confused message systems and propositions should result in a more readable text when compared with the less coherent original version. If revised for clarity, a well-edited text would be preferable.

Institutional or classroom needs may also dictate reading of edited or excerpted texts. The concept "edited texts" has received a bad name largely because the term has become a catchword for readings in beginning textbooks: Dick and Jane stories to be read for language practice rather than meaning. Editing can, however, serve other objectives. For example, many L1 survey courses depend on anthologies rather than ask their students to read an overwhelming corpus of texts in the original. Content courses in L2 will probably find it necessary to use at least some anthologized or excerpted materials of many authors at the expense of in-depth treatment of only a few.

Nonetheless, a plea can be made for longer texts on the basis of general pedagogical considerations. One such consideration is that texts of more than 500 words seem to activate different reading strategies and recall than their shorter counterparts (Kintsch & van Dijk). In other words, the findings in L1 research suggest that reading of longer texts involves styles of comprehension and recall of that comprehension different from the comprehension and recall of shorter passages. If students are going to apply their knowledge of the second language to continue study or advance in their work environment, they are probably going to have to read longer texts. Consequently, longer works should be represented in L2 course offerings.

In sum, length *per se* has no special virtue, but it is a pedagogical consideration.

What would be an illustration of a selection suitable for a content course?

Let us assume a course whose topical focus is societies. One segment of this course will be devoted to the ethics of medical experimentation or the ramifications of extending life. For a literary treatment of this subject, we have chosen an excerpt from Stanislaw Lem's novel *The Futurological Congress*.

As an excerpt, it exhibits several important features. The passage has a clear beginning and an end. It is comprehensible without additional facts from the longer work. In other words, the observations of Tichy, the protagonist, can be read either independently of a larger context or as part of a related whole. The entry has episodic closure. The referential system of the segment will be evident even to the cursory reader without text-extrinsic information. The passage contains a sufficient number of adverbs of time and place to locate it as occurring during Tichy's initial weeks after being revived. If the diary excerpt is identified for the reader as an early segment in a longer series, students can easily predict a larger scenario. The reader prompted to think in this direction can foresee that the problems Tichy apprehends at this juncture will be discussed subsequently in greater detail and probably augmented by a series of personal, social, political, and economic elaborations. Here, then, is the text.

5 VIII 2039. Four more days and I leave the revivificarium. There are presently 29.5 billion people inhabiting the planet. Nations and boundaries, but no conflicts. Today I learned the fundamental difference between the new people and the old. The key concept is psychem. We live in a psychemized society. From "psycho-chemical." Words such as "psychic" or "psychological" are no longer in usage. The computer says that humanity was torn by the contradictions between the old cerebralness, inherited from the animals, and the new cerebralness. The old was impulsive, irrational, egotistical and hopelessly stubborn. The new pulled in one direction, the old in the other. (I still find it difficult to express myself when it comes to more complex, sophisticated things.) The old waged constant war against the new. That is, the new against the old. Psychem eliminated these internal struggles, which had wasted so much mental energy in the past. Psychem, on our behalf, does what must be done to the old cerebralness—subdues it, soothes it, brings it round, working from within with the utmost thoroughness. Spontaneous feelings are not to be indulged. He who does so is *very bad*. One should always use the drug appropriate to the occasion. It will assist, sustain, guide, improve, resolve. Nor is it *it*, but rather part of one's own self, much as eyeglasses become in time, which correct defects in vision. These lessons are shocking to me, I dread meeting the new people. And I have no intention of ever using psychem myself. Such objections, says the preceptor, are typical and natural. A caveman would also resist a streetcar. (67–68)

The language of the entry is syntactically and semantically straightforward, since it relates physical features of an alien culture in simple sentences and with a minimum of conjecture and opinion—reporting rather than analyzing or criticizing. At the macro-level the selection has many features which are familiar to American students or ESL students in the Americas. The protagonist is frozen and "reanimated," a procedure which has been depicted in other contemporary texts, in books, in movies, and in discussions in the scientific community.

If we select texts for which students possess background knowledge, as in the case of the Lem passage, why talk about it before assigning reading?

We have stated that shared background knowledge facilitates reading. However, like our students' command of L2, the specifics of shared background knowledge will vary widely. To be applicable, that background must be identified and then linked to the focus of the text. If, for example, students have read some George Orwell or Frank Herbert or seen Spielberg's *Star Wars*, their background represents a range of concepts, not all of which are equally appropriate for the Lem excerpt. *Star Wars* is about ancient myths updated into interplanetary heros and bogeymen. Lem's novel takes place on earth and explores the theme of mind control. The perspective used by Lem is closer to Orwell's *1984* than to Herbert's *Dune*, because Lem avoids myths and interplanetary travel.

As an East Bloc writer in the pre-Gorbachev era, Lem makes no explicit political commentary. Like Orwell, his science fiction focuses on a future era on earth in which technology has destroyed individuality and human values. Typical for that subgenre, Lem depicts a future earth in which people have become soulless creatures under soulless conditions.

Accessing what students know about typical scenarios in science fiction is relatively easy. The prereading challenge for teachers is to construct tasks that activate prior knowledge in order to reveal the focus of a particular reading passage. Teachers who attempt to link student knowledge to a text are confronted with two temptations. First, they are tempted to tell students what connections should be seen. Second, it is tempting to ask students to express that connection themselves. Yet these tactics often subvert the goal of introducing a text.

In the first instance, teacher explanations fail to engage the students' points of view and specific types of background which they possess. Explanations impose an *additional* point of view and, if conducted in the second language, impose additional burdens in the students' cognitive processing of unfamiliar language. In the second instance, soliciting student viewpoints, the combination of conceptual and linguistic demands frequently proves to be beyond most students' abilities to respond.

To be oriented to the Lem text, for example, students must recognize that science fiction has several subclassifications. Only then can they appreciate the particular type of science fiction to which Lem's novel belongs. The question "What are the major types of science fiction?" would probably not elicit much useful clarification. First, the question has not been put into a clear frame of reference. Second, none but very fluent speakers make such comparisons without prior linguistic orientation. Interpretation can occur only after students have had practice in thinking about the concepts that underlie a possible interpretation.

How do we get students to think about the concepts in texts?

A good case can always be made for identifying key concepts through matching the students' vocabulary with that of the text. Vocabulary need not be introduced in prescriptive lists. Students are quite capable of scanning a text for unfamiliar words. The resultant list, while more learner-centered than a prescription, would still be random. A more explicit framing asks students to create a list that reveals how the text deals with a given topic. Generally this can be accomplished by having students scan for words that suggest the microdetails of a macroconcept.

In the Lem excerpt, students can locate the various references evoked by the word *psychem.* The resultant list (*psycho-chemical, eliminated internal struggles, subdues, guide, part of one's own self,* etc.) can then be subdivided into categories the teacher suggests by asking "What words describe the characteristics of drugs which you normally expect? Which characteristics strike you as unusual?" When vocabulary is clarified through exercises that frame the contextual function of those words, students seem to be aided in their general reading comprehension.

Why must background knowledge of students be activated through problem-solving?

Texts intend to say something. However, for readers to identify that something, they must engage in problem-solving. That is, readers must bring background knowledge to bear on the new information presented in the text. The intense problem-solving nature of this interaction can be illustrated even with texts that are presumed to be simple as far as their linguistic demands are concerned. Consider the reading of maps. This is an activity which requires minimal command of language; however, different maps offer different kinds of information—hence they need to be encoded in different ways. What information the reader is challenged to uncover will depend on what the map is designed to do: maps of city streets, maps of public transportation, planning maps, aerial maps, geological maps, maps that tell people how to get to someone's house all require readers to apply their background knowledge in different ways.

For a stranger in New York, some maps will be easier to read than others, depending on whether that reader is, for example, a farmer from rural India, a real estate agent from Chicago, or an alien from another planet. Someone who wants to use maps to locate things she knows exist somewhere has an easier problem to solve than someone who has never been to a large city in a westernized society. Tourists looking at a subway map will only be able to use it if they know that subways run underground.

Tichy's reluctant caveman or visitors from distant planets would need to relate the concepts "streetcars" or "subways" to something in their experience before they would be able to use a transit map to get somewhere, even if they understood all the rules about how maps work. Like the caveman, unless L2 readers can match the intersecting colored lines on a transit plan with a real-world correlative, which colored lines go where is meaningless information. Before L2 students can engage in this kind of problem-solving, they must be able to connect textual information with their own experience. And before that can happen, teachers must guide students in identifying the real-world correlatives they possess.

Why do questions about the facts in a passage fail to activate problem-solving?

Correct answers to factual questions will confirm that students prepared for class, but they will not confirm whether students have identified the coherent messages of the text. Questions like "When will Tichy leave the revivificarium?" or "How many people inhabit the planet?" ask students to look at individual thoughts expressed in individual sentences. Alternatively, questions that *connect* facts, such as "What words describe the difference between the old and the new people?" offer a tactic which not only teaches language, but also reveals that students understand how text language relates to meaning.

Students who practice selecting facts which belong together are engaging in guided problem-solving. They are conceptualizing relationships through selection of non-prescriptive language. Discrete questions offer only practice in prescribed selection of language. The difference between discrete-point and problem-solving questions can be illustrated as follows: an assignment that asks students to be responsible for informational detail in a travel brochure of a town has those students confirm detail for its own sake, whereas an assignment that asks the students to read the brochure in order to plan a sightseeing tour has them apply the same details to achieve an objective. Unless applied to solve a problem, factual knowledge creates no direct linkage between language and meaning. Hence students who read for a particular problem-solving activity are more likely to find that linkage in their search for the functional use of a text's language as it expresses relationships and potential realities.

What kinds of classroom activities lead to problem-solving?

The teacher will have to frame a problem-solving orientation to a text. Initially that framing can be achieved through three pedagogical strategies—a task design that (1) narrows the field of inquiry, (2) is nonprescriptive in its expectations, and (3) demands minimal use of language. When, for example, a teacher asks students what books or movies come to mind in conjunction with the term "science fiction," they need only to provide names of familiar books and movies from their experience. Such nonprescriptive answers are linguistically undemanding and minimize use of L1.

The instructor can next ask students to decide which of the resultant titles they would group together, or suggest two or three categories for grouping. As students proceed to sort the original list, the concept of subgenres begins to develop contours. By focusing attention on different treatments within the science fiction genre, the sorting activity will focus reader expectations. Which of the works mentioned are about exploration and control of outer space, and which ones are about earth in the future? Which works will probably present negative images, which are more likely to represent a positive view of future societies?

Through limiting the frame of reference for the subgenres, students have eliminated extraneous possibilities in plot and character development. A brief session about the relationship between genre and subject matter narrows a reader's field to a limited number of likely scenarios—in the Lem excerpt, the ways in which the problems confronting people in outer space probably differ from those of people who live in a futuristic society on earth.

Do careful orientation and problem-solving assignments render actual reading superfluous?

Some teachers are concerned that once students know what the text is about, they won't have a reason to read it. This, of course, depends on how the assignments are constructed. Orientation activities introduce the students to problem-solving at the macrolevel. The actual tasks of identifying the specific features of that problem, the microlevel, are still the students' tasks. We would argue that these procedures actually lead to more rather than less reading of the assignment. When, for example, students must identify features of the new and the old world as Tichy describes them in *The Futurological Congress*, they will have to read the passage not once, but several times.

Writing activities like the matrix assignment motivate rereading, a process which has several pedagogical advantages. Students who reread spend more time on task. They are also engaged in cognitive activity which connects language and meaning. Implicit in thoughtful rereading is a focal attention on meaning which ultimately should encourage automatic processing of vocabulary and structures of the text. Like information, language only partially understood on initial reading is more likely to be fully grasped on second or third readings.

Will rereading result in boredom?

Roland Barthes suggests that all readers need to reread in order to replace their prior expectations with insights gleaned from reexamination of a text.[1] Boredom results when readers *fail* to reread, because without rereading they tend to apprehend only their own preconceptions. They reread the same message in different texts rather than experiencing the stimulation of confronting entirely novel perspectives. In both literature and nonfiction, new perspectives are revealed in the way key concepts appear within the total discourse of a selection. Unless students understand the discourse of a text in terms of a larger system of meaning, they will probably be unable to apprehend what is new or stimulating about it.

As an illustration, whether students recognize the term *cerebral* as a cognate or look it up in a dictionary, most readers of Tichy's diary entry will probably understand the word as a reference to the human intellectual or rational faculty. Consequently, when they read this word, students whose preconception is that cerebral means "rational faculty" will be puzzled by the textual distinction between "old" and "new" cerebralness. Only after they equate "old cerebralness" with "stubborn, irrational, inherited from animals," can readers appreciate that Lem is referring to the reptilian brain or cerebellum. In Tichy's world, the new cerebralness, the cerebrum no longer needs to mediate between rational and irrational. Psychem replaces its mediating function and in so doing, the decision-making function of the new cerebralness. In this way texts, not dictionaries, define words.

What keeps a matrix assignment from being a copying exercise?

Since students select language in a passage to execute their assignment, a matrix always involves copying. It also, however, involves more than copying. When students look for language that maps meaning, for words and phrases that serve a particular function in the story, they will have to ask themselves questions about what that language signifies, as the example above concerning the definition of "cerebral" illustrated. It is the matrix assignment's demand for reader assessment in selecting the item to be copied that precludes it from being a mechanical task.

Is there a preferable organization (a right matrix) for textual information?

The answer to this question depends on teacher and reader goals. Reading Lem for implied features of life under a totalitarian regime may yield a different sorting of information than a reading centered on text-explicit information. A reading for positive and negative features of Tichy's world would yield virtually the same information subsumed under the same comparative logic as old versus new society: bad can be equated with language such as "impulsive," "irrational," "egotistical," or "waste of mental energy," whereas good is implied by phrases such as "internal struggles eliminated," "psychem subdues old cerebralness," and the like.

But not all categories will work for all texts.

Different texts have different logics depending on their context and informational objectives. Some choices of organization are not reflected in the text or may demand that students generate language before they comprehend its meaning. For example, if students wanted to set up a causality logic using Lem's passage, they would have to generate one-half of the matrix. They would have to speculate that "as a result of taking psychem people probably . . ." Not only would that logic demand sophisticated language use, it would also focus on textual implications rather than on what the text says. Before proceeding to the text's implications, students should identify that the conflict-free utopia which Tichy innocently describes at face value is the result of self-deception. Only after rereading and creating a matrix of explicit information can students pinpoint how psychem eliminates freedom of choice and decision. Only thereafter can they infer that what sustains the "new cerebralness" in this society is the fact that the drugs people choose render them incapable of caring about what they think or feel. Students may then speculate that probably chemicals eliminate mental struggle at the price of judgment, that psychemized human beings turn themselves into robots.

Such insights are the central implications of textual information unavailable in the surface language of the text. Only after students have looked at what is said, at the information which compares the non-psychemized with the psychemized behavior, are they really using the text (rather than their own, text-extraneous opinions) to draw conclusions about what this comparison probably implies, namely a new definition of human behavior.

Can these procedures work with any text, trivial as well as literary ones?

Most literature addresses significant issues. In the novel from which our illustrative passage was chosen, Lem depicts rationality gone mad. The information Tichy provides in later entries about the temptation to live in a dream world rather than reality and the use of psychem for criminal purposes makes it clear that in a society where the will and the judgmental faculty are co-opted, moral values are irrelevant.

Not all readings have significant messages, and neither students nor teachers want to read significant literature all the time. A case can be made for periodic selection of trivial readings, since a popular text often reflects unquestioned acceptance of behaviors criticized in a literary work. When ads, reviews, or magazine articles are read in conjunction with literature, the contrasts between cultural clichés in the trivial texts and criticism of these clichés in literary texts can be informative. As an illustration, the following article presents the general topic of prolonging life from the perspective of a popular magazine.

DISNEY ON ICE
by Carol Cioe

To set the record straight, Walt Disney's body is not frozen. But James Bedford's has been for eighteen years. When the seventy-three-year-old Glendale, California, psychologist died in 1967, he became the first human placed in cryonic suspension. There he lies, his blood replaced by chemicals, his body frozen solid until scientists discover a cure for cancer—not to mention a way to bring frozen corpses back to life.

Cryonics disciples admit the movement's fervor has chilled somewhat since the Sixties and Seventies, when as many as forty persons were frozen in storage capsules. Only eleven bodies remain, according to Arthur Quaife, president of Trans Time of Emeryville, California. "Many didn't make the proper legal and financial arrangements and had to be thawed," he says. Quaife's organization requires members to pay a minimum of $80,000, usually through life insurance—$20,000 pays to prepare the body for freezing, while the rest is invested to cover maintenance. The South Florida Cryonics Society will not consider anyone with less than a $100,000 policy. But skyrocketing costs aside, the most significant factor against recruitment is the lack of a track record. Medical science is far closer to finding a cure for cancer than a cure for death, and cryonics researchers are struggling for funds to continue their work. "The progress in research is slow. We can't show we can freeze a person today and bring him back tomorrow," says Quaife. "It's hard to sell on that basis."

The organizations, four in California and one each in Florida and Michigan, do continue to sell hope. And, however slim, hope is enough for most members. The faithful total more than 125 nationwide and include a high percentage of computer specialists, physical and mathematical scientists, and teachers—"people who have an appreciation of the power of modern science, who think it's better to be alive than dead," says Quaife. Austin Tupler, president of South Florida Cryonics, finds solace in such medical strides as the freezing of blood, sperm, and limbs. "I don't think I have much chance of coming back. I feel I'm donating my body to science," he says. "But my three sons will have a 15-percent better chance than I do. It's worth it for that reason." And for those who look askance and joke about "corpsicles," Tupler has a rejoinder: he just might have the last laugh.

A comparison of the two passages reveals how much difference orientation makes. Tichy worries about adaptation to the new world. The problems that the Cryonics Society talks about are mainly financial and scientific. In addition, there are some implications about social class which are totally missing in Lem's text. In the magazine article, only the very rich can afford to be frozen. Thus in this different genre, the same topic is put in a frame of reference quite different from that of Lem's novel. Fictional actuality (Tichy's diary) is reframed here by a journalistic description of a potential actuality. A completely different logic is at work. If the magazine article is read in conjunction with the Lem excerpt, students have two distinct message systems about the same subject: freezing and reviving dead people.

What if the magazine article seems to offer only facts and lacks a clear message system?

Most texts lack an explicit message system. The problem-solving that faces a reader is the creation of a consistent system which reflects the messages of the text, yet arranges them coherently in a manner which may not be self-evident in the textual presentation. Just as "Disney on Ice" may appear at first glance to offer nothing more than incidental facts about the Cryonics Society, many texts appear on first reading to be no more than collections of information on a given subject. If reading is to be meaningful, however, the reader needs to reflect about the metacategories of those facts as cause or effect, a contrast, or features and implications.

Viewed from a metaperspective, some facts in "Disney on Ice" can be understood as features of the Cryonics Society, other facts as problems facing the group: skyrocketing costs—and the fact that reviving the dead is far from a reality. If indeed most of the information in the text can be organized by focusing on the facts of its topic—the status of the cryonic movement—and problems that movement is currently confronting, the reader has succeeded in uncovering reasonable metacategories. After a few trials, students will start to recognize that journalistic treatments frequently present facts in a manner that suggests that some facts are features of a situation and other facts constitute problems or the impact of those features. In the case of "Disney on Ice," such a sorting of textual information might yield the following matrix:

Features	*Problems*
first human in cryonic suspension died in 1967	no cure for cancer, no way to bring frozen corpses back to life
forty people frozen, only eleven remain	many didn't make proper legal, financial arrangements
pay a minimum of $80,000	skyrocketing costs, lack of track record
four organizations in California, one each in Michigan & Florida, (about) 125 members nationwide, members are computer specialists, scientists, and teachers	progress in research is slow, researchers struggling for funds, sell hope, can't show we can freeze a person today and bring him back

How can students who lack a large vocabulary set up a valid matrix?

The answer to that question is that the ability to think about the text needs to be practiced as a skill separate from decoding L2 vocabulary and grammar. Teachers sometimes take a few minutes out of initial class time to introduce the concept of matrix design applied to L1 texts. Another way to practice conceptualizing the message systems of a text is to use class time to have students skim a passage dealing with a familiar topic, yet written in an entirely unfamiliar foreign language. If the passage mentions dates, names, and places or has sufficient cognates in a familiar alphabet, the class can work together to puzzle out stages in idea development or story episodes. They recognize that their relative success is grasping the gist of a text written in an unknown L2 resulted from their reliance on an information pattern to help them map meaning.

Will students find it easy to execute a matrix if they have never done so before?

Students totally unfamiliar with this procedure require initial guidance. Generating a matrix is no easy task for students who have never approached reading in this way. Only after five to six weeks of practice with partial matrices can readers be expected to create their own. Until then students should work with a partial matrix which identifies major category types and some of the answers appropriate to those categories (e.g., Grellet, Vansant et al.). These assignments will facilitate reading and serve as models for later independent analysis.

In conjunction with a partial matrix, class time devoted to small group work gives two or three students an opportunity to problem-solve together. When a class is structured so that student groups can consult with each other and with the instructor, readers discover the virtue of multiple strategies: identifying words from context, noting discourse markers as indicators of text development, or recognizing parts of speech to establish whether, for example, the word "cryonics" names something or describes an action.

Prereading sessions will have to orient the class to the subject of the text (a society that arranges for the freezing of corpses in the hopes of bringing them back to life) in terms of key phrases that express details of that topic such as "cryonic suspension" (a technical term) or "financial arrangements" (the euphemism for $80,000). Particularly in initial stages of reading for meaning, prereading work should help students establish the metacategories of textual information and representative textual language that elaborates these categories.

How can students achieve better understanding of vocabulary meaning by selection of words for a matrix?

Even though students may only understand the unbracketed words in the statement "progress in [research] is slow," the decision to put the entire statement in the problem category reduces the range of the unfamiliar word's possible meanings in this particular text. The progress must have something to do with difficulties facing the cryonic society. If the list is examined vertically (reading all the problems from top to bottom), one sees entries like "no way to bring frozen corpses back to life" or "can't show we can freeze a person and bring him back to life." It is this scientific problem area in which progress is slow. Failure to decode "research" has not inhibited reading or led to misreading. At a later point, if a standard definition of "research" is sought or provided in class, the word should be more memorable for having been the object of prior, relatively non-frustrating reflection about its generic meaning within this discourse.

To return to an example from the "Disney" matrix, compare the feature entry "eleven people out of the original forty still frozen" with the problem entry "absence of proper legal, financial arrangements." Once students grasp the causality of "thawing bodies" and "lack of proper arrangements," words like financial and legal become logical particulars of lack of proper arrangements. Even without a precise mapping for "legal and financial arrangements," students can link this language to resultant problems such as thawing corpses.

Certainly misreadings and faulty guesswork will occur. With a written matrix, however, a teacher can diagnose these difficulties because the written assignment reveals a total pattern of student perception. A teacher who reads the phrases in the two columns can quickly determine whether students have understood the text well enough to speculate about whether the chances of being brought back to life after freezing are good or not good. Misapprehensions can be clarified through a classroom review of perceptions about which information belongs under which heading. Once students see an underlying or metapropositional meaning linking three statements within a category or in a juxtapositioned category, vocabulary meanings emerge. Words such as "track record" are in the same column with the phrases "sell hope" and "struggling for funds." A poor track record has contributed to the low probability that hopes will be rewarded or funds found.

How can a matrix be used to help students talk about a text in a grammatical and meaningful way?

Student participation in a language class will depend on the teacher's sensitivity to a task hierarchy. The initial speaking stage is reading aloud that text language which illustrates its information pattern. At the next stage the student is ready to use that information pattern as the basis for speaking and writing, first at the sentence level and subsequently in connected discourse. The sentence and discourse types which emerge will depend on the informational systems of *The Futurological Congress* or "Disney on Ice"—what kind of sentence-level grammar is implied by their information pattern. As with the comprehension tasks, students' success with activities that enable them to express meaning will depend on the way the teacher frames those tasks.

The following example illustrates some of the framing features to consider. An assignment that asks students to read to compare features of the new and old cerebralness in the Lem excerpt would result in sentences such as "The old cerebralness was more impulsive than the new one" or "The old cerebralness was impulsive, but is eliminated by psychem." Consequently, one optimal use of such a matrix at lower levels would be to teach or review comparison of adjectives, or with more advanced students, the discourse markers that signal contrast.

Another framing feature to keep in mind is that assignments must encourage fidelity to textual meaning. The concern for accurate reflection of textual meaning frames grammar usage. For example, it is misleading to ask students to write sentences such as "The old cerebralness was impulsive, but the new cerebralness soothes." The problem with this wording is that, unlike Tichy's prose, this construction implies that the new cerebralness is the agent for a feeling of comfort. However, as the text depicts this form of cerebralness, it is not an agent itself, but the result of a use of psychem. Because it is caused by the drug, the "new person" or "new cerebralness" is in actuality the experiencer rather than the actor.

The teacher can help students identify such distinctions by creating exercises that point out the inherent meaning (semantics) of certain syntactic forms. In this case, students are asked to produce constructions that use "people" ("People feel soothed," "People are improved"), and contrast these with sentences that involve psychem. In the case of the use of "people," the construction conveys a sense of people experiencing something. In contrast, students will likely place "psychem" in the subject position and use an active verb, resulting in the meaning of "active agent" ("Psychem soothes," "Psychem improves"). The resultant sentences are not only grammatically correct, they also correctly mirror in their syntax the semantics of the text.

Why is writing a sentence based on the matrix any more integrative than writing a dehydrated sentence or filling in a blank with the correct form?

Compare the task of writing a series of sentences in the past tense based on the matrix for the Lem text with an assignment that asks students to write sentences based on the cues "Psychem / to eliminate / internal struggles (past tense)." Transformation of "to eliminate" into "eliminated" does not let the student reflect about whether it matters if the verb chosen is "eliminate," "soothe," or "help." The dehydrated sentence exercise dictates that students transform formal features, not ideas. Presumably, students will pay more attention to meaning if they are transforming the information they consider relevant.

Additionally, if the language is drawn exclusively from the matrix, the resultant sentences will necessarily reflect the larger informational coherences in the text. Consequently they constitute a first stage in the development toward expanded discourse. It is a relatively easy step for students to transform their factual statements about the messages of the text to illocutionary statements in which they discuss the implications of a passage and express their own opinions about it.

What kinds of assignments bridge the gap between sentences and connected discourse?

Once students have demonstrated comprehension of textual messages and the ability to express those messages in simple sentences, they are equipped with the cognitive and linguistic tools to take positions on the fundamental issues raised by a passage. They have command of key concepts in both texts presented in this chapter: Lem's psychemized world which eliminates the need for reality and the Cryonic Society's pragmatic world which exists within realistic economic and social constraints. At this point in the exercise sequence it is reasonable to ask students to reframe either message by introducing their text-extrinsic point of view. Grammar usage will not be more complex but consistent within the framework of a given scenario. For example, students can practice expressing simple active or entailed sentences that advertise the use of psychem. That assignment would result in sentences such as "Psychem (can, will) assist, sustain."

For a framing that is linguistically more demanding, a review of the subjunctive, the teacher can ask students to speculate about their personal reactions if put in Tichy's situation. The result would be a series of sentences modeled along the lines of "If I took psychem, it would not soothe me." Similarly, for "Disney on Ice," students asked to argue whether they would or would not consider joining the Cryonics Society must review their matrix and decide whether or not they would spend $100,000 this way or speculate about whether scientists will someday be able to thaw corpses and bring them back to life.

The foregoing assignments would be based on the assumption that students knew how to use subjunctive forms. It is, however, a simple matter to frame opinion questions which need no subjunctive features. If students have had active practice in only present and past tenses, modals, conjunctions, and comparison of adjectives, they will be able to express their ideas in an essay question such as "Which world do you want to live in—Tichy's or ours?" This formulation avoids the pitfall of a too demanding task such as use of the subjunctive, yet allows the individual student to examine textual messages and practice expressing those reflections in connected discourse.

Why is it important to reflect about a text, even a factual report such as "Disney on Ice"?

From the standpoint of the reader *all* writing is the real world once removed. The text's information, how that information is weighted and organized, the goal intended by the writing—that reality is the writer's text. The reader's job is bidirectional: to use real-world knowledge to interact with the text's reality and to do so without distorting it. Even when a text seems to consist of nothing but real-word facts or cultural clichés, neither the facts nor the clichés are its meaning. A text's meanings emerge from the reader's perception of its information pattern, and the implications and significance of those patterns.

The foregoing questions are by no means an exhaustive inventory of pedagogical concerns. Several large realms of inquiry remain, each of which deserves separate discussion: the introduction of reading in beginning instruction, testing reading for meaning, teaching reading in advanced content and literature courses, and identifying the curricular implications of these approaches. The remaining chapters in this book address each of these concerns in turn.

NOTE TO CHAPTER 8

1. The full quotation is: "Rereading, an operation contrary to the commercial and ideological habits of our society, which would have us 'throw away' the story once it has been consumed ('devoured'), so that we can then move on to another story, buy another book, and which is tolerated only in certain marginal categories of readers (children, old people, and professors), rereading is here suggested at the outset, for it alone saves the text from repetition (those who fail to reread are obliged to read the same story everywhere), multiplies it in its variety and its plurality: rereading draws the text out of its internal chronology ('this happens *before* or *after* that') and recaptures a mythic time (without *before* and *after*); it contests the claim which would have us believe that the first reading is a primary, naive, phenomenal reading which we will only afterwards have to 'explicate,' to intellectualize (as if there were a beginning of reading, as if everything were not already read: there is no *first* reading, even if the text is concerned to give us that illusion by several operations of *suspense*, artifices more spectacular than persuasive); rereading is no longer consumption, but play (that play which is the return of the different)" (15–16).

Nine

Testing Reading for Meaning

Tests that measure classroom achievement of learner-based instruction require rethinking of item types and their goals. As Omaggio points out, the traditional achievement test with its single-sentence format and discrete-point items (fill in the blanks, translation, matching) evaluates only formal accuracy in decontextualized situations (1986, 311). In her discussion of readability criteria, Nuttall concludes that "no mechanical test . . . can be completely reliable" (29). She suggests that a test's difficulty depends on more than linguistic factors: e.g., reader objectives in independent reading, classroom reading, general information, or research. Tests that value comprehension of meaning must reward "propositional and illocutionary development beyond the sentence level, as well as the interaction between language behavior and real-world phenomena" (Wesche 552–53). In sum, learner-centered tests reveal students' cognitive processes. They are tests that reward a communicative or proficiency-based learning style.

For tests of reading, an interactive approach suggests four processing factors to be considered: informational background (the reader's context), metacognition (how does the reader structure comprehension?), intent (why is the text being read?), and the reader's language proficiency. These factors, in turn, have their correlative in the text. Each text has context (Who is Madame X? Where is she? What is she doing?), a structure of information (Does Madame X arrive before or after the rain begins?), an authorial intent (Is this passage written to teach language? To entertain? To argue a particular point of view?), and a particular choice of vocabulary and usage. According to L1 interactive theorists, the successful reader processes these components in a parallel rather than a linear way, i.e. either a top-down or bottom-up sequence. Until recently, tests looked only at individual aspects of reader processing because combination items were considered unreliable. The problem with tests of single factors in reading comprehension is that they fail to measure the *way* a reader comprehends.

In sum, tests of reading should diagnose not only text-based products, but reader-based processing. What processes characterize successful L2 readers? Based on the research cited in earlier chapters, there seem to be at least six general tendencies. Successful readers: (1) correct misreadings, (2) link concepts between sentences rather than focusing solely on information within sentences, (3) identify textual organization, (4) express comprehension more fully in the native tongue than in the second language, (5) engage in a gamut of reasoning strategies not necessarily identical with those of fellow classmates or the constructor of the test, and (6) understand both what is written and how to apply what is written to their own purposes or views. How can these tendencies be acknowledged in tests?

1. Reading tests should assess student schemata as a factor in text selection.

Initial misapprehension of a text can result in consistent misreading, yet a misreading that is viewed diagnostically may reveal success in several of the processes listed above. Bernhardt (1986c), for example, reports on a passage dealing with ecological issues unfamiliar to American students. One student in her study encoded the word *Waldkrankheit* as *Weltkrankheit*. The notion of a *sick woods* is unfamiliar to the American student. Hence a schematic change from *sick wood* to *sick world* is a reasonable reading for someone who is familiar with ecological issues, but has not been previously exposed to the popular or scholarly debates concerning Germany's dying woods. The evidence in favor of a schema-driven reconstruction is that this same student read a subsequent passage and recalled *Wald* as *woods*. The correct recall in the second passage suggests that the initial misreading (*Waldkrankheit* > *Weltkrankheit*) resulted from a failure to grasp the message systems of the first passage (attributed above to L1 schema interference—an encoding problem) rather than failure to "know" the dictionary meaning of *Wald* (a decoding problem).

Bernhardt's evidence suggests that the issue of misreading is often a cultural rather than a language problem (see also Johnson; Steffensen et al.). In other words, L2 tests need to be sensitive to reading problems arising from cultural ignorance. To avoid assessments based on cultural rather than linguistic deficiencies, tests should solicit data about student background on the subject of the passages they read. Alternatively, the teacher can make an effort to ascertain shared academic or personal interests of a class. If determined at the outset of the school year or semester, that information can be a factor in selection of passages on a test. Only then can selections challenge students with a similar level of schematic difficulty. The issue is not that readings must be familiar, only that students who read them must share a similar degree of familiarity or unfamiliarity with the subject matter.

2. Reading tests should include items that reveal a grasp of intersentential links.

Frequently L2 readers fail to register logical connectors (e.g., *since, because, nevertheless*), words that they process automatically and quickly in their native language (Mackay & Mountford). Increasingly, researchers suggest that discourse practices vary among languages. Some believe that conflicting L1 / L2 ways of organizing information (style) may cause special difficulties for readers. For example, Bernhardt's (1987) eye-movement study revealed that native speakers of German spent more time on words linking sentences and so-called function words (prepositions, conjunctions) than did non-native readers—even non-natives with considerable reading proficiency. Others have found that the presence or absence of connectors (Chaudron & Richards), or factors such as contrasting word order may, in and of themselves, inhibit comprehension (LoCoco).

In short, reading problems facing the L2 student may vary from one language to the other. L2 research suggests that, among other problems, poor readers are less able to connect ideas than successful readers. Increasingly, researchers point out that words like *nonetheless, in spite of that,* and *because* often introduce "macromarkers," since such adverbs and conjunctions signal major shifts in textual logic and link concepts in particular patterns. Student awareness of how syntactic markers link ideas seems to affect their reading comprehension as much as does their command of vocabulary (Barnett 1986). Consequently, a reading test needs to be sensitive about whether student failure to connect ideas is caused by ignorance of semantic items or a failure to schematize that language's syntactic markers.

3. Reading tests should enable students to demonstrate their view of textual organization.

Closely allied with the foregoing discussion about intersentential markers is a body of L1 and L2 research that explains why it is so important for students to be able to recognize macromarkers. We have discussed evidence about students who recall a particular textual organization—cause/effect, problem/solution, contrast, issue/implication. Apparently, when students perceive a particular textual organization they have better understanding of the text than when they perceive only random information or descriptions. Their recall is also significantly higher.

4. Reading tests should, if feasible, allow some reader conceptualization of text meaning in the native language.

Selective use of the native language, particularly in early stages of language learning, seems to allow a fuller assessment of students' rhetorical schematizing and command of detail. Lee (1986a) conducted L2 studies on the effect of background, in part to assess measurement variables that may distort results. In an earlier study, Carrell (1983) had compared the effects of background knowledge on native and non-native speakers and concluded that the effects, while significant for natives, were not significant for the non-natives' reading comprehension.

Lee challenged that conclusion. To do so, he used the identical texts and evaluative techniques as those employed by Carrell, with the single exception that his L2 students wrote their recall protocols in English, their native language, whereas Carrell's ESL students, who also used English, were writing in their second language. Lee's results indicate that background factors are significant when students are allowed to write about an L2 text in their native language. He concludes that "assessing comprehension with the native language allows learners to more fully demonstrate their comprehension" (353). Similar findings in ESL studies suggest that, for an as yet unspecified period of time, asking questions in the native tongue (Tan & Ling) and allowing students to provide longer narrative answers in L1 results in better student performance.

5. Reading tests should ascertain the reasoning behind a student's conclusions.

Tests should enable students to use both the first and the second language to express ideas. Here information about how students arrived at their conclusions is more important than language. Students use multiple strategies to comprehend. The key distinction in processing is not what strategies students use, but the ultimate objective of those strategies, whether their aim is to decode or to encode text language.[1] A student who brings prior knowledge to information in a text tends to encode, i.e., create patterns of meaning with language. In the alternative reading mode, decoding, the reader matches L1 and L2 surface language without necessarily anchoring patterns to meaning. This reader looks at linear sequences of words and explicit information. Encoding, the process by which the student constructs meaning, occurs when a reader connects facts and draws inferences.

Assessment of encoding often involves a mingling of skills (e.g., comprehension and writing). Students must not only recognize that Madame X arrives before it starts raining, they should also be able to identify text language or information which confirms facts and inferences. While unorthodox in the sense of strict skills separation in testing, Oller and others who argue for *unitary proficiency* (ability in one skill transferring to another) actually conclude that tests with mixed skills may have greater validity.

Practical problems abound with tests of mixed skills. Foremost among these is the way teachers weight errors in L2 written language. To weight meaning as well as form, a teacher must judge whether the faulty language usage inhibits or distorts the picture of student reading comprehension. The biggest problem we see with such formats is the teacher's tendency to weight language errors so punitively that students' substantive command of text content cannot offset their language deficiencies. When left to individual judgment, weighting of errors can be arbitrary—differing from one instructor to the next. This problem emerges in studies about disparities in native and non-native speakers' or teachers' and laypersons' assessments of error severity (e.g., Eisenstein). Such difficulties will be addressed in the section on production exercises later in this chapter.

6. Reading tests should enable students to demonstrate a grasp of the text's cultural and authorial characteristics.

If teachers want to encourage reading for meaning, tests of reading must go beyond the level of what a text says to the level of whether the L2 student can think about or do something with what the text says (e.g., Perrig & Kintsch). If we apply the procedural model proposed in Chapter 5, testing reading for meaning involves testing both the grammar rules of language and their function—the context and intent of the passage's information and ideas.

Written discourse creates its own context—its own culture. In a text, cultural appropriateness is also created by the author. For example, the boundaries between correct usage and functional use in the text often result from intentional authorial ploys

(Brecht's biblical formulations, or Pinter's use of profanity, for example). Tests that distinguish between the cultural background of the text and the text's interpretation of that cultural background might ask students to identify either diachronic factors (comparison of historical developments) or synchronic ones (comparison of contemporary phenomena).

As an illustration, the book *Megatrends*, written in the early 1980s, looks at shifting demographics in the United States sunbelt due to economic factors (a developing electronics industry) and changing standards of living (a commuter population with leisure time). By the late 1980s, environmental factors such as water shortages and air pollution began to assume the status of economic issues. At the time it was written, the book was a best-seller with prophetic vision. Today readers may find the book symptomatic of a problem in cultural attitudes of the eighties: short-sightedness with regard to natural resources. A test about *Megatrends* would have readers first ascertain what the text says and then elicit those readers' verbal interpretations about what the text says to *them*. To have read the book and to be able to do no more than identify pieces of its information is hardly training for real-world applications of the second language in school or in the workplace.

THREE IMPLICATIONS FOR L2 TEST DESIGN

A test of reader processes, then, looks at multiple cognitive and linguistic skills in order to see if the student can (1) account for a text's pragmatic as well as its informational and formal features, (2) link comprehension to L2 production in a cognitive sequence, and (3) acknowledge individual variance in answers. Objective reading tests have the great virtue of readily-assessed item validity. They are subject to serious criticism, however, on the grounds that they fail to reflect interactive processes. Bernhardt (1986b) sums up the problem quite aptly by questioning whether tests reveal proficient texts or proficient readers. Similarly, Lee (1987a) points out that any test which ignores the significance of reader background probably rewards bottom-up processing. Reading tests that fail to account for the reader deny an interactive hierarchy. To acknowledge reader interaction, questions must discriminate between different focuses of reader perception. What types of questions achieve this goal?

COMPONENTS OF AN INTERACTIVE TEST FOR READING

1. Diagnostic rather than objective items. A holistic approach to language learning redefines the tester's task. Traditionally, reading tests have been constructed by practitioners who ask students to replicate textual facts. In effect, the L2 reader is asked to match textual and test language. When the student reads the question "When did Mary arrive?", finding the textual answer ("at seven p.m.") results from matching the lexical meaning of individual words and phrases. The student may or may not realize that due to a series of circumstances alluded to indirectly in the passage, Mary barely made the appointment on time. A discrete-point question fails to incorporate multiple units of information implied by the text as a whole, such as "rain," "car breakdowns," and the vagaries of buses. Single-item questions may, but rarely do, integrate contextual factors like the time of year in the passage, or the size of the community in which Mary lives.

Most standardized tests in reading use multiple choice items. This practice has inevitably influenced L2 classroom testing. Two problems occur with this item type. First, since multiple choice questions ask students to match the test item's language with textual language, they tend to be text-based. They often emphasize vocabulary matching rather than drawing conclusions or making inferences about the text. Second, the emphasis on surface language discourages interactive reading. When test items stress proficiency with text language—the ability to match synonyms or confirm textual facts—an integrated perspective on the part of the reader is superfluous and may even prove a handicap. When confronted with a unidirectional test, bidirectional readers may find their dual perspective a disadvantage.

Interactive reading is thwarted when multiple choice items trigger only a bottom-up strategy for reading (letter to word to phrase). Often correct answers depend on correct usage—"walked *into* the room" versus "walked *by* the room" or an idiom such as "went to pieces" for "became hysterical." Such tests have clear advantages for quantifiable results. They yield norms. But the exclusive use of standardized tests is inappropriate for achievement testing in the classroom because objective items fail to motivate integrated or bidirectional reading. Instead, multiple choice questions force students to think about competing patterns, only one of which is correct. Consequently, objective tests cannot help us diagnose the basis for a misreading, e.g., determine whether a misreading results from inadequate vocabulary, syntax, or schemata. By default, multiple choice tests evaluate primarily students' command of the grammar and vocabulary of the passage rather than their comprehension of the text.

Even when they strive to target global comprehension, multiple choice items have limitations. They necessarily have a replicative, text-based focus. Even when the item asks for the main idea of a passage, the student only matches test items against statements in the text. Instead of examining one of the text's multiple meaning factors (context, intent, information), the student reader is asked to evaluate an encoding of text meaning. Success depends on how well the student maps a test's equivalencies. To diagnose reader comprehension, items must assess discrete interactive processes of the individual reader.

2. *An item sequence from comprehension to production.* To be able to think about or do something with a reading passage involves major readjustment in our current tests of reading. Tests of reading must reveal that students are able to comprehend textual meaning *and* utilize or express views about that meaning. Assessing a mixture of comprehension and production skills is sometimes referred to as *hybrid testing*. In current practice, most hybrid items test discrete points of language usage and vocabulary (Omaggio 1986: 312–26). In other words, the focus of hybrid tests in the past has been on language mastery, not textual meaning, inferences, or implications of the text.

One hybrid test which has made small inroads in national achievement testing is the cloze procedure. Cloze is increasingly viewed as a discrete-point or sentence-level test (e.g., Oller 1983; Alderson 1983). As a comprehension measure, it is generally unpopular with students, who seem to prefer other test types (Shohamy 100). The items elicit no more than a single word in context. Thus, as a reading test, even a flexible cloze (i.e., one that gives credit for any acceptable selection) is completely text-based.

As another alternative to multiple choice items, Omaggio (1986) suggests a variety of elicitation techniques, such as choosing the best paraphrase for the main idea or a combination of short answers and multiple choice answers. But does such a combination *necessarily* address the problem of meaningfulness or reader interaction? In other words, as long as combinations of short-answer and multiple choice items test only reader registration of what the text says, they fail to reveal how the reader constructs the gist, ideas, and implications of the text. As previously suggested, one pitfall of the short answer is that, unless it is linked to other segments of the text, it credits students with correct item identification without necessarily revealing whether they understand any implications of that knowledge for the rest of the passage (Jones).

Beyond cloze and short-answer questions, longer tests of production are generally not considered hybrid. Instead, they are classified as writing exercises, separate from reading comprehension. The bridge between comprehension of factual or ideational content and extended production of language is tacitly ignored. Yet it is precisely in the process of connecting these two capabilities, not only in choosing the best paraphrase, but also in being able to generate one as well, that student learning appears to be considerably enhanced (Gagné). Therefore, the second feature of the reading-comprehension test presented here is that it connects a student's comprehension of the text to the expression of the ideas that the reader has about what has been comprehended. One of the test's goals should be to elicit either L1 or L2 discourse that expresses a reader's views of textual implications.

3. Flexibility in acknowledging individual interpretations and speech acts.

A procedural test asks students to use the text as a grammar model for language usage. When text language is chosen for meaningfulness, students select phrases and sentences that convey meaningful information. Ultimately, this process should foster individual expression. Cognitive evidence in L1 research confirms that propositional rather than verbatim language is the expected result of comprehension of meaning (e.g., Osgood). Yet many of our evaluative tools for language production, such as cloze or blank-completion answers, ask for a form of verbatim comprehension—for particular rather than generic choices. Tests of writing (e.g., discrete-point answers and most cloze items) tend to reward the precise replication of language rather than the creation of propositional meaning. An essential feature of processing—the capacity to express meaning in one's own terms—is absent in such items.

Any textual comprehension involving "reading between the lines," i.e., reading inferences or assessing significances, depends on reader background and reader analytical style. Since individual processing is significant, it should be accounted for. In that case, some portion of the test instrument should allow individual variance about what is comprehended in a text: variance in the student's choice of language, subject matter, and intent.

The comprehension exercises we are about to present are all text-based. They are hybrid items that commence with macropropositions (encoding text content and intent). They are followed by questions about how the text develops these propositions in informational details and text language expressing that information. In all instances, the emphasis is not on a particular answer, i.e., whether an answer is "true" or "false," "a" or "b." Instead, the items try to establish whether reader judgment about the text's messages corresponds to reader-selected textual language.

COMPREHENSION EXERCISES:
IDENTIFYING MACROPROPOSITIONS

1. Focus on content or text schema

One problem all readers share is attending to the text—to the precise language that conveys a particular inference for them. While ostensibly "objective," the items below attempt to forge this link without necessitating more than a recognition task on the part of the reader. To understand the topical macropropositions of stories, readers generally need to encode descriptive schema about the sex, companions, destination, and activities of leading characters (e.g., Bensoussan). Similarly, in an expository text, students will need to be able to state *who, what, where,* and *when.* Such questions are often sufficient to establish global comprehension of subject matter.

> INSTRUCTIONS: Skim the first page. Answer the questions below and include the paragraph and page numbers from which you have taken your answers:

Sample questions:

who or what the passage is about: _____

where events take place: _____

when events take place: _____

Note: The answers involve no language creation. Students copy selectively and are graded on the basis of those selections.

> INSTRUCTIONS: Skim the first page of the text. Which of the following statements are true, and which are false? Regardless of your answer, give each sentence the number of the paragraph in which the correct information is found.

Sample:

1. The person traveled alone. (number of significant persons)
2. The person traveled for six weeks. (time frame)
3. S/he went to large urban areas. (location)
4. The person is a young man. (sexual identity of significant persons)

Assertions above T/F?   *Sentence and paragraph where*
                                 answer is found

1. _____   _____

2. _____   _____

2. Focus on intent

Sample: (for initial readings):

Skim the text entitled _____ . This text is a(n):
   (a) newspaper report
   (b) advertisement
   (c) government brochure
Write down two words, phrases, or other textual features (features of paragraphs, transitions, pictures, etc.) which substantiate choices.

If only one type of text is being used, students may need to recognize the intended audience in order to be able to predict its rhetorical features.

> The following science article is written for what audience?:
>
> (a) specialist (specialized terms, narrow focus on a particular aspect of a topic, detailed proofs and argumentation)
> (b) people with a general knowledge of science (terms defined in the text, broad implications of the issue linked to focus of the passage)
> (c) popular (general discussion of global issues, few specialized terms, detail)
>
> Write down two words or phrases which substantiate your choice.

Again, macroprocessing relies on reader familiarity with subject matter and organizational features in the text, features such as location, number or identity of significant persons, time frames, or major activities. Like questions about the people, events, and settings in stories, or the subject matter of expository texts, items about genre and audience reveal how students arrive at their answers. Questions about genre and audience prompt readers to consider their expectations about register (word choice) and information probable for this text. Answers about text situation and intent help teachers discover where global reading problems start. Macrofeatures of situation and intent must be addressed separately, because otherwise the source of a student's comprehension problem cannot be addressed.

3. Focus on information

Students who answer the questions below must demonstrate that they can map informational details to language in terms of the macroconcepts in the text.

> INSTRUCTIONS: Where in the text do you find information about the following topics? Write down paragraph and line numbers next to the relevant topics (some may be in more than one place):
>
> *Sample*:
> 1. The history of Haägen Dazs _____
> 2. Current plans for expansion in Europe and South America _____
> 3. The current financial status of Haägen Dazs _____

If the instructor feels the students can generate their own topics, the exercise might be a completion task.

> INSTRUCTIONS: This text is an encyclopedia entry about Brazil. List the subtopics of the text and complete the chart below.
>
> *Sample*:
>
> | *Topic* | *Student answer* |
> | --- | --- |
> | History | _____ |
> | _____ | 3rd paragraph, lines 22–24 |

4. Focus on grammatical competence

Apparently L2 students who recognize both syntactic and semantic grammar functions not only decode, but also encode more successfully than those who do not (Barnett 1986; Phillips). Items that link meaning and formal features can reinforce these reading behaviors as well as reveal problems in sentential processing.

Sample #1:

Underline the subject and circle the verbs in each sentence of this paragraph.

In your view which item below best describes the underlined subjects:

1. a shift from abstract to concrete nouns
2. a shift from nouns to pronouns
3. a shift from third person to first person
4. the use of concrete nouns throughout the text

Note: In FL or ESL classes that share a common native language, students should comment briefly on the inferences that can be drawn from the choice of nouns, pronouns, and verbs that describe a subject in a text, e.g., the shift from general nouns to impersonal pronouns (people → one) or a change in person or tense in a story that signals a shift in perspective. If reading is purposeful (i.e., more than just an exercise in recognizing parts of speech), it will be more memorable as well (Kintsch 1976).

Sample #2a:

Find and underline or give the line numbers of the sentences in the text which are in the passive voice.

Note: As with example 1 above, the shifts can be commented on or assessed in a parallel item using multiple choice, e.g.:

Sample #2b:

Which item below best describes the function of the passive voice in this passage?

1. Information in sentences in the passive voice contrasts with information in the sentences in the active voice.
2. No contrast is apparent between active and passive sentences.
3. Since sentences in the passive voice dominate this paragraph, the sentences in the active voice are highlighted.

The example below illustrates a further degree of sophistication in that patterns of sentence intent (in this case, a contrast) are linked to schematic features.

Sample #3:

Find sentences expressing a contrast. Give the line numbers, and decide if these sentences contrast a place, a person, or properties or degrees. Write down the words which signal the contrast.

> Line 6: Anny is tall, and Joe is short.
>   + properties: tall / short
> Line 8: Sarah is taller than Joe.
>   + degree: taller than

DIAGNOSTIC GOALS OF QUESTIONS THAT REVEAL UNDERSTANDING OF GRAMMAR FUNCTION

Like the foregoing segments, these samples ask students to link meaning and language use. The particular focus in the samples above: (1) they reveal functional command of grammar topics taught for mastery, and (2) they reveal problems in linking formal features to meaning function. The identification demonstrates students' proficiency in details of morphology and syntax such as tense formation, verb inflections, or comparison of adjectives. Yet it makes no demands on active command of vocabulary (i.e., words extraneous to the text).

Grading such sections is straightforward. In the case of compound tenses, the passive or subjunctive constructions, for example, all verbs must be recognized. Weighting in such instances (total points or fractional points) is an issue of classroom emphases and the individual teacher's goals.

COMPREHENSION OF DISCOURSE RESTRICTIONS

In contrast to the emphasis on subject matter in the preceding exercises, discourse items require the reader to look for a text's cohesion and coherence—how the subject matter is developed. Like the preceding comprehension tasks, they ask students to confirm answers with language from the text. In this case, however, the objective is to see if students can focus on how ideas connect within the text as a whole, rather than as points of information.

Sample #1:

INSTRUCTIONS: Which information did you find in this text [again: an assumed encyclopedia description of Brazil]:

   (a) historical developments in Brazil
   (b) problems and implications of Brazil's debt structure
   (c) the impact of Portuguese colonialism on Brazil's problems today
   (d) a contrast between life in Portugal and Brazil

What textual clues substantiate your choice? [e.g., for "a," several references to dates followed by names and events]

Sample #2:

INSTRUCTIONS: The best rewrite for the sentence "Although no longer as young and impetuous as he once was, Captain Kirk still leads the crew" (from a paragraph critical of the *Star Trek* movie) would be:

   (a) The aging Captain Kirk is still in charge.
   (b) Captain Kirk still looks pretty foolish piloting the Starship.
   (c) Captain Kirk is still young and impetuous.

Briefly explain the reason for your choice.

[Reasons may refer to grammar, word choice, diction level, or lack of coherence]

Sample #3:

INSTRUCTIONS: Locate the topic changes in the text, and write down the line
numbers. After you do that, make lists of the connectives or
words which told you that the topics changed (because, the
next thing, in 1955, etc.)

EXAMPLE: *line 5—the first day* _____

_____

_____

On the basis of your list, what is the logic pattern of the text?

–chronological organization
–cause and effect
–compare / contrast
–problem / solution

The foregoing exercises can be written in either the L1 or L2, depending on
instructional goals and stages of instruction. At initial stages of reading, these exercises
encourage encoding. As test items, such questions would be useful with excerpts from
longer texts. Answers would ascertain whether students can use content and discourse
clues in initial paragraphs.

RECALL PROTOCOLS FOR A FOCUS ON HOLISTIC COMPREHENSION

Bernhardt (1983a) suggests applying a research measure, *recall protocols*, to classroom
testing. Protocols—reader summaries of textual content—are appealing because they
reveal what students remember about the text as a whole. Whereas language level was
previously considered the key variable in reading comprehension, today we recognize
compensatory factors such as schemata and text logic. Indeed, reader perspective, purposes, and background may be more decisive factors than language level (Devine). Particularly when protocols for L2 texts are written in the students' native language, they
reveal how the readers' logical manipulations—their predicting, organizing, and inferencing about textual meaning—interact with their recognition of textual vocabulary and
syntax.

Native-language protocols enable L2 students to give fuller accounts of their comprehension. Several pragmatic objections can be raised. First, how should protocols be
graded? Regardless of their language, testers need to decide whether to rate recall protocols as reader- or text-based organization. Rating standards in which some ideas are
ranked more heavily than others (as pieces of "macro-" versus "micropropositions")
alter scores. Thus, until a ranking system is devised that accounts for reader schemata,
the evaluation of protocols will be open to question. Moreover, assessment of protocols
demands some sophistication about weighting and analyzing propositions. In sum, standardized grading is still problematic.

Possibly, computer programs which can assess propositions will eventually be designed. While individual institutions report using protocols with success,[2] probably their
widespread use in achievement testing must wait for computer grading of protocols.
Such grading would be standardized and would replace the relatively time-consuming
evaluation of idea units in current practice.

The second objection concerns the fact that recall protocols are in the native rather than the second language. This makes them inappropriate for many ESL situations. In FL classrooms, anything more than the very limited use of English raises the issue of motivation. If the FL students are tested predominantly in English, it may be done at the cost of incentive to practice cognitive bonding between comprehension and production of the second language. Nonetheless, recall protocols provide excellent spot tests or serve well as a crosscheck against L2 sections of a longer reading examination.

Holistic alternatives to the recall protocol are procedural matrices, idea maps, and story grammars (Chapters 5 and 7). Used routinely in class, such tasks reinforce instructional approaches and the use of the second language. Students who express the topic of a text and illustrate its rhetorical organization in a matrix have revealed a grasp of both macro- and micropropositions as well as their own point of view. For confirmation about whether they can apply textual information, students at elementary levels of language learning can be asked to address briefly the implications of the text in their native tongue.

PRODUCTION ITEMS FOR TESTS AND CLASSROOM USE THAT ENCOURAGE EXPRESSION OF STUDENT PERSPECTIVE

Production of language based on reading stresses two levels of discourse: the text's and the student's. For cognitive ease, the items, like the procedural exercises presented in Chapter 7, build from production of textual words and phrases through descriptive sentences to the assumption of a student's active control of textual discourse, i.e., the ability to generate meaning. Consequently, the test items that emphasize understanding of formal features (paradigms, tense use, and the like) must be separated from those that look at the students' competence in functional use of the language. The functional competencies will involve the contexts and intents of a text.

1. Focus on situational context

Items of this type ask students to integrate text semantics and reader schemata. The task is skimming an unfamiliar text in the second language. Based on the words they think articulate the gist of that text (the *who, what, where,* and *when* words), students are asked to formulate a descriptive statement. The exercise has a two-fold cognitive component: active recall of words that express macropropositions and active synthesis of those words into a sentence that students create.

Sample #1

INSTRUCTIONS: Skim the first paragraph (page) of the text. Identify and write down five words which suggest the main people, places, events or ideas—the *who, what, where,* and *when*—of the text. Then write a sentence (or two short sentences) that expresses the main subject matter of the text.

Note that rewarding an admixture of reasonable apprehension of content on the one hand and a grammatical expression of that content on the other distinguishes between the readers' comprehension difficulties and their linguistic ones. If students perform poorly on the grammar aspect of this exercise, review of textual language use is indicated. When students monitor the text, they focus on morphological and syntactic features such as gender of nouns, cases, adverbial usage, and word order. Guiding students in monitoring input facilitates their comprehension. We suggest that it also aids production ability. The student who fails to hear or read a difference between "he go to the store" and "he goes to the store" can hardly be expected to produce one form over another except on a random basis.

A more teacher-structured version of the foregoing might be:

Sample #2

INSTRUCTIONS: Identify and write down key words from the text which provide the following information about the main idea of the text:

who: _____   what: _____

when: _____   where: _____

Using these words, write a sentence expressing the main idea of the text.

This formulation of the exercise is particularly useful for beginning students, in that it prescribes the information which they will be required to produce. The text may, for example, just be about people and objects with no reference to time or location. In that case, the teacher might want to guide students by asking only for "who" and "what."

2. Focus on information

This task rewards students for developing their own strategies for vocabulary building. It can be expanded to "other ways of saying" or to "expressions which show that the country was hot," as discourse-building work. To minimize decoding, it can be a timed item, with a minimum of correct answers being prescribed, and additional ones counting as bonuses.

Sample

INSTRUCTIONS: Find synonyms or references from the text for the following words:

EXAMPLE: Spock (Sample Answer: "a *vulcan* [has] a major role in the film" etc.)

The following exercise asks students to locate the significant information of a text in a rhetorical organization—a systematic or logically-grounded framework of their own choosing. Since the language is selected from the text, problems of grammar are restricted. Monitoring of text usage is practiced, but in terms of grammar functions (which concepts are conveyed by nouns, time phrases, and the like).

Sample

(based on the Artmann story, Chapter 7, "The Story of a Railroad-Crossing Tender")

INSTRUCTIONS: You have decided that the story describes when events occur and what happens as a consequence. Fill in the following chart with information from the text. Your entries should show a relationship between events in the story.

When event occurs	What happens
train at 9:35 p.m. every day	_____
_____	an unannounced train rolls by
the next morning	_____

Note: If the passage has been read in class, the exercise can be conducted from memory. It is also a useful way to assess comprehension of a sight passage.

3. Focus on grammatical competence

These items ask students to align the logic of textual information with a probable syntax. The actual syntax exercise will vary with the rhetorical and informational logic of the text. As was illustrated in Chapter 7, the information matrix becomes the vocabulary and the syntax for this exercise. Since students only recreate textual facts, the resulting statements are descriptive or locutionary. The preceding exercise asking students to establish "when" and "what happened at that time," might look like this:

Sample #1

INSTRUCTIONS: On the basis of the information pattern above, write sentences with the propositional form *when* + *what*. Use the simple past tense.
Example: towards 11 p.m. + the train appears
Illustration: Towards 11 p.m., the train appeared.

In a test situation, in which the teacher may not want the students to recapitulate the entire information system, this exercise can be modified into an evaluation question by telling students which story is referred to and reminding them of the informational logic.

Sample #2

INSTRUCTIONS: In the story, events and their timing are of major importance. Write two sentences about major events in the story.

situation: around 11 p.m.
information: time + what happened
sentence model: simple sentences, simple past tense.
Illustration: Around 11 p.m. the train appeared. It made no noise.

Both sentences focus on the students' syntactic competencies. The important variable is syntax—in this case adverbial markers of time—not vocabulary. Students are rewarded whether they write "The train made no noise" or "Next day he pasted the book together." Unless students are given a matrix, the full scope of the story is fair game. In other words, the tester is not requiring that the student remember a particular verb form or a particular noun to get this question "right."

For intersentential practice, the exercise can be varied, i.e.:

Sample #1

INSTRUCTIONS: The sequence of events in this story is important. On the basis of the [hypothetical] information matrix above, write sentence pairs expressing the sequence of two events in the story. Contrast past perfect and past tenses in German.

sentence model: At 9:30 p.m. + the train appears // after that + a man waves

Illustration: At 9:30 p.m. the train had appeared as usual. After that a man waved.

The instructions above assume that the student has access to the text or an information item. The item will generate a sentence series whose number should be specified. A shorter or two-sentence version of the item above would be:

Sample #2

situation: the gatekeeper's adventure
information: two events + their times
sentence model: two sentences; one event in past perfect, and one in past.

4. Focus on intent

With the aid of propositional cues, students are asked to create illocutionary sentences. Such sentences must express an intention or restrict an idea not necessarily stated in the text. Yet they must also reflect appropriate usage, i.e., formal accuracy and vocabulary, as reflected in the reading passage in question.

Sample #1

INSTRUCTIONS: Write sentences expressing the state of mind of the crossing tender. Use the propositional cues:

what (he felt) // what + when
Write two-clause sentences, using *because, since,* or other causal connectives.

Illustration: Because the crossing tender had premonitions, he pasted the book shut the next morning.

OR

Sample #2

INSTRUCTIONS: Write sentences expressing what the crossing tender should
or should not have done. Use the subjunctive mood (speculations), and propositional cues:

who + what // what

and "if–then" as the connectives (any tense).

Illustration: If he hadn't read the book, then the train wouldn't have come.

PRODUCTION EXERCISES THAT EXPRESS DEVELOPMENT OF A POINT OF VIEW

In contrast to the text-based items described above, discursive items require not only a textually-determined grammatical and vocabulary competence, but also the students' ability to integrate a personal view with views expressed by the text. Students must not only fulfill requirements prescribed by the teacher, they must also indicate which requirements need to be fulfilled, by using connectors indicating contrasts, speculation, or the like.

Sample #1:

Write five sentences for or against the following statement. Use causal sentences to justify your position. Start: "The crossing tender should [not] read beyond page 77, because . . . ."

OR

Sample #2:

Write a paragraph of five sentences in length which explains an alternate ending to the story. Use subjunctive. Start: "The crossing tender would have continued reading, if . . . ."

OR

Sample #3:

Compare the situation of the crossing tender before and after thinking about reading past page 77. Use contrast sentences. Start: "The crossing tender had a very uneventful life. However, after he decided . . . ."

OR

Sample #4:

In the story of the crossing tender, we think that many things happened. Retell only those events in the story which actually did happen. Use sequence sentences to connect the narrative. Start: "He was reading the book. After he had read for a while, ..." Write at least 4 or 5 sentences.

ITEM EVALUATION

In grading hybrid questions a major problem is consistency. It is, of course, always possible to grade for one particular aspect of the question, e.g., meaningfulness, clarity, accurate reproduction of text content or formal grammar. As a practical matter, however, we suggest that instructors divide error assessment between content and form. Students who know, for example, that fractional points are deducted for spelling or formal errors tend to write more carefully than if this is not the case. As long as such fractional points constitute no more than one quarter to one half of the total possible points in a section, formal accuracy is not the sole dimension in assessment.

In general we suggest that assessment of errors be weighted so that the bulk of the points go for correct and consistent information. True, many instructors feel that students are doing "C" level work if their writing exhibits flagrant disregard for spelling and morphology. By the same token, answers on a reading examination that miss what happened at a given time, mix up the sequence of events, or confuse facts probably reveal equally serious deficiencies in comprehension.

One motivational solution to the weighting problem is to award those grammar items of major importance (i.e., those prescribed in the item directions) full point deductions, while grammar items not explicitly addressed receive fractional-point deductions. Students will see the pragmatic value of learning rules emphasized in class. As a diagnostic aid, teachers find it useful to compare errors in form and content in individual items in order to determine whether the students' reading problems originate in faulty comprehension or result from deficiencies in the second language.

Essays pose a different grading problem. We know from L1 and L2 studies on the impact of correction style that students' writing rarely improves with correction of formal features (e.g., Raimes; Zamel 1975). Essays are, after all, a communicative synthesis, merging the concepts and language of both text and reader. If, for example, an essay counted thirty points, certain specifications could be made in advance. In our hypothetical instance the essay could divide formal and informational features equally. Students are told that their essay must contain at least five complete, discursively- and thematically-connected sentences. Those sentences must develop a particular argument or point of view (e.g., why the crossing tender is foolish, why *Star Trek* movies are popular). A percentage of points could be deducted for grammar problems, a percentage for flaws in logic or connected argumentation.

How would these principles operate in practice?

Grading grammar.   If each sentence or clause is worth five points, in grading grammar, there might be a maximum of one or two minus points. Instructions must state which syntactic structures to use and which to avoid. *Speculate about* implies, but does not explicitly solicit, the subjunctive. In many instances, one language's cultural rules call for forms that are not germane to the English speaker or ESL student. In German, indirect discourse generally is expressed in a subjunctive form. The French prefer to make requests with impersonal constructions rather than expressing them directly. Differences need to be spelled out for students and test evaluators. Everyone involved needs to know the game rules, e.g., that well-executed answers will have sentence sequences that use adverbs of time such as *before,* and *afterwards,* or a series of causal statements expressed in complex sentences that commence with conjunctions like *because,* and *since.*

Depending on the language, it may be motivationally useful to be consistent in deducting one point for major usage errors—the three or four features stressed during that particular semester, such as incorrect verb choice (in Spanish, for example, the use of *ser* versus *estar*). Morphological and spelling errors are deducted in fractional points. Overall, no more than three points per sentence would usually be deducted for grammar problems.

Grading content. The first axiom in grading essay content is to reward the student who comes to grips with the issue at hand. Conversely, it seems reasonable to grade harshly (up to fifty percent) for student failure to address the essay question. Some students can produce elegant tangents, but fail to reflect knowledge of textual issues and information. Conversely, an insightful analysis of story meaning needs to be rewarded. Often, imaginative students falter in expressing sophisticated ideas. Full content points, when appropriate, compensate learners who are trying to stretch their minds at the cost of linguistic accuracy. Such stretching appears to be an intermediary step towards higher proficiency in language (Magnan 1988).

In a five-sentence essay, we suggest deducting six points for every sentence under five—a ploy that renders attempts more valuable than no effort at all. Such suggestions are anything but axiomatic. In the event of a clear essay that has several carefully executed subordinate clauses, for example, fewer than five sentences should suffice. These are questions of individual class objectives and test instructions. Some weighting should, nonetheless, be constant. Probably at least one point should always be deducted when sentences fail to develop a logical thread of thought, e.g., reveal the absence of inter-sentential connectors or logically related propositions. Similarly, sentences have to express ideas that can be verified in or inferred from the text.

CONCLUSION

We have tried to illustrate the hierarchy of the three test criteria presented at the outset of this chapter. The criteria attempt to (1) account for a text's pragmatic as well as its informational and formal features, (2) link comprehension to L2 production in a cognitive sequence, and (3) acknowledge individual variance in answers—an individual reader's horizon. Central factors in such a hierarchy are the metalinguistic cues that aid the learner by linking reader and text perspectives. These cues account for an individual language user's comprehension of the way the text says things in conjunction with that text's usage of formal features and discourse patterns.

Despite current emphasis on the reader's role, L2 testing practice has remained largely text-centered. Consequently, tests of reading comprehension often fail to assess a vital component: the student's construction of textual meanings based on that individual's cognitive and background schemata. The fundamental criterion for reader-based items presented in this chapter is that test items reveal the way students connect text meaning. In format such items differ from text-based questions in at least one of the following respects:

1. Items are hybrid—in either a mixed language or mixed L2 skills format which asks for a match of reader concept (keyed in English or the L2) to the language of the text (*matching propositions between languages and then locating the L2 realization in surface language*);

2. Items ask students to reveal how they connect information between sentences and larger units of information (*uncovering patterns of text structure*);

3. Items distinguish between explicit textual statements and reader-based views of what these statements imply (*interfacing text and reader propositions*).

The rationale behind these options is that in tests of classroom achievement, students of a second language need to practice cognition in the second language before they are rated for their production of discourse. The production will be conditioned by comprehension if learners are to have more than rote command of a grammar point. In challenging students' comprehension before their production, and evaluating their competence in this area, teachers will be ascertaining two things: (1) whether the meanings of various grammatical or expressive problems have been comprehended by the students, and (2) what their significance is to the student learner. Only after comprehension has been ascertained can the students integrate form and function, combine correct "endings" or "vocabulary" and correct usage in the broader cultural sense.

The reading test that assesses integrative processes will ask students about both types of features. However, it is asking too much to do this all at once, or to expect these abilities to develop automatically. A testing instrument must discriminate among cognitive subtasks that promote communicative competence. Equally important, it is antithetical to a learner-oriented approach to expect twenty or thirty students to all learn the same information in the same way. The first step in becoming a proficient speaker or writer in L2 involves having a secure grasp of *one's own* command of L2, as opposed to trying to know everything. Hence the communicative test must afford latitude in allowable information. Finally, but by no means least of all, such a test must reward various processing factors by weighting item types so that cognitive as well as linguistic abilities are acknowledged.

NOTES TO CHAPTER 9

1. These terms are defined differently by different researchers. Goodman (1982), for example, argues that "decoding" means many things, including "rethinking" from speech to another modality (phonological or orthographic) and reconceptualizing.

2. Personal communication, Ray Wakefield and Catherine Baumann, University of Minnesota.

Ten

Using Classroom Contexts: Instructional Strategies

Throughout this book we have emphasized ways to join comprehension of content to learning a second language. *These precepts represent instructional strategies, not methodologies.* Methods prescribe teaching techniques as well as the ordering and presentation of content to the learner audience. Instructional strategies represent the techniques for ordering and presenting content in view of the learner's needs, interests, and ability level. Because meaningfulness is a key component in both attention and memory functions of learners, we have suggested instructional strategies for the reading of authentic texts. These strategies must be applied in ways that help students use their language knowledge in the real world. To achieve communicative ability, students need to practice language functions in a social context. While reading provides the content of that practice, it is the teacher and the students who determine the social context of communication about how that content is discussed.

In this chapter we suggest strategies that link context to classroom language practice. Context itself can activate different styles of cognitive awareness, since human perspective is both individual and social. The perspective with which we as individuals or citizens of the United States or France or Colombia view nuclear disasters, the war on drugs, or sitcom TV series—our relationship to the content of a text—all contribute to the complexities of understanding that text. In the pages that follow we will first illustrate how personal perspective increases situational complexity, and second, how shifts in student perspective can help the class expand a linguistic range that is built on the progress and grammatical accuracy exhibited at the previous control stage. We also will indicate how shifts in perspective can correspond to stages in our students' conceptual development.

What kinds of conceptual stages are we talking about? They parallel the cognitive development of children, who move from concrete situations and proceed to levels of abstract reasoning. The most concrete of all entities is the self, the *me*, and hence the first cognitive and linguistic stage for the child is the *subject focus*—the ability to *talk about one's feelings and state of being*. In the next stage, rapidly following the first, the child begins looking at the world in an *object focus*, and develops the ability to *describe the relationships between people and objects*. Stage three is a leap into abstraction. This third level, a *visualization focus*, is reflected in the child's capacity to *visualize and describe things not concretely available* to touch or point to. Finally, at the fourth and last stage of maturation, children undertake *abstract thinking*. For purposes of interactive reading this means they are able to *analyze someone else's verbal information and generalize about someone else's patterns of thought*.

What do these stages have to do with a mature L2 student's reading comprehension and linguistic development? Perhaps the easiest way to answer this question is to look at each stage in turn and consider its relevance to reading and speech production. These stages reveal how linguistic demands are triggered by a particular text focus, when the complexity of students' locutions and illocutions arises out of expressive options which the teacher can control. These controls, however, are contextual rather than managerial.

THE INITIAL STAGES OF CONTEXTUALIZATION: THE SELF AND THE OBJECTIVE WORLD

As with the child, the adult beginner's context is the self. In fact, the first few lessons in many textbooks tend to be about people who speak predominantly in the first person. Activities and characteristics of these people automatically produce highly restricted communicative patterns suggested by a first-person focus. The information structure of typical utterances will contain a subject + verb + verbal complement or adverb ("I play the piano"; "I jog slowly") or a subject + the verb "to be" + a predicate adjective or nominative ("I am slow"; "I am a jogger"). Not only is this language highly redundant, it also establishes a metaschema for the learner. "Subject + verbs + verbal complements" or "subject + verb 'to be' + a predicate adjective or nominative" all refer to realities within the immediate experience of the speaker. One of the notably successful realizations of this focus is Total Physical Response (hereafter TPR). Responding to commands, students move according to instructions or undertake activities with classroom objects.

Although they are only asked to react physically, students soon learn to produce commands themselves ("Go to the door," "Hop three times"). This is, as Asher (1982) emphasizes, in part due to the kinesthetics of learning through motion coupled with visual input. But a concomitant reinforcement is provided through the contextual situation of TPR. The learner schema is concrete, and the focus is on generating rather than thinking about activities. Additionally, student propositions are realizable in a consistent language pattern. TPR can be used to enhance comprehension of reading texts, review functional use of a grammar point, or as an independent activity. While TPR has proven advantages, the point here is that any activity with a self and objective-world focus will limit the vocabulary and grammar demands it poses (Di Pietro 1982).

CLASSROOM PRACTICE IN CONCRETE CONTEXTUALIZATION OF THE SELF

A focus on the self is an ideal context from which to move from comprehensible input to speech production. Thinking and talking about ourselves reflects our most immediate concept schema, that of personal roles and their descriptive features. Linguistically, this context focuses talk on first and second person singular or plural pronouns, verbs expressing feelings or state of being, negation, predicate adjectives, verbal complements, fixed prepositional phrases, and word order of basic sentence types. If these limits are structured by classroom instructions, the result is a *contextual drill*—an activity whose linguistic constraints are prescribed by speech context, not by requests to manipulate a particular morphology or syntax.

Mechanical drills have students manipulate language to achieve the automatic use of formal features. Contextual drills have students manipulate language to express ideas. Contextual limits dictate repetition of a restricted number of formal features. If well executed, contextual drills can therefore combine the advantages of practice in automaticity with practice in meaningful creation of language. When, for example, students play games such as "Twenty Questions" or "What's My Line?," they are in a language situation whose references and logic frame comprehension. Yes / No answers to simple sentences or questions are entirely adequate for questions such as "Do you want a small car?" or "Are you happy at your work?" The discourse frame limits the linguistic frame.

While the linguistic demands made on them are comparatively simple, students are nonetheless evaluating a relatively complex conceptual situation in the target language: juxtaposing other people's language with their own gestalt. The way is also paved to have students ask simple questions as well as answer them. Consider the restricted complexity for those questions. The verb forms need only reflect the present tense; there will be frequent use of the verbs "to be," "to live," "to want," verb forms for action words, and predicate adjectives or adverbs ("Are you young? Old? Do you work? Do you have money?").

Because attention is to one's self ("I") + activity or state of being, the context is concrete: The people talking or being asked about themselves are in the classroom. Vocabulary, particularly new nouns and adjectives, can be restricted by game instructions: "Think of a profession, an interest, a favorite food." An instructor can, after a series of "Twenty Questions," change the context from a real "self" being described to an imaginary person ("Pretend you are a movie star" or "Pretend you are a piece of furniture in this room") and thereby initiate not only a good deal of fun, but a shift in vocabulary concepts as well. Similarly, recontextualizing can change the linguistic rules. To practice the past tense, for example, instructions can ask about something seen yesterday; for plurals, students become multiple instead of single entities (a couple in a small business, or a pair of bookends).

As an illustration of an activity with a focus on the self, here is a typical second-week class's game of "Twenty Questions." The subject of the game is professions:

QUESTION 1:	Do you work in Texas?
ANSWER:	Yes.
QUESTION 2:	Do you work in a city?
ANSWER:	No.
QUESTION 3:	Do you work in the country? etc.

In one such game, the individual was a diver and the class ran out of question options before arriving at the correct answer. The teacher asked the class to reiterate what was known and not known about the interviewee. Sample answers: "She does not work in a city" and "She lives in Texas." Through this expedient the question syntax was transformed into a series of statements. Additionally, the activity became a contextual drill in simple negation and third-person pronouns. Once the answer is known, the instructor will find it profitable to ask the students to review their inquiry strategies and generate questions which might have lead them to the correct answer, such as "Do you work near water?" or "Is your work unusual?" The class is thereby encouraged to review the relationship between comprehended concepts and language capability.

In the phase which focuses on the self, such a class hour might look like this:

1. Focus on classroom objects: Review with TPR (5 minutes)
   (Point to the desk. Open the drawer. Count the drawers, etc.)
2. "Twenty Questions" object game (10 minutes)
   (Are you in the room? Do I sit on you? Are you square? etc.)
3. Question review before guessing the answer (5 minutes)
   (She's not large. She is round. She is useful, etc.)
4. Have students write guesses on a sheet of paper and add one or two answers which lead them to their particular conclusion—with resultant discussion in the target language. (10 minutes)
5. Repeat sequence or introduce new word fields for additional focus or breadth as student progress and interest dictate.

Just as contextual drills such as TPR are recommended for brief review throughout the language-learning experience (Glisan; Wolfe & Jones), the subject-focus activities are appropriately part of the class's repository of potential review experience. After the initial weeks of class and the introduction of more challenging problem solving, periodic return to contextual activities with a focus on the self will mean that the learner's attention is no longer on new conceptualization. Instead, attention can be on acquisition or review of vocabulary and linguistic features. We strongly suggest, therefore, that five- to ten-minute intervals of this type be part of subsequent lesson planning or applied to figures or objects in readings.

SECOND STAGE OF CONTEXTUALIZATION: THE OBJECTIVE WORLD

The second level of context moves away from the subject focus into self / objective-world relationships. The difference is between imagining and articulating from the personal standpoint (first-person pronouns, verb forms) to an impersonal one (third person). The increased grammatical complexity of the focus on the objective world is illustrated with the "Twenty Questions" game. The change takes place when an interviewee who expresses experiential reality becomes an interviewee who describes himself, another person or an object. Instead of questions based on a "me / you" relationship, speakers must now add an "it." Consequently, students will need to ask if one object is larger or smaller than another, whether it exists in a city or in this room, whether one can eat it or see it.

Appropriate questions will still be very short and syntactically simple ("Is it made of wood?" or "Is it larger than a house?"), but the logical range of potential juxtapositions of nouns and adjectives has been exponentially expanded from "Do you drive?" to "Do you drive people?" (direct object) or "Do people pay you?" (indirect object). The object focus also accelerates demands for speech. Instead of responding now with merely a "yes" or "no," the interviewee must provide short sentence answers. This will naturally afford opportunities for alternative word orders employed for emphasis ("Sometimes I drive" implying a neutral option and "I sometimes drive" implying a possible contingent necessity) and a review of negation options ("No, I never drive" as opposed to "I don't drive") as well as an opportunity to contrast verb endings in the present tense ("They see me. I don't see them.").[1]

Opportunities for grammatical fine tuning will shift from pronouns and verbs (focus solely on the self) to noun and adjective morphology. Because self / objective-world distinctions utilize more grammatical markers, contrastive forms can be linked to their meaning function. The instructional inquiry "Does she drive to the country or drive around in the countryside?" (the German case distinction of *"aufs Land"* and *"auf dem Land,"* the French prepositional distinction made between *"à"* and *"à travers de"*) has, for example, an informative or acquisition function as a clarification of meaning based on a morphological distinction.

Linking meaning and form helps students monitor their production errors as communicative interference factors rather than personal failings. Teacher interjection will be for purposes of clarification rather than admonition ("You really mean you drive around in the country every day, not that you drive to the country every day?"). To cite one instance of functional as well as linguistic confusion, many students have trouble distinguishing between subject / object pronouns or use of singular and plural pronouns. They fail, for example, to contrast "who" and "whom." Such confusion is often evident in students' ungrammatical L2 questions such as: "Who (rather than 'whom') do you see?" and "Whom (rather than 'who') is the person?"

To show how clear use of interrogatives clarifies exchange of ideas—the functional use of distinctions in form—the teacher might have the class play "Guess the interrogative." In this activity, instructor or students make a declarative statement which involves a person as either subject or object of the sentence, i.e., "We want to study French" or "I gave him the book." The class then proceeds to match an interrogative with the noun or pronoun in the sentence which the teacher specifies, i.e. "Who or whom? What interrogative matches 'we'?" (who) or "Which one matches 'him'?" (whom). Variations of that activity apply as well to a variety of pronoun usages in European languages.

In addition to training in functional use of a language's formal properties, such comprehension activities provide practice with another ability as well—filling in gaps in partially-understood speech. Even among native speakers, successful communication exchanges demand listener speculation about how to fill in gaps in oral language, currently discussed as "speech gambits" (i.e., contextual practice in natural discourse). Ability to play with pieces of language information in terms of probable global meaning is an essential strategy for comprehending input (Joiner).

Apparently this ability accounts for the native speaker's higher success rate at deciphering partially-heard utterances. Students who can ascertain questions on the basis of answers ("Where or where to—The answer is 'at my Dad's house'—What was the question?" [answer: where]) can correlate systematic recurrence of grammatical form to conceptual meaning. They are also being sensitized to the cues a native speaker will deem of high communicative importance.

A functional approach to fine tuning cultivates the awareness that minimal distinctions often signal schematic meaning in normal speech situations. These are lessons which cannot be learned in a system in which all grammar features are equal. A contextual system offers an alternative to this practice because it makes some linguistic rules more important than others in terms of their communicative value. Students who learn the culturally sanitized language of carefully edited textbooks are unprepared for the fact that, in authentic cultural situations, the identical vocabulary and syntax can mean different things under different circumstances. Awareness of contextual frames is the first step in comprehending how such frames shift meaning systems.

It follows from linking fine tuning to meaningful utterances that students need to listen to each other. This listening involves both linguistic and factual recall because understanding information will depend on clear, accurate language. The self / objective-world stage is ideal for starting listening confirmation exercises since the data are restricted to brief, simple sentence descriptions of concrete objects and activities. As we have seen, such statements are more memorable than abstract or complex concepts. Listening-*qua*-monitoring practice can begin in small-group sessions, whenever individual participants act as spokespeople for others in their group, reporting on the subject assigned ("Jay has a little dog. He's called 'Spike'. He is eight months old.").

Later the instructor can ask the class to recall what they know about Jay's dog. Characteristically, the information will be remembered in several ways: "That dog is small. His name is 'Spike.' He's pretty young. I don't remember how old exactly." It is precisely these differences which encourage practice in careful listening to the multiple ways information is conveyed through language. Monitoring others increases awareness of propositional similarities in dissimilar surface language. Students will learn that "He's called Spike" and "His name is Spike" or "He's a tiny dog" and "That dog is small" are linguistically different, but propositionally similar. That knowledge enables encoding of the redundant propositions of a text.

Redundant and restricted propositional content results from the fact that the subject / object framing is ostensive only, referring to real-world people and things. Qualifying, speculating, and analyzing are excluded in this focus. Linguistically, this means speakers have no need for compound modal verbs expressing restrictions on intent ("I wish to go," "can do it," "must run off"), the subordinating clauses or infinitive phrases needed to express causality ("because," "in order to," "since"), or the subjunctive constructions necessary for speculating ("if only I had time," "if we were rich," "I believe that," etc.). As a result of limited contextual options, students can express themselves using the level of vocabulary and syntax that they already possess. Beginners are less likely to be enticed into complex translation efforts. Malapropisms such as the ESL student's request for a *bloody* steak (Fr. *seignant*—rare, bleeding, bloody).

USING CONCRETE CONTEXTS TO FACILITATE COMPREHENSIBLE INPUT

The point in the semester when shifts between contextual focuses occur will, of course, be contingent on the instructional program as a whole. Whether contextual drills of comprehension use TPR or other activities, student response is the best gauge for deciding when to introduce increasingly complex conceptual options for students to articulate. Most high school and college students actually want to begin speaking (i.e., using more than a word or two) after a two- to three-week comprehension period. We therefore suggest concomitant use of a self / objective-world emphasis with contextual activities.

Initially, typical classroom behaviors in that case might be as follows: After a series of student-generated commands such as "Point to the ceiling," the instructor would begin to describe the execution of commands which students gave ("Mark points to the ceiling"). The initial teacher task will always be to check whether any grammatical fine-tuning, in this case a shift in word order and verb form, is comprehensible. The practice of mini-comprehension / contrast drills is expedient for both teaching and ascertaining comprehension. To contrast word order usage in questions and commands, for example, the teacher says: "I am describing. Do I say 'Mark point to the ceiling!' or 'Mark points to the ceiling'?" or "When I make a request do I say 'Maureen, comb your hair' or 'Maureen combs her hair'?"

The minimal comprehension / contrast exercises can also be varied as conceptual pantomime games, in which students are asked to assess whether verbal statements describe a demonstrated action. The teacher may rub her nose and say "I'm closing the door." The class must recognize that the actions do not suit the words. Similarly, students can demonstrate an action which the class describes. As soon as students begin speaking, such exercises readily adapt to student participation. If made as an assignment ("Come prepared tomorrow to demonstrate three or four actions which you will describe either accurately or inaccurately"), students will review not only vocabulary and phonology, but will also be confronted with the reality of language as a descriptive tool. The consensus of the group concerning the validity or lack of validity in matching oral and visual experience reinforces the learner's sense of being able to convey a concrete message to peers, and removes the teacher from a position of sole monitor-authority.

When the class is ready for focus solely on the objective world, the material of initial lessons can be reviewed profitably from the perspective of this additional communicative complexity. Now, instead of the self-orientation of statements such as "I am closing the door," the students are more likely to be describing the door itself ("The door is large. It's in the middle of the wall."). In removing themselves from the center of the communicative message, they are practicing the first step towards abstraction, the consideration of an "other." In the focus on the self, the objects of the world exist in terms of our power to act on them ("Open the door," "Close the window"). When we introduce the relational equivalence of self and objects or even the possible emphasis on objects, the speaker has greater command of descriptive details. Objects, in and of themselves, are only identifiable in terms of contrasts with other objects. Whereas in the phase that focused on the self, objects existed exclusively through someone's mode of interacting with them (Heidi has the book), they now have the option for autonomous existence (a red book on a shelf). In languages with an extensive morphology, morphological markers are frequently linked to a shift in a conceptual focus.

Another way to review the concrete vocabulary of current and previous lessons is through pantomimes. Here the focus advantage is that even unfamiliar language is intelligible when students have a clear context. The difference between "I can see the object in this room" and "I see the object in this room" will not inhibit the understanding that the unknown object is in the classroom. In this way the teacher can introduce new grammatical constructions (here the use of modals with other verbs) as comprehensible input.

Let us assume that the vocabulary of a typical lesson revolves around the objects in the classroom, and the formal considerations are the introduction of contrasting cases with various prepositions. By the seventh or eighth week a class hour might look like this:

> TPR review (focus on the self, imperative, topic: moving around indoors) (5 minutes)
>
> Comprehension confirmation (focus on objective reality, declarative: teacher describes class manipulating the objects indoors, class pantomimes) (5 minutes)
>
> Introduction of modals as intentionality shifts in the foregoing sentences ("Can I open the door" versus "May I open the door" as a request for permission)
>
> Contrast confirmation (teacher equates formal distinctions with meaning, class identifies distinctions) (5 minutes)
>
> Student-initiated pantomime (student acts out, and teacher articulates) (5 minutes)
>
> Students direct pantomimes for fellow students to articulate (5 minutes)
>
> After monitoring frequency of errors, teacher selects four or five representative problems for form / meaning contrasts in sentences with / without modals (5 minutes)
>
> Class breaks up into small group exchanges on the topic "Where to look for a microdot" (each student must come up with at least one viable place to search) (5 minutes)
>
> Spokesperson for each group tells where individual members have suggested looking (5 minutes)
>
> Class as a whole writes down three or four suggestions while the peripatetic teacher monitors individual statements for clarity and orthographic accuracy (may be optionally collected for assessment) (5 minutes)
>
> Assign outside reading of a textbook explanation about conjugating modal auxiliaries

Student behaviors in the foregoing hour would be characterized by practice in making verbal distinctions about meaning. If statements such as "I saw Michael put something under the eraser" lead to examination of an eraser, or if students stop looking when someone says "I think Kevin already looked there," the speaker has really done something with words—a true perlocution. Perlocutionary responses to language use confirm that the linguistic input is comprehensible and reinforce that comprehension with physical responses.

FROM OBJECTS TO VISUALIZATION

The language level used in classes with a focus on self and the objective world may include a range of linguistic features, e.g., noun / pronoun substitution, adjective endings, tense, coordinating or subordinating conjunctions. However, only when students are directed to visualize that concrete reality in their minds does the use of more complex linguistic features become a necessity. To narrate and describe requires that the speaker conceptualize space (comparing size, dimensionality, intensity, which necessitates quantifiers, possessives) and time (expressing sequence or hierarchy, which necessitates tense, first- versus second-reference distinctions).

Before this stage, students have been communicating information within a tangible, fixed environment. Now they will be asked to add a major variable: perception of and expression of a reality that is anchored in an individual mind (verbal definitions) rather than in the world at large (ostensive definitions). Consequently, the visualizations that students imagine and identify will reveal their individual and cultural histories. The difficulties that listeners face will be in matching their gestalt of reality with that of another person. Comprehension difficulties will result from concept as well as language mismatch. A major class goal is student awareness of concept mismatch. Once students are *aware* of the need to negotiate better understanding, their practice with discourse gambits ("Just a minute—what size is the desk?") will follow more naturally (e.g., Kramsch 1981; Di Pietro 1983).

VISUALIZATION FOCUS

Visualization activities use pictures or scenarios (picture sequences). These pictures should be of two kinds: those originating in the mind of the student and those originating in an external source (Omaggio 1979b). Visualization activities provide an interim step between language use that represents the objective world and use that represents abstract thinking. A person's visual image is an interpretation of tangible reality. If two students are asked to draw a tree, whether one draws a tree with leaves and one draws one without leaves is a question of detail and total reference (were students asked to draw any trees? trees in wintertime? etc.).

Even when the teacher says "Make the tree in the lower right-hand corner of your picture larger than the tree in the upper left-hand corner" no two students will draw the same tree. How we visualize depth and details varies just as our surface language varies, despite our sharing an underlying proposition. For example, do trees have needles or leaves? Are they bushy or thin? Are branches visible or not?

The fact that linguistic meaning is not absolute and is, in actual practice, a result of a series of cultural assumptions (the pragmatic rules of a community of speakers), is perhaps most readily recognized in simple picture drawing exercises based on a teacher's oral description.

As a further illustration, consider what occurs when American students are instructed to draw a French railway station. The teacher may specify many of the details: "There are three sets of tracks. In front of these tracks which run parallel to the building is a large platform on which several people are standing. There is a large clock facing the platform." In actual practice, however, differences in cultural preconceptions will emerge. If they live on the East Coast, students might draw a commuter station. In the West, drawings will probably depict a relatively small station with cattle or freight cars.

Such variance introduces cultural features as perceptual distinctions and prepares students for the realization that even shared cultural artifacts are not necessarily subject to identical applications or functions. To fine-tune comprehension and point out cultural differences, the instructor can compare the drawings: "John drew a very large clock on one train platform. Most European train stations have a clock on each platform, since trains often arrive at close to the same time, and travelers cannot see from one platform to the other."

Drawing tasks are neither juvenile nor inappropriate for adults. First, as is the case with TPR and language games in general, drawing puts no one "on the spot." There are no expectations about elegant draftsmanship. Consequently, even public discussion of drawings generally involves minimal embarrassment. Second, from a discourse standpoint, this is a task which demonstrates sophistication in putting linguistic pieces together. At the same time it confirms comprehension of detail. Consider the alternatives for a moment. What happens when interrogative questions ("How many trees are in the yard?") are asked? The correct answer provides a piece of meaning rather than a system of relationships ("How are the trees arranged? Which are larger? Which shade the house?").

In a drawing task, the teacher rewards a comprehension of relationships. A missed detail will not vitiate the total picture. Instead of an absolute standard of right or wrong, most students experience variation in their completed executions—an experience that prepares them for variation in reading comprehension. Details which are missed or incorrectly understood can be recovered in the comparison and review session. Not least of all, self-generated visualization reviews learning of language and information (Omaggio 1979b).

THE PRAGMATIC USE OF VISUALIZATION

Perspective about relationships, not a necessary feature of either a subject or subject / object focus, is central to grasping someone else's visualized message. As listeners, we have to know whether we are hearing about a close-up or a wide-lens shot, a satellite picture or a child's-eye view. Otherwise the information makes no sense. A satellite photo shows Racine, Wisconsin, as "in close proximity to" Chicago. A five-year-old who travels by bus to visit Grandma Elly may conclude that the two cities are light years apart. Only if the listener understands the message perspective will these discrepancies make sense.

Some grasp of metalanguage helps make another person's perspective more intelligible. Students who understand that perspective is introduced when sentences begin with "I think that" or "obviously" may be able to appreciate the importance of the surface language that expresses those perspectives and their relationships to one another. Visualization introduces the language of perspectives and relationships: main clause contrasts ("My clock is small, but it is easy to read"), the use of "that" in subordinate and relative clauses ("I see that your clock is large. My clock, which is smaller, looks funny"), referential structures that express contrasts ("There are three clocks, but they aren't all the same size"), and referential structures that express relativity ("There is a large clock which reads 1 p.m."). In exercises using text pictures, the choice of linguistic rules or syntax and vocabulary is expanded considerably for the students, because they must express their own speech intentions within a text or an environment designated by the teacher. The descriptive language used in previous focuses no longer suffices.

ACTIVITIES AND EVALUATION

After drawing practice directed by the teacher, visualization exercises can be adapted from texts. Consider a few of the integrative possibilities: One student can read a description aloud while a second student draws what is understood on the blackboard;

different groups in the class can be assigned pictures from various episodes of a reading text; groups can be told to vary the text version, thereby introducing a test of comprehension if the class must identify the incorrect or extraneous feature ("The car was big, not little" or "There is no clock in the station").

If the student fails to recreate a scene from a passage in the way that others in the class envision it, the class exercise will prompt negotiation of meanings between text and various perceptions by various students. Moreover, a discussion will develop in class about the reasons for differing visualizations (due to misunderstanding of schema? vocabulary? syntax?). Such discussion arises out of curiosity about why people see things differently—a situation that corresponds to ordinary communication in real life. Yet, since the environment and the information in the conversation remain restricted within a particular range of illustration, the language competence in such discussions will revolve around the students' realization of their personal language intents.

Drawings can encourage beginning students to concentrate on an aspect of language learning that is essential for successful reading comprehension: a grasp of relationships. They also afford opportunities to weight comprehension vis-à-vis production. The teacher will have to decide whether a student who misspells "clock," but draws it appropriately in the middle of the train station, should receive an equivalent or higher grade than the student who spells "clock" correctly, but draws it outside the building. In either case, consistent rewards for precision in comprehension as well as precision in formal production cannot be overemphasized in an acquisition approach. If we believe that comprehensible input is essential, grading systems must reflect this conviction in terms of percentage weighting. In this case, neither student is exactly correct, but a correctly placed, albeit misspelled, clock may be communicatively more valuable than the clock in the wrong place in the visual world.

USING VISUALIZATION IN THE CLASS HOUR

Initial introduction to visualization correlates logically with an introduction to reading, since the processes of speculation—the answer to the question "What alternative reality is being constructed here?"—are similar conceptual problems. Having students describe pictures that correspond to short reading texts is, then, an excellent introduction to reading on several counts. Assuming an accurate picture–text correspondence, students will be formulating preliminary reading hypotheses as they identify features of a picture ("A man is lying in a bed. Two people are standing next to him. One is holding the man's wrist. He must be in a hospital."). Drawings force students to think about and use important vocabulary of the text in a connected way. They review vocabulary and syntax from the reading in terms of their own picture of the textual world, an exercise in depth of processing.

Since visualization necessitates applying complex grammar rules to complex conceptualization, it is best to avoid new vocabulary. The teacher resituates or refocuses familiar situations to enable student comprehension and expression of additional perspectival options. Starting with a focus on the self, the instructor can, by the ninth or tenth week of class, move quickly through a series of conceptually- and grammatically-discrete stages toward progressive abstraction. Such a class hour might typically be broken down as follows.[2]

Stage 1. *Focus on the self—comprehension*
A first person narrative / demonstration of driving a car ("First I start the car. I take the key. I insert it, etc."). (5 minutes)

Stage 2. *Focus on the self—production*
Teacher reviews the sequence and asks students to participate using TPR confirmation through actions ("Take the key. Insert the key, etc."). (5 minutes)

Stage 3. *Focus on the objective world—comprehension*
The teacher now pantomimes the sequence, asking the class to articulate (identify) what they see being done ("You take the key. You put it in the lock. Now you look around in both directions, etc.") The teacher can reinforce this stage by asking different students to demonstrate actions in or out of sequence and have fellow students articulate the action. (5 minutes)

Stage 4. *Focus on the objective world—production in simulated real world*
Students are asked to generate a simulated situation by means of speech, i.e., the teacher pretends to need driving instructions. Students tell her what to do and she pantomimes, i.e., using the teacher as an object of manipulation. (5 minutes)

Stage 5. *Students respond to intents expressed by the instructor*
The teacher narrows the focus from all aspects of driving a car to a particular application (thereby introducing intentionality), i.e., driving to a specific location under particular constraints ("You are at the Capitol and want to go to the river"—students combine acting out and word / phrase articulation of appropriate behaviors). (5 minutes)

Stage 6. *Visualization variation: Individual student intents expressed*
Teacher now makes the situation open-ended (no goal is specified). Student language usage takes place at a simulated intersection and situation-dependent directions demand that students generate logical chains of reasoning in the foreign language. Students simulate vehicles, pedestrians, and road signs. Appropriate mobile units ask their fellow classmates for permission to drive or walk in a particular direction. All constraints (traffic, lights, policemen, etc.) must be accounted for. ("I'm a truck heading north. What can I do?" [answer] "You have to stop for the stop sign and turn left," etc.). Students take full active responsibility for communicating their variant on the visualized situations, their intentionality, and its implications. (10 minutes)

Stage 7. *Visualization variation: Writing*
Picture dictation series—stages of driving a car. Each stage is to be accompanied by a brief caption. Key details are to be labeled. (10 minutes)

Stage 8. *Visualization variation: Textual reality and its implications*
Students preview a car ad with an accompanying two- or three-paragraph text. The teacher cue, "What can you do in this car?," establishes open conditions ("If I drive this car I can go about 150 kilometers an hour."). Their reading assignment will be to come to class the next day prepared to list the features of the car in the ad and comment about why they like or dislike those features ("I don't want a big car. It uses too much gas."). (10 minutes)

Visualization practice is also a post-reading activity that fosters partial control of language. If students can refer to the text after reading two or three paragraphs, their pictures will use a broader range of language than if those students worked only from memory. Many of the verbal blanks are filled in with additional information from the text ("The man in the bed is not really sick. He just fell asleep. The two doctors don't know who he is. The one thinks that he is a patient. The other is not so sure.").

Since there is no single "right" answer when students are asked to describe a picture, they need not be called on for specific responses. The minimal teacher cue "Describe the picture" can prompt an extensive series of individual responses such as those exemplified above in terms of the additive logic implied in any visual scene. Unlike texts, which frequently present causal connections (issues and their implications, problems and solutions), the available logic systems of visualization are only contrastive and additive. Hence pictures can be described at great length without the requisite use of modal verbs, the subjunctive, or those subordinating conjunctions which express causal relationships (*so that, because, since*).

FROM EXPLICIT VISUAL MEANING TO IMPLIED MEANINGS IN READING TEXTS

Students take their first conceptual step towards increasing abstraction when they identify the contingencies in a text—when they discover how one thing leads to another. Causality is necessarily more abstract than either the additive or contrastive logic patterns which are applied in comparing visualizations, since causality is based on an author's conjecture. Linguistic markers signal when and how to guess, but this function of grammar is rarely emphasized. For this reason, let us briefly explore how linguistic markers signal causal relationships in order to illustrate why a reading context presents L2 readers with special conceptual difficulties.

STRUCTURES OF SOCIAL CONVENTION

Simple causality, expressed in most European languages in subordinate clause constructions, is always marked by a word or words which ascribe predication, i.e., "because there is no gas in the car" (we can't go to the store) or "since the dog is so big" (the flea problem is horrendous). These relationships are, in this sense, a social convention expressed in the connectives of cause and effect.[3] Quantities of fleas and bigness have equivalent claims to existence, as does gas in the car and a visit to the store. Consequently the conceptual problem of sorting heads and tails can easily occur for students. As Burt and Kiparsky point out, non-native students often make the "global" error of putting, for example, a subordinating conjunction with the wrong information ("Because the dog has a lot of fleas, he is really big.").

Before they can produce the language structures of created causalities, students must become comfortable with two-clause sentences whose topics sort out as two independent, declarative statements. In the two-clause sentence "Daniel went to the store because his mom needed some milk," an initial comprehension assignment would ask students to make two simple sentences out of one. Working backwards in this way enables students to see that "Daniel went to the store" / "His mom needed some milk" are independent ideas until the word "because" is introduced. Only then does the relationship become explicit.

The interference factor that makes the sentence "wrong" is not so much a problem with word order or morphology, as a failure to separate what is an issue and what is an implication. To solve this problem, students need a monitor for the linguistic forms of causality rather than formal practice *per se*. Assignments that ask students to sort out issues and implications provide such practice. When they are working with a picture of a big dog followed by a series of pictures showing expensive food purchases and a yard with no grass, connectives become tools to convey causality. Answers such as "Because the dog is small, it costs a lot to feed him" or "In order to have a yard, Irene needs a dog" are rejected on the basis of faulty meaning rather than form. These exercises prepare students for the less secure, implied causalities that represent their next major expressive hurdle: the spectrum of contingency and credibility entailments.

Pictures are an ideal way to practice when modals are used to clarify a speaker perspective or entailment. Once the content of a picture has been established, alternative conditions (entailed information) can be introduced as conceptual substitutions that differ from factual assertions. With the cue "What can happen to alter the course of the story?", the teacher using a picture can model or elicit such responses as "The man can wake up and tell the doctors he is not sick" or "The doctors may look at the patient's chart and see 'he' is supposed to be a woman." To focus fine-tuning, the teacher will cue specific modality options (e.g., "What should he do? What does he want to do? What must he do?").

At the threshold between the fixed reality of focus on the self and the objective world, picture drawing was used to introduce the variable of speaker speculation about a concrete reality ("I think that the patient is sick. He sees that the doctor is puzzled."). With modals, speculation about that reality now becomes a question of contingent degree, a percentage play whose probability of being realized will depend on other options within the given contextual reality, i.e., "The person in bed may not be a patient at all" (he may be a visitor), or "He's supposed to be operated on" (but he may need some blood tests first).[4]

The next step towards more abstract student processing is that of open conditions. Open conditions project an effect or consequence of a present reality, i.e., "If the doctors think that man is their patient [open condition], he'll be operated on [consequence of condition being accepted as reality]." Note that the probability, the situation's result, is more clearly optional in the statement of open condition than it was with modal verbs. The fact of a completed operation absolutely depends on the condition's being realized. An open condition selects one piece of information and projects it into a future beyond the environment of the picture. An assertion made with a modal verb ("He is supposed to [must, can, may] be operated on any time."), states no explicit conditions to be fulfilled in a future, but only a range of options with their probability shading (wants to, can, is not allowed to). Modals describe the entailments which limit the situation; an open condition expands its frame.

The last stage of entailments are those available solely in linguistic description— as variants of the objective world described with contrary-to-fact subjective forms. These entailments speculate about alternative realities expressed in closed conditions. Here again, visualization activities can be structured to practice an alternative conceptual system without introducing unfamiliar vocabulary or new contexts. To minimize processing, the subjunctive is cued to an alternative found in previous lessons, i.e., "If Jay had a very little dog, then . . . (it probably wouldn't eat very much)." Contrary-to-fact conditions describe a pseudo-reality which denies the facts. "If I were king" suggests a possible reality which is contrary to the actual case. English speakers have lost awareness of most formal distinctions between open (indicative) and closed (subjunctive) conditions. Hence, activities that ask students to create alternative realities are a vital conceptual practice stage on which any learning of morphological or syntactic realizations must be built.

THE CONTEXTUAL PRECONDITIONS OF FREE VARIATION

To be able to function at the free variation stage which follows the variations on visualizations, students must be capable of comprehending and manipulating alternative reality constructs. Longer texts, films, or tapes of target language information will come from unfamiliar and possibly even antithetical frames of reference (a propaganda film from Cuba, a documentary on universal health coverage from Canada). If health coverage information or longer texts in a foreign language are to be recognized as alternative constructions of reality, students must be able to apprehend and articulate the degree to which that alternative reality modifies or negates their own world construct.

A bidirectional perspective on reading or listening acknowledges learner expectations without allowing them to skew interaction with the text toward subjectivity on the one hand, or attention only to random facts that are devoid of schematic connections on the other. Students who integrate their perspectives with the text might say something like the following before viewing the films mentioned in the preceding paragraph: "In this film all references to communism are probably going to be positive, those to capitalism generally unfavorable—let's see how that's handled," or "Since no mention is made about drug prices, the price of medication must be included in Canada's definition of 'universal coverage'—a lot different from our Medicare, which audits prescription prices."

The expectation of the viewer / listener / reader will focus any foreign-language text in much the same fashion as a camera aperture focuses an image. Without the ability to adjust conceptual framing, distortion results. And, as the schema evidence testifies, distortion can render both global and local messages unintelligible. Preconceptions ("That's all propaganda," or "Socialized medicine doesn't work.") inhibit bidirectional reading about Castro's government or government-subsidized medicine in Canada.

When the frame of the language use is rejected or distorted by the student, the information and language represented will not be acquired for use in the patterns and frequency expected by a native speaker. Thus, though we have been specifying visual contexts, a teacher undertaking a series of contextual tasks is also preparing students to deal with abstract alternative realities: the range of restrictions, contingencies, and relational variables which create new or "foreign" implications out of familiar issues. All longer discourses, all authentic texts in a foreign language create contexts for new implications. They are recreations of reality whose information can only be comprehended if the student also understands both its creator's intent and the environment in which the text originally served a communicative function.

It is for this reason that, as early as the first semester of language learning, teachers must begin to introduce samples of extended discourse in reading texts, tapes, or films as practice in identifying and reconstructing alternative systems of meaning. These systems create a conceptual grammar located only in the discourse patterns themselves. In the next chapter we will consider those discourse patterns, where they originate, and how to identify and use them.

NOTES TO CHAPTER 10

1. The need for students to hear word order contrasts for listening comprehension, particularly those not characteristic of L2 students' native language, is well-established in research (e.g., LoCoco). In instructional practice, however, this and other listening comprehension abilities have, until recently, been virtually ignored (Joiner).

2. The hour described here was taught by Phyllis Manning. A videotape of that hour is available under the title "From Comprehension to Production in Context: Excerpts from a Beginning Sixth-Week Hour" from the University of Texas Language Lab for the price of copying the original plus postage.

3. Ernst Mach defines causality as a consequence only of the habituation of the human to his life world, not as an ontic reality—we become used to seeing certain data in sequence and, therefore, conceptualize one as "causing" the other.

4. An extension of this presentation of the modal verbs could be to reframe their meaning as subjective use of the modals. "He's supposed to be a good photographer" means not "he must, by *law*," but "*everyone* says." Similarly: "He must be a good photographer" = "I assume to ninety percent credibility, since he was hired for the prince's wedding." For English, see Joos.

Eleven

Text Readability
and Content Orientation

PEDAGOGICALLY-APPROPRIATE TEXTS
AS COMPONENTS OF LANGUAGE LEARNING

Increasingly, L2 textbooks for beginning language students are introducing authentic readings in initial chapters. Even for beginners, familiar genres such as ads, biographies, and letters need pose no greater difficulty than carefully edited readings. Indeed, authentic materials may be easier to comprehend. As Grellet, Honeyfield, and others have pointed out, simplifying texts by eliminating redundancy or deleting discourse markers often results in increased reading difficulty. In such instances students have been denied the redundant clues which characterize a genre and sort its textual message systems. The point here is not that edited texts are *per se* inferior to authentic texts. Edited texts can retain important discourse and message features. As with the selection of authentic readings, it is readability and pedagogical function, not labels such as "authentic" or "edited," that determine the merits of texts.

Text type and text format encourage specific student reading behaviors. The apparatus accompanying texts edited in traditional fashion—more than occasional vocabulary glosses and questions restricted to isolated information—discourages those strategies that lead to schematizing of textual meanings. Editing that encourages reading word for word *discourages* student efforts to establish the conceptual patterns of the text. Traditionally graded or edited texts were tailored expressly to limit students to vocabulary and morphological structures suitable for a designated learner norm. Those objectives focus on language features rather than on content and meaning. Throughout this book we have argued that, even in beginning language classes, reading should promote broader applications of language learning.

Toward a definition of pedagogically-appropriate texts. Pedagogically-useful texts, oral or written, are texts whose primary intent is to communicate meaning. Such texts are generally written by native speakers of the language to be read by other native speakers—the usual definition of authentic in L2 teaching (e.g., Bacon). However, whether texts are intended for native speakers of the language is not the relevant issue. Instead, questions about appropriateness center on issues of quality and suitability for the L2 classroom.

In Chapter 8 we presented nine features to consider when selecting texts—features that seem to be significant variables in reading research: topic familiarity, interest level, discernible plot or message system, clear sequential development, well-marked episodes, a recognizable agent or concrete subject, a restricted amount of description, unambiguous intent, and appropriate length. Not every text, authentic or edited, will be representative of all these features.

Choice of texts, then, presents instructors with more new criteria for decision-making about readability than have been identified in the past (Schulz). If they understand the classroom parameters involved, the opinions of native speakers should be sought in decisions about materials because educated native speakers can tell us about readability in terms of cultural messages and language processing. In order to establish factors such as topic familiarity and interest level (e.g., whether readings should be in science, social science, literature, or other text types), teachers can make use of a general questionnaire administered and assessed at the onset of the high school year or college semester (see Appendix, this chapter). Such inquiries are essential because interests vary with institutions and individual classes.

Aside from appropriate schemata, features such as unambiguous intent and readily-discernible message systems activate several styles of cognitive processing.[1] If appropriate authentic texts are read for varying degrees of information, e.g., gist or language detail or both, such texts can be employed to augment an existing curricular program without subverting or replacing it. They prepare students for reading authentic texts in a content area. Aside from serving purely academic concerns, authentic texts introduce students to the feasibility of "pleasure reading"—outside reading which students select on the basis of personal interest.[2] As has been stressed in earlier chapters, without quantitative reading outside of class, we can hardly expect students to develop or improve their comprehension of vocabulary and increase their reading speed.

INDIVIDUALIZING READING TASKS

The definition of comprehension presented in this book—the identification of information systems and their implications—changes L2 curricular objectives for reading. Establishing what a text means has now become the responsibility of the student, whereas earlier, text meaning was largely the purview of the teacher. The pitfall here is that, unless teachers and student readers can agree in advance about what kinds of meanings they are looking for, chaos can result. A comparison between the comprehension of various readers of the same text can be uninteresting if students indulge in subjective speculation. Discussion can be uninformative if students replicate textual facts as a random gloss on unrelated information.

To read interactively, students must do more than answer questions about text content. Readers must see how those pieces fit into a whole, and what the sum of a text's parts implies to them. To encourage these reading behaviors, the teacher asks fewer questions about specific details of text meaning and uses tasks that reveal what students think about it. Yet a reader's thinking must be objective rather than subjective— recall the readers Block describes as non-integrators who often fail to apprehend textual messages because they superimpose their personal perspectives on textual data. One operating premise of the reading model presented in Chapter 5 is that texts cannot be read for propositional meaning unless readers are capable of separating textual messages from their own preconceptions. In order to avoid misreadings and to develop cultural literacy, readers must be able to distinguish between the two. Since the distinction between textual and personal views is fundamental to applications of reading, in this chapter we will review features of text structure that promote objective assessment.

SORTING THE MACROFACTORS OF ILLOCUTION— TEXT CONTENT, CONTEXT, AND AUTHORIAL INTENT

How context impinges on content. Context is the framing for any reading. A cursory look—twenty seconds of skimming or scanning for nouns and verbs—answers the questions *who, what,* and *where.* A stage description of a middle-class home with nineteenth-century furnishings and a woman in long skirts and a high-buttoned blouse will more likely be Ibsen or Wilde than either Shakespeare or Euripides. Similarly, a first paragraph of a text with words such as *ignorance, reading instruction, television viewing, malaise,* and *school* suggests a newspaper article or essay concerning literacy problems in the media age. These terms rarely introduce, for example, a murder mystery or a treatise on Social Security. Such an initial assessment of textual subject matter as a prereading exercise limits the range or scope of reader speculation. Most topics (at least as discussed by competent writers) have distinctive vocabulary and discourse markers. Conscious application of this knowledge allows the reader to restrict guesswork about a passage's vocabulary.

Intent and textual semiotics. After ascertaining context, the reader's next global task is to identify the scenario or authorial intent of the text. Even longer works such as plays, novels, and expository books reveal their objectives in their opening statements or initial pages. In the first three minutes of Chekhov's *The Cherry Orchard,* the merchant Lopakhin waits for a train bringing the aristocratic landowners back to their estate. During this initial scene, the merchant mentions his money and his peasant origins. He orders the landowner's servant girl to bring him a drink, chastising her for dressing too much like a lady. After such an introduction, the action or direction of the play is suggested: a depiction of the aristocratic class confronting the practical middle-class merchant Lopakhin. Such initial assessments of text intent (in this case, a "subtext" with social or cultural implications) give the semantic environment (who, what, where) its propositional syntax, the answers to the questions "how" and "why."

Students must avoid assessing *The Cherry Orchard* in terms of their cultural experience in the 1990s (the subjectivity factor or non-integration mentioned above). If readers schematize events according to their historical schema rather than the text's, Lopakhin can easily be viewed as a clown, an absurd figure. To avoid misreading, students must view Lopakhin within an information pattern that is verifiable in textual events and characters. Readers can, for example, contrast the behaviors of Lopakhin and the aristocratic family in the play. Such a contrast would reveal how these figures represent two distinct economic, social, or intellectual worlds. If students further reflect on the origin (Russia) and time of the play (the close of the nineteenth century), they can avoid making an erroneous interpretation according to their own culture.

In this book we have been framing textual patterns (their semiotics) in four ways: as institutions, events, problems, or ideas (representative people, places, events, etc.).[3] Depending on how information is structured within these frames, the identical surface topic can have four textual realizations. For example, if a text deals with the global issue of unemployment, the topic can be expressed within four frames:

IDEA—a representative unskilled worker looks for a job;

INSTITUTION—operations of an employment agency;

PROBLEM—the difficulties confronting unskilled workers seeking jobs;

EVENT—the impact of a recent recession on unemployment problems.

Each frame will present different information and will require a different logic of presentation. This is another way of saying that, from the standpoint of reading for meaning and establishing a model for cognitive processing of information, it is insufficient that the reader grasp only that a text treats a specific issue, in this case, unemployment. Consideration of unemployment in isolation is uninformative because without a frame for that topic, reader attention cannot focus on the organization of textual subject matter, i.e., whether information illustrates an idea, an institution, an analysis of a problem, or an assessment of an event.

A major reading difficulty arises when edited or culturally sanitized texts eliminate discourse markers of authorial intent—for example, adverbs which emphasize something is true or colloquial superlatives to sell a product. Textual intents can be straightforward information, questions, answers, demands, greetings, or thanks and congratulations which contain no motives other than those expressly stated in the surface of the language, as in letters from institutions that begin, "We wish to thank you . . . ," "This is to inform you that . . . ."[4]

On the other hand, in many expositions, particularly those in longer texts, the straightforward expression of intent and the surface language are not the same as the subtextual objective. In such cases readers must locate discrepancies between author-stated and implied intent. They must find words or phrases that state what the authors say they want done and correlate such assertions with consequences. With this matrix, students uncover the propositional logic underlying the surface assertions of texts such as Swift's "A Modest Proposal." Once students note that starvation among the Irish is made worse by administrative policies, suggestions for macabre governmental solutions emerge as criticism of all governmental practice.

In Chapters 7 and 8 we illustrated how readers can practice finding patterns of information. To make global assessments about the way a text is structured, students must be able to think in terms of the three options for textual information: (1) lists and descriptions (stages, objects, or people, and their respective attributes); (2) comparisons and contrasts (in scale or degree, or plus and minus); (3) causation—clearly arranging specified events or situations as results of another set of events (issue and implication, problem and solution, and the like).

In the real world outside the classroom, students choose what they want to read on the assumption that the objectives of the authors they choose match their expectations as readers. People buy a particular newspaper, for example, assuming its journalists will present information in ways already familiar to them. Similarly, readers select trivial paperback thrillers to escape from what's going on in the world and will be dismayed if the author tries to distract them by taxing their intellect. In interactive reading, students must sort out comprehension options—recognize and distinguish between the text's, the teacher's, and their own personal perspectives. They integrate textual information with textual illocution—its content, context, and intent.

SORTING LOCAL FACTORS—
INFORMATION AND LANGUAGE

After previewing to establish a text-based reading prediction, i.e., identifying the global factors of a text's subject matter (content), time and place (context), and focus (intent), the student can proceed to read for detail. Without predicting the topic and perspective of the reading, the reader is unable to systematize text information. This is a theoretical way of saying that assertions about cherry orchards in a Chekhov play will not be classified according to the same system as assertions found in a nursery catalogue. In the play, the dying orchards are a metaphor for the demise of Russian aristocracy. In the catalogue, cherry trees are real-world entities. A global prediction defines such message systems as metaphors or real world. The subsequent reading process confirms how informational details apply to each system.

In previous chapters we have illustrated how readers can structure information from actual texts. In this chapter we want to illustrate how textual logic affects readability. Writers alter their messages by deciding to frame topics as representative ideas instead of representative institutions, problems, or events. This decision is further modified by the writer's choice of rhetorical organization. The author who describes unemployment problems (features and elaborations) automatically creates a different set of implications than the author who contrasts the life of unemployed and employed persons. Similarly, if unemployment is explored in terms of causality, text meaning will vary if structured as issues and implications, problems and results, or problems and solutions.

In newspaper "human interest" stories, magazine articles, and literary treatments, for example, an unskilled worker is implicitly a representative of the unemployed in similar circumstances. As such, the logic of the personal or anecdotal information which follows will be descriptive: features of this individual's life and elaborations on characteristics of those features. Using these categories, a reader can more easily identify subtopics available in a hypothetical text:

Features of Situation	*Characteristics*
loss of income	negative feelings
long job search	part-time or low-paying jobs
mounting debts	loss of possessions, etc.

The arrangement of information will vary with the text, but the possibility of introducing concepts outside the range of reader expectation is relatively remote. Readers with low language competencies can develop a global prediction such as "Reading to find out what happens when an unskilled worker loses his / her job in this society today." Although L2 students may not be able to define the words "possessions" or "part-time," they can nonetheless recognize that these terms belong under the category "characteristics of the unemployment dilemma." Subsequent class discussion can confirm such analyses and also provide more precise lexical meanings for vocabulary.

An essay, pamphlet, or book-length text with an institutional focus such as the Office of Health and Human Services or a local employment agency will probably differ from the human interest story in the *kind* of detail and the greater degree of impersonality it uses. In a treatment of an employment agency or other institution which aids workers in finding jobs, the reader will probably be confronted with a descriptive logic. Frequently, statements about institutions make generalizations about (1) what the institution does (features), and (2) how it does it (characteristics).

Alternatively, if the text is critical of the institution, a problem logic will dictate a different arrangement of textual facts. Critiques or negative analyses of institutions will categorize information as (1) what's wrong (problem), and (2) what happens as a consequence (results) or what these problems imply. Typically, the informational detail in a critical analysis might look like this:

Economic Problem	*Institutional Problems That Result*
1. High unemployment	1. Agency has insufficient resources to meet demand
2. Need for retraining programs	2. Agency unable to reallocate existing funds, etc.

If students are asked to compare the logic of an institutional focus with that of a focus on the problem of unemployment, the contrast might be as follows:

Source of Problem	*Economic Implications*
1. Too many unskilled workers	1. Without retraining, jobless remain unemployed
2. Need for retraining	2. Continued unemployment more costly than retraining, etc.

These examples demonstrate how the respective focuses (institution / problem) restrict the implications of textual information. When texts consider only institutional implications, one problem seems to generate a set of new problems (e.g., breakdown in administrative capabilities as in the first example). Similarly, problems and implications tend to offer negative assessments. Alternatively, when the *idea* of unemployment is both the textual frame and focus of a matrix, the implied likelihood of a solution seems greater. Data are more neutrally aligned with cause and effect, not conditioned by preexisting limitations.

Unemployment Issues	*Implications*
1. Unemployment strains the economy, lowers tax base	1. Fewer funds for job retraining = more expense in the long run than high unemployment
2. Increase in poverty = increase in crime	2. Larger police force, more incarceration, more jails

Similarly, if contrast patterns are applied to the same information, yet another set of message options emerges. Texts which contrast two similar institutions (employment agencies with distinctly different approaches, for example), problem areas, or specific events offer a relatively easy reading-comprehension task. For example, a description of the problems of unskilled workers would revolve around how their monetary, social, and personal habits are affected by being unemployed. To explore the impact of two events—the depression of 1929 and the recession of the late 1970's—a text might compare such features as who was unemployed, what social conditions were characteristic, and what impact these events had on the economy.

Unemployment in Early 1930s	*Unemployment in the 1970s*
1. No government funds	1. Unemployment insurance, Social Security
2. Dust bowl, crop failures, many farmers bankrupt	2. Disaster legislation, price supports for farmers

Even readers totally unfamiliar with the depression of 1929 would find such contrast messages anchored within the range of their existing schema: expectations about the ways in which the serious economic recession of the thirties changed attitudes in the United States about the role of government. A comparison of the respective situations suggests that government entitlement programs have responded to the type of economic dislocations which were characteristic of the thirties.

We have argued that the vocabulary of lists, descriptions, and illustrations is more comprehensible if read within straightforward logical patterns than if read as random collections of data. Paramount for comprehensibility will be the consistency with which a given focus is maintained throughout the text, the extent to which reasonable reader prediction is confirmed by the reading process. Subject matter which shifts in midstream from problems to events or representative figures will confuse any reader (e.g., Anderson & Armbruster; Kintsch & Vipond). Similarly, the failure to provide clear discourse markers and coherence between sentences, paragraphs, and episodes can subvert the reading task. These potential interferences are located in the language of texts and need to be addressed as such.

TEXT LANGUAGE AND READABILITY STANDARDS

Any readability notions that consider the reader's non-linguistic as well as linguistic interactions with a text deviate from traditional thinking about readability measures and text selection. As the foregoing section indicates, text structures—their message systems—are key non-linguistic factors. Since authentic materials are not edited for a particular language level, the clarity of their messages assumes paramount importance as a readability factor. At the same time, teachers cannot forego consideration of such issues as sentence length or rapid introduction of new and unfamiliar vocabulary. Long sentences with complex embedded structures or extended adjectival constructions are no more desirable than series of compound nouns.

The point is not to discard traditional measures of readability but to expand them and shift criteria for what constitutes readable texts. Assessment of language difficulty should begin with the global factors of content, context, and intent—are they clear and consistently realized throughout the text? One way to check these features in text language is through the presence of cohesion. Markers of cohesion—generally adverbs or conjunctions—refer to preceding or forthcoming information.

Logical organization in textual structure relies on these markers to establish intersentential relationships. Contrast logic uses words and phrases such as *conversely, on the other hand, instead, but then,* and *nevertheless.* A logic of issues and implications often uses sentences with *therefore, consequently, as a result, thus, hence.* Readings that utilize a particular logic often employ not only a restricted number of semantically-related connectives, but ones which are characteristic of an authorial style or narrational level as well. The connectives of *A Clockwork Orange* will, after all, not be interchangeable with those of *Great Expectations.*

When students look at the logic of a text's intersentential connectives, they attend to grammar function at the level of both gist and detail. With guidance, students may be able to recognize the function of these words as markers of discourse logic even though they are unable to define the connectives with precision. To read authentic texts for meaning rather than decoding, students must be comfortable with the fact that some of the phrases they select will be semantically unfamiliar. However, as long as they know that the discourse markers of the text indicate, for example, that these words specify advantages or disadvantages of a job or aspects of the operation of an employment agency, they can begin to trace patterns in the language according to textual message.

In the procedural model that we suggest, a textual message is identified and substantiated in that text's language before students articulate opinions or views on that message. In initial tasks, reader opinion and comprehension are differentiated. The instructional approach allows learners to move in stages of linguistic sophistication: comprehension achieved in stages of pre-production (the word or phrase identification involved in ascertaining global meaning), reproduction (the sentence level of confirming the global meaning in the identification and articulation of textual information), and free production (the extended discourse level of student expression of opinions or views concerning the global and local messages of the text).

EARLY INTRODUCTION OF AUTHENTIC TEXTS FOR LANGUAGE AND COGNITIVE PRACTICE

The learning focuses suggested in Chapter 10 should guide initial selection of authentic texts. Texts in which people talk about themselves or which can be adapted to activities in which students can talk about themselves tend to be easily comprehended. Short interviews or monologues about concrete activities such as school, home life, vacation experiences, or job preferences, for example, are likely to be comprehensible for a range of reasons. They usually contain relatively few pronouns and unmarked tense changes (always troublesome for beginners), since such texts are in the first person. They focus on a single subject which implies redundant use of vocabulary—action verbs such as *make, learn,* and *work.* In a text on professions, for example, recognizable cognates abound for terms such as *engineer, computers, cosmetics, flight attendant,* and *electrician.*

These readability factors can be used to enhance student awareness of features they might expect from a different genre. For example, many stories will shift between dialogue and third person + narrative perspective. Story intent is less explicit than a first-person monologue. The schema monologue almost always features expression of desires, beliefs, or convictions. If written as a verbalization of someone's thoughts, a monologue will further reduce reader uncertainty because it is linked to a particular logic, e.g., "speaker preferences + reasons."

Once this connection is made, the global concept of monologue suggests a pattern of local information, and a reading hypothesis is then possible. The narrational logic and therefore the reader logic for these texts is most frequently "jobs (narrational topic) + elaborations (narrational comment)." Students' hypotheses about text structure narrow their search for recognizable language to words that suggest particular features of a particular profession.

At this early stage in reading, students will be best able to read in terms of semantic fields—locating the vocabulary of familiar topics. Texts about well-known figures in the L1 culture, particularly those that describe sensational events or unusual activities, encourage students to read for what they will recognize rather than be overwhelmed by unknown vocabulary. Moreover, L2 texts about the student's native culture can promote insights about different cultural perspectives.

REPRODUCTION OF TEXT MESSAGE—MATRICES

The purpose of the information details assignment is to ask students to examine how textual language confirms global propositional meaning. In the hypothetical case of a monologue about professional preferences, a reading assignment might look something like this:

Sample Matrix Assignment
INSTRUCTIONS: Note words and phrases in the text "Vocational Aspirations" which indicate the following:

Choice of Profession	*Desirable Features of Profession*
wholesaler	local workplace
electrician	own business
flight attendant	a lot of travelling

To create sentences about textual information, students must next assess the text's mini-"universe of discourse" by identifying its consistencies and manipulating its words and structures. To illustrate how texts can forestall the interference that normally occurs when students create sentences based on L1 models, German illustrations are added. Depending on the actual language of the text read, an illustration of such an assignment might be:

Sample Reproduction Exercise: Sentence Level

1. One can express professional wishes with the modal sentence
   I want to become an X. / Ich will X werden.

2. Find other structures in the text which fulfill this function!
   SAMPLE ANSWERS: I like learning X. / Ich lerne gern X.
   I would like to be an X. / Ich möchte X werden / sein.
   Ich wäre gern X, etc.

Employing a foreign language text as a reference for the formal structures which express particular meanings helps students attend to usage in conjunction with comprehensibility. Note, for example, that in the second sample answers, the professional goal is expressed in German without an indefinite article, whereas English requires one (I want to be *a* flight attendant, *a* teacher, *a* doctor). Rather than teaching a formal rule as an abstract principle (e.g., "After *sein* and *werden*, German does not use an indefinite article with nouns of profession unless they are further modified."), the text is a model for the way grammar conveys meaning. In effect, the assignment procedure insists that students pay attention to specific target language functions (formal accuracy) as subsets of global meaning.

This is not to claim that teachers should never explain rules of formal accuracy, but rather that it is desirable for students to learn formal language operation as a part of their comprehensible input. Rule learning is tedious and less productive if it occurs in the abstract, i.e., not linked to input. Assignments that focus learner attention on surface form as an integral part of textual message (information pattern) encourage learners to integrate both the formal and the functional features in their language acquisition.

ASSESSING MESSAGE IMPLICATIONS—FREE VARIATION IN LANGUAGE PRODUCTION

If the purpose of the information structure assignments is to have students confirm textual messages, the purpose of the production exercises is to enable students to use the matrix to express their reactions to these messages. The following exercise manipulates textual language to help readers express their own views. Nonetheless, textual messages and their language can be the basis for these statements:

Sample Production Assignments

STUDENT TASK: Describe a career choice. The class must be able to guess the career.

Note what happens to text context and intent:

1. Context shifts from text-generated to student-generated choices that are now hypothetical rather than real, hence broader in potential range;

2. Intent shifts from the text's assertion to a student's disguised assertion, i.e., making the description of a career choice hard to guess without being unfair.

STUDENT TASK: Interview a candidate for a particular career.

1. Again, context is student-generated, e.g., an American corporation, such as Boeing or IBM;

2. Intent shifts from monologues to interviews, e.g., from assertions to questions and answers.

These tasks dictate speaker intent. For example, the task "Select an occupational choice of the interviewees in these monologues and decide why you would or would not like their desired job," prescribes a causal logic which necessitates the use of modals and subordinate conjunctions such as "can," or "have to," and "because, since."

Such tasks are intersentential. To express a point of view students must do more than state facts or judgments. The assertion "A flight attendant has a good job" is not explicit. Only a connected sentence or subordinate clause, i.e., "a flight attendant has a good job, because . . . (s/he can travel a lot, s/he will meet many interesting people, etc.)" answers the question "Why does this person believe it is a good job?" Similarly, the task "Name a job and describe its working conditions" suggests the subordination and superordination of descriptions whose associated grammar topics are relative pronouns, adverbs of time, and pronoun / noun substitutions, i.e., "I work in an office that has a computer. Usually several people work with the computer. It is easy to use, etc." The instructor briefly points out or assigns review of grammar topics that have particular relevance or likelihood of frequency in conducting these tasks.

FINDING AUTHENTIC TEXTS FOR BEGINNERS

Given the common textbook disjuncture between so-called "active" language applications on the elementary level and the usual "passive" treatments of reading in advanced stages, even a few minutes weekly of communicatively-based exposure to authentic materials can have both motivational and practical value. High school or college teachers concerned with having their students make a transition from elementary instruction to a more reading-oriented curriculum in second-year or upper-divison courses can provide needed practice in predicting and confirming textual messages in conjunction with expanding communicative competence.

Since the reading procedures suggested here are unfamiliar to students or are employed as unconscious rather than conscious operations, we have found it helpful to introduce these techniques with another European language, related but unfamiliar to the class. The Dutch text analyzed in Chapter 2 is appropriate to introduce a class to schematizing and information structuring. Asking students to identify the subject matter and environment of a passage in an unfamiliar European language brings home to them the enhanced comprehension which occurs when information is organized or perceived as existing in a textual system.

Nothing convinces students like their independent success. Most classes have fun, for example, when they locate all the historical events mentioned in a Danish shoe advertisement and note the footwear types connected to these events in the text. After mapping the text in this way, they have no difficulty recognizing the implication that a particular shoe company represents a culmination of technology in the field. Since the abstract notion of implications is relatively unfamiliar to most students, repeated use of these reading techniques is vital to illuminate the uses of systematic reading. Only after practice can students be expected to apply similar strategies with more demanding L2 readings.

Advertisements provide a transition to challenging reading because their visual format and exaggerated intent provide the reader with maximum contextual clues. Since Western sales techniques constitute a universe of discourse, students recognizing the genre "advertisement" expect that one product will be compared with another, or that the text will promise that, as a result of purchasing a particular item, readers will be better looking, have more money, more prestige, and the like. Ads are designed to reach readers with a minimal demand on their time and intelligence, and the information patterns are clearly marked. Because students know what the ad intends, their attention focuses on locating details which reinforce the selling intent with particular information.

Similarly, government pamphlets, business prospectuses, and travel brochures can activate student schemata. The educational, social, and cultural ministries of most nations provide free materials on a wide variety of topics on request. International information agencies such as UNESCO also publish documents in many languages. Writing to a foreign corporation or business which advertises in foreign-language publications will often yield catalogues and illustrative materials of high interest value for students (e.g., computer or sports equipment). Teachers should also check on the policies of local libraries in regard to back issues of out-of-date foreign newspapers and magazines. Libraries that maintain microform files may be willing to give back issues to teachers.

The readability of these materials will depend on the degree to which they reflect an uncomplicated assertion of intent to enumerate features of a single topic, e.g., job or educational opportunities, youth hosteling, study abroad, welfare and health care. The most readable examples keep "fine print" to a minimum and abound with visually-interesting charts, graphs, and cartoons illustrating answers to questions such as how one goes about getting a job or what the relative availability of jobs will be upon completion of studies. Newspaper and magazine articles must be carefully scrutinized because journalistic writing often exhibits unpredictable shifts from human interest (representative ideas) to the broader circumstances (institutions or events) to problems associated with the topic. Particularly for readers of low language ability, such leaps in logical structuring must be noted in advance of an assignment through techniques such as semantic mapping in which students skim for word fields associated with a particular topic, or Directed Reading, Directed Thinking Activity, in which students confirm initial reading hypotheses.

INTERMEDIATE-LEVEL READING: PLEASURE READING, READING NOTEBOOKS, AND PEER REVIEW

After students are both comfortable and relatively articulate in expressing the messages of shorter readings such as ads, short articles about familiar, even sensational topics, and interviews, they are prepared to read longer texts on the basis of special interests or to engage in "pleasure reading" as an outside activity. Students can select their authentic reading without modifying an existing curriculum. Semke reports positive results with a corrective focus on meaning rather than form. In other words, teacher feedback about content leads to significantly higher gains in written fluency than instructional feedback on error. In this same vein, practitioners have reported positive results with a logical variant of the focus on meaning—the response or dialogue journal in which teacher and student exchange ideas (Dvorak 158). Improved attitudes toward writing are a key advantage to assignments that focus on meaning. With a content emphasis, the teacher can become a reader rather than a taskmaster who examines a paper only to find fault. Assignments that encourage students to express their comprehension tend to make L2 writing more satisfying than the intimidating experience of having writing monitored only for formal accuracy.

Writing practice in a reading notebook can fulfill these objectives. Recent work in ESL suggests that short essay writing—like reading authentic texts—can profitably be engaged in earlier in the language-learning process than heretofore thought. Compositions, whether a paragraph or a page, reinforce the language being learned and spoken.

In a study using think-aloud protocols, Raimes found that ESL writers engage in a mix of attention to surface-level editing and changes that affect meaning. The eight students in the study had tested at a similar language level, yet, as in the reading performance of Devine's students, strategy differences resulted in performance differences. Students edited both their language and understanding of meaning, but some techniques appeared to improve the quality of writing of some students more than others. Raimes suggests that a middle ground is called for to mediate between increases in language proficiency and "instruction and practice in generating, organizing, and revising ideas" (250).

Zamel's research (1985), however, reveals that teacher response to student writing tends to be almost exclusively at the level of surface editing rather than responding to the content and thought of student essays (for FL, see Kassen). The suggestions that follow are based on the following suppositions: (1) Students need a language model to improve their own writing; (2) They need to practice both rhetorical structure and surface structure in their L2 writing; (3) To accomplish the foregoing it is useful to combine reading and writing tasks.

We call the format suggested here a *précis*—a format for written analysis of textual messages and their significance to the reader. The first half of the précis presents a text's focus, argument, and a rhetorical structure in the form of a matrix (see Chapters 5 and 7). The second half consists of a short analysis which comments on the implications of the text as the student sees them. In initial reading practice with the précis format, beginning students often write their comments on the implications of the L2 text in their native language. In this way the teacher can confirm L1 understanding of implications that are cross-referenced with the L2 matrix. After they are familiar with the précis format, students can begin to write short compositions in the L2.

In introducing the précis as an ongoing task during the semester, the following instructions may be useful:

Précis guidelines: articulating main ideas and their implications

1. At the metalevel, texts can only focus on four kinds of topics.

KEY TERMINOLOGY:

event structure
EXAMPLE: economic and political events that have led to specific programs and changes in the status of L2 instruction in the United States

institution, movement structure
EXAMPLE: the emergence of both private language schools and business enterprises to teach ESL and FL

issue, problem structure
EXAMPLE: despite current interest in L2, lack of qualified teachers, problems in availability of technologies (computer software, laser disks, etc.), uncertainty about learning goals and realistic expectations, questions about the value of immersion programs and starting with language study in grade school, etc.

idea structure (often depicting a representative participant)

EXAMPLE: a businessman at Chrysler Corporation talks about the company's joint effort with Mitsubishi to create a school to meet the language needs of Japanese as well as American students in a community where a plant was built

STUDENTS WRITE: A sentence characterizing the event, institution, problem or idea in question noting the *who, what, where,* and *when* of the event, issue, concern, or movement.

EXAMPLE: The text describes the impact of a sister-city relationship on the languages and cultures taught in an elementary and high school system in Bloomington, Illinois

2. The students' second sentence will expand the focus by stating how topics are treated: for example, a comparison of two problems, causes of a problem and its solutions, or stages in the problem and what occurred as a result. NOTE: Sentences 1 and 2 may coalesce into a single statement as long as that statement is clear and explicit. Typical concepts to add:

Causes	**Goals**
Stages	**Conditions**
Characteristics, features	**Impact, results, effects**
Solutions	**Sources, origins**

STUDENTS WRITE: A sentence describing the logic pattern or structure of the topic.

EXAMPLE #1: "This essay talks about how private language schools are filling a gap in the training of businesspeople going abroad." (the institution's goals and how they are met)
Sample language needed to express such statements:*
The passage deals with _____ (e.g., goals, objectives) **in order to show** _____ (relationship to the specific results).

EXAMPLE #2: "The text compares L2 learning in the United States and Canada." (a comparison of two institutions in two countries)
Sample language needed to express such statements:*
The text compares _____ (e.g., features of two institutions).

EXAMPLE #3: "This story traces the relationship between the sister-city idea and the joint venture developed by Chrysler and Mitsubishi." (the economic problems facing a community and the corporate solutions in which the community participated)
Sample language needed to express such statements:*
This article describes _____ (features or problems) and **their solution** _____ (specific examples).

* L2 cues: *discourse markers that introduce various styles of logic.*

3. Students exemplify the logic pattern above by locating key words or phrases (not necessarily sentences) *in the text* which correspond clearly to these categories. Three such pairs are generally sufficient to assess the scope of the argument; more than five are generally superfluous.

STUDENTS WRITE: Two category headings, and corresponding examples from the text.

EXAMPLE: *Stages in setting up school*   *Positive impact on the community*

4. After completing 1–3, students analyze the implications of the pattern arrangement they have identified. They reflect on their matrix (but must convince readers that they understand what was written in 1–3) and tell them *why the passage is significant or interesting*; what is the author's covert, unstated program; how do the conclusions suggested by the text (the contrasts or implied causalities) correspond to the student's view of reality?

5. Based on feedback from the group or partner, students will revise portions of their précis.

The précis format complements L2 programs designed to teach content. Content-based approaches de-emphasize mechanics of language and unidirectional reading in that they focus on synthesis and interpretation of content. Similar to L1 approaches to writing across the disciplines (e.g., Beach & Bridwell), the L2 writing exercises are linked to understanding of subject matter, the attention of both the learner and the instructor are on what ideas are presented and how effectively (e.g., Krashen 1982: 168). "Treatments of matters of form (organization, grammar, mechanics) and style do not dictate the composition course syllabus, but rather follow from writers' needs" (Shih 624).

At the same time, particularly valuable in a redrafting stage, the précis lends itself to some attention to mechanics or what Raimes calls surface-level editing. Systematic reference to textual usage serves as a check for students—they reread the passages relevant to their arguments and look at the precise way in which the text expresses concepts or information. Reinforcement for this style of attention can be achieved by deducting points for inaccurate copying. Generally, students become aware of this style of attention with only a minimal penalty (e.g., five to ten percent). If, for example, the grade for overall précis content is eighty percent, poor attention to correct spelling, gender and case of nouns, tense and person of verbs clearly marked in the passage would then reduce that percentage to seventy-five.

As research on motivation emphasizes, L2 students respond positively to precision in assessment standards for an L2 course. Without the security of word lists and charts, students often find themselves uncertain about how to study because they are uncertain about how they will be graded. They want to know what has to be done in order to become successful language learners as measured by grades and grade-point averages. Consequently, directions for written work should state the criteria for evaluation of précis assignments: which features will be penalized and to what degree. Our practice is to assign minimal penalties for problems in legibility, neatness, or accuracy in copying language from the text. The bulk of the overall grade is awarded on the basis of content. Each précis must have:

- a clear statement of the *who, what, where, when* of the text + the logic of that data
- a consistent and clear matrix of information from the text as a whole
- a statement in the L2 that sums up the new concepts or information which the reader has gleaned from the passage and, based on the précis matrix, reader inferences about those concepts (see Chapter 7).

These criteria encourage monitoring and repair strategies which L1 students use to their advantage when they encounter comprehension difficulties: restatement or paraphrase of the original, backtracking or rereading, and puzzling out relationships (Bereiter & Bird).

The format suggested here integrates written work with comprehension monitoring on the part of the student. Students can revise their papers and think critically about the work of their peers, both tasks that provide the language teacher with a basis for assessing a student's understanding of a passage. Moreover, that assessment encompasses attention to accuracy.

It is not necessary, however, nor even desirable, that the instructor assume the full burden of assessment. Written work can also be the basis for both group activity and peer correction for second drafts. Pica and Doughty's research on interaction in peer groups supports the notion that students in these groups benefit not only from having more opportunities for speaking practice, but also from interactions focusing on comprehension of language meaning. Students seem to engage in behaviors such as clarification requests and confirmation checks as much when working together as they would with a teacher-directed group. As Long (1985) has stressed, it is not group interaction *per se* that aids comprehension, but rather whether the group clarifies and confirms comprehension. One way to structure such exchanges is to have students read and react to each other's précis as evaluators either in their native language or in the L2.

The demands on peer evaluators will vary with their language level. We recommend students identify no more than three to five surface-errors. Often linguistic problems solve themselves once the thinking behind a statement is sorted out. If comments address purely linguistic issues, however, the critique must be supported by the textbook or reference grammar students use in that course. Directions for this phase of peer-evaluation might be as follows:

Directions for evaluating errors in formal features:
- Choose inaccuracies that interfere with comprehension, or linguistic structures emphasized in class.
- Circle three to five problems such as instances of confusing word order, incorrect usage of prepositions, spelling, cases, and endings.
- **Note sections in the class's reference grammar or dictionary which were consulted.** Guesswork receives no credit.

More important for comprehension monitoring and rewriting will be the way members of the group address the content of each other's précis. We suggest, therefore, that more than half of any grade for peer evaluators, regardless of their learning level, be awarded on the basis of thoughtful responses to content. Such directions might read as follows:

Directions for evaluating the précis of a fellow student:

Does the author *extend my knowledge, clarify, or contradict* ideas I have about the text? Was the précis interesting and easy to follow?

Please comment in a sentence with a "because" or "consequently."

To suggest ways to rewrite the précis, comment on:

* how the main idea of the reading might be more clearly addressed,
* how the argument of the essay (logic of presentation) might be improved,
* in what ways examples or arguments might be more consistent,
* what discourse markers could help change assertions into analysis.

These suggestions help to structure connections between comprehension and production. These interactions are based on materials which inform; learner attention is on content. A definite impetus toward teaching content, even in skills courses, is emerging in the professional literature (e.g., Giauque). Large institutions report that they are integrating area studies and FL instruction (Dannerbeck, Sternfeld 1989). Concurrently, we find renewed interest in the role of literature in L2 study (e.g., Adelson; Harper; Oster; Spack). In Chapter 12 we will examine why, within the context of emphasis on content, composition, and recognition of cultural values expressed in authentic texts, literature is being singled out as a category of special significance.

NOTES TO CHAPTER 11

1. Stevick links acquisition, affective factors, and cognitive processing, stressing that only through acquisition processes is material sufficiently meaningful to be memorable: "In acquisition the image from which we reconstruct what we are after is rich and well integrated, while in learning it is impoverished and unintegrated. The higher the quality of the image—that is, the richer and better integrated it is—the more easily we will be able to get back one part of it when we encounter another part. In addition, the affective side of what we acquire is usually of a kind which causes us to welcome the recall of an image" (25). These assertions are commensurate with the overlap established in the taxonomy of the affective domain; see Bloom et al. 1964: 49–50.

2. Frank Smith (1971, 1973, 1978) has long argued that the best way to learn to read is by reading. Stephen Krashen advocates that foreign-language reading be conducted on the precepts of Smith's work in first language, particularly urging student self-selection of texts for pleasure reading (1982: 164–67).

3. These are the available cultural artifacts Michel Foucault (1976) identifies as representing the thought structures of a given geographical and historical location. His work explores the way a cultural-historical frame of reference and the underlying patterns of conceptualization are manifested in the goals and behaviors of scientific, social, and political institutions.

4. For a chart of illocutionary speech acts, see Searle, 66–67.

APPENDIX TO CHAPTER 11

Interest Inventories: Literature, Social Sciences, Science

A. *Purpose* The following inventories may be administered to assess students' interests in reading various types of literature.

B. *Description* The sample interest inventory may be adapted to survey students' interests in subject content, genre, biographical subject, author preferences, television viewing, career information, newspapers, and magazines.

C. *Procedure* Administer as a group test. Survey and summarize each student's responses to determine individual interests. A composite summary of all students' responses will provide direction for planning teaching units and selecting literature for students.

SAMPLE READING INTEREST INVENTORY FOR LITERATURE

1. Listed below are some topics you can read about in books. Check the topics listed below about which you would enjoy reading.

arts and crafts	_____	aviation	_____
religion	_____	hobbies	_____
jobs	_____	sailing	_____
government	_____	fairy tales	_____
cooking	_____	adventure stories	_____
detective stories	_____	history	_____
sports	_____	animals	_____
comedy	_____	space	_____
mystery	_____	war	_____
westerns	_____	spy stories	_____
love stories	_____	other _____	

2. Check below the kinds of writing listed below you enjoy reading.

long stories (novels)	_____
short stories	_____
poetry	_____
plays	_____
biographies	_____
essays	_____

3. List below persons' life stories you would be interested in reading.

   _____   _____
   _____   _____

4. List below authors whose books you enjoy reading.

   _____   _____
   _____   _____

5. Name three of your favorite television programs.

   _____
   _____
   _____

6. Name three careers (jobs) you might consider after you finish school.

   _____
   _____
   _____

7. Check any of the following newspaper sections you enjoy reading.

   News   _____   Sports   _____
   Editorial   _____   Business   _____
   Classified   _____   Entertainment   _____
   Comic   _____   Personal Advice Columns _____
   Advertisements_____

8. Check any of the following magazines you would enjoy reading. Teachers should allow students to browse through sample copies of magazines before asking students to complete the item).

   National Geographic   _____   *Reader's Digest*   _____
   Mad Magazine   _____   *Life*   _____
   Newsweek   _____   *Glamour*   _____
   Time   _____   *Popular Mechanics*   _____
   Ebony   _____   *Sports Illustrated*   _____
   U.S. News and World Report   _____   Other (specify)   _____

9. Books I have read and would recommend to my friends are:

   _____
   _____
   _____
   _____

10. Which of the following reasons for reading describe why you read most often:
    _____ to solve a problem (e.g., to pass a test; to build or cook something)
    _____ to feel that I am on top of what is going on in the world
    _____ to learn new information
    _____ to find ideas/opinions that agree with my own
    _____ to enjoy literature that is beautifully written
    _____ to forget my own problems for awhile
    _____ to experience events/places that I have not experienced first-hand

SAMPLE READING INTEREST INVENTORY FOR SOCIAL STUDIES

1. What two countries would you enjoy reading about?

   _____   _____

2. The world has many problems, and solutions to many problems have been proposed. Which of the following world problems would you be interested in reading about?

   ending world hunger   _____
   advances in ending racial inequities   _____
   improved life for city dwellers   _____
   improved medical care   _____
   inflation   _____
   threats of nuclear war   _____
   other _____   _____

3. Several countries are listed below. Check to the right of each country the aspects about the country you would be interested in reading about.

	Religion	Arts/ Crafts	Geography	Imports/ Exports	Other (write in)
Japan					
France					
Spain					
West Germany					
Brazil					
Other (write in)					

4. If you were to read about students from other countries, which of the following topics would you be interested in learning more about?

   clothes   _____   employment   _____
   school life   _____   holidays   _____
   music and dances   _____   transportation _____
   food   _____   education   _____
   recreation   _____

SAMPLE READING INTEREST INVENTORY FOR SCIENCE

Listed below are questions and surveys you may adapt to form a reading interest inventory related to scientific materials.

1. *Scientific Magazines*

   Look at the sample magazines being passed around. Below, check the titles of any you think you would enjoy reading regularly.

Popular Science	_____	*Space Frontiers*	_____
Mechanics Illustrated	_____	*Fantasy and Science Fiction*	_____
Scientific American	_____	*Science News*	_____
Popular Mechanics	_____	*Science World*	_____
National Geographic	_____	*New Scientist*	_____
Science Digest	_____	*Nature*	_____
Science	_____		

2. *Biography and Autobiography of Scientists*

   Listed below are some famous men and women in science. Check five to ten people you would like to know more about.

   _____ Jacques Cousteau (underwater sea explorer)
   _____ Lee Iacocca (engineer and the man most responsible for the original Ford Mustang)
   _____ Dr. Edward Teller (father of the H-Bomb)
   _____ Marie Curie (known for work on radioactivity and on radium)
   _____ Sir Isaac Newton (English mathematician and physicist; considered by many to be greatest scientist who ever lived)
   _____ Thomas Edison (inventor; developed a complete electrical distribution system for light and power)
   _____ James Watt (Scottish inventor; improved the steam engine. The watt, a unit of electrical power, was named for him)
   _____ Albert Einstein (German-American physicist known for the relativity theory)

3. *Scientific Related Agencies*

   Below are agencies and companies involved in science. Check three or four you would like to visit.

_____ oil refinery	_____ nuclear power plant
_____ space agency	_____ water treatment plant
_____ planetarium	_____ lapidary shop
_____ museum of natural science	_____ arboretum
_____ chemical plant	_____ city health department
_____ zoo	_____ federal drug abuse agency
_____ hospital	_____ other _____

4. *Careers in Science*

   The following careers require scientific backgrounds. Put a check mark beside careers that you already know something about. Put an "x" beside the ones you would like to learn more about. If you know someone that works in one of the jobs, put a circle (○) beside it. Put a "c" beside any career you think you might like to pursue.

Health Services:

_____ physician

_____ psychiatrist

_____ surgeon

_____ pharmacist

_____ osteopath

_____ veterinarian

_____ chiropractor

_____ dietitian

_____ registered nurse

_____ dental lab technician

_____ optometrist

_____ medical x-ray technician

_____ obstetrician

_____ physical therapist

_____ radiologist

_____ dental assistant

_____ practical nurse

_____ orderly

_____ nurse's aide

Education:

_____ elementary science teacher

_____ high school science teacher

_____ college professor

_____ adult school science teacher

Social Sciences:

_____ anthropologist

_____ geographer

_____ archaeologist

Aeronautics:

_____ aeronautical engineer

_____ aerospace engineer

_____ flight engineer

_____ navigator

Natural Science:

_____ biologist

_____ geologist

_____ geophysicist

_____ meteorologist

_____ microbiologist

_____ oceanographer

_____ chemist

_____ physicist

_____ astronomer

_____ research scientist

Conservation and Ecology:

_____ ecologist

_____ forester

_____ marine biologist

_____ soil conservationist

_____ agricultural scientist

_____ fish and wildlife conservationist

Miscellaneous:

_____ criminologist

_____ engineer

5. *Scientific Topics*

Put a check beside any of the following topics about which you would like to read.

_____ birds	_____ African animals	_____ engines
_____ the oceans	_____ genetics	_____ navigation
_____ stars	_____ ecology	_____ astrology
_____ flowers	_____ the future	_____ atomic power
_____ space	_____ mummies	OTHERS: _____
_____ airplanes	_____ bees	_____
_____ fossils	_____ insects	_____
_____ prehistoric man	_____ diseases	_____
_____ snakes	_____ weather	_____

6. *Scientific Equipment*

Put a check beside any piece of equipment you think you would be interested in teaching fellow classmates how to use.

_____ ammeter	_____ graduated cylinder
_____ spring balance	_____ electroscope
_____ platform balance	_____ galvanometer
_____ triple-beam balance	_____ convex/concave lens
_____ Bunsen burner	_____ meter stick
_____ collision balls apparatus	_____ stopwatch
_____ compass (magnetic)	_____ thermometer (chemical)
_____ conductivity testing apparatus	_____ voltmeter

7. *Science Fiction*

Some fiction writers base their stories on scientific possibilities. Check any science fiction writer whose stories you have read.

_____ Andre Norton	_____ Ray Bradbury
_____ Isaac Asimov	_____ Jules Verne
_____ J. R. R. Tolkien	

8. Which television show would you like to watch as an assignment in science?

_____ National Geographic	_____ The Body Human
_____ Wild Kingdom	_____ That's Incredible
_____ Real People	

From Betty M. Criscoe and Thomas C. Gee, *Content Reading: A Diagnostic / Prescriptive Approach* (Englewood Cliffs, NJ: Prentice Hall, 1984).

Twelve

Literature,
Literary Criticism,
and Cultural Literacy

In previous chapters we have looked at how authentic texts can foster reading comprehension in conjunction with listening, speaking, and writing. In this chapter, we turn to L2 reading of literary texts and how they pose both the greatest challenges and the greatest potential benefits in this enterprise. Reading literature is different from reading expository writing or reading for entertainment because of the extra demands a literary text imposes on its readers. Expository texts are read most often for information—their content is the reader's primary focus. In contrast, literary texts frequently challenge readers with discomfiting perspectives and linguistic techniques that deviate from standard usage.

Entertainment literature serves a function more similar to expository writing than to serious literature because the reader of popular fiction confronts familiar rhetorical structures and thematic components. Entertainment literature such as westerns, criminal and science fiction, romances, comics, and popularizations of current topics in science, business, history and the like tend to be formulaic. Louis L'Amour buffs all expect the desirable woman to despise the hero at the outset and be taken in by the villains, who manage to inflict grievous bodily injury on the hero before he escapes and recovers in a hidden valley. L'Amour fans anticipate these components and will be able to read westerns by other authors with greater facility because of their familiarity with a formula. Popular nonfiction books about, for example, raising children or how to dress, eat, or act to ensure success in the business world, each have their own sets of similarly-predictable components.

Perhaps the major difference between serious and popular literature, then, is that the former is not formulaic. As a result, when second-language students read literature, they must make inferences not only about what the text says, but how it says it—its metaphors, ordering of information, omissions, and narrative point of view. At the same time, literary texts reflect culture. They convey "the codes and preoccupations that structure a real society" (Collie & Slater 4).

For the L2 student, these are the extraordinary merits of literature. Collie and Slater sum up these virtues—linguistic, cultural, and personal—in a resource book of ideas and activities for the teaching of literature in a second language. In their exemplification of exercise types for plays, short stories, poems, and full-length novels, the authors make a strong case for the instructional feasibility of literary texts.

Literary texts have long been the traditional reading material in FL courses after the first year of language study. Within the past decade, however, expository texts, particularly ones dealing with social issues and lifestyle, have made inroads into intermediate anthologies for FL and ESL students. Emphasis on reader background has, to some extent, contributed to this trend. Many expository texts link facts to events or actions in a straightforward manner. That clear linkage is less characteristic of fiction. One considerable challenge of literary texts is that they contain densely-written propositions which characteristically imply multiple meanings. Even for L1 readers, a high inference load often creates a readability problem (Kintsch 1977b). Students who read literature need to engage in more interpretation than is necessary for most expository texts.

Along with the challenge of density of ideas, L2 students face a second formidable challenge that is more uniquely their own special problem: unfamiliar cultural allusions. Literary works abound with references to cultural detail. By contrast, both content and context are relatively predictable in trivial texts such as Harlequin romances and thrillers, or expository writing in nonacademic or popular culture articles. Rather than challenging the reader to think, these entertainments offer the reader an escape from having to think. Their content and context are familiar.

Since content and context are important readability factors, expository texts anchored in the reader's real-world experience or trivial texts with familiar schemata may be better than literary texts for reading for information and increasing automaticity with L2 vocabulary. Most L2 content courses can rely on the fact that their students are somewhat familiar with the subject matter of the text and often with the treatment as well (e.g., Dubin et al.). The context and content of United Press stories, business letters, or governmental policy reports are well defined. These structures are shared to a large degree by most European languages. The same cannot be said of the content and context of literature. Even within a single language, content and context will vary with the age, geographical location, ethnicity, socio-economic status, and educational background of the author, to mention only a few variables.

Along with hurdles of high inference load and the likelihood of unfamiliar cultural allusions, literary texts are also encumbered by a scholarly tradition that has done little to encourage their reading by L2 students. In her summary of this tradition, Horner points out that our current scholarly approach to the teaching of literature is of relatively recent vintage. In eighteenth-century England the purpose of English studies had been to unite the teaching of rhetoric—persuasive oral and written discourse—with an understanding of literary culture. By the mid-nineteenth century, colleges in the United States had adopted this model. At Harvard "theme writing, declamations, and the study of rhetorical principles in passages from great literary works were part of a single, undifferentiated process" (Graff 41).

Not until the late nineteenth century did literature become a distinct field of study in the United States. The first meeting of the Modern Language Association was in 1883 and at that time scholars warned that English must become a science (Graff 67–68). Prior to this time, in both England and the United States, the term "literature" had been defined differently than it is today (Kinneavy 14–17). The concept had had a strong classical component (Latin and Greek). It also included history and biography, expository and didactic works, scientific writing, poetry and fiction. Towards the close of the century, however, English studies began to change in several ways. First, the range of texts to be dealt with in the field narrowed more specifically to a canon of literary works. Second, the subdisciplines of literature and composition emerged. Third, instructional focus on the constituents of a literary work shifted to instructional acts of interpretation. As Spack observes, "literature, once concerned primarily with the study of the creative act, became more concerned with the study of reading, or the interpretive act" (707).

It is this third development that has had a particular impact on current thinking about the role of literature in the L2 classroom, because current scholarly approaches to literature are almost all critic-centered rather than reader-centered. With the exception of work in phenomenology, notably Iser's *The Act of Reading*, and the related field of reader-response represented by such critics as Fish and Scholes, most scholars provide students with expert interpretations—that is, critics' interpretations—of the meanings and implications of what they have read.[1] The significance of this procedure is clear to our students, especially to non-native speakers: they see their task as a passive one. Such students read a literary text for its surface information or explicitly-stated facts and depend on a teacher-expert to reconstruct the cultural and aesthetic coherences available beneath its surface. They do not see themselves as capable of serious independent interpretation.

Such a perception deprives L2 students of interaction with the text. They interact with the instructor's comprehension of the text rather than their own, thereby reducing their view of literature to that of a story line and a compendium of cultural facts. Such a view fails to develop student awareness of the unique character of literary discourse, of the communicative potential of language beyond its purely utilitarian uses (Widdowson).

Consequently, students who are encouraged to read only for facts in a literary text are at a great disadvantage. When students read only to collect facts they have lower levels of reading comprehension than when they engage in structuring those facts. Studies in metacognition indicate that students generate scenarios or use rhetorical patterns to organize textual information. Research comparing students reading to "collect" facts with those arranging facts according to a particular logic (cause and effect, comparison) or a particular point of view (as a housewife or policeman), has led to consistent results for both first- and second-language readers: students who schematize text structure learn more from a text and remember it better.[2]

What about students who accept the teacher's schema, the critic-imposed interpretive system? Certainly an imitative approach is a valid tool for teaching structuralism, semiotics, reception theory, or whatever the favored method happens to be. Teaching students critical approaches, however, is not quite the same thing as teaching them to discover what texts mean. And L2 students need to learn to uncover the messages of a poem, novel, or story, not what that work means to an expert critic. Due in part to the traditions in literary criticism since the nineteenth century, this is not generally encouraged. We in modern language studies have been engaged in interpreting texts for each other and our students, rather than facilitating and developing the interpretive strategies of those students. Consequently, we produce disciples who defer to the experts when it comes to questions of textual meaning and significance. Such students are culturally illiterate.

Our aim in this chapter is to explore the practical ramifications of cultural literacy for student readers of English and foreign languages. To do so, we will first propose a definition of cultural literacy and then present an application of the concept in classroom reading. Finally, we will suggest some implications of teaching cultural literacy in English and foreign-language curricula.

A PROCEDURAL DEFINITION OF CULTURAL LITERACY

A culture has a historically- and geographically-identifiable infrastructure, consisting of its language, artifacts, and institutions. Recent debate has centered on the facts people must know to appreciate literary or historical allusions. Scholars such as Allan Bloom and E. D. Hirsch (1987) argue that these references have been neglected in public school and undergraduate college education in the United States. Two issues emerge from efforts to address this problem. First, in an era of proliferating information, the question of selection is acute. One of the reasons Hirsch has been at the center of debate is that many scholars disagree with the particulars of the culture he suggests we learn. What should be included and what not? True, we need familiarity with our own cultural heritages, but in a melting-pot nation, multiple heritages abound. Cultural prescriptions soon become political issues (e.g., Scholes). Western Heritage courses, for example, necessarily ignore the reality that many of their students will be from non-European cultures.

Second, some object that knowledge of culture is more than knowledge of facts. Like textual language, cultural facts must be embedded in a discourse to assume meaning. This assertion implies that L2 students need to comprehend culture much as they comprehend texts—as sign systems. Cultural historians suggest that an examination of the surface of a cultural infrastructure will reveal consistent patterns that express regularities in that culture's underlying system of thought. Foucault calls these regularities epistemes.

If we accept this division of culture into surface manifestation and subsurface thought-system, then an individual who is culturally literate must be capable of reading not only the surface structures and signs of a culture, but also the underlying configuration of meanings from which those surface structures emanate.

Culturally literate students can, for example, locate the status of the middle class in the phenomenon of Renaissance architecture. They might begin by recognizing a pattern of worldliness that is implied by the shift from the ethereal church structures that dominated Gothic communities to the new emphasis on relatively unimposing Renaissance city halls, libraries, and private homes, all of which were built to a scale intended to facilitate rather than confound human comprehension. Such an architecture, in turn, was possible only in fifteenth- and sixteenth-century Europe, because its humanist social and historical message—the conscious imitation of ancient Greek scholars and merchants—was eclipsed in the seventeenth century by the emergence of the absolutist monarchs of Europe, who sent out very different architectural, social, and political messages in the following three hundred years.

Educators who face an American audience cannot assume their students' ability to link such social, artistic, historical, and political events. Our students seldom make the leap from the explicit facts of one discipline to the implied relationship of those facts to other disciplines. Student readers of Anthony Burgess' *A Clockwork Orange* rarely apply the referential system of that book to their courses in psychology (behavioral conditioning), communication (subliminal advertising techniques), or sociology (origins of societal attitudes). Teachers of English and foreign-language literature cannot be assured that reading the literature of a culture will produce students who are culturally literate, students who will automatically see the implications of that literature and the ways in which its messages connect with a range of related real-world phenomena.

What measures, then, can be undertaken to encourage cultural literacy among our students?

UNCOVERING CULTURAL MESSAGES: STAGES AND PROCEDURES

Our first job is to refocus our students' perceptual procedures by encouraging them to correlate the surface information of a literary work with the underlying referential systems that are implied by the surface arrangement. Robert Scholes illustrates the surface / subsurface distinction in his discussion of teaching the "cultural code" (his term) of Ernest Hemingway's *In Our Time*. Scholes suggests that references to "bombardment," "shelling," and "trench" evoke "the whole world of World War I," whereas other vocabulary is incidental. For instance, the words "Fossalta" and "Mestre," he points out, "are not essential for comprehension of Hemingway's messages" (28–29). Reading assignments focus on thematic connections that help students identify such cultural coding: the referential system of a work's words and syntax. Students must be aware that the messages of a textual system will emerge as they undertake backward and forward inferencing, associating the features and implications of later actions or reactions with earlier ones, or predicting behaviors and events on the basis of the informational patterns they perceive at any given point in their reading.

Depending on the genre and messages of the text, different associative features will apply. In Kafka's "Metamorphosis," for example, shifts in scene play a minimal role, but shifts in the attitudes of Gregor and his family toward his altered state reveal a consistent development. Gregor's initial preoccupation with his job and his employer, coupled with his resentment against the constraints of a life that revolves around the demands of work and family, diminish in direct relationship to the family's increasing indifference toward him. Attitudinal and behavioral changes in his parents and sister occur in tandem with Gregor's gradual acceptance and exploration of his new role as a cockroach.

Reading for such correlations or schemata is not an exercise in open-ended speculation, because the schematizing point of view is anchored in the discourse of "Metamorphosis." The resultant reading perspectives must interface with that discourse. They do not displace the text as the center of reader attention. Students who have been asked to organize textual information in terms of the contrast between Gregor's attitudes and behaviors and those of his family come to class prepared to draw inferences derived solely from their experience with the text. The students' opinions or personal reactions to the subject matter have been set aside. They will discuss the patterns of Kafka's work rather than their personal judgments based on text-extrinsic information and experience.

Instead of comparing a set of subjective reader-responses to the surface of the text (in this case the plot or situation *per se*), students have been given an analytical frame whose scope admits only textual messages for discussion. Instead of reacting on the basis of their preconceptions, students can see how the text is built and how Gregor's world functions.

Class time can be spent in assembling the student readers' pieces of the textual puzzle, excluding extraneous pieces, anachronisms, or prejudices ("nobody should live with their parents"). The patterns that result from such group work will vary in their particulars, but independently assembled sets of facts about attitudes and behaviors in "Metamorphosis" will overlap significantly, no matter what previous experience the students have had with the culture from which the work derives. Students will pinpoint aspects of Gregor's initial feelings of guilt and self-recrimination in response to unexamined family and occupational demands. They will locate some of Gregor's subsequent stages of self-analysis, which include criticizing the behavior of his parents and his sister and, ultimately, ceasing to think about work and obligations altogether. They will discover at what juncture in the story Gregor begins to experience his new condition as a cockroach by climbing walls and having sensations of physical well-being in dark, cramped places. They can then correlate Gregor's concomitant discovery with a series of increasingly positive potentials in his new life, such as mobility and explorative capacities.

INFORMATION PATTERN AND TEXTUAL IMPLICATIONS

What purely textual implications emerge from this pattern? Once the shifts in surface behaviors have been schematized, the connotational system in Kafka's story is straightforward. Gregor's life prior to his metamorphosis consisted of meeting societal demands. Once he is no longer capable of meeting these demands, two things happen: First, he discovers a range of new experiences and sensations; second, he rejects his society and his family.

It is of course possible to create alternative interpretations of the information in "Metamorphosis." However, the issue is not that a common pool of textual information be assembled and interpreted, but rather that a systematic process of grouping the information patterns be undertaken. Moreover, this process must be undertaken before the words and the data of literature (or, indeed, any type of text) can be properly linked to its underlying, necessarily culture-bound meanings. If such links are not made by the student reader, the instructor's presentations about style, imagery, or comparisons with other literatures will lack significance in the hermeneutic sense: They cannot be the basis for further inquiry because cultural implications are mediated by the student's frame of reference and the coherences the student perceives in a text.

That mediation is a direct result of the breadth of student reading in what today would be called non-literary as well as literary texts. In other words, if our definition of literature had a nineteenth- rather than twentieth-century breadth, the term would encompass not only poetry and fiction, but also history and biography, expository and didactic works, and scientific writing. Students who are aware of the links between these diverse "literatures" are more likely to have frames of reference that illuminate textual patterns.

Kafka's story illustrates the value of merging content courses and literary works. Consider the L2 student taking area-study courses in the history, sociology, or the art and music of Germany and Austria. If Kafka is read in conjunction with expository texts covering such topics, this L2 student has a cognitive base from which to view Gregor's behaviors and attitudes—to connect Gregor and his family with societal behaviors and attitudes of nineteenth- and early twentieth-century Europe. The paintings, music, and events from the revolution of 1848 onward all point to the severe social and political limits imposed on the bourgeoisie by repressive governments which were mirrored in patriarchal family structure. Deviation of any kind was punished harshly in public and in the home. The only option for an individualist was to make a complete break, a metamorphosis whose consequences would place that person ouside the pale of society. In Gregor's case, that isolation proved fatal. These insights about "Metamorphosis" have clear applications outside their particular time and place.

TEXTUAL IMPLICATIONS AND CULTURAL SIGNIFICANCES

If our goal is cultural literacy, then our students' connections between the real world and the literary text must originate with their knowledge of history and geography on the one hand, and appreciation of literature as a cultural artifact on the other. Only after students can view a story as a cultural artifact can they go on to consider its contemporaneous relationship to seemingly-disparate phenomena. "Metamorphosis" can be linked to a spectrum of early twentieth-century cultural hallmarks: Freud's conclusions about hysteria and the dream world, or Wilde's comedies of manners, or even the suicidal patterns of trench warfare. A variant of the same paradigm—the domination of the young by their parents and parental social institutions—applies in each case. One underlying theme in Freud's work was that neuroses originate in suppressed resentments or guilt about parental or societal demands. Wilde's comedies attacked the episteme of societal repression by making people laugh about it. And a "lost" generation in the twenties and thirties, disabused of parental veneration, took their parents' society to task for the insanities of World War I, of which trench warfare was only one. While students do not need to know all these things, they must be aware that such connections need to be made between literature and the time and place in which it was written.

If we take seriously E. D. Hirsch's dictum that "the value of knowledge is realized in its application," (1978:156), then our primary instructional task as L2 teachers and humanists is to enable students to discover the fundamental meanings within texts and to link or apply those meanings to the cultures from which the texts derive. Assignments that facilitate the students' discovery of meaningful patterns in a work of literature are commensurate with our scholarly training. The result, however, is not a finished interpretation, but rather a *pre-interpretation*, a matrix of the essentials in which a finished interpretation would need to be grounded.

The resultant macrostructure is neither simplistic nor reductionist. The difference between teaching interpretation and pre-interpretation can be compared to teaching students the regulative rules of a specific board game like Monopoly as opposed to teaching the premises or constitutive rules of all board games from Clue to Trivial Pursuit.[3] Regulative rules specify the conditions for a particular game. For Monopoly, regulative rules define procedures such as acquiring property or building houses, whereas constitutive rules are the generalized patterns of any board game: the use of dice to determine moves; the possibility of landing on penalty squares; the additional chance function of cards to penalize or reward. Interpretation asks students to learn a particular critical game; pre-interpretation asks students to learn the conditions for successful play.

What is the interpretive difference between learning the premises of playing a game (constitutive rules) and learning game-specific rules (its regulations)? For instance, the structuralist interpretative game for "Metamorphosis" would probably employ regulative rules of binary distinctions (animal / human categories, for example), whereas a semiotic analysis would use quite different regulative principles such as the functions of public and private channels for communicating signals (which events are known only to Gregor?), and a psychoanalytic interpretation would probably correlate Gregor's plight with biographical details of Kafka's relationship to his own parents. In each example, the reader would use different interpretive codes (the regulative rule system for that method) to uncover different facets of "Metamorphosis"' textual codes.

Pre-interpretation, on the other hand, asks students to look only at textual codes. The reading process involved directs students toward finding related patterns of events, environments, attitudes, behaviors, or ideas. Our scholarly training prepares us to identify the reader point of view that will link surface and subsurface textual features. Our job as teachers of literature is to enable students to identify those features and to uncover the underlying patterns that render them culturally significant. Only then are our students really ready to interpret or appreciate expert interpretations.

PRE-INTERPRETATION AS INTERACTIVE READING

The hallmark, then, of the approach to reading suggested in this book is not that we must teach one specific pattern in a literary work. To teach a single "truth" is to function as the critical expert, not the pre-interpretive guide. Rather, teachers of literature should construct assignments and syllabi that require the students to read analytically, perceiving surface information as a function of underlying implications.

To be meaningful, reading of plays, novels, and longer expository prose must address both detail and gist. Hence, with the exception of short stories and poetry, the challenges facing a reader of literature are those facing readers of longer texts. As argued in earlier chapters, L2 students need to read more than they currently do.

Naturally, which texts they read will depend on their course work, but regardless of differences in course content or emphases, if reading is made an important component of L2 learning, reading of longer, authentic texts must commence earlier than has been standard practice. And considerably more reading must be done outside of class.

Reading outside of class is an independent activity. Consequently, clear guidelines are essential. Students need to diagnose their progress. Instructors need an instrument to verify that students are reading and to evaluate the quality of that reading. Moreover, the guidelines must be easy for students to use, yet substantive enough to reveal their comprehension of longer works. And, of course, guidelines should reflect the goal underlying the entire agenda of this book—students need tasks that foster reading for meaning.

To encourage and confirm meaningful reading, assignments must help students use a task hierarchy with two kinds of system—semantic and syntactic—the components of meaning and the way those components relate. The semantic and syntactic charts that follow illustrate the relationships of detailed information to larger patterns in longer texts. Because meaning in a longer text is cumulative, the different layers in these charts must be read vertically as well as horizontally.

To appreciate literature, readers need to appreciate the layers of discourse within a literary work. To exemplify the layers of discourse which students must identify, we chose the novel *Alice's Adventures in Wonderland*, a work that is familiar to most readers. Of course, this multilayered approach is appropriate for all styles of longer texts.

SUMMATIVE CHARTS FOR THE PROPOSED

A. SEMANTIC SUBSYSTEMS—LAYERS OF TEXT AND READER INTERACTION

> ***Layer 1. Predictive semantic reader associations** (things / idea / activities)*
> EXAMPLE: Students speculate that a text entitled *Alice's Adventures in Wonderland* might mention talking animals, frightening people or places, surprising events.

Layer 2. Semantic realizations at the word level (primarily nouns, verbs, and adjectives and adverbs modifying nouns and verbs—the who, what, where, when)

    EXAMPLE: Alice, curious little girl, talking rabbits, pocket watch

Layer 3. Semantic coherence / cohesion at the sentence and intersentential level = common propositional content is related

coherence: an implicit connection

    EXAMPLE: The rabbit actually took a watch out of his waist-coat pocket. Alice burned with curiosity.

cohesion: an explicit connection

    EXAMPLE: The rabbit actually took a watch out of his waist-coat pocket. That made Alice very curious.*

Layer 4. Implicit / explicit connections at the paragraph or episode level

implicit connection: two neutral objectifications with an implied connection (characteristic, possible event)

    EXAMPLE: Paragraph 3 describes Alice watching the rabbit. Paragraph 4 is a single sentence stating that Alice followed the rabbit down the rabbit hole "never once considering how in the world she was to get out again."

explicit connection: two mutually-defining scenes

    EXAMPLE: Paragraph 1 describing Alice watching the rabbit followed by a statement that her curiosity prompted her to follow the rabbit.*

Layer 5. The relationship between context and information in a chapter or article

context: the scenario for a plot segment or argument segment

    EXAMPLE: In Chapter 1 the reader learns that Alice will miss her cat. Subsequent interaction with animals may reflect this affection for her cat or a general love of animals, but such a relationship is not specified.

(Chart A continues on page 224)

MODEL OF READING

B. SYNTACTIC SUBSYSTEMS—LAYERS OF TEXT AND READER INTERACTION

Layer 1. Predictive syntactic reader associations = a scale such as worse to better, larger to smaller, parts to whole, chronology, and relationships in the sense of super- and subordination

EXAMPLE: Students would speculate that a text entitled *Alice's Adventures in Wonderland* suggests a comparison with a less adventurous real life.

Layer 2. Syntactic realizations at the word level (case relationships, adverbs, adjectives, prepositional phrases, connectives)

EXAMPLE: Students locate words that suggest progressive stages developing in the text: *the first* [question], *at last, then, the next* [thing], *in a little while.*

Layer 3. Syntactic coherence / cohesion at the sentence level or between two sentences or propositions = common propositional content is related

coherence: an implicit connection

EXAMPLE: The rabbit actually took a watch out of his waist-coat pocket. Alice started to her feet.

cohesion: an explicit connection

EXAMPLE: Because the rabbit actually took a watch out of his waist-coat pocket, Alice started to her feet.*

Layer 4. Implicit / explicit connections at the intersentential or episode level

implicit connection: forward and backward connections must be inferred by the reader

EXAMPLE: During her fall, Alice misses her cat. Later in the pool of tears, she describes the cat.

explicit connection: forward and backward references (deixis) overtly state relationships

EXAMPLE: During her fall, Alice misses her cat. Later, in the pool of tears, she attributes virtues to the cat that animals in Wonderland lack.*

Layer 5. The relationship between intent and language usage in a chapter or article

intent: what the speaker or writer has in mind, sometimes referred to as authorial *stance:* explicit or implicit indications of the author's aims

EXAMPLE OF IMPLICIT

EXPRESSION OF AIMS: Chapter 1 describes Alice's solitary adventures

(Chart B continues on page 225)

Chart A (continued from page 222)

information: stated relationships at the plot level or article argument level

    EXAMPLE: A subsequent segment in which Alice might observe that her fondness for her cat reflects a preference for the society of animals over human company.*

Layer 6. The relationship between word fields in the real world and text vocabulary = **book length or longer finished work**

word fields: all vocabulary appropriate to the topic (text extrinsic)

    EXAMPLE: the concrete vocabulary of a child's world, fairy tales, games

text vocabulary: only the author's words (text intrinsic)

    EXAMPLE: The author's word choice in describing or explaining how fantasy and adventure stories reflect a child's perception of actual people and events.*

---

* Note: Starred items reflect examples not found in *Alice's Adventures in Wonderland*

Chart B (continued from page 223)

(landing at the bottom of the rabbit hole, following the rabbit, finding the small door, shrinking to ten inches, etc). In Chapter 2 Alice meets a mouse in the pool of tears. In Chapter 3 she engages in story-telling with all the animals who have swum out of the pool of tears with her.

EXAMPLE OF EXPLICIT
EXPRESSION OF AIMS: As above except that each chapter links stages with macromarkers that specify a developmental relationship between chapters (*First we will find out what Alice does when she is alone in peculiar circumstances. In the following chapter the author shows how Alice behaves when conversing with a single creature from Wonderland. In subsequent chapters we see how she accepts the challenges posed by groups of stange animals, objects, and people.**)

language usage: the adequacy of markers used to achieve intent, also *process, style,* or *execution*, i.e., the clarity and consistency the author uses in achieving his or her aims

EXAMPLE: In the actual Carroll narrative, the pattern of Alice's adventures emerges as stages in increasingly complex socialization. The development of these stages is consistent. The book does not, for example, suddenly engage in tangents about Colonial policies or social hypocrisy in Victorian England, references unrelated to the textual logic—a sequence of fairy-tale adventures.

Layer 6. Discourse structures / discourse markers = **fully-developed discourse of book length**

discourse structures: genre

EXAMPLE: Gothic novel, scholarly biography, comedy of manners

discourse markers: starts and finishes or closure (some genres, such as the short story, characteristically lack these features)

EXAMPLE: rhythm of episodes, progression of settings, stock characters and scenes

---

The connections illustrated above are rarely made spontaneously. Yet we have found that locating these layers promotes interactive reading because the reader must identify and connect key factors in textual comprehension. Throughout this volume we have discussed texts in terms of these multiple interrelated factors: the text and the reader's context, topic focus, information, and language. These charts illustrate the hierarchy of those factors in longer texts. The resultant pre-interpretation enables students to assess textual messages at every layer and to augment their evolving comprehension. What follows illustrates a hypothetical use of these charts.

Layer 1: Pre-reading or activating strategies

The first layer in the charts begins where reading usually begins—the title. With the title and the frontispiece to a book, the reader can already make assumptions about pieces of content (textual semantics) and how those pieces relate to one another (textual syntax). At the pre-semantic level we have Wonderland—a place of illogical connections. The predictive syntax of Wonderland is chronological. The reader anticipates a sequence of one wonder after another, much in the sense of the tales of E. T. A. Hoffmann or Baron Münchhausen. The common thread of the story will probably be the title character, Alice—the single point of continuity in a world otherwise full of unexpected surprises.

Layer 2–3: Close reading for detail

In Chapter 1, page one, we encounter the semantic field of "a hot day," a child "tired of sitting," with "nothing to do," and feeling "very sleepy and stupid." Here is a bored, tired child. She sees a rabbit who says to himself "Oh dear! Oh dear! I shall be too late!" and who takes "a watch out of its waistcoat-pocket" (5–6). Alice runs after the white rabbit and follows it down the rabbit hole. The bored child has become the curious and adventurous child who unquestioningly engages in behavior that challenges the laws of the real world. Now readers can establish relationships for the semantic features observed: the juxtaposition of Alice's Wonderland activities and their consequences with her prior lassitude. Even at this early juncture in the reading, this juxtaposition reveals that Alice is an active participant in Wonderland rather than the passive object of events.

Looking to substantiate these insights between sentences and paragraphs, the reader will find semantic confirmation in all of the events that follow once Alice descends down the rabbit hole. Nothing ordinary occurs. She falls "down what seemed to be a very deep well," but "had plenty of time as she went down to look about her" and when she lands, "not be a bit hurt." The semantic list of Chapter 1 would be of discoveries and speculations ("I wonder how many miles I've fallen?").

To establish the text's relationships, the reader looks particularly for markers of logic, sequence, location, or time at the sentence and intersentential layers. Sentences— particularly sentences that start paragraphs—are introduced with "presently," "soon," or "after a while." Particularly toward the close of the chapter, sentences end or are connected with "when suddenly," "then," or "sometimes." As the reader has already anticipated, the text presents a sequence of events, and that perception is reinforced semantically by temporal markers.

These perceptions bring the reader to the essentially artificial boundary between semantic and syntactic distinctions in meaning. A reader's prediction that *Alice's Adventures in Wonderland* would be full of chronological events may not be realized at the syntactic layer of word meaning, but the peculiarity of those events will. When Alice falls down the rabbit hole, for example, the statement "down, down, down" introduces two paragraphs. As complete statements, the normally-expected syntactic proposition ("Alice was falling down further and further") is reduced to a single word. Observations such as "curiouser and curiouser" not only reduce propositions ("Things were getting more and more curious"), they also underscore that deviation in their non-standard morphology. Such violations in word usage support the reader's sense of the peculiarity and unconnectedness of events described. The sense of discontinuity is further foregrounded by the sentence and intersentential syntax in the story's episodes.

During the initial phase of Alice's fall down the rabbit hole, for example, her questions to herself are unusually well-formed (e.g., "I wonder how many miles I have fallen by this time?"). She is, the reader is told, practicing showing off her knowledge. By the third paragraph, however, the questions have become repetitive and shorter. The query "But do cats eat bats, I wonder?" is reversed into a sing-song of "Do cats eat bats? Do bats eat cats?" With such syntactic reversals, Carroll draws Alice and the reader into the semantic absurdities of Wonderland. Subsequent dialogues about courses in reeling and writhing or playing croquet with flamingos are conducted with complete syntactic propriety. Throughout the story, syntactically-normed discourses are isolated from an expected standard of meaningfulness. This disjuncture between syntax and semantics at the sentence level foreshadows anomalies to come: the mouse's tale written in the shape of his tail or Alice reciting poems in which the words do not come out the same as they used to.

Layer 4: Episodes and gist

Differences in reader perception of patterns in longer and shorter texts occur at the junction between paragraphs and episodes. In short passages, information is arranged between sentences and paragraph segments. In longer texts, information patterns involve shifts of topic, setting, and character. Consequently, for extensive reading of longer works of literature, the reader's focus will be on such changes and how each episode relates to succeeding ones.

In well-written literature, the semantic and syntactic patterns at the word and intersentential layer are expanded, elaborated, and intensified. As in the discussion about *Alice's Adventures*, they are not, however, substantively altered at the episode layer. In the shifts of setting and character in all the chapters of *Alice's Adventures in Wonderland*, the syntax of activities and consequences emerges. All Alice's actions—the explicit story developments—lead to new problems. After Alice has "finished off the cake," she finds herself "growing . . . more than nine feet high," only to find herself shrinking again and "that the cause of this was the fan she was holding, and she dropped it hastily, just in time to save herself from shrinking away altogether" (17–23).

The semantics of episodes, however, places a different and altogether harmless light on these disasters. Although she is periodically daunted, the pace of events for Alice (and the reader) in new episodes removes any suggestion of permanency. Matters get "curiouser and curiouser," but every disaster Alice initiates is consistently followed by a successful narrow escape. Both Alice and the reader "read" this pattern as a fixed expectation of Wonderland. The sole difference is from whom or where the challenges emanate and what results occur when Alice responds to them.

At the episode layer, a vertical as well as a horizontal reading of the matrix is needed to uncover the implicit messages in textual juxtapositions. When readers consider the semantic longitude of the story, they will see that all episodes mingle real-world and Wonderland elements. In Chapter 1 the bottle says "DRINK ME," something which bottles never say, yet Alice looks to see if "this bottle was marked 'poison'" before she drinks it, something well-brought-up little girls are taught to do in the real world. In Chapter 2 Alice has a conversation with a mouse, but his unmouselike behavior is followed by that animal's very normal fright at the mention of cats and dogs. Implicitly, then, most episodes confront the usual with the unusual, the behaviors and values of the real world with those of Wonderland. As Alice notes, "Everything is so out-of-the-way down here, that I should think very likely it [the mouse] can talk" (25). Alice is constantly having to puzzle out a new game of social interaction. She must socialize with animals and cards who swim, walk, and talk with her. In order to survive, she must apply her own knowledge about human interaction to uncover the regulative rules of the new environment.

What happens when the reader considers the implied pattern of that learning process? In terms of the spectrum of episodes from beginning to end, a developmental sequence emerges. The initial challenges are to Alice's physical self: falling down the rabbit hole, shrinking and growing precipitously, virtually drowning in tears. By Chapter 3, however, some of the challenges begin to shift to the realm of human interaction. Alice socializes with peers—individuals with whom one needs to do business, but who also provide useful information and keep one from being lonely. Alice must relate to such creatures in a number of different ways. She must, for example, provide prizes for the animals gathered to hear the mouse's tale. By Chapter 4 Alice must engage in her own recitation efforts and finds she has "never been so much contradicted in all her life before" (66). At the mad tea party in Chapter 7, she needs only to engage in polite conversation. Consistently, socializing problems have to do with the unpredictability and hypersensitivity of the animals she deals with. "I wish these creatures wouldn't be so easily offended" (66), Alice thinks to herself while talking to the caterpillar. However, these traits take on threatening dimensions only when Alice confronts figures of authority—the King, Queen, and Duchess.

Longitudinally, the implied syntax of episodes reveals that Alice's challenges have paralleled the challenges of a growing child, the challenges emerging from changes in physical size and the resulting advantages and disadvantages. Social questions follow: negotiation with peers, and the acceptance or rejection of the behavior of social equals. Finally, the book addresses a child's difficulties in interacting with the escalating demands of authority figures.

Layer 5: Implications

The inventory of layers 1 through 4 reveals the semantics of Carroll's text, the everyday events in a child's world when that world is turned upside down. Even if the reader knows nothing about the 1860s in England, it is relatively easy to infer details about Alice's social status: She lives in a sheltered nursery where proper behavior is a paramount virtue. Alice worries, for example, about whether she can curtsey while falling down the well. Older women wield arbitrary and therefore frightening power ("Off with their heads!"). Occasionally that power is mitigated by a protective but largely passive King ("Consider my dear, she is only a child."). Inferences about behavioral norms in Victorian households are easy to draw if the L2 reader has studied the era, the relationship between Queen Victoria and her consort, the patterns of English colonialism in the nineteenth century, or the role of men and women in upper-middle-class society of the day.

The text's explicit semantics are simple and concrete throughout. On the few occasions when Alice experiments with big words, she is glad no one is listening as they do not "sound right at all." When authority figures employ high-sounding phrases from the adult world, their words are quickly deflated by Alice's matter-of-fact questions or ensuing events. The King's order to "read the accusation," for example, is followed by the famous quatrain that begins "The Queen of Hearts, she made some tarts."

Again, as with the preceding layers, it is the pattern of semantic information that illustrates the function of this concrete language. In Wonderland Alice discovers literal meanings for murky, abstract terms. At the trial she watches a guinea-pig being put in a bag and sat upon by the officers of the court and observes "I've so often read in the newspapers, at the end of trials 'There was some attempt at applause, which was immediately suppressed by the officers of the court,' and I never understood what it meant till now" (155). This treatment of language, which abounds throughout the book, reveals Carroll's intent, as well as the fascination of this children's book for adult readers. The author has reduced the complex dilemmas of the adult world—with all their moral and logical diffuseness—to very literal terms. There are neither moral nor intellectual predicaments in Wonderland. What Carroll did was translate Victorian values into an amusing sequence of scenarios. As a consequence, rather than stifling Alice's curiosity and intimidating her independent spirit, in Carroll's hands those values present harmless challenges to a child's imagination.

Layer 6: Significance

The genre of a "child's fantasy book" frees Carroll from the necessity to create realistic situations, probable characters, or emotional authenticity. Such features would have rendered the story's innocuous events disturbing. To prevent any misunderstandings about that intent, the novel has a clear beginning and end—starting with Alice's initial boredom on a hot summer afternoon and concluding with the reflections of her older sister after Alice awakes, retells her dream, and runs off to tea. It is the sister's thoughtful resumé of Alice's dream that explicitly locates where dream and reality meet: The rattling teacups become tinkling sheep-bells, and the Queen's shrill cries, the voice of the shepherd boy. The real world of Victorian England, now foregrounded in the narrative, is referred to as "dull reality." From this retrospective the word field of the preceding chapters, its frequent reprimands ("You're late!," "Get up!," "Keep your temper!," "And be quick about it!") and Alice's explanation for odd behavior ("Maybe it's always pepper that makes people hot-tempered"), reveal the degree to which Wonderland expectations parallel adult expectations in this child's real world.

Practice in looking for these fundamental stages in interpretive analysis must, of course, rely heavily on the language of the text. If students use that language to express their sense of the story's messages and implications, the results may not always be the most appropriate English or foreign-language usage. But with systematic practice in isolating levels of textual messages, a reader will be able to use the L2 text's language to convey connected ideas about its meaning, its larger as well as smaller pieces. Most of us who are not native speakers will, in the normal course of our speech and writing, lack absolute confidence about word choice and appropriate use of formal features. Textual language, while it is not always colloquial, enables students and teachers to share a common vocabulary without recourse to translation. At the same time, non-native speakers can monitor the accuracy of their language usage against a language model which integrates formal correctness with functions of meaning. At the point when students can use textual language to express that work's messages, implications, and significance, the text becomes a grammar, a model of language usage. And literary texts make beautiful grammars.

QUANTITATIVE READING AND THE FOREIGN-LANGUAGE STUDENT

To learn to read longer texts in terms of related systems we and our students must, in most instances, revise long-standing perceptions about L2 reading (Barnett 1990). As was emphasized in earlier chapters, most skills-oriented classrooms inhibit students from reading in a foreign language the way they read in English. Trained and tested for mastery of vocabulary and grammar, students assume that reading, even light reading, should be conducted along the same premises as language learning—as if reading were an activity predicated wholly on language mastery. Most first-year and even second-year textbooks imply that the preconditions for reading comprehension are similar to those for production of the language. Both in reading texts and in producing language, these textbooks encourage students to think word for word rather than to understand ideas. The questions and exercises that accompany reading assignments also suggest that a grasp of the text's information level is sufficient for adequate comprehension. Yet foreign-language reading research suggests that reading strategies focusing on a text's logical coherences (sometimes referred to as "main meaning") seem to compensate significantly for inadequate command of the language (e.g., Hosenfeld).

This is not to suggest that reading in foreign languages is not concerned with the surface. Clearly, some grammaticality is essential if anything at all is to be understood. But even complete command does not guarantee good comprehension.[4] Comprehension goes beyond surface information. The reader must identify the underlying, culture-bound coherences suggested by that surface. In short, surface content and structure alone will not make the text's message-spectrum intelligible. Like the readers of English literature, students of foreign languages must learn that surface structures and information are fully meaningful only in conjunction with their subsurface referential systems, and with the sign systems of the culture that generated them (Steffensen et al.).

CURRICULAR SUGGESTIONS

The recommendation to read literary and non-literary texts as cultural artifacts has important implications for the choice of reading assignments. At present, foreign-language textbooks tend to provide students with culturally sanitized language rather than with examples of genuine communication in that language. To be genuine or "authentic" communication, texts must be produced in contexts that are plausible to real speakers of the language. Instead of such readings, our students often confront contrived text language. The selections in the average anthology have been simplified or especially written to conform to word-frequency lists and formulae for ascertaining the appropriate syntactical and semantic models and levels of difficulty. In such formulae, sentence length and syllable counts are decisive factors, not meaningfulness. Such formalistic criteria desiccate the language and render it an artifact standardized by *our* culture, rather than presenting it as the unique artifact of an identifiably different culture. Particularly in view of academia's renewed interest in interdisciplinary programs, it is time for the foreign-language profession to re-evaluate its stance and to develop alternatives to the current norms for choosing reading materials. Exposure to reading selections that more closely approximate the topics and cultural interests of native speakers has pragmatic benefits for students intending to work in, for example, business or diplomacy.

This chapter has attempted to present the rationale for reading more texts, for reading texts with significant content, and for reading literature in second-language classes from the beginning of instruction. Implicit in this rationale is a different definition of reading than that which has characterized our practice up to now, a different concept of the reading process.

A major argument of this book has been that pre-interpretive procedures are essential to reading for meaning or cultural literacy. Submitting a text's surface information to an assessment of its focus and arrangement requires intellectual activity. Readers who look for culture-specific significances of that arrangement must analyze a work with respect to their own prior experience. This kind of reading comprehension is a schematization process in which information is not only recognized, but also reconstructed in terms of its implications. Only texts that are meaningful and appropriately written (see discussion, Chapter 8, pages 137–140) are suitable for such a procedure, since only they will provide information that richly and consistently reflects the cultural characteristics of a specific time, place, and society. And the significant texts of any culture must include its literature.

Redefining reading, seeing it as a process through which a text is actively assessed for implications and significances, can help to solve one of the central problems of English and foreign-language faculties. We have too readily accepted skill separation, dividing our functions into "composition" and "literature," or "grammar" and "reading." Arguments against this separation are mounting. Oller concludes his exhaustive analyses of the implications of current research in language teaching with the following assertion: "In spite of all the remaining uncertainties, it seems safe to suggest that the current practice of many ESL programs, textbooks, and curricula of separating listening, speaking, and reading and writing activities is probably not just pointless but in fact detrimental" (1979: 457–58). Joiner, Bernhardt, and Dvorak reach similar conclusions in their analyses of FL research in listening, reading, and writing.

These divisions have plagued the curriculum of English and foreign-language teaching in recent decades. We need to look at the older definitions of literacy that encompassed expository texts of all kinds along with literary ones. In having disengaged literature from composition in English studies, or from the "skills" in foreign languages, we have really disengaged ourselves as educators from teaching the analytical processes that render texts informative and readers informed. Recognition of the cultural implications that underlie the informational norms of texts is the basis for examining those facets of rhetorical structure and language that characterize a fine literary text as opposed to trivial imitations. This ability also clarifies the contrast between standard and poetic language, whether one is reading literature, magazines, or travel brochures. The aesthetic features of a text are vital components in the construction of textual implications (e.g., Mukarovsky).[5]

Ultimately, literature involves cultural ideology in the sense that it presents us with value systems that reflect culture-specific significances. It is easy to be so suspicious of ideologies that we fail to make the distinction between teaching students a particular system of beliefs, and teaching students the strategies for recognizing and analyzing different systems of thought. Because language, cultural artifacts, and institutions all reflect systems of thought, to become culturally literate L2 students need to be taught to identify and analyze these systems. Such an ability is the hallmark of educated people and characterizes those individuals who can interact with, rather than simply react to, cultural messages implied by the written word.

NOTES TO CHAPTER 12

1. Wolfgang Iser's *The Act of Reading* expands on the theories of Roman Ingarden. For both Ingarden and Iser, text apprehension is an individual experience. Stanley Fish argues that text apprehension is conditioned by an interpretive community. In his book *Textual Power: Literary Theory and the Teaching of English*, Robert Scholes rejects this aspect of Fish's theory and makes the case for accepting multiple reader interpretations in classroom practice, though they must be guided by the teacher.

2. For a brief, thorough summary of the first- and second-language research substantiating these claims, the reader is referred to Patricia Carrell (1985). For a seminal L1 study, see Bransford and Johnson.

3. John Searle employs the terms "regulative" and "constitutive" to distinguish between different domains for the application of rules within a culture (33–53). For a collection of papers exploring this subject, see the anthology edited by Giglioli.

4. Depending on research variables, investigators' conclusions differ with regard to which factors are most essential and how these factors interact. Alderson and Urquhart give an excellent analysis of research and related issues (1–27). On the basis of his research Koh concludes that "knowledge of the language was a necessary but insufficient condition for reading comprehension" (375).

5. The renewal of interest in modern rhetoric has been signaled by, among other things, excellent translations of such classic European works as the *Encyclopedic Dictionary of the Sciences of Language* (Ducrot & Todorov) and *A General Rhetoric* (Dubois et al.)

Conclusion

Conceptual Competence and the L2 Curriculum

This book has suggested ways to integrate reading comprehension and the logical propositions of that comprehension into second-language instruction. While equally applicable for work in beginning language instruction, our emphasis has been on encouraging the practice of extensive reading, particularly in intermediate and upper-division programs in FL and intermediate or advanced work in ESL. The thrust of our suggestions has a subtext: that meaningfulness is a component missing in many language programs. The usual academic emphasis in language courses, even at the post-secondary level, has been on acquiring factual knowledge. We have argued a case for _applications of factual knowledge_. Factual knowledge can be found in texts. Applications are the reader's purview.

But applications rarely set the standard for performance in academic work. Reader purviews are seldom acknowledged or measured in L2 classes. In advanced college courses, linguistic competence with subject matter is the measure of success. Particularly in ESL and FL study, that measure may fall short of the mark in meeting the needs of students who want to apply their knowledge to a spectrum of real-world situations.

In a period when both immersion studies and interdisciplinary programs are gaining status in college curricula, departments across the country are taking a hard look at what kinds of competences ESL and FL students need beyond the first years of instruction. Indeed, the profession is also reconsidering emphases in the first years of L2 instruction in view of increasingly positive indications about immersion programs and course work with a content orientation (Swain & Lapkin).

Demographics are also changing at the college level. Students over twenty-five will soon be in the majority, and this change in student population signals the need for changes in materials, techniques, and topics for the L2 curricula (Dannerbeck). Comparisons between the cognitive styles of more mature adults and their relatively-younger counterparts reveal that the more mature the students, the more adept they are at synthetic reasoning. Graduate students, for example, use organizational features of texts far more effectively than do undergraduates, who, in turn, have more success than high school students (Meyer & Freedle). Learner-centered approaches are a virtual necessity with adult students, who tend to seek a partnership with the teacher rather than an authoritarian relationship.

How can the learner-based competences presented in this book be applied to the goals of ESL and FL programs?

LANGUAGE ABILITIES AND COGNITIVE CONTEXTS

Students, particularly mature adults, seem to experience greater success in L2 learning with integrative approaches that stress reading and writing in conjunction with listening and speaking. Such integration is essential for students who want to attain measurable skills or knowledge in a content area such as business or engineering. Hence it plays a key role in the programs such as those promoted by the Council of Europe (Trim et al.) or being devised in this country under the umbrella of content courses.

Applications of knowledge in any content area call upon higher-order or synthetic reasoning. That reasoning ability, in turn, can only be acquired through practice with carefully-structured discourse. A major source for such discourse is well-constructed texts. Consequently, reading appropriate texts affords students practice in comprehending a significant discourse style very different from that of listening to everyday conversation.

To make a convincing statement about women's rights, for example, or to propose a solution to the country's drug problem, a well-written text must link sentences and use a broad spectrum of syntactic and morphological features. Far less linguistic sophistication is needed in a dialogue about how to mail packages or locate a hotel. Even dialogues in which speakers are persuasive or argumentative will probably reveal less linguistic sophistication than is characteristic of longer narrative or expository prose which argues or persuades. Thus, readers of such texts are starting out on the long road of engaging in the use of the thought patterns and linguistic markers characteristic of educated people. Empowering our students through such abilities represents the ultimate goal of humanist education.

When texts can also be used as the basis for verbalizing ideas, L2 students have the opportunity to participate in classroom discourse at their educational level. Traditionally ESL and FL courses have followed the pattern of language instruction for children—the profession has assumed that concrete situations, because they are most readily articulated, represent a requisite stage that our students must master before they can comprehend and express abstract thought. This assumption seems to be unwarranted, however, for adult learners who already possess cognitive sophistication in their native language.

As discussed in Chapter 4, beyond the level of initial instruction, it is difficult to establish whether reader problems are rooted in inadequate language proficiency, inadequate knowledge of their field, problems in native-language reading ability, or lack of clarity about reading objectives. The components of a competence threshold for reading for meaning have yet to be determined. Experimental studies give no straightforward conclusions about what reader competences matter, in part because "the cognitive level of objectives has not received much attention in the learning objectives literature" (Royer et al. 68). In his postscript to Alderson's analysis of the problem, Urquhart observes that the evidence in their anthology suggests the following conclusions: (1) There is a difference between language competence and reading skills; (2) a good L1 reader will probably transfer skills to L2; (3) some knowledge of the FL is necessary to read it with any facility (25–26).

Most colleges and universities in the United States tacitly assume that such a threshold is established in the first year of college language instruction. Evidence about reading comprehension suggests that, in *all* levels, background knowledge and higher-order reasoning play a large role. Again, there is no evidence that L2 skills alone guarantee students who can read for meaning.

KNOWLEDGE VERSUS APPLICATIONS OF KNOWLEDGE

If our job as teachers of ESL and FL is to prepare students to do things with their L2 knowledge, then our programs must also equip them with conceptual tools enabling them to connect command of language with their work in other disciplines. Such cognitive connections parallel the function of propositional cues for thinking about texts. They link topics and comments. Content areas are really metatexts, the large body of coherent information and schemata in any subject field. If the goal of a language major is to be able to "read" Spanish history or French architecture, then the first job of the department is to establish the conceptual boundaries of the specialized language these disciplines use. Similarly, an ESL program that prepares students for college work will expose them to the different expectations of work in, for example, liberal arts and the natural sciences.

At present, most ESL programs focus on language acquisition as the prerequisite to applications of language. Most FL departments offer courses in knowledge rather than applications of knowledge: composition and stylistics rather than the styles of persuasion and argumentation, surveys of literary or cultural periods rather than the relationships between them. In individual course descriptions, instructors rarely specify the conceptual or disciplinary patterns students are to learn.

Consequently, we often train students who can define a genre but, at the same time, can't apply the concept and generate an interpretation based on principles as, for example, rising and falling action or closed structure. Such students are only competent at the level of subject-matter replication. They lack practice in applying knowledge to generate new ideas. This problem is, then, one of "competence as knowledge" versus "competence as application of knowledge."

If L2 courses ask only that students define and describe content, they are teaching the established norms of that field, not what those norms are good for. To be able to use those concepts to think and express ideas about the texts in a discipline, students must learn to analyze problems. And they can only analyze problems if they are equipped with the relevant inferential tools. They need a metastructure from which to generalize.

Students need to be able to work with the metastructure of disciplines if they are to be able to interpret textual messages. Unless students understand, for example, that genres have conventions of form as well as of subject matter, the implications of genre or authorial treatment may be largely lost on them. The content of the discipline (the rules of odes, the language proficiency to decode the text) is inadequate for interpretive purposes. Data are not enough. Students who lack the conscious inferential premises of a discipline lack the framework within which to conceptualize and later reapply the data of that discipline.

In a century of rapid technological change and "information explosion," the true danger of cultural illiteracy is that it may produce a population incapable of informing itself about the implications of the social, economic, and political thought that conditions its life. In a democracy it is precisely the capacity to shape information, to penetrate past a surface denotation in order to perceive connotational patterns that makes possible a critical interchange between a representative government and its citizens. In this sense, teaching students how to read actively means transmitting an essential skill for cultural survival.

How can curricular planning aid students in schematizing their subject areas? What are the consistent tensions in particular fields of study? And how do the schemata of a discipline correlate with a departmental track in literature, or an interdisciplinary program in international business or geology?

We argue that the procedures suggested in this book make viable a close connection between language and content instruction. The conceptual ability to be developed does not reflect a particular interpretive method or an exhaustive knowledge of facts. Instead, these procedures teach students both to recognize and to transcend disciplinary boundaries. Our practices promote just such objectives: grasp of the implications of events, ideas, or institutions in a discipline. In that sense they apply the insights of philosophers and intellectual historians who suggest examination of cultural metahistory—the consistent patterns that emerge when we explore authentic texts of a culture at a given time and place (e.g., Braudel; White).

In FL departments we have to apply these precepts in our various content courses for advanced levels. To illustrate the point, departments concerned about whether to teach culture as "big C" (the historical events and monuments of the linguistic community) or "little c" (the contemporary mores and behaviors of the language group) are looking at the wrong issue. Command of facts at the knowledge level calls on lower-order cognition. The ability to synthesize those facts involves higher-order cognition at the application level (e.g., Bloom et al.'s taxonomy). At the application level, the ultimate goal of a program in a specific culture must be to see whether students can correlate features of its different subdisciplines—the history, sociology, art, music, and architecture of a culture.

Frequently, FL departments have English language courses in these adjunct fields. The concept "French, Spanish, or German Studies" is emerging as a new umbrella for amalgamating cross-disciplinary needs. One of the reservations about these programs concerns our expertise. Neither ESL nor FL teachers are trained as social scientists, experts in business, or historians. Aside from a language background, do L2 teachers need special qualifications to teach courses containing components that are ordinarily associated with other disciplines? We suggest that our emphasis should be on knowing what we are looking for. Language teachers don't need to be historians or business specialists to teach history or business as long as we can agree on the frames of reference our students should uncover when learning about history and business.

The need for such a focus can be illustrated by looking at the problems facing ESL students who leave their language training to move into the academic world (Bramki & Williams; Koh). Language ability fails to compensate for the inability to read for meaning and apply that meaning to real-world situations. When students study with and are tested with questions at the application level (Piaget's formal operations) in their native language, they learn differently (e.g., Watts & Anderson). Presumably these same constraints hold true for all students who study in a second language. Most ESL programs strive to prepare their foreign-born students for multidisciplinary work in the academy in the United States. Most disciplines in that academy are themselves interdisciplinary at the upper-division level. Pieces of history, sociology, philosophy, business, art, and music appear in most courses in the humanities and social sciences. That range of disciplines is germane (if less evident) for natural sciences, engineering, and business fields as well.

How do theories about teaching higher-order skills apply to actual curricula? As a case in point, let us look briefly at the most traditional track in FL departments, the literature sequence. The established course types are familiar as the desirable training for language majors. Traditionally and typically, a "literature track" offers its students an "Introduction to Literature" focused on either historical epochs, representative texts, or genres (or a combination). A higher-level literary history course then presents trends and the development of national identity and literary form. Subsequent specialty courses offer more detailed works on defined problems ("The Concept of Classicism"), themes ("Alienation"), genres, critical methods ("Feminist Approaches to . . ."), or periods ("Literature in the Third Reich").

In designing such courses, most departments agree that readings and lectures for the students should replicate aspects of the canon for the literature, especially in introductory, genre, and period courses; readings in specialty courses may range further afield in order that the problems be adequately represented (for instance, in "Feminist Approaches" to periods, standard canons contain few women writers in certain centuries, and so unfamiliar names must necessarily be included).

From the perspective of the metastructure of these courses, each of them represents contexts, flexible groupings of subject matter. Yet each of these contexts carries with it some less visible baggage, tacit cultural assumptions about what can and cannot be said about a given subject. Genre, for example, has established formal and conventional definitions, but these definitions rest on a set of inferences about society, the reader, and subject matter. The "death of the novel" and the notion of reader response, whether in literary criticism or psycholinguistics, are both twentieth-century modifiers on the act of reading. Rather than learning only the facts of genre (i.e., definitions), students need to cross-reference genre and changes in social attitudes. When, for example, critics talk about the "death of the novel," this hardly implies that novels are no longer written, but it does signal a change in features of the genre. As author Peter Schneider points out, novels have become far less plot-oriented and more essay-like. Consequently, the twentieth-century novel genre assumes different dimensions from its nineteenth-century predecessors that stressed personal development or the clash of social forces, and is much closer to eighteenth-century antecedents such as *Tristam Shandy* in the sense of dealing more with the general human condition and giving psychological portraits short shrift.

To clarify formal definitions of genre, students need to understand the behavioral rules suggested by such definitions, e.g., characteristics of nineteenth- versus twentieth-century novels. They must also be aware of how echoes and references to earlier practices condition audience reception. Otherwise students are in the position of the individual who sees Woody Allen's film *Play it Again, Sam* without having viewed *Casablanca*. In short, a literate reader, like a literate film-goer, is aware of audience expectations about materials, plots, or images in a cultural artifact or event. These organizing and evaluative criteria are part of text meaning, not mere facts to memorize about genre. This interplay of features controls a literate reader's interpretive results and goals.

MODES OF TEXT SELECTION THAT HELP ESL AND FL STUDENTS PRACTICE IN INFERENCING

If readings in a course prove difficult for L2 students, the problem may not be that the materials were too long, difficult, or obscure for the class's language level, but rather that the course presupposed a basis for inferencing that was nonexistent. Sociological approaches can work well for learners who are aware of the implications of social class and economic status; students lacking such practice may, on the other hand, fail to recognize sociological patterns of explanation by themselves. An essay with the ambiguous banner "Create Jobs that Pay as Well as Crime" may confuse an ESL student unfamiliar with the prevalence of crack sales and teenage pushers in the big-city ghettos where employment for this age group is restricted to low-paying jobs.

To grasp the context of this particular problem, students need texts that juxtapose various aspects of the drug problem in the United States: social (crime rates), political (relationships with countries such as Colombia and Peru), economic (the cost in productivity, the burden on taxpayers). A range of perspectives is also essential: comparison between attitudes about drugs in the sixties and today (e.g., the drug heroes in *Easy Rider*), or interviews that depict the plight of Peruvian farmers.

Byrnes (1990) suggests that students first need to develop sensitivity about alternative ways of seeing their own culture—reading about the second-language culture (C2) in their native language (L1)—before graduating to L2 statements about C1 and ultimately, observations expressed in the L2 about the C2. Only after students recognize contrasting attitudes, assumptions, and behaviors in L1 texts can they be expected to recognize similar features in a foreign-language text. Like language acquisition, higher-order applications result from cognitive practice.

Overloading students with unfamiliar applications *and* a foreign language probably defeats both cognitive and linguistic aims. Students who learn first to "read between the lines" that depict events and people in a foreign culture learn cultural encoding. In other words, they possess strategies that substitute for "expert knowledge." Their cultural literacy is that of the competent reader in the field: the knowledge of the correlations and patterns which render facts meaningful.

There are some practical reasons for adopting this point of view. If, as Carlos Fuentes' unborn hero suggests, "history is faster than fiction," the proliferation of facts in today's cultures outstrips our students' ability to acquire them. Moreover, a focus on facts leaves students with a sense that the course material is unrelated to the work done in other disciplines or even other language courses. On the face of it, fifteen weeks spent studying "Nazi Germany" appear irrelevant to a degree in linguistics. Yet the aims and institutional manifestations of Nazi ideology apply very directly to approaches in sociolinguistics. Only the explicit connection is lacking.

COURSE SEQUENCES AND READER INFERENCE

How would inferential reading apply to a course sequence? As an illustration, the introductory culture sequence might be a cultural history, given in the foreign language over two semesters. Here, the program has two choices: a sociological approach to history in the classroom, or a history of the country's political dates, its battles, and its cultural monuments.

For purposes of illustration, assume that a sociological approach is used. In this case information is presented as a tension between conflicting social forces. The forces vary with time and place. However, once students establish the principle of an interaction between two opposing social orders, it is relatively easy for them to frame readings and discussions around principles that remain linguistically constant. Whether the conflict is between the Romans and the Germanic tribes, Islamic culture and Christian forces, or emperors and princes, propositional cues that express these conflicts are in a consistent analytical mode. Their surface language expression will access such features as comparative and superlative structures, subordinate clauses, or adverbial markers of contrast. In most of these cases, the "big C" or historical account presents a particular series of events initiated by one group and the response of the opponents. In a "small c" or sociological depiction, authors tend to contrast features of the two factions.

Once students grasp these organizational principles, they can apply them as communicative strategies to encode their reading assignments and talk about them in class. A procedural format for written work reinforces the conceptual schemata of readings because it asks students to do in writing precisely what is expected in oral response: (1) to identify the major forces discussed in the text, pinpointing the time and place; (2) to identify the account's logical organization of information. The analytic pattern students create to comprehend and retain essential textual information can vary as long as the information in that pattern is recognizable in the text. In other words, if the assessment model in Chapter 9 is applied, students perform equally well on tests about the Middle Ages regardless of whether they view the emperor as under attack by the princes or the princes as exploited by the emperor.

Students need not be language majors to benefit from these approaches. Any course that encourages them to uncover their substantiated inferences about texts—whether in the sciences, social sciences, or literature—informs other disciplines. Literature courses offer expansions of historical approaches. An advanced culture seminar can, for example, trace German aesthetics with slides, music, and essays on art. The aim is not to be exhaustive, but to teach students how Germans conceived the place and purpose of the work of art and the artist in the nineteenth and twentieth centuries. Connections between art and society emerge when, for example, essays are correlated with the rise of the bourgeoisie. Wagner's early newspaper articles on the Germans and history present a key to his dramaturgy as conceived for this new audience: for the emerging entrepreneurial class and German nobility, myths that revolve around giants, fighters, and confrontations. As a later expression of the relationship between society and art, the fact that *Bauhaus* affirmed beauty in mass production echoes democratizing impulses in the Weimar Republic. In such a format, developments in art are linked to cultural values and image-building. Students who learn to see parallels between art forms and their audiences, materials, and means of distribution can begin to see beyond the dictates of individual texts or coursework to the broader substance of humanist thought.

CONCLUSION

In these last pages, we have briefly suggested how the meaningfulness criteria for reading procedures can apply to curricula. We have argued throughout this volume that, when our ESL and FL courses are anchored in a coherent rationale for processing textual meaning, students can learn to read beyond the surface language of the texts despite their lack of cultural schemata. By the same token, while language teachers cannot be experts in all things, we can ourselves be competent readers of a culture. The competence required to teach a course in business is not the subject *per se*, but the language appropriate to a particular business context: whether students can recognize and utilize levels of social consciousness, protocol, and interaction.

A standard of meaning can validate the existence of language departments as "interdisciplinary," of language teachers as specialists in the discourses of a target country and its representative institutions and artifacts, including language itself. This, we feel, is a more fruitful approach than efforts to foster advanced course work in language study based on knowledge of facts alone. Just as language is a vehicle for communication, factual knowledge is the vehicle for articulate points of view. A standard of meaning in teaching of L2 texts empowers our students by rewarding comprehension and application of those texts as cultural artifacts. Ultimately, when we teach language, we teach meaning.

Bibliography

1. ABRAMOVICI, SHIMON. "Lexical Information in Reading and Memory." *Reading Research Quarterly* 19 (1984): 173–87.
2. ADAMS, MARILYN J. "Models of Reading." *Language and Comprehension.* Eds. Jean-François Le Ny & Walter Kintsch. Amsterdam: North-Holland, 1982. 193–206.
3. ADAMS, SHIRLEY. "Scripts and Recognition of Unfamiliar Vocabulary: Enhancing Second Language Reading Skills." *Modern Language Journal* 66 (1982): 155–59.
4. ADELSON, LESLIE A. "History, Literature, and the Composition and Conversation Class." *Modern Language Journal* 72 (1988): 13–20.
5. AHMAD, KHURSHID, G. CORBETT, M. ROGERS, & R. SUSSEX. *Computers, Language Learning, and Language Teaching.* Cambridge: Cambridge UP, 1985.
6. ALDERSON, J. CHARLES. "The Cloze Procedure and Proficiency in English as a Foreign Language." *Issues in Language Testing Research.* Ed. John Oller. Rowley, MA: Newbury, 1983. 205–17.
7. ———. "Reading: A Reading Problem or a Language Problem." *Reading in a Foreign Language.* Eds. J. Charles Alderson & A. H. Urquhart. Essex: Longman, 1984. 1–24.
8. ——— & A. H. URQUHART, Eds. "Postscript on Alderson." *Reading in a Foreign Language.* Essex: Longman, 1984. 25–27.
9. ALLEN, EDWARD D., ELIZABETH B. BERNHARDT, MARY THERESE BERRY, & MARJORIE DEMEL. "Comprehension and Text Genre: An Analysis of Secondary School Foreign Language Readers." *Modern Language Journal* 72 (1988): 163–87.
10. ALLEN, VIRGINIA F. *Techniques in Vocabulary Teaching.* New York: Oxford UP, 1983.
11. ALLINGTON, RICHARD, & MICHAEL STRANGE. "Effects of Grapheme Substitutions in Connected Text upon Reading Behaviors." *Visible Language* 11 (1977): 285–97.
12. ALLWRIGHT, RICHARD L. "Turns, Topics, and Tasks: Patterns of Participation in Language

Learning and Teaching." *Discourse Analysis in Second Language Research.* Ed. Diane Larsen-Freeman. Rowley, MA: Newbury, 180. 165–87.

13. American Council on the Teaching of Foreign Languages. *ACTFL Proficiency Guidelines.* Hastings-on-Hudson, NY: ACTFL Materials Center, 1986.

14. ANDERSON, THOMAS. "Readable Textbooks, or, Selecting a Textbook is Not Like Buying a Pair of Shoes." *Reading Comprehension: From Research to Practice.* Ed. Judith Orasanu. Hillsdale, NJ: Erlbaum, 1986. 151–62.

15. ——— & BONNIE ARMBRUSTER. "Studying." *Handbook of Reading Research.* Ed. P. David Pearson. New York: Longman, 1984. 657–79.

16. ANDERSON, RICHARD C. "Substance Recall of Sentences." *Quarterly Journal of Experimental Psychology* 26 (1974): 530–41.

17. ——— & JAMES W. PICHERT. "Recall of Previously Unrecallable Information Following a Shift in Perspective." *Journal of Verbal Learning and Verbal Behavior* 17 (1978): 1–12.

18. ———, JAMES W. PICHERT, & LARRY L. SHIREY. "Effects of the Reader's Schema at Different Points in Time." *Journal of Educational Psychology* 75 (1983): 271–79.

19. ——— & P. D. PEARSON. "A Schema-Theoretic View of Basic Processes in Reading Comprehension." *Interactive Approaches to Second Language Reading.* Eds. Patricia L. Carrell, Joanne Devine, & David E. Eskey. Cambridge: Cambridge UP, 1988. 37–55.

20. ARIEW, ROBERT, & ANNE NERENZ. *C'est à dire.* Boston: Heinle & Heinle, 1989.

21. ARMBRUSTER, BONNIE B. & THOMAS H. ANDERSON. "The Effect of Mapping on the Free Recall of Expository Text." *Tech. Rep. No. 160.* Urbana: U of Illinois, Center for the Study of Reading, 1980.

22. ———. Idea Mapping: The Technique and its Use in the Classroom. (Tech. Rep. No. 36). Urbana: U of Illinois, Center for the Study of Reading, 1982.

23. ASHER, JAMES J. "Children's First Language as a Model for Second Language Learning." *Modern Language Journal* 56 (1972): 133–39.

24. ———. "Comprehension Training: The Evidence from Laboratory and Classroom Studies." *The Comprehension Approach: An Evolving Methodology in Foreign Language Instruction.* Ed. Harris Winitz. Rowley, MA: Newbury, 1981. 187–222.

25. ———. *Learning Another Language through Actions: The Complete Teacher's Guidebook.* Los Gatos, CA: Sky Oaks Productions, 1982.

26. ATKINSON, RICHARD C., & RICHARD M. SHIFFRIN. "Human Memory: A Proposed System and its Control Processes." *The Psychology of Learning and Motivation: Advances in Research and Theory.* Vol. 2. New York: Academic Press, 1968. 89–195.

27. AUSTIN, J. L. *How to Do Things with Words.* 2nd ed. Eds. J. O. Urmson & M. Sbisa. Cambridge, MA: Harvard UP, 1962.

28. AUSUBEL, DAVID. *The Psychology of Meaningful Verbal Learning.* New York: Grune & Stratton, 1963.

29. ———, JOSEPH NOVAK, & HELEN HANESIAN. *Educational Psychology: A Cognitive View.* 2nd ed. New York: Holt, Rinehart, & Winston, 1978.

30. BACON, SUSAN M. CAMERON. "Mediating Cultural Bias with Authentic Target-Language Texts for Beginning Students of Spanish." *Foreign Language Annals* 20 (1987): 557–63.

31. BAKER, LINDA, & ANN BROWN. "Metacognitive Skills and Reading." *Handbook of Reading Research.* Ed. P. David Pearson. New York: Longman, 1984. 353–94.

32. BARNETT, MARVA. "Syntactic and Lexical / Semantic Skill in Foreign Language Reading: Importance and Interaction." *Modern Language Journal* 70 (1968): 343–49.

33. ———. "Teaching Reading Strategies: How Methodology Affects Language Course Articulation." *Foreign Language Annals* 21 (1988a): 109–19.

34. ———. "Reading through Context." *Modern Language Journal* 72 (1988b): 150–59.

35. ———. *More than Meets the Eye.* Englewood Cliffs, NJ: Prentice Hall, 1990.

36. BARTHES, ROLAND. *S / Z.* Trans. Richard Miller. New York: Hill & Wang, 1974.

37. BARTLETT, FRÉDÉRIC C. *Remembering: A Study in Experimental and Social Psychology.* Cambridge, UK: Cambridge UP, 1932.

38. BATEN, LUT. "Text Comprehension: The Parameters of Difficulty in Narrative and Expository Prose Texts: A Redefinition of Readability." Diss. Univ. of Illinois, 1981.

39. BEACH, RICHARD, & LILLIAN BRIDWELL. "Learning through Writing. A Rationale for Writing across the Curriculum." *The Development of Oral and Written Language in Social Contexts.* Eds. A. D. Pellegini & T. D. Yawkey. Norwood, NJ: Ablex, 1984. 183–98.

40. BECK, ISABEL, & MARGARET G. McKEOWN. "Developing Questions that Promote Comprehension: The Story Map." *Language Arts* 58 (1981): 913–18.

41. ———. "Instructional Research in Reading: A Retrospective." *Reading Comprehension: From Research to Practice.* Ed. Judith Orasanu. Hillsdale, NJ: Erlbaum, 1986. 113–34.

42. BELASCO, SIMON. "The Plateau: Or the Case for Comprehension: The Concept Approach." *Modern Language Journal* 51 (1967): 82–88.

43. BENEDETTO, ROSEMARY ANN. "A Psycholinguistic Investigation of the Top-Level Organization Strategies in First and Second Language Reading: Five Case Studies." Diss. New York Univ., 1984.

44. BENSOUSSAN, MARSHA. "Beyond Vocabulary: Pragmatic Factors in Reading Comprehension— Culture, Convention, Coherence and Cohesion." *Foreign Language Annals* 19 (1986): 399–407.

45. ———, & BATIA LAUFER. "Lexical Guessing in Context." *Journal of Research in Reading* 7 (1984): 15–32.

46. ———, DONALD SIM, & RAZELLE WEISS. "The Effect of Dictionary Usage on EFL Test Performance Compared with Student and Teacher Attitudes and Expectations." *Reading in a Foreign Language* 2 (1984): 262–76.

47. BEREITER, CARL, & M. BIRD. "Use of Thinking-Aloud in Identification and Teaching of Reading Comprehension Strategies." *Cognition and Instruction* 2 (1985): 131–56.

48. BERMAN, RUTH A. "Syntactic Components of the Foreign Language Reading Process." *Reading in a Foreign Language.* Eds. J. Charles Alderson & A. H. Urquhart. Essex: Longman, 1984. 139–56.

49. BERNHARDT, ELIZABETH. "Testing Foreign Language Reading Comprehension: The Immediate Recall Protocol." *Die Unterrichtspraxis* 16 (1983a): 17–33.

50. ———. "Three Approaches to Reading Comprehension in Intermediate German." *Modern Language Journal* 67 (1983b): 111–15.

51. ———. "Text Processing Strategies of Native, Non-Native Experienced and Non-Native Inexperienced Readers of German: Findings and Implications for the Instruction of German as a Foreign Language." Diss. U of Minnesota, 1984.

52. ———. "Reconstructions of Literary Texts by Learners of German." *New Yorker Werkstattgespräch: Literarische Texte im Fremdsprachenunterricht.* Ed. Manfred Heid. München: Kemmler & Hoch, 1985. 254–89.

53. ———. "Reading in the Foreign Language." *Listening, Reading, Writing: Analysis and Application.* Ed. Barbara H. Wing. Middlebury, VT: NEC, 1986a. 93–115.

54. ———. "Proficient Texts or Proficient Readers?" *ADFL Bulletin* 18 (Spring, 1986b): 25–28.

55. ———. Participant Handouts. "Second Language Reading Research. A Cognitive Perspective." Guest Lecture. University of Texas, Austin, October, 1986c.

56. ———. "Cognitive Processes in L2: An Examination of Reading Behaviors." *Delaware Symposium on Language Studies: Research on Second Language Acquisition in the Classroom Setting.* Eds. James Lantolf & Angela LaBarca. Norwood, NJ: Ablex, 1987. 35–50.

57. ———. "A Model of L2 Text Reconstruction: The Recall of Literary Text by Learners of German." *Issues in L2: Theory as Practice / Practice as Theory.* Ed. Angela LaBarca. Norwood, NJ: Ablex, 1989.

58. ——— & VICTORIA C. BERKEMEYER. "Authentic Texts and the High School German Learner." *Die Unterrichtspraxis* 21 (1988): 6–28.

59. BIALYSTOK, ELLEN B. "A Theoretical Model of Second Language Learning." *Language Learning* 28 (1978): 69–83.

60. BLOCK, ELLEN. "The Comprehension Strategies of Second Language Readers." *TESOL Quarterly* 20 (1986): 463–94.

61. BLONSKY, MARSHALL, ed. *On Signs*. Baltimore: Johns Hopkins UP, 1985.
62. BLOOM, ALLAN DAVID. *The Closing of the American Mind: Education and the Crisis of Reason*. New York: Simon & Schuster, 1987.
63. BLOOM, B. S., M. D. ENGELHART, E. J. FURST, W. H. HILL, & D. R. KRATWOHL, eds. *Taxonomy of Educational Objectives: Cognitive Domain*. New York: David McKay, 1956.
64. BOLINGER, DWIGHT. "Meaning and Memory." *Forum Linguisticum* 1 (1976): 1–14.
65. BORLAND, RON, & AUGUST FLAMMER. "Encoding and Retrieval Processes in Memory for Prose." *Discourse Processes* 8 (1985): 305–17.
66. BRAMKI, DOUDJA, & RAY WILLIAMS. "Lexical Familiarization in Economics Text, and its Pedagogic Implications in Reading Comprehension." *Reading in a Foreign Language* 2 (1984): 169–81.
67. BRANSFORD, JOHN, *Human Cognition: Learning, Understanding and Remembering*. Belmont, CA: Wadsworth, 1979.
68. ———, & M. K. JOHNSON. "Contextual Prerequisites for Understanding: Some Investigations of Comprehension and Recall." *Journal of Verbal Learning and Verbal Behavior* 11 (1972): 717–26.
69. ———, J. RICHARD BARCLAY, & JEFFERY FRANKS. "Sentence Memory: A Constructive versus Interpretive Approach." *Cognitive Psychology* 3 (1972): 193–209.
70. BRAUDEL, FERNAND. *On History*. Trans. S. Methew. Chicago: Chicago UP, 1980.
71. BROWN, ANN. "Metacognition in Reading and Writing: The Development and Facilitation of Selective Attention Strategies for Learning from Texts." *Directions in Reading: Research and Instruction*. Ed. Michael Kamil. Washington, DC: National Reading Conference, 1984. 21–43.
72. BURGESS, ANTHONY. *A Clockwork Orange*. New York: W. W. Norton, 1963.
73. BURT, MARINA K., & CAROL KIPARSKY. *The Gooficon: A Repair Manual for English*. Rowley, MA: Newbury, 1972.
74. ———, & HEIDI DULAY. *New Directions in Second Language Learning, Teaching and Bilingual Education*. Washington, DC: TESOL, 1975.
75. BYRNES, HEIDI. "Proficiency as a Framework for Research in Second Language Acquisition." *Modern Language Journal* 71 (1987a): 44–49.
76. ———. "Speech as Process." *Foreign Language Annals* 20 (1987b): 301–10.
77. ———, & MICHAEL CANALE, eds. *Defining and Developing Proficiency: Guidelines, Implementations, and Concepts*. Lincolnwood, IL: National Textbook Co., 1987c.
78. ———. "Beyond the Form / Meaning Debate: Correction Strategies in Adult Learner Languages." Unpubl. paper, Symposium on Research Perspectives in Adult Language Learning & Acquisition, Ohio State Univ., Columbus, October 21–22, 1988.
79. ———. "Reflections on the Acquisition of Cross-Cultural Competence in the Foreign Language Classroom." Ed. Barbara S. Freed. *Foreign Language Acquisition Research and the Classroom*. New York: D. C. Heath & Co., 1990.
80. CABELLO, SUSAN. Pacific University. Personal Communication, 1988.
81. CANALE, MICHAEL. "Considerations in the Testing of Reading and Listening Proficiency." *Foreign Language Annals* 17 (1984): 349–68.
82. CARPENTER, PATRICIA A. & MARCEL JUST. "Reading Comprehension as Eyes See It." *Cognitive Processing in Comprehension*. Eds. Patricia A. Carpenter & Marcel Just. Hillsdale NJ: Erlbaum, 1977. 109–39.
83. ———. "What your Eyes Do while your Mind is Reading." *Eye Movements and Reading: Perceptual and Language Processes*. Ed. Keith Rayner. New York: Academic Press, 1983. 275–307.
84. CARRELL, PATRICIA. "Three Components of Background Knowledge in Reading Comprehension." *Language Learning* 33 (1983): 183–207.
85. ———. "Facilitating ESL Reading by Teaching Text Structure." *TESOL Quarterly* 19 (1985): 727–52.
86. ———. "Text-boundedness and Schema Interference." *Interactive Approaches to Second*

Language Reading. Eds. Patricia L. Carrell, Joanne Devine, & David E. Eskey. Cambridge: Cambridge UP, 1988. 101–13.

87. ———. "Metacognitive Awareness and Second Language Reading." *Modern Language Journal* 72 (1989): 120–34.

88. ———, & JOAN C. EISTERHOLD, "Schema Theory and ESL Reading Pedagogy," *TESOL Quarterly* 17 (1983): 553–73.

89. CARROLL, JOHN. "Learning Theory for the Classroom Teacher." *The Challenge of Communication. The ACTFL Review of Foreign Language Education* 6. Skokie, IL: National Textbook Co., 1974.

90. ———. *The Foreign Language Attainments of Language Majors in the Senior Year: A Survey Conducted in U.S. Colleges and Universities.* Cambridge, MA: Graduate School of Education, Harvard Univ., 1967. [ED 013 343]

91. ———. "Learning Theory for the Classroom Teacher." *The Challenge of Communication. The ACTFL Annual Review of Foreign Language Education* 6. Ed. Gilbert A Jarvis. Skokie, IL: National Textbook Co., 1974. 113–49.

92. ———. "Development of Reading Comprehension." *Cognition, Curriculum and Comprehension.* Ed. John T. Guthrie. Newark, NJ: International Reading Association, 1977. 1–15.

93. ———. "Psychometric Theory and Language Testing." *Issues in Language Testing.* Ed. John. W. Oller. Rowley, MA: Newbury, 1983. 80–107.

94. ———, PETER DAVIES, & BARRY RICHMAN. *Word Frequency Book.* New York: American Heritage, 1971.

95. CARROLL, LEWIS. *Alice's Adventures in Wonderland.* NY: Heritage Press, 1941.

96. CATES, G. TRUETT, & JANET K. SWAFFAR. *Reading a Second Language.* Arlington, VA: CAL, 1979.

97. CHAFE, WALLACE. *Meaning and the Structure of Language.* Chicago: Chicago UP, 1970.

98. ———. "Creativity in Verbalization." *Discourse Production and Comprehension.* Ed. Roy Freedle. Norwood, NJ: Ablex, 1982. 41–55.

99. CHASTAIN, KENNETH D. "A Methodological Study Comparing the Audio-Lingual Habit Theory and the Cognitive Code-Learning Theory—A Continuation." *Modern Language Journal* 54 (1970): 257–66.

100. ———, & FRANK J. WOERDEHOFF. "A Methodological Study Comparing the Audio-Lingual Habit Theory and the Cognitive Code-Learning Theory." *Modern Language Journal* 52 (1968): 268–79.

101. CHAUDRON, CRAIG, & JACK C. RICHARDS. "The Effect of Discourse Markers on the Comprehension of Lectures." *Applied Linguistics* 7 (1986): 113–27.

102. CHIESI, HARRY L, GEORGE J. SPILICH, & JAMES F. VOSS. "Acquisition of Domain-Related Information in Relation to High and Low Domain Knowledge." *Journal of Verbal Learning and Verbal Behavior* 18 (1979): 257–74.

103. CHOMSKY, NOAM. "Review of Skinner's *Verbal Behavior.*" *Language* 35 (1959): 26–58.

104. ———. *Aspects of the Theory of Syntax.* Cambridge, MA: MIT Press, 1965.

105. ———. *Language and the Problems of Knowledge. The Managua Lectures.* Cambridge, MA: MIT Press, 1986.

106. CHRISTISON, MARY ANN, & SHARRON BASSANO. *Look Who's Talking.* Hayward, CA: Alemany Press, 1981.

107. CIRILO, RANDOLPH, & DONALD FOSS. "Text Structure and Reading Time for Sentences." *Journal of Verbal Learning and Verbal Behavior* 19 (1980): 96–109.

108. CLARKE, DAVID. "Computer-Assisted Reading—What Can the Machine Really Contribute?" *System* 14 (1986): 1–13.

109. ——— & I. S. P. NATION. "Guessing the Meanings of Words from Context: Strategy and Techniques." *System* 8 (1980): 211–20.

110. CLARKE, MARK. "The Short-Circuit Hypothesis of E. S. L. Reading—or When Language Competence Interferes with Reading Performance." *Modern Language Journal* 64 (1980): 203–9.

111. ——. "Reading in Spanish and English: Evidence from Adult ESL Students." *Language Learning* 29 (1979): 121–50.

112. COADY, JAMES. "Research on L2 Vocabulary Acquisition: Putting It in Context." International TESOL. Chicago, IL, March 8–13, 1988.

113. COHEN, ANDREW. "The Processing of Feedback on Student Papers." *Learner Strategies in Language Learning.* Eds. Anita L. Wenden & Joan Rubin. Englewood Cliffs, NJ: Prentice-Hall, 1987.

114. ——, & EDNA APHEK. "Retention of Second-Language Vocabulary over Time: Investigating the Role of Mnemonic Associations." *System* 8 (1980): 221–35.

115. COLLIE, JOANNE, & STEPHEN SLATER. *Literature in the Language Classroom.* Cambridge: Cambridge UP, 1987.

116. CONNOR, ULLA. "Recall of Text: Differences between First and Second Language Readers." *TESOL Quarterly* 18 (1984): 239–56.

117. ——. "Research Frontiers in Writing Analysis." *TESOL Quarterly* 21 (1987): 677–96.

118. COOPER, MALCOLM. "Linguistic Competence of Practiced and Unpracticed Non-Native Readers of English." *Reading in a Foreign Language.* Eds. J. Charles Alderson & A. H. Urquhart. Essex: Longman, 1984: 122–35.

119. Cowie, Tony., "Review of *Vocabulary in a Second Language.*" *Reading in a Foreign Language* 2 (1984): 198–205.

120. CRAIK, FERGUS I. M., & ROBERT S. LOCKHART. "Levels of Processing: A Framework for Memory Research." *Journal of Verbal Learning and Verbal Behavior* 11 (1972): 671–84.

121. —— & ENDEL TULVING. "Depth of Processing and the Retention of Words in Episodic Memory." *Journal of Experimental Psychology* 104 (1975): 268–94.

122. CRISCOE, BATTY L. & THOMAS C. GEE. *Content Reading: A Diagnostic / Prescriptive Approach.* Englewood Cliffs, NJ: Prentice-Hall, 1984.

123. CROW, JOHN T. "Receptive Vocabulary Acquisition for Reading." *Modern Language Journal* 70 (1986): 242–50.

124. ——, & JUNE QUIGLEY. "A Semantic Field Approach to Passive Vocabulary for Reading Comprehension." *TESOL Quarterly* 19 (1985): 497–513.

125. CUROE, PHILLIP. "An Experiment in Enriching the Active Vocabularies of College Seniors." *School and Society* 49 (1939): 522–24.

126. ——, & WILLIAM WIXTED. "A Continuing Experiment in Enriching the Active Vocabularies of College Seniors." *School and Society* 53 (1940): 372–76.

127. CZIKO, GARY A. "Language Competence and Reading Strategies: A Comparison of First- and Second Language Oral Reading Errors." *Language Learning* 30 (1980): 101–14.

128. DANEMAN, MEREDYTH, & PATRICIA CARPENTER. "Individual Differences in Working Memory and Reading." *Journal of Verbal Learning and Verbal Behavior* 19 (1980): 450–66.

129. DANNERBECK, FRANCIS J. "Adult Second-Language Learning: Toward an American Adaptation with a European Perspective." *Foreign Language Annals* 20 (1987): 413–19.

130. DASCH, ANNE. "Aligning Basal Reader Instruction with Cognitive Stage Theory." *The Reading Teacher* 36 (1983): 428–34.

131. DE BEAUGRANDE, ROBERT. *Text, Discourse and Process: Toward a Multidisciplinary Science of Texts.* Norwood, NJ: Ablex, 1980.

132. ——. "Design Criteria for Process Models of Reading." *Reading Research Quarterly* 16 (1981): 261–315.

133. ——. "General Constraints on Process Models of Language Comprehension." *Language and Comprehension.* Eds. Jean-Francois Le Ny & Walter Kintsch. Amsterdam: North-Holland, 1982. 179–92.

134. DENHIERE, GUY, & JEAN-FRANÇOIS LE NY. "Relative Importance of Meaningful Units in Comprehension and Recall of Narrative by Children and Adults." *Poetics* 19 (1980): 147–61.

135. DE SAUSSURE, FERDINAND. *Course in General Linguistics.* Trans. Wade Baskin. New York: McGraw-Hill, 1966.

136. DEVINE, JOANNE. "ESL Readers' Internalized Models of the Reading Process." *On TESOL*

'83. Eds. Jean Handscombe, Richard Orem, & Barry Taylor. Washington, DC: TESOL, 1984. 95–100.

137. DILTHEY, WILHELM. *Ideen über eine beschreibende und zergliedernde Psychologie Gesammelte Schriften.* Vol. V. Leipzig: Teubner, 1924.

138. DI PIETRO, ROBERT. "Strategic Interaction from Texts: Converting Written Discourse into Spoken Conversation." *Linguistics and Literacy.* Ed. W. Frawley. New York: Plenum, 1982. 387–97.

139. ———. "From Literature to Discourse: Interaction with Texts in the ESL / EFL Classroom." *The Canadian Modern Language Review* 40 (1983): 44–50.

140. DOUGLAS, DAN. "Context in SLA Theory and Language Testing." Ed. Grant Henning. *Language Acquisition and Language Assessment* (forthcoming).

141. DUBIN, FRAIDA, DAVID E. ESKY, & WILLIAM GRABE, eds. *Teaching Second Language Reading for Academic Purposes.* Reading, MA: Addison-Wesley, 1986.

142. DUBOIS, J., F. EDELINE, J.-M. KLINKENBERG, P. MINGUET, F. PIRE, & H. TRINON. *A General Rhetoric.* Trans. Paul B. Burrell & Edgar M. Slotkin. Baltimore: Johns Hopkins UP, 1981.

143. DUCROT, OSWALD, & TZVETAN TODOROV. *Encyclopedic Dictionary of the Sciences of Language.* Trans. Catherine Porter. Baltimore: Johns Hopkins UP, 1979.

144. DULAY, HEIDI, MARIA K. BURT, & STEPHEN KRASHEN. *Language Two.* New York: Oxford UP, 1982.

145. DUNBAR, RONALD W. "Discourse Pragmatics and Contrastive Analysis: Some Parallel Constraints on English and German Subordinate Clauses." *The Contrastive Grammar of English and German.* Eds. Walter F. Lohnes & Edwin A. Hopkins. Ann Arbor, MI: Karoma Publishers, Inc., 1980. 152–61.

146. DUNKEL, PATRICIA. "Computer-Assisted Instruction (CAI) and Computer-Assisted Language Learning (CALL): Past Dilemmas and Future Prospects for Audible CAL." *Modern Language Journal* 71 (1987): 250–60.

147. DVORAK, TRISHA. "Writing in a Foreign Language." *Listening, Reading, and Writing: Analysis and Application.* Ed. Barbara H. Wing. Middlebury, VT: Northeast Conference on the Teaching of Foreign Languages, 1986. 145–67.

148. ECO, UMBERTO. *A Theory of Semiotics.* Bloomingdale: Indiana UP, 1976.

149. ———. "How Culture Conditions the Colours We See." *On Signs.* Ed. Marshall Blonsky. Baltimore: Johns Hopkins UP, 1985. 157–75.

150. EISENSTEIN, MIRIAM. "Native Reactions to Non-Native Speech: A Review of Empirical Research." *Studies in Second Language Acquisition* 5 (1983): 160–76.

151. ELLEY, WARWICK B. "L2 Reading Difficulties in Fiji." *Reading in a Foreign Language.* Eds. J. Charles Alderson & A. H. Urquhart. Essex: Longman, 1984. 281–301.

152. ELY, CHRISTOPHER M. "Personality: Its Impact on Attitudes Toward Classroom Activities." *Foreign Language Annals* 21 (1988): 25–32.

153. FAERCH, CLAUS, & GABRIELE KASPER, eds. *Strategies in Interlanguage Communication.* New York: Longman, 1983.

154. FANSELOW, JOHN F. *Breaking Rules. Generating and Exploring Alternatives in Language Teaching.* New York: Longman, 1987.

155. FARHADY, HOSSEIN. "New Directions in ESL Proficiency Testing." *Issues in Language Testing Research.* Ed. John W. Oller. Rowley, MA: Newbury, 1983. 253–69.

156. FARR, ROGER, & ROBERT CAREY. *Reading: What Can Be Measured.* Newark, DEL: International Reading Association, 1986.

157. FEENY, THOMAS. "Vocabulary Teaching as a Means of Vocabulary Expansion." *Foreign Language Annals* 9 (1976): 485–86.

158. FELIX, SASCHA W. "The Effect of Formal Instruction on Second Language Acquisition." *Language Learning* 31 (1981):87–112.

159. FILLMORE, CHARLES. "The Case for Case." *Universals in Linguistic Theory.* Eds. Emmon Bach & Robert T. Harms. New York: Holt, Rinehart, & Winston, 1968.

160. FISH, STANLEY. *Is There a Text in This Class?* Cambridge, MA: Harvard UP, 1980.

161. FLAMMER, AUGUST, & M. TAUBER. "Changing the Reader's Perspective." *Discourse Processing.* Eds. August Flammer & Walter Kintsch. Amsterdam: North-Holland, 1982. 219–38.

162. FLAVELL, JOHN H. "Metacognitive Development." *Structural / Process Theories of Complex Human Behavior.* Eds. Joseph M. Scandura & Charles J. Brainerd. Alphen a. d. Rijn, Netherlands: Sijthoff & Noordhoff, 1978. 217–45.

163. FLOYD, PAMELA, & PATRICIA CARRELL. "Effects on ESL Reading of Teaching Cultural Content Schemata." *Language Learning* 37 (1987): 89–108.

164. FOUCAULT, MICHEL. *The Archaeology of Knowledge.* Trans. A. M. Scheridan Smith. New York: Harper & Row, 1976.

165. ———. "What Is an Author?" *Language, Counter-Memory, Practice, Selected Essays and Interviews.* Trans. Donald Bouchard. Ithaca, NY: Cornell UP, 1977. 113–38.

166. FREDERIKSEN, CARL. "Acquisition of Semantic Information from Discourse." *Journal of Verbal Learning and Verbal Behavior* 14 (1975): 158–69.

167. ———. "Processing Units in Understanding Text." *Discourse Production and Comprehension.* Ed. Roy Freedle. Norwood, NJ: Ablex, 1982. 57–87.

168. FREEDLE, ROY. "Introduction to Volume I." *Discourse Production and Comprehension.* Ed. Roy O. Freedle. 2nd ed. Norwood, NJ: Ablex, 1982. xv-xix.

169. FUENTES, CARLOS. *Christopher Unborn.* Trans. Alfred MacAdam. New York: Farrar, Straus, & Giroux, Inc., 1989.

170. "Fund for the Improvement of Postsecondary Education Resources: The Comprehensive Project Descriptions 1987–1988." Washington, DC: U. S. Department of Education, 1987.

171. GAGNÉ, ELLEN. *The Cognitive Psychology of School Learning.* Boston: Little, Brown & Company, 1985.

172. GARNER, RUTH, & RON REIS. "Monitoring and Resolving Comprehension Obstacles: An Investigation of Spontaneous Text Lookbacks Among Upper-Grade Good and Poor Comprehenders." *Reading Research Quarterly* 16 (1981): 569–82.

173. GASS, SUSAN M., & LARRY SELINKER, eds. *Language Transfer in Language Learning.* Rowley, MA: Newbury, 1983.

174. GASS, SUSAN M., & CAROLYN G. MADDEN, eds. *Input in Second Language Acquisition.* Rowley, MA: Newbury, 1985.

175. GAUDIANI, CLAIRE. *Teaching Writing in the Foreign Language Curriculum.* Language in Education: Theory and Practice. Washington, DC: Center for Applied Linguistics, 1981.

176. GENESSEE, FRED. "Second Language Learning through Immersion: A Review of U. S. Programs." *Review of Educational Research* 55 (1985): 541–61.

177. GEVA, ESTHER. "Facilitating Reading Comprehension Through Flow Charting." *Reading Research Quarterly* 18 (1983): 384–405.

178. ———, & ELLEN B. RYAN. "Use of Conjunctions in Expository Texts by Skilled and Less Skilled Readers." *Journal of Reading Behavior* 17 (1985): 331–46.

179. GIAUQUE, GERALD. "Teaching for Content in a Skills Course: Greek Mythology in French." *Foreign Language Annals* 20 (1987): 565–69.

180. GIGLIOLI, PIER PAOLO, ed. *Language and Social Context.* Baltimore: Penguin Books, 1972.

181. GILLET, JEAN WALLACE, & CHARLES TEMPLE. *Understanding Reading Problems: Assessment and Instruction.* Boston: Little, Brown & Co., 1982.

182. GLISAN, EILEEN W. "Total Physical Response: A Technique for Teaching all Skills in Spanish." *Foreign Language Annals* 19 (1986): 419–28.

183. ———. "Reading: A Psycholinguistic Guessing Game." *Journal of the Reading Specialist* 4 (1967): 126–35.

184. ———. "Decoding: From Code to What?" *Language and Literacy. The Selected Writings of Kenneth S. Goodman.* Ed. Frederick Gollash. Boston, MA: Routledge & Kegan Paul, 1982. 53–60.

185. GOODMAN, KENNETH, & OLIVE S. NILES, eds. *Reading: Process and Program.* Urbana, IL: National Council of Teachers of English, 1970.

186. GOODWIN, CRAUFURD, & MICHAEL NACHT. *Abroad and Beyond*. New Rochelle, NY: Cambridge UP, 1988.

187. GOUGH, PHILLIP. "Word Recognition." *Handbook of Reading Research*. Ed. P. David Pearson. New York: Longman, 1984. 225–53.

188. GRABE, WILLIAM. "Reassessing the Term 'Interactive'." *Interactive Approaches to Second Language Reading*. Eds. Patricia L. Carrell, Joanne Devine, & David E. Eskey. Cambridge: Cambridge UP, 1988: 56–70.

189. ———, & J. ZUKOWSKI-FAUST. "On the Acquisition of Vocabulary from Context." International TESOL Twentieth Annual Convention, Anaheim, CA, March 3–7, 1986.

190. GRAFF, GERALD, *Professing Literature. An Institutional History*. Chicago: Chicago UP, 1987.

191. GREIMAS, A. J. *Structural Semantics: An Attempt at a Method*. Trans. Daniele McDowell, Ronald Schleifer, & Alan Velie. Lincoln, NE: Nebraska UP, 1983.

192. GRELLET, FRANÇOISE. *Developing Reading Skills. A Practical Guide to Reading Comprehension Exercises*. Cambridge: Cambridge UP, 1981.

193. GRIMES, JOSEPH. "Narrative Studies in Oral Texts." *Current Trends in Textlinguistics*. Ed. Wolfgang Dressler. Berlin: Walter de Gruyter, 1978. 123–32.

194. GUARINO, REGINA, & KYLE PERKINS. "Awareness of Form Class as a Factor in ESL Reading Comprehension." *Language Learning* 36 (1986): 77–82.

195. GUMPERZ JOHN J., ed. *Language and Social Identity*. Cambridge: Cambridge UP, 1982.

196. HAGUE, SALLY A. "Vocabulary Instruction: What L2 Can Learn from L1." *Foreign Language Annals* 20 (1987): 217–25.

197. HALFORD, GRAEME S. "A Structure-Mapping Approach to Cognitive Development." Special Issue: The Neo-Piagetian Theories of Cognitive Development. *International Journal of Psychology* 22 (1987): 609–42.

198. HALLIDAY, MICHAEL A. K., & RUQAIYA HASAN. *Cohesion in English*. London: Longman, 1976.

199. HAMP-LYONS, LIZ. "Two Approaches to Teaching Reading: A Classroom-Based Study." *Reading a Foreign Language* 3 (1985): 363–73.

200. HARPER, SANDRA N. "Strategies for Teaching Literature at the Undergraduate Level." *Modern Language Journal* 72 (1988): 402–8.

201. HARRI-AUGSTEIN, SHEILA, & LAURIE F. THOMAS. "Conversational Investigations of Reading: the Self-organized Learner and the Text." *Reading in a Foreign Language*. Eds. J. Charles Alderson & A. H. Urquhart. Essex: Longman, 1984. 250–76.

202. HAYES-ROTH, BARBARA, & FREDERICK HAYES-ROTH. "The Prominence of Lexical Information in Memory Representations of Meaning." *Journal of Verbal Learning and Verbal Behavior* 16 (1977): 119–36.

203. HAYNES, MARGOT. "Patterns and Perils of Guessing in Second Language Reading." *On TESOL '83*. Eds. J. Handscombe, R. A. Orem, & B. P. Taylor. Washington, DC: TESOL, 1984.

204. HEIMLICH, JOAN E., & SUSAN D. PITTELMAN. *Semantic Mapping: Classroom Applications*. Newark, DE: International Reading Associaition, 1986.

205. HENNING, GRANT H. "Remembering Foreign Language Vocabulary: Acoustic and Semantic Parameters." *Language Learning* 15 (1973): 167–79.

206. ———. "The Influence of Test and Sample Dimensionality on Latent Trait Person Ability and Item Difficulty Calibrations." *Language Testing* 5 (1988): 83–99.

207. HIGGS, THEODORE. "Language Acquisition and Language Learning: A Plea for Syncretism." *Modern Language Journal* 69 (1985): 8–14.

208. HILL, DEBORAH J., ed. *Innovative Approaches to Curriculum Design in the Study Abroad Program*. Columbus, OH: Renaissance Publications, 1987.

209. HINDS, JOHN L. "Contrastive Rhetoric: Japanese and English." *Text* 3 (1983): 183–95.

210. HIRSCH, ERIC DONALD. *The Validity of Interpretation*. New Haven, Yale UP, 1967.

211. ———. *The Aims of Interpretation*. Chicago: Chicago UP, 1978 (1976).

212. ———. *Cultural Literacy: What Every American Needs to Know.* Boston, MA: Houghton Mifflin, 1987.

213. HOLMES, GLYN, & MARILYN E. KIDD. "Second-Language Learning and Computers. *The Canadian Modern Language Review* 38 (1982): 503–16.

214. HONEYFIELD, JOHN. "Simplification." *TESOL Quarterly* 11 (1977): 431–40.

215. HOPPER, PAUL. "Discourse Analysis: Grammar and Critical Theory in the 1980s." *Profession* 88 (1988): 18–24.

216. HORNER, WINIFRED BRYAN. "Historical Introduction." *Composition and Literature: Bridging the Gap.* Ed. Winifred Bryan Horner. Chicago: Chicago UP, 1983. 1–13.

217. HORWITZ, ELAINE K. "Preliminary Evidence for the Reliability and Validity of a Foreign Language Anxiety Scale. *TESOL Quarterly* 70 (1986): 559–62.

218. ———. "The Beliefs about Language Learning of Beginning University Foreign Language Students." *Modern Language Journal* 72 (1988): 283–94.

219. HOSENFELD, CAROL. "A Preliminary Investigation of the Strategies of Successful and Non-Successful Readers." *System* 5 (1977): 110–23.

220. HUDSON, THOM. "The Effects of Induced Schemata on the 'Short-Circuit' in L2 Reading Performance." *Language Learning* 32 (1982): 1–30.

221. HUSSERL, EDMUND. *Phenomenological Psychology.* The Hague: M. Nijhoff, 1977.

222. HYMES, DELL. *Language in Culture and Society: A Reader in Linguistics and Anthropology.* Ed. Dell Hymes. New York: Harper & Row, 1964.

223. ———. *Toward Communicative Competence.* Philadelphia: Pennsylvania UP, 1972.

224. INGARDEN, ROMAN. *The Literary Work of Art.* Evanston, IL: Northwestern UP, 1973.

225. ISER, WOLFGANG. *The Act of Reading.* Baltimore: Johns Hopkins UP, 1981.

226. JAKOBOVITS, LEON A. "Research Findings and FL Requirements in Colleges and Universities." *Foreign Language Annals* 2 (1969): 436–56.

227. JARVELLA, ROBERT J. "Effects of Syntax on Running Memory Span for Connected Discourse." *Psychonomic Science* 19 (1970): 235–36.

228. ———. "Syntactic Processing of Connected Speech." *Journal of Verbal Learning and Verbal Behavior* 10 (1971): 409–16.

229. JOHNS, TIM, & FLORENCE DAVIES. "Text as a Vehicle for Information: The Classroom Use of Written Texts in Teaching Reading in a Foreign Language." *Reading in a Foreign Language* 1 (1983): 1–19.

230. JOHNSON, DALE, & P. DAVID PEARSON. *Teaching Reading Vocabulary.* New York: Holt, Rinehart, & Winston, 1978.

231. JOHNSON, PATRICIA. "Effects of Building Background Knowledge." *TESOL Quarterly* 16 (1982): 503–15.

232. JOINER, ELIZABETH G. "Listening in a Foreign Language." *Listening, Reading, and Writing: Analysis and Application.* Ed. Barbara H. Wing. Middlebury, VT: Northeast Conference on the Teaching of Foreign Languages, 1986. 43–70.

233. JONES, RANDALL L. "Testing the Receptive Skills: Some Basic Considerations." *Foreign Language Annals* 17 (1984): 365–79.

234. JOOS, MARTIN. *The English Verb: Form and Meanings.* Madison: Wisconsin UP, 1964.

235. JUEL, CONNIE. "Comparison of Word Identification Strategies with Varying Context, Word Type, and Reader Skill." *Reading Research Quarterly* 15 (1980): 358–76.

236. JUST, MARCEL, & PATRICIA CARPENTER. "A Theory of Reading: From Eye Fixations to Comprehension." *Psychological Review* 4 (1980): 329–54.

237. KAMIL, MICHAEL. "Current Traditions of Reading Research." *Handbook of Reading Research.* Ed. P. David Pearson. New York: Longman, 1984. 39–62.

238. KANT, IMMANUEL. *Critique of Pure Reason.* Trans. N. K. Smith. New York: St. Martin's Press, 1965.

239. KASSEN, MARGARET ANN. "Native Speaker and Non-Native Speaker Teacher Response to FL Composition. A Study of Beginning, Intermediate, and Advanced Level French." Diss. U of Texas. 1990.

240. KAST, BERND. "Literarische Texte für Anfänger im kommunikativen Fremdsprachen-unterricht." *Literarische Texte im kommunikativen Fremdsprachenunterricht: New Yorker Werkstattgespräch 1983.* Ed. Manfred Heid. München: Kemmler & Hoch (1985): 132–54.

241. KATZ, JERROLD J. *Semantic Theory.* New York: Harper & Row, 1972.

242. KEMPER, SUSAN. "Measuring the Inference Load of a Text." *Journal of Educational Psychology* 75 (1983): 391–401.

243. KERN, RICHARD G. "Second Language Reading Strategy Instruction: Its Effects on Comprehension and Word Inference Ability." *Modern Language Journal* 73 (1989): 135–49.

244. KING, JANET, FREDA HOLLEY, & BETTY NANCE WEBER. "A New Reading." *Perspective: A New Freedom. The ACTFL Annual Review of Foreign Language Education* 7. Ed. Gilbert A. Jarvis. Skokie, IL: National Textbook Co., 1975. 169–217.

245. KINNEAVY, JAMES. *A Theory of Discourse.* New York: Norton, 1980.

246. KINTSCH, WALTER. "Recognition Memory in Bilingual Subjects." *Journal of Verbal Learning and Verbal Behavior* 9 (1970): 405–9.

247. ———. *The Representation of Meaning in Memory.* Hillsdale, NJ: Erlbaum, 1974.

248. ———. *Memory and Cognition.* New York: John Wiley & Sons, 1977a.

249. ———. "On Comprehending Stories." *Cognitive Processes in Comprehension.* Eds. Marcel Just & Patricia Carpenter. Hillsdale, NJ: Erlbaum, 1977b. 33–62.

250. ———, & JANICE M. KEENAN. "Reading Rate as a Function of the Number of Propositions in the Base Structure of Sentences." *Cognitive Psychology* 5 (1973): 257–74.

251. ———, & TEUN A. VAN DIJK. "Towards a Model of Discourse Comprehension and Production." *Psychological Review* 85 (1978): 363–94.

252. ———, & DOUGLAS VIPOND. "Reading Comprehension and Readability in Educational Practice and Psychological Theory." *Perspectives on Memory Research.* Ed. Lars Göran Nilsson. Hillsdale, NJ: Erlbaum, 1979. 329–65.

253. ———, & J. CRAIG YARBROUGH. "Role of Rhetorical Structure in Text Comprehension." *Journal of Educational Psychology* 74 (1982): 828–34.

254. KLEIMAN, GLENN M. "Speech Recoding in Reading." *Journal of Verbal Learning and Verbal Behavior* 14 (1975): 323–39.

255. KOH, MOY YIN. "The Role of Prior Knowledge in Reading Comprehension." *Reading in a Foreign Language* 3 (1985): 375–80.

256. KORJAKOVCEVA, N. F. "Zur Bestimmung der Niveaustufen der Lesefähigkeit in der Fremdsprache." *Deutsch als Fremdsprache* 15 (1977): 280–86.

257. KRAMSCH, CLAIRE. *Discourse Analysis and Second Language Teaching.* Language in Education: Theory and Practice 37. Washington, DC: Center for Applied Linguistics, 1981.

258. ——— "The Proficiency Movement: Second Language Acquisition Perspectives." Review Article. *Studies in Second Language Acquisition* 9 (1987): 355–62.

259. KRASHEN, STEPHEN. *Second Language Acquisition and Second Language Learning.* Oxford: Pergamon Press, 1982.

260. ———. *The Input Hypotheses: Issues and Implications.* Harlow: Longman, 1985.

261. KRUSCHE, DIETRICH. "Die Chance des fremdkulturellen Lesers: Konkrete Poesie im Anfangsunterricht—und danach?" *Literarische Texte im kommunikativen Fremdsprachen-unterricht: New Yorker Werkstattgespräch 1983.* Ed. Manfred Heid. München: Kemmler & Koch, 1985. 444–81.

262. KUFNER, HERBERT L. The Grammatical Structures of English and German. Chicago: Chicago UP 1962.

263. KUHN, THOMAS. *The Structure of Scientific Revolutions.* 2nd ed. Chicago: Chicago UP, 1970.

264. LABERGE, DAVID, & S. JAY SAMUELS. "Toward a Theory of automatic Information Processing in Reading." *Cognitive Psychology* 6 (1974): 293–323.

265. LADO, ROBERT. "Linguistics across Cultures." Reprinted in *Language Transfer in Language Learning*. Eds. Susan M. Gass & Larry Selinker. Rowley, MA: Newbury, 1983: 21–31.

266. LADO, ROBERT, BEVERLY BALDWIN, & FELIX LOBO. *Massive Vocabulary Expansion in a Foreign Language beyond the Basic Course: The Effects of Stimuli, Timing and Order of Presentation.* Final Report, Project No. 5-1095. ERIC Microfiche No. ED 013 046. Washington, DC: U.S. Department of Health, Education, and Welfare, 1967.

267. LAEUFER, CHRISTIANE. "Theoretical and Pedagogical Implications of Recent Research on Phonetic / Phonological Interference in Adult Foreign Language Acquisition." Unpubl. paper, Symposium on Research Perspectives in Adult Language Learning & Acquisition, Ohio State Univ., Columbus, October 21–22, 1988.

268. LAMBERT, RICHARD, & BARBARA FREED, eds. *The Loss of Language Skills.* Rowley, MA: Newbury, 1982.

269. LAUFER, BATIA, & DONALD SIM. "Measuring and Explaining the Reading Threshold Needed for English for Academic Purposes Texts." *Foreign Language Annals* 18 (1985): 405–11.

270. LEBLANC, RAYMOND, & GISELE PAINCHAUD. "Self-Assessment as a Second Language Placement Instrument." *TESOL Quarterly* 19 (1985): 673–87.

271. LEE, JAMES F. "The Effect of Research Design on Free Written Recall as a Measure of Reading Comprehension in a Second Language." *TESOL Quarterly* 19 (1985): 782–93.

272. ———. "Background Knowledge and L2 Reading." *Modern Language Journal* 70 (1986a): 350–54.

273. ———. "On the Use of the Recall Task to Measure L2 Reading Comprehension." *Studies in Second Language Acquisition* 8 (1986b): 83–93.

274. ———. "Toward a Professional Model of Language Program Direction." *ADFL Bulletin* 19.1 (1987a): 22–25.

275. ———. "Comprehending the Spanish Subjunctive: An Information Processing Perspective." Modern Language Journal 71 (1987b): 51–57.

276. ———, & TERRY LYNN BALLMAN. "The Ability of Foreign Language Learners to Recall and Rate the Important Ideas of an Expository Text." *Foreign Language Learning: A Research Perspective.* Eds. Bill VanPatten, Trisha Dvork, & James Lee. Cambridge, MA: Newbury, 1987. 108–18.

277. ———, & DIANE MUSUMECI. "On Hierarchies of Reading Skills and Text Types." *Modern Language Journal* 72 (1988): 173–87.

278. LEM, STANISLAW. *The Futurological Congress.* Trans. Michael Kandel. A Continuum Book. New York: Seabury Press, 1974.

279. LE NY, JEAN-FRANÇOIS, MARYVONNE CARFANTAN, & JEAN-CLAUDE VERSTIGGEL. "Accessibility from Working Memory and Role of Reprocessing in Sentence Comprehension." *Language and Comprehension.* Eds. Jean-François LE NY & Walter Kintsch. Amsterdam: North Holland, 1982. 123–34.

280. LEVINE, ADINA, & THEA REVES. "What Can the FL Teaching Teach the Motor Tongue Reader?" *Reading in a Foreign Language* 3 (1985): 329–39.

281. LEVINE, MARTIN, & GEORGE HAUS. "The Effect of Background Knowledge on the Reading Comprehension of Second Language Learners." *Foreign Language Annals* 18 (1985): 391–97.

282. LIGHTBOWN, PATSY M. "Input, Interaction, and Acquisition in the SL Classroom." *Classroom Oriented Research in Second Language Acquisition.* Eds. Herbert W. Seliger & Michael Long. Rowley, MA: Newbury, 1983: 217–43.

283. LISKIN-GASPARRO, JUDITH. "The ACTFL Proficiency Guidelines: Gateway to Testing and Curriculum." *Foreign Language Annals* 17 (1984): 475–89.

284. LITTLEWOOD, WILLIAM. "Social Interaction Activities." *Communicative Language Teaching: An Introduction.* Cambridge: Cambridge UP, 1981. 43–64.

285. LOBO, FELIX A. "10,000 Spanish Word Vocabulary Expanded from 3,000 English Cognates." Diss. Georgetown Univ., 1966.

286. LoCoco, VERONICA. "Learner Comprehension of Oral and Written Sentences in German and Spanish: The Importance of Word Order." *Foreign Language Learning: A Research Perspective.*

Eds. Bill VanPatten, Trisha Dvorak & James Lee. Cambridge, MA: Newbury, 1987. 119–29.

287. LONG, MICHAEL. "Process and Product in ESL Program Evaluation." *TESOL Quarterly.* 18 (1984): 409–25.

288. ———. "Input and Second Language Acquisition Theory." *Input in Second Language Acquisition.* Eds. Susan M. Gass & Carolyn G. Madden. Cambridge, MA: Newbury, 1985. 377–93.

289. ———, & PATRICIA A. PORTER. "Group Work, Interlanguage Talk, and Second Language Acquisition." *TESOL Quarterly* 19 (1985): 207–28.

290. LONGACRE, ROBERT E. *An Anatomy of Speech Notions.* Lisse: deRidder, 1976.

291. LOUGHRIN-SACCO, STEVEN J., ELLEN M. BOMMARITO, & WENDY SWEET. "Anatomy of an Elementary French Class." Unpubl. paper, Symposium on Research Perspectives in Adult Language Learning & Acquisition, Ohio State Univ., Columbus, October 21–22, 1988.

292. LUDWIG, JEANNETTE. "Native-Speaker Judgments of Second Language Learners' Efforts at Communication: A Review." *Modern Language Journal.* 66 (1982): 274–83.

293. LYONS, JOHN. *Semantics.* Cambridge: Cambridge UP, 1968.

294. MACH, ERNST. *The Analysis of Sensations, and the Relation of the Physical to the Psychical.* Trans. C. M. Williams. NY: Dover Press, 1959.

295. MACKAY, RONALD, & ALAN MOUNTFORD. "Reading for Information." *Reading in a Second Language.* Eds. Ronald Mackay, Bruce Barkman, & R. R. Jordan, Rowley, MA: Newbury, 1979. 106–41.

296. MAGNAN, SALLEY SIELOFF. "Assessing Speaking Proficiency in the Undergraduate Curciculum: Data from French." *Foreign Language Annals* 19 (1986): 429–38.

297. ———. "Grammar and the ACTFL Oral Proficiency Interview: Discussion and Data." *Modern Language Journal* 72 (1988): 266–76.

298. MANDLER, JEAN M., & NANCY S. JOHNSON. "Remembrance of Things Parsed: Story Structure and Recall." *Cognitive Psychology* 9 (1977): 111–51.

299. ———. "Recent Research on Story Grammars." *Language and Comprehension.* Eds. Jean-François Le Ny & Walter Kintsch. Amsterdam: North-Holland, 1982. 207–18.

300. MCCLELLAND, JAMES & DAVID E. RUMELHART. "An Interactive Activation Model of the Effect of Context in Perception." *Psychological Review* 88 (1981). 375–407.

301. MCCONKIE, GEORGE W., & DAVID ZOLA. "Language Constraints and the Functional Stimulus in Reading." *Interactive Processes in Reading.* Eds. Charles A. Perfetti & Alan M. Lesgold. Hillsdale, NJ: Erlbaum, 1981. 155–75.

302. MCLAUGHLIN, BARRY. *Theories of Second-Language Learning.* Edward Arnold: London, 1987.

303. ———, TAMMI ROSSMANN, & BEVERLY MCLEOD. "Second Language Learning: An Information-Processing Perspective." *Language Learning* 33 (1983): 135–58.

304. MEARA, P. M., ed. *Vocabulary in a Second Language. Specialized Bibliography 3.* London: Centre for Information on Language Teaching and Research, 1983.

305. MELENDEZ, E. JANE, & ROBERT H. PRITCHARD, "Applying Schema Theory to Foreign Language Reading." *Foreign Language Annals* 18 (1985): 399–403.

306. MEYER, BONNIE, J. F. *The Organization of Prose and its Effects on Memory.* New York: North Holland, 1975.

307. ———. "Reading Research and the Composition Teacher: The Importance of Plans." *College Composition and Communication* 33 (1982): 37–49.

308. ———. "The Structure of Text." *Handbook of Reading Research.* Ed. P. D. Pearson. New York: Longman, 1984, 319–51.

309. ———, DAVID M. BRANDT, & GEORGE J. BLUTH. "Use of Top-Level Structure in Text: Key for Reading Comprehension of Ninth-grade Students." *Reading Research Quarterly* 16 (1980): 72–103.

310. ———, & ROY O. FREEDLE. "Effects of Discourse Type on Recall." *American Educational Research Journal* 21 (1984): 121–43.

311. MICHAELS, SARAH. "Sharing Time: Children's Narrative Styles and Differential Access to Literacy." *Language in Society* 10 (1981):423–42.

312. MILLER, GEORGE A. "The Magical Number Seven, Plus or Minus Two." *Psychological Review* 63 (1956):81–97.

313. ———. "Dictionaries in the Mind." *Language and Cognitive Processes* 1 (1986): 171–85.

314. MILLER, JAMES R., & WALTER KINTSCH. "Readability and Recall of Short Prose Passages: A Theoretical Analysis." *Journal of Experimental Psychology: Human Learning and Memory* 6 (1980): 335–54.

315. ———. "Knowledge-based Aspects of Prose Comprehension and Readability." *Text* 1 (1981): 215–32.

316. "MLJ Readers' Forum." *Modern Language Journal* 72 (1988): 450–57.

317. MOORE, DAVID W., & JOHN E. READENCE. "A Quantitative and Qualitative Review of Graphic Organizer Research." *Journal of Educational Research* 78 (1984): 11–17.

318. MORRIS, C. DONALD, JOHN D. BRANSFORD, & JEFFERY J. FRANKS. "Levels of Processing versus Transfer Appropriate Processing." *Journal of Verbal Learning and Verbal Behavior* 16 (1977): 519–33.

319. MOULTON, WILLIAM G. *The Sounds of English and German.* Chicago: Chicago UP, 1962.

320. MUKAROVSKY, JAN. "Standard Language and Poetic Language." *A Prague School Reader.* Ed. Paul L. Garvin. Washington, DC: Georgetown UP, 1964. 17–30.

321. MURDOCK, BENNET B. "The Retention of Individual Items." *Journal of Verbal Learning and Verbal Behavior* 16 (1977): 519–33.

322. MUSUMECI, DIANE. "Early-stage Learners' Strategies in the Comprehension of Tense." Unpubl. paper, Symposium on Research Perspectives in Adult Language Learning & Acquisition, Ohio State Univ., Columbus, October 21–22, 1988.

323. NAGLE, STEPHEN, & SARA SANDERS. "Comprehension Theory and Second Language Pedagogy." *TESOL Quarterly* 20 (1986): 9–26.

324. NAGY, WILLIAM E., & RICHARD C. ANDERSON. "How Many Words Are There in Printed School English?" *Reading Research Quarterly* 19 (1984): 304–30.

325. NAISBITT, JOHN. *Megatrends: Ten New Directions Transforming our Lives.* NY: Warner Books, 1982.

326. NATION, I. S. P. "Beginning to Learn Foreign Vocabulary: A Review of the Research." *RELC Journal* 13 (1982): 14–36.

327. NEMOIANU, ANCA. "Reading between the Lines: Written Texts as Input for Second Language Development." Diss. Univ. of California, Berkeley, 1987.

328. NUTTAL, CHRISTINE. *Teaching Reading Skills in a Foreign Language.* Practical Language Teaching Series No. 9. London: Heinemann, 1982.

329. OLLER, JOHN W. "Evidence for a General Language Proficiency Factor: An Expectancy Grammar." *Issues in Language Testing.* Ed. John W. Oller. Rowley, MA: Newbury, 1983:3–10.

330. ———. *Language Tests at School.* London: Longman, 1979.

331. OLSEN, JUDY E. *Communication Starters: Techniques for the Language Classroom.* Oxford: Pergamon Press, 1982.

332. OMAGGIO, ALICE C. *Games and Simulations in the Foreign Language Classroom.* Washington, DC: Center for Applied Linguistics, 1979a.

333. ———. "Pictures and Second Language Comprehension: Do They Help?" *Foreign Language Annals* 12 (1979b): 107–16.

334. ———. *Language Teaching in Context. Proficiency Oriented Instruction.* Boston, MA: Heinle & Heinle, 1986.

335. OSGOOD, CHARLES. "Where Do Sentences Come from?" *An Interdisciplinary Reader in Philosophy, Linguistics and Psychology.* Eds. David Steinberg & Leon A. Jakobovits. London: Cambridge UP, 1971. 497–531.

336. OSTER, JUDITH. "Seeing with Different Eyes: Another View of Literature in the ESL Class." *TESOL Quarterly* 23 (1989): 85–103.

337. OSTYN, PAUL, & PIERRE GODIN. "Ralex: An Alternative Approach to Language Teaching." *Modern Language Journal* 69 (1985): 346–55.

338. OXFORD, REBECCA, & MARTHA NYIKOS. "Variables Affecting Choice of Language Learning Strategies by University Students." Unpubl. paper, Symposium on Research Perspectives in Adult Language Learning & Acquisition, Ohio State Univ., Columbus, October 21–22, 1988.

339. PALINSCAR, ANNEMARIE, & ANN BROWN. "Reciprocal Teaching of Comprehension Fostering and Comprehension-Monitoring Activities." *Cognition and Instruction* 1 (1984): 117–75.

340. PERFETTI, CHARLES A. *Reading Ability.* New York: Longman, 1985.

341. PERRIG, WALTER, & WALTER KINTSCH. "Propositional and Situational Representations of Text." *Journal of Memory and Language* 24 (1985): 503–18.

342. PHIFER, SANDRA J., & JOHN A. GLOVER. "Don't Take Students' Word for What They Do While Reading." *Bulletin of the Psychonomic Society* 19 (1982): 194–96.

343. PHILLIPS, JUNE. "Practical Implications of Recent Research in Reading." *Foreign Language Annals* 17 (1984): 285–96.

344. PIAGET, JEAN. *Genetic Epistemology.* New York: Norton, 1971.

345. PICA, THERESA, & CATHERINE DOUGHTY. "Input and Interaction in the Communicative Language Classroom: A Comparison of Teacher-Fronted and Group Activities." *Input in Second Language Acquisition.* Eds. Susan M. Gass & Carolyn G. Madden. Rowley, MA: Newbury, 1985. 115–32.

346. PIKE, KENNETH. "Nucleation." *Modern Language Journal* 44 (1969): 291–95.

347. POSTOVSKY, VALERIAN. "Effects of Delay in Oral Practice at the Beginning of Second Language Learning. *Modern Language Journal* 58 (1974): 583–86.

348. *President's Commission on Foreign Language and International Studies. Strength through Wisdom: A Critique of U.S. Capability.* Washington, DC: Superintendent of Documents, U.S. Government Printing Office, 1979.

349. PRESSLEY, MICHAEL. "Children's Use of the Keyword Method to Learn Simple Spanish Vocabulary Words." *Journal of Educational Psychology* 69 (1977): 465–72.

350. PROPP, VLADIMIR. *Morphology of the Folktale.* Trans. L. Scott. Pub. 10, Bloomington: Indiana University Research Center in Anthropology, Folklore and Linguistics, 1958.

351. RAIMES, ANN. "What Unskilled ESL Students Do As They Write: A Classroom Study of Composing." *TESOL Quarterly* 19 (1985): 229–58.

352. RATYCH, JOHANNA. "Zwei Jahrzehnte literarischer Lehrbücher." *Literarische Texte im kommunikativen Fremdsprachenunterricht: New Yorker Werkstattgespräch.* Ed. Manfred Heid. München: Kemmler & Hoch, 1985. 68–84.

353. REDFIELD, JAMES. "The Politics of Language Instruction." *ADFL Bulletin* 20 (1989): 5–12.

354. REICHER, GLENN M. "Perceptual Recognition as a Function of Meaningfulness of Stimulus Material." *Journal of Experimental Psychology* 8 (1969): 275–80.

355. REYNOLDS, RALPH E., & ROBERT M. SCHWARTZ. "Relation of Metaphoric Processing to Comprehension and Memory." *Journal of Educational Psychology* 75 (1983): 450–59.

356. RICH, ELAINE. *Artificial Intelligence.* New York: McGraw-Hill, 1983.

357. ROBB, THOMAS, STEVEN ROSS, & IAN SHORTREED. "Salience of Feedback on Error and Its Effect on EFL Writing Quality." *TESOL Quarterly* 20 (1986): 83–95.

358. RODGERS, THEODORE S. "On Measuring Vocabulary Difficulty: An Analysis of Item Variables in Learning Russian-English Vocabulary Pairs." *IRAL* 7 (1969): 327–43.

359. ROLLER, CATHY M. "The Effects of Reader and Text-Based Factors on Writers' and Readers' Perceptions of the Importance of Information in Expository Prose." *Reading Research Quarterly* 20 (1985): 437–57.

360. ROSENBLATT, LOUISE. *Literature as Exploration.* New York: D. Appleton-Century, 1938.

361. ROYER, JAMES M., JOHN A. BATES, & CLIFFORD E. KONOLD. "Learning from Text. Methods of Affecting Reader Intent." *Reading in a Foreign Language.* Eds. J. Charles Alderson & A. H. Urquhart. London: Longman, 1984. 65–85.

362. RUBENSTEIN, HERBERT, LONNIE GARFIELD, & JANET MILLIKAN. "Homographic Entries in the Internal Lexicon." *Journal of Verbal Learning and Verbal Behavior* 9 (1970): 487–94.

363. RUMELHART, DAVID E. "Notes on Schema for Stories." *Representation and Understanding.* Eds. Donald G. Bobrow & Allan Collins. New York: Academic Pres, 1975. 211–36.

364. ———. "Toward an Interactive Model of Reading." *Attention and Performance.* Vol. 4. Ed. Stanislav Dornic. New York: Academic Press, 1977. 573–603.

365. ———, & JAMES L. McCLELLAND. "Interactive Processing through Spreading Activation." *Interactive Processes in Reading.* Eds. Alan M. Lesgold & Charles A. Perfetti. Hillsdale, NJ: Erlbaum, 1981. 37–60.

366. SALLING, AAGE. "Essays in Comparative Vocabulary Studies." *Modern Language Journal* 42 (1958): 222–25.

367. SAMUELS, S. JAY, & MICHAEL L. KAMIL. "Models of the Reading Process." *Handbook of Reading Research.* Ed. P. David Pearson. New York: Longman, 1984: 185–224.

368. SANFORD, ANTHONY J., & SIMON C. GARROD. *Understanding Written Language.* New York: John Wiley & Sons, 1981.

369. SAPIR, EDWARD. *Culture, Language and Personality.* Berkeley, CA: California UP, 1956: 45–64.

370. SARAGI, T., I. S. P. NATION, & G. F. MEISTER. "Vocabulary Learning and Reading." *System* 6 (1978): 72–78.

371. SAVIGNON, SANDRA. *Communicative Competence: Theory and Classroom Practice—Texts and Contexts in Second Language Learning.* Reading, MA: Addison-Wesley Publishing Company, 1983.

372. ———. "Evaluation of Communicative Competence: the ACTFL Provisional Proficiency Guidelines." *Modern Language Journal* 69 (1985): 187–93.

373. SCHANK, ROGER C. *Reading and Understanding: Teaching from the Perspective of Artificial Intelligence.* Hillsdale, NJ: Erlbaum, 1982.

374. ———, NEIL GOLDMAN, CHARLES RIEGER, & CHRISTOPHER RIESBECK. *Conceptual Information Processing.* Amsterdam: North Holland, 1975.

375. SCHALLERT, DIANE L. "The Significance of Knowledge: A Synthesis of Research Related to Schema Theory." *Reading Expository Material.* New York: Academic Press, 1982. 13–48.

376. ———, SARA L. ULERICK, & ROBERT J. TIERNEY. "Evolving a Description of Text through Mapping." *Spatial Learning Strategies: Techniques, Applications, and Related Issues.* Eds. Charles D. Holley & Donald F. Dansereau. New York: Academic Press, 1984. 255–74.

377. SCHERER, GEORGE A., & MICHAEL WERTHEIMER. *A Psycholinguistic Experiment in Foreign Language Teaching.* New York: McGraw-Hill, 1964.

378. SCHMID, RICHARD F. "Prior Knowledge, Context Familiarity and the Comprehension of Natural Prose." Diss. Arizona State Univ., 1977.

379. SCHNEIDER, PETER. "The Light at the End of the Novel." *The New York Times Book Review.* Section 7, July 26, 1987.

380. SCHOLES, ROBERT. *Textual Power: Literary Theory and the Teaching of English.* New Haven / London: Yale UP, 1985.

381. SCHRIER, LESLIE. "The Culture of a Spanish Literature Classroom and Its Effects on Reading Comprehension." Northeast Conference on Foreign Languages, New York, April 7–9, 1988.

382. SCHUBERTH, RICHARD E., & PETER D. EIMAS. "Effects of Context on the Classification of Words and Nonwords." *Journal of Experimental Psychology: Human Perception and Performance* 3 (1977): 27–36.

383. SCHULZ, RENATE. "Literature and Readability: Bridging the Gap in Foreign Language Reading." *Modern Language Journal* 65 (1981): 43–53.

384. SCIARONE, ABONDIO G. *Woordjes Leren in het Vreemdetalenonderwijs.* Muiderberg: Continho, 1979.

385. SEARLE, JOHN R. *Speech Acts: An Essay in the Philosophy of Language.* Cambridge: Cambridge UP, 1969.

386. SEBEOK, THOMAS A. *Linguistics in Western Europe.* The Hague: Mouton, 1972.

387. SEIBERT, LOUISE C. "A Study on the Practice of Guessing Word Meanings from a Context." *Modern Language Journal* 29 (1945): 296–322.

388. SELINKER, LARRY, & JOHN T. LAMENDELLA. "Two Perspectives on Fossilization in Interlanguage Learning." *Interlanguage Studies Bulletin* 3 (1978): 143–91.

389. SEMKE, HARRIET. "The Comparative Effects of Four Methods of Treating Free-Writing Assignments on the Second Language Skills and Attitudes of Students in College Level First Year German." Diss. Univ. of Minnesota, 1980.

390. SHIFFRIN, RICHARD, & WALTER SCHNEIDER. "Controlled and Automatic Human Information Processing: I & II. Perceptual Learning, Automatic Attending, and a General Theory." *Psychological Review* 84 (1977): 127–90.

391. SHIH, MARY. "Content Approaches to Teaching Academic Writing." *TESOL Quarterly* 20 (1986): 617–48.

392. SHOHAMY, ELANA. "Does the Testing Method Make a Difference? The Case of Reading Comprehension." *Language Testing* 1 (1984): 147–70.

393. SIM, DONALD. "Links between Context and Selected Features of Grammatical Cohesion in English, and Performance in Advanced Reading Comprehension for Overseas Students." Diss. Univ. of Manchester, England, 1979.

394. ———, & MARSHA BENSOUSSAN. "Control of Contextualized Function and Content Words as It Affects EFL Reading Comprehension Test Scores." *Reading in a Second Language*. Eds. Ronald Mackay, Bruce Barkman, & R. R. Jordan. Rowley, MA: Newbury, 1979. 36–44.

395. SIMMONS, L. V. T. "A Vocabulary Count Based on Three German Dramas." *Modern Language Journal* 14 (1929): 33–36.

396. SINGER, HARRY, & D. DONLAN. "Active Comprehension: Problem-Solving Schema with Question Generation for Comprehension of Complex Short Stories." *Reading Research Quarterly* 17 (1982): 166–86.

397. SMITH, FRANK. *Understanding Reading*. New York: Holt, Rinehart, & Winston, 1971.

398. ———. *Psycholinguistics and Reading*. New York: Holt, Rinehart, & Winston, 1973.

399. ———. *Reading without Nonsense*. New York: Teachers College Press, 1978.

400. SMITH, PHILLIP D., JR. *A Comparison of the Cognitive and Audiolingual Approaches to Foreign Language Instruction*. Philadelphia: Center for Curriculum Development, 1970.

401. SPACK, RUTH. "Literature, Reading, Writing, and ESL: Bridging the Gaps." *TESOL Quarterly* 19 (1985): 703–25.

402. STANOVICH, KEITH E. "Toward an Interactive-Compensatory Model of Individual Differences in the Development of Reading Fluency." *Reading Research Quarterly* 16 (1980): 32–71.

403. STEFFENSEN, MARGARET, SW., CHITRA JOAG-DEV, & RICHARD C. ANDERSON. "A Cross-Cultural Perspective on Reading Comprehension." *Reading Research Quarterly* 15 (1979): 10–29.

404. STEIN, BARRY S., C. DONALD MORRIS, & JOHN D. BRANSFORD. "Constraints on Effective Elaboration." *Journal of Verbal Learning and Verbal Behavior* 17 (1978): 707–14.

405. STEIN, NANCY L. "What's in a Story: Interpreting the Interpretations of Story Grammars." *Discourse Processes* 5 (1982): 319–35.

406. ———, & CHRISTINE G. GLENN. "An Analysis of Story Comprehension in Elementary School Children." *New Directions in Discourse Processing*. Ed. Roy O. Freedle. Norwood, NJ: Ablex, 1979. 53–120.

407. STEPHENS, DONALD, & JANET SWAFFAR. "The Comprehension-Based Class in Theory and in Practice." *The Comprehension Approach: An Evolving Methodology in Foreign Language Instruction*. Ed. Harris Winitz. Rowley, MA: Newbury, 1981. 254–74.

408. STERN, H. H. "A Quiet Language Revolution: Second Language Teaching in Canadian Context—Achievements and New Directions." *The Canadian Modern Language Review* 40 (1984): 506–24.

409. STERNFELD, STEVEN. "The Applicability of the Immersion Approach to College Foreign Language Instruction." *Foreign Language Annals* 21 (1988): 221–26.

410. ———. "The University of Utah's Immersion / Multiliteracy Program: An Example of an Area Studies Approach to the Design of First-year College Foreign Language Instruction." *Foreign Language Annals* 22 (1989): 341–54.

411. SWAFFAR, JANET. "Reading Authentic Texts." *Modern Language Journal* 69 (1985): 16–34.

412. ———. "Reading and Cultural Literacy." *The Journal of General Education* 38.2 (1986): 70–84.

413. ——, & MARGARET WOODRUFF. "Language for Comprehension: Focus on Reading: A Report on the University of Texas German Program." *Modern Language Journal* 62 (1978): 27–32.

414. SWAIN, MERRILL. "Communicative Competence: Some Roles of Comprehensible Input und Comprehensible Output in its Development." *Input in Second Language Acquisition.* Eds. Susan M. Gass & Carolyn G. Madden. Cambridge, MA: Newbury, 1985. 235–53.

415. ——. "Second Language Testing and Second Language Acquisition: Is there a Conflict with Traditional Psychometrics?" Unpublished paper. Georgetown University Round Table on the Interdependence of Theory, Practice, and Research, Georgetown, 17 March, 1990.

416. ——, & SHARON LAPKIN. "Canadian Immersion and Adult Second Language Teaching: What's the Connection?" *Modern Language Journal* 73 (19890: 150–58.

417. TAN, SOON HOCK, & CHU POH LING. "The Performance of a Group of Malay-Medium Students in an English Reading Comprehension Test." *RELC* 19 (1979): 81–89.

418. TARNÓCZI, LORÁNT. "Wortbestand, Wortschatz, Wortfrequenz." *IRAL* 9 (1979): 297–318.

419. TAYLOR, BARBARA, & RICHARD W. BEACH. "The Effects of Text Structure Instruction on Middle Grade Students' Comprehension and Production of Expository Work." *Reading Research Quarterly* 19 (1984): 134–46.

420. TESCHNER, RICHARD V. "A Profile of the Specialization and Expertise of Lower-Division Foreign Language Program Directors in American Universities." *Modern Language Journal* 71 (1987): 28–35.

421. TESNIÈRE, LUCIAN. *Éléments de syntaxe structurale.* Paris: Klincksieck, 1959.

422. THOMAS, JENNY. "Cross-Cultural Pragmatic Failure." *Applied Linguistics* 4 (1983): 92–112.

423. THORNDIKE, ROBERT. *Reading Comprehension Education in Fifteen Countries.* New York: John Wiley & Sons, 1973.

424. THORNDYKE, PERRY W. "Cognitive Structures in Comprehension and Memory of Narrative Discourse."*Cognitive Psychology* 9 (1977): 77–110.

425. TIERNEY, ROBERT J., JOHN E. READENCE, & ERNEST K, DISCHNER, eds. *Reading Strategies and Practices.* Boston: Allyn & Bacon, 1985.

426. TOLLEFSON, JOHN W., BOB JACOBS, & ELAINE J. SELIPSKY. "The Monitor Model and Neurofunctional Theory: An Integrated View" *Studies in Second Language Acquisition* 6 (1983): 1–16.

427. TOMPKINS, JANE P. "An Introduction to Reader-Response Criticism." *Reader Response Criticism: From Formalism to Post-Structuralism.* Ed. Jane P. Tompkins. Baltimore: Johns Hopkins UP, 1980, ix–xxvi.

428. TRIM, JOHN L. M., RENE RICHTERICH, JAN A. VAN EK, & DAVID A. WILKINS. *Systems Development in Adult Language Learning.* Prepared for the Council of Europe. London: Pergamon Press, 1980.

429. TULVING, ENDEL, & CECILLE GOLD. "Stimulus Information and Contextual Information as Determinants of Tachistscopic Recognition of Words." *Journal of Experimental Psychology* 66 (1963): 319–27.

430. TWYFORD, CHARLES W. "The Effect of Syntactic Information, Pragmatic, Expectation, and Cognitive Style on Learners' Comprehension of a Second Language." Diss. Indiana Univ., 1980.

431. ULIJN, JAN. "Foreign Language Reading. Conceptual and Syntactic Strategies and Their Consequences for the Role of the Native Language." *IRAL* 22 (1984): 71–73.

432. URQUHART, A. H. "The Effect of Rhetorical Ordering on Readability." *Reading in a Foreign Language.* Eds. J. Charles Alderson & A. H. Urquhat. London: Longman, 1984. 160–75.

433. VALDÉS, GUADALUPE, ENRIQUE LESSA, MARIA PAZ ECHEVERRIARZA, & CECILIA PIÑO. "The Development of a Listening Skills Comprehension-Based Program: What Levels of Proficiency Can Learners Reach?" *Modern Language Journal* 72 (1988): 415–25.

434. VALDES, JOYCE MERRILL, ed. *Culture Bound: Bridging the Cultural Gap in Language Teaching.* Cambridge: Cambridge UP, 1986.

435. VAN DIJK, TEUN A. "Semantic Macrostructures and Knowledge Frames in Discourse Comprehension." *Cognitive Processes in Comprehension.* Eds. Marcel Just & Patricia Carpenter. Hillsdale, NJ: Erlbaum, 1977. 3–32.

436. ———, & WALTER KINTSCH. *Strategies of Discourse Comprehension.* New York: Academic Press, 1983.

437. VAN KLEECK, ANNE. Editor's Foreword. *Topics in Language Disorders* 7 (1987): vi–vii.

438. VANSANT, JACQUELINE, JANET SWAFFAR, KATHERINE ARENS, SANDRA D. SHATTUCK, & MARIE-LUISE GÄTTENS. *Blickwechsel.* Boston, MA: Houghton Mifflin, 1990.

439. VIGIL, VIRGINIA DOROTHEA. "Authentic Text in the College-Level Spanish I Class as the Primary Vehicle of Instruction." Diss. Univ. of Texas at Austin, 1987.

440. VIPOND, DOUGLAS. "Micro- and Macroprocesses in Text Comprehension." *Journal of Verbal Learning and Verbal Behavior* 19 (1980): 276–96.

441. WADSWORTH, BARRY. *Piaget for the Classroom Teacher.* New York: Longman, 1978.

442. WALTERS, JOEL, & YUVAL WOLF. "Language Proficiency, Text Context and Order Effects in Narrative Recall." *Language Learning* 36 (1986): 47–63.

443. WATTENMAKER, WILLIAM, GERALD DEWEY, TIMOTHY MURPHY, & DOUGLAS MEDIN. "Linear Separability and Concept Learning: Context, Relational Properties, and Concept Naturalness." *Cognitive Psychology* 18 (1986): 158–94.

444. WATTS, GRAEME H., & RICHARD C. ANDERSON. "Effect of Three Types of Inserted Questions on Learning from Prose." *Journal of Educational Psychology* 62 (1971): 387–94.

445. WEAVER, CONSTANCE. *Psycholinguistics and Reading: From Process to Practice.* Cambridge, MA: Winthrop, 1980.

446. WESCHE, MARJORIE BINGHAM. "Communicative Testing in a Second Language." *Modern Language Journal* 67 (1983): 41–55.

447. WESTFALL, ALFRED. "Can College Students Expand their Recognition Vocabularies?" *School and Society* 73 (1951): 25–28.

448. WHALEY, JILL FITZGERALD. "Readers' Expectations for Story Structure." *Reading Research Quarterly.* 17 (1981): 90–114.

449. WHEELER, DANIEL. "Processes in Word Recognition." *Cognitive Psychology* 1 (1970): 59–85.

450. WHITE, HAYDEN. *Metahistory: The Historical Imagination in Nineteenth Century Europe.* Baltimore: Johns Hopkins UP, 1973.

451. WIDDOWSON, HENRY G. *Stylistics and the Teaching of Literature.* London: Longman, 1975.

452. WIMSATT, W. K., JR. with MONROE C. BEARDSLEY. *The Verbal Icon: Studies in the Meaning of Poetry.* NP: U of Kentucky, 1954.

453. WINITZ, HARRIS, ed. *The Comprehension Approach: An Evolving Methodology in Foreign Language Instruction.* Rowley, MA: Newbury, 1981.

454. WITTGENSTEIN, LUDWIG. *The Blue and Brown Books.* New York: Harper & Row, 1958.

455. WITTROCK, MERLIN C., CAROLYN MARKS, & MARLEEN DOCTOROW. "Reading as a Generative Process." *Journal of Educational Psychology* 67 (1975): 484–89.

456. WOLFE, DAVID, & GWENDOLYN JONES. "Integrating Total Physical Response Strategy in a Level I Spanish Class." *Foreign Language Annals* 15 (1982): 273–80.

457. WOLFF, DIETER. "Some Assumptions about Second Language Text Comprehension." *Studies in Second Language Acquisition* 9 (1987): 307–26.

458. WRIGHT, ANDREW, DAVID BETTERIDGE, & MICHAEL BUCKBY. *Games for Language Learning.* Cambridge: Cambridge UP: 1979.

459. WYATT, DAVID. "Computer-Assisted Teaching and Testing of Reading and Listening." *Foreign Language Annals* 17 (1984): 393–407

460. YOUNG, DOLLY, & ELAINE HORWITZ. *Language Anxiety: Second Language Learning and Performance.* Englewood Cliffs, NJ: Prentice Hall, 1991.

461. ZABRUCKY, KAREN. "The Role of Factural Coherence in Discourse Comprehenseion." *Discourse Processes* 9 (1986): 197–220.

462. ZAMEL, VIVIAN. "Teaching Composition in the ESL Classroom: What We Can Learn from Research on the Teaching of English." *TESOL Quarterly* 10 (1976): 67–76.

463. ———. "Responding to Student Writing." *TESOL Quarterly* 19 (1985): 79–101.

464. ———. "Recent Research on Writing Pedagogy." *TESOL Quarterly* 21 (1987): 697–715.

Index